The Main Line French:
3 ♞c3

Steffen Pedersen

First published in the UK by Gambit Publications Ltd 2001
Reprinted 2006

ISBN-13: 978-1-901983-45-6
ISBN-10: 1-901983-45-5

DISTRIBUTION:
Worldwide (except USA): Central Books Ltd, 99 Wallis Rd, London E9 5LN, England. Tel +44 (0)20 8986 4854 Fax +44 (0)20 8533 5821.
E-mail: orders@Centralbooks.com

Gambit Publications Ltd, 99 Wallis Rd, London E9 5LN, England.
E-mail: info@gambitbooks.com
Website (regularly updated): www.gambitbooks.com

Edited by Graham Burgess
Typeset by John Nunn
Printed in Great Britain by The Cromwell Press, Wiltshire.

10 9 8 7 6 5 4 3 2

Gambit Publications Ltd
Managing Director: GM Murray Chandler
Chess Director: GM John Nunn
Editorial Director: FM Graham Burgess
German Editor: WFM Petra Nunn
Webmaster: Dr Helen Milligan WFM

Contents

Symbols

+	check	Wch	world championship
++	double check	WCup	World Cup
#	checkmate	Ech	European championship
!!	brilliant move	ECC	European Clubs Cup
!	good move	Ct	candidates event
!?	interesting move	IZ	interzonal event
?!	dubious move	Z	zonal event
?	bad move	OL	olympiad
??	blunder	jr	junior event
+−	White is winning	wom	women's event
±	White is much better	mem	memorial event
⩲	White is slightly better	rpd	rapidplay game
=	equal position	sim	game from simultaneous display
∞	unclear position	corr.	correspondence game
⩱	Black is slightly better	1-0	the game ends in a win for White
∓	Black is much better	½-½	the game ends in a draw
−+	Black is winning	0-1	the game ends in a win for Black
Ch	championship	(*n*)	*n*th match game
Cht	team championship	(*D*)	see next diagram

Transpositions are displayed by a dash followed by the moves (in *italic*) of the variation to which the transposition occurs. The moves start with the first one that deviates from the line under discussion. All the moves to bring about the transposition are given. Thus, after 1 e4 e6 2 d4 d5 3 ♘c3 dxe4 4 ♘xe4 ♘d7 5 ♘f3 ♘gf6 6 ♘xf6+ ♘xf6 7 ♗d3 c5 8 dxc5 ♗xc5 9 ♕e2 0-0 10 ♗g5 ♕a5+ the comment "11 ♗d2 ♕c7 – *9...♕c7 10 ♗d2 0-0* ±" signifies that the reader should locate material on 1 e4 e6 2 d4 d5 3 ♘c3 dxe4 4 ♘xe4 ♘d7 5 ♘f3 ♘gf6 6 ♘xf6+ ♘xf6 7 ♗d3 c5 8 dxc5 ♗xc5 9 ♕e2 ♕c7 10 ♗d2 0-0, to which play has transposed. The '±' sign indicates the overall assessment of that line; such signs are only given when it is meaningful to do so.

Bibliography

Minev: *French Defense 2*, Thinkers' Press, 1998
Tiemann: *Die Französische Verteidigung* (Band 1), Reinhold Dreier, 1991
McDonald and Harley: *Mastering the French*, Batsford, 1997
Watson: *Play the French* (new edition), Cadogan, 1996
Uhlmann: *Winning With the French*, Batsford, 1995
Psakhis: *The Complete French*, Batsford, 1992
Gufeld and Stetsko: *The Classical French*, Batsford, 1999
McDonald: *French Winawer*, Everyman, 2000
Korchnoi: *C18-C19*, Šahovski Informator, 1993
ECO, volume C (2nd, 3rd and 4th editions), Šahovski Informator,
    1981/1997/2000
Nunn, Burgess, Emms, Gallagher: *Nunn's Chess Openings* (NCO),
    Gambit/Everyman, 1999

Informator (up to 80)
ChessBase Magazine (up to 81)

Introduction

The French Defence provides good evidence that opening theory in chess is far from being exhausted. Take a look at one of the world's best players, Russian GM Alexander Morozevich, and you will quickly notice that even in extensively analysed positions he has been finding plenty of room for new ideas. Therefore this book is far from 'the ultimate truth' of the opening. However, it is rather a detailed coverage of the various lines beginning after White's 3rd move, 3 ♘c3 (D).

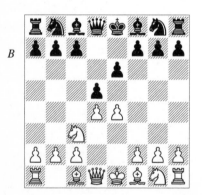

I have opted for a predominantly theoretical coverage, but I hope that the frequent verbal explanations of plans and strategies help the reader develop a good understanding of the general

ideas that are most important in these lines of the French.

This book is the first of two volumes that between them will cover the entire opening complex of the French Defence, 1 e4 e6. The second volume will cover the Tarrasch Variation, Advance Variation, and others. This book only concentrates on the positions arising after 2 d4 d5 3 ♘c3. I have divided the book into four parts:

1) The Rubinstein and Burn Variations (3...dxe4 and 3...♘f6 4 ♗g5 dxe4);

2) The Classical French (3...♘f6);

3) The Winawer (3...♗b4);

4) Rare 3rd moves.

I could easily have written a whole book on each of the first three parts. Hence, in many lines, I have ruthlessly cut down on non-relevant lines and endeavoured to give the most important lines for both sides.

The French Defence is full of various transpositions. I have used the system developed by Graham Burgess to navigate around these, i.e. moves which transpose elsewhere are given followed by a dash and the exact move-order where the reader should locate the material in *italics* (for a more detailed description, see page 4).

In most cases, an assessment is also given, so the reader can quickly see whether the transposition is worth following.

I think that the French Defence offers something to all kinds of players. There are sharp lines and there are more strategic/positional lines, but remember: the only way to learn the finesses of an opening is to try it out yourself, so good luck with the French Defence!

Steffen Pedersen
July 2001

1 Rubinstein Variation: 4...♗d7 and others

1 e4 e6 2 d4 d5 3 ♘c3 dxe4 4 ♘xe4
(D)

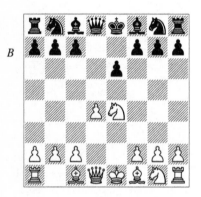

The Rubinstein Variation is a solid choice. White obtains a space advantage but Black can develop fairly freely and can later hope to exert pressure on White's centre. There are various ways of playing the Rubinstein Variation but the key question for Black is how to develop his light-squared bishop. Ideally, it would like to be on b7, but this is not always a suitable solution. It very much depends on how Black continues on his next move. In this chapter we discuss:

Black's main option, 4...♘d7, is examined in the next chapter.

The immediate 4...b6?! deservedly has a poor reputation, mainly based upon the game Tal-Kholmov, Moscow 1975, where White quickly obtained a very promising position with a series of active moves: 5 ♕f3! c6 6 ♗f4 ♗b7 7 0-0-0 ♘f6 8 ♘xf6+ ♕xf6 9 ♕g3 ♘d7, and now Tal suggests 10 ♗d3 ±.

A)
4...♕d5

This move is not so bad, but it is definitely not one that will cause White many sleepless nights. The best Black can hope for is a transposition to an inferior reply to an innocuous line of the Winawer.

5 ♗d3

5 ♘c3 ♗b4 is a rather tame line of the Winawer (3...♗b4 4 exd5 ♕xd5?!) but Black has recaptured with the queen rather than the much simpler capture with the e-pawn. This offers White good chances of an advantage; for example, 6 ♘f3 (6 ♘e2 is a safe

alternative; another line is 6 ♕g4 but 6...♘c6 7 ♘f3 ♘ge7 8 ♕xg7 ♖g8 9 ♕xh7 e5! gives Black excellent dynamic play) 6...♘f6 7 ♗d3 and now:

a) 7...♘e4 8 0-0!? ♘xc3 9 bxc3 ♗xc3 10 ♖b1 ♘c6 11 ♗e3 ♗d7 12 ♖b5 ♕d6 13 ♖xb7 ♘b4 (13...♗xd4 14 ♘xd4 ♘xd4 15 ♗xd4 ♕xd4 16 ♖xc7 ♕b6 17 ♕f3 ♕xc7 18 ♕xa8+ ♗c8 19 ♖b1 ± Sax-Stroebel, Vraca 1975) 14 ♘e5 0-0 15 ♗e4 ♗a4 (T.Wall-Crouch, Newcastle 1995) 16 a3 ♘d5 17 ♕d3 +−.

b) 7...b6!? 8 0-0 ♗xc3 9 bxc3 ♗a6 10 ♖e1 0-0 11 ♗xa6 ♘xa6 12 ♕d3 ♘b8 13 c4 ♕b7 14 ♗a3 ♖e8 15 d5 ♘bd7 16 dxe6 ♖xe6 17 ♖xe6 fxe6 18 ♖e1 ♖e8 19 ♘d4!? ± B.Lengyel-Hoang Than Trang, Budapest 1997.

5...♘f6

Or:

a) 5...f5 doesn't really come into consideration, since after 6 ♘g3 ♕xg2 7 ♘f3 Black has spent too much time with his queen only to win a pawn.

b) 5...♘c6 is an alternative. There are then three options for White:

b1) 6 c3 e5 7 ♕e2 ♗e6 8 ♘f3 exd4 9 0-0 0-0-0 10 ♖d1 gave White compensation in Mitkov-Sulava, Yugoslav Ch (Kladovo) 1991, but is not altogether clear if Black just develops sensibly.

b2) 6 ♘e2 and now instead of 6...♗d7?! 7 ♘2c3 ♗b4 8 ♕g4 ♕xd4 9 ♗e3 h5? 10 ♗xd4 hxg4 11 ♗xg7 ♖h5 12 ♘f6+ ♘xf6 13 ♗xf6 ± Lie-Goddard, Molde 1990, Black should try 6...♘b4.

b3) 6 ♘f3 ♘b4 7 0-0 ♘xd3 8 ♕xd3 ♘f6 9 ♘xf6+ gxf6 10 ♗f4 c5 11 c4 ♕d7 12 ♖ad1 ± Pavičić-Raičević, Yugoslavia 1976.

6 ♘xf6+ gxf6 7 ♘f3 *(D)*

7 ♕f3 would be quite good if only Black were incautious enough to take the d4-pawn. Then White would get a huge advantage in development and a very good position, but Black should play 7...♕xf3 8 ♘xf3 ♘c6 9 c3 ♗d7 with a solid game.

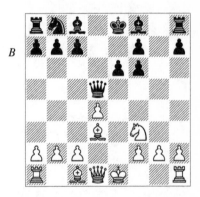

7...♖g8

7...♗d7 8 c4 ♕d6 9 0-0 ♘c6 10 ♗e3 ♘e7 11 b4 ♘g6 12 c5 ♕d5 13 b5 ± Mortensen-Crouch, Copenhagen 1995. This is obviously a much too passive strategy.

8 0-0 ♘c6 9 ♖e1 ♗d6 10 g3 *(D)*

10 ♗e4 ♕h5 11 c4 ♗d7 12 d5 ♘e7 13 dxe6 fxe6 14 g3 0-0-0 15 ♕b3 and now 15...b6? 16 ♘d4 ♗c5 17 ♗e3 left White with a very good position in Tolnai-Hoang Than Trang, Budapest 1996. Later Hoang Than Trang demonstrated that 15...c6 is more tenacious

and produced a dangerous attack against Z.Varga in Budapest 1998; following 16 ♘d4 e5 17 ♘c2 f5 18 ♗f3 ♕g6 19 ♗e3 f4 20 ♗xa7 ♗f5 Black had good compensation for the pawn, with the thrust ...e4-e3 on the agenda. 15...♗c6 doesn't look like a bad idea either. Then if White goes for the e-pawn with 16 ♗xc6 ♘xc6 17 ♖xe6, 17...♗e5 somewhat embarrasses the rook.

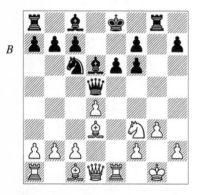

B

10...♕h5 11 ♗e2 ♕h3 12 d5 ♘e7 13 dxe6 ♗xe6

13...fxe6 14 ♘d4 is pleasant for White. He easily evades the checks after 14...♗xg3 15 fxg3 ♖xg3+ 16 hxg3 ♕xg3+ 17 ♔f1 ♕h3+ (17...e5 18 ♗h5+ ♘g6 19 ♕f3+–) 18 ♔f2, by walking his king towards the centre.

14 ♗b5+ ♗d7 15 ♗xd7+ ♕xd7 16 ♕d4

White is better, Glek-Hoang Than Trang, Budapest 1998.

B)

4...♗e7

This is a solid but not very common line.

5 ♘f3 ♘f6

5...♘d7 – 4...♘d7 5 ♘f3 ♗e7 ±.

6 ♘xf6+ ♗xf6 7 c3 (*D*)

7 ♗d3 is also possible, but then 7...c5 8 dxc5 ♘d7 gives Black reasonable chances of equality; e.g., 9 0-0 (9 c6!?) 9...♘xc5 10 ♗b5+ ♗d7 11 ♕e2 0-0 12 ♗e3 ♗xb5 13 ♕xb5 b6 14 c3 ♕c7 with equality, V.Belov-Radjabov, KasparovChess Cadet GP 2000.

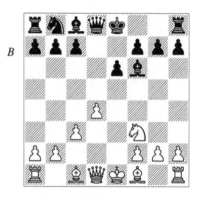

B

7...b6

7...♘d7 8 ♗e3!? ♕e7 (8...0-0 9 ♗d3 c5 10 ♕c2 h6 11 0-0 cxd4 12 ♗xd4 ♗xd4 13 ♘xd4 ± Peek-Carlier, Ostend 1991) 9 ♕c2 c5 10 dxc5 (10 ♗d3 is maybe better, with the idea of recapturing with the pawn after 10...cxd4) 10...♘xc5 11 ♗b5+ ♗d7 12 ♗xc5 ♕xc5 13 ♗xd7+ ♔xd7 14 0-0 ♖ad8 15 ♖ad1+ ♔e7 16 ♖xd8, Piket-Krudde, Dutch Cht 1992, and now the continuation 16...♔xd8 17 ♖d1+ ♔c8 should be fine for Black.

8 ♗d3!?

The thematic manoeuvre 8 ♗b5+ c6 9 ♗d3 is here well met by 9...♗a6!, when Black equalized in Adorjan-Romanishin, Hastings 1976/7: 10 0-0 ♗xd3 11 ♕xd3 0-0 12 ♗f4 ♘d7 13 ♖ad1 ♕e7 14 ♖fe1 ♖fd8 15 h3 ♖ac8 16 ♕a6 ♘f8 17 a4 ♘g6 18 ♗g3 ♕d7 =.

8...♗b7 9 ♕e2 ♘d7 10 ♗f4 0-0 11 0-0-0 ♖e8 12 h4 ♘f8 13 ♔b1

In this position White has slightly the better prospects, Kreiman-Blatny, New York 1998.

C)

4...♘f6

This is another rather unpopular line, but again Black is solid and White's only advantage is his possession of slightly more space.

5 ♘xf6+ gxf6 (D)

This leads to similar positions to lines in the Burn Variation in which Black recaptures with the g-pawn, only here has White exchanged a knight instead of a bishop. The other capture, 5...♕xf6, is worse as the queen is too exposed: 6 ♘f3 h6 7 ♗d3 ♘c6 8 0-0 ♗d6 9 c3 0-0 (9...♗d7 10 ♕e2 0-0-0 11 b4 g5 12 b5 ♘e7 13 c4 ♗f4 14 ♗b2 g4 15 ♘e5 ♗xe5 16 dxe5 ♕g5 17 ♗e4 ± Zarnicki-Jerez Infante, Villa Martelli 1997) 10 ♘d2! e5?! (this is premature but the alternatives also leave White better) 11 ♘e4 ♕d8 12 ♕h5 exd4 13 ♗xh6! gxh6 14 ♕xh6 ♗f5 15 f4 ♖e8, Gufeld-Alburt, USSR 1974, and now Gufeld suggests 16 ♖f3!, with the possible variation 16...♖e6 17 ♖g3+ ♖g6

18 ♗c4 ♗xe4 19 ♖xg6+ ♗xg6 20 ♕xg6+ ♔h8 21 ♕h5+ ♔g8 22 ♕xf7+ ♔h8 23 ♕h5+ ♔g7 24 ♖e1 +−.

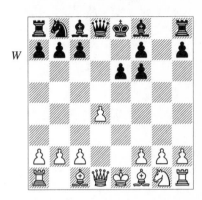

6 ♗e3! b6

6...♘c6 7 ♗e2!? ♗d7 8 ♗f3 ♕e7 9 ♕d2 0-0-0 10 0-0-0 ♕b4 11 ♕xb4 ♘xb4 12 a3 ♘c6 13 ♘e2 ♘e7 14 ♘g3 ♗c6 15 ♗xc6 ♘xc6 16 ♘h5 ♗e7 17 g4 and White is slightly better, Borge-K.Rasmussen, Danish League 1996/7.

7 ♕f3 c6 8 0-0-0 ♗b7 9 ♘h3 ♘d7 10 ♘f4 ♕e7 11 ♗d3 0-0-0 12 ♗e4 ♕d6 13 g4

± Timoshenko-Lukov, Paris 2000.

D)

4...♗d7 (D)

5 ♘f3

This is the most natural but there is another plan worth mentioning: 5 c4 ♗c6 6 ♘c3 ♘f6. Rather than controlling the centre with his minor pieces, White has chosen a slightly more aggressive set-up with the pawn on c4. The drawback of this plan is that White must take care not to fall too far behind

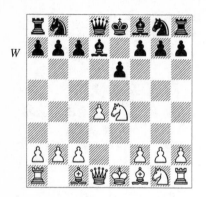

in development and that the d-pawn may become vulnerable. White now has a choice:

a) 7 ♘f3 ♗xf3! 8 ♕xf3 ♘c6! (8...c6 9 ♗e3 ♘bd7 10 ♗e2 ♗d6 11 0-0 0-0, as in Nunn-Karpov, Wijk aan Zee 1993, is solid but slightly passive) 9 d5 (9 ♗e3 ♘xd4 10 ♗xd4 ♕xd4 11 ♕xb7 ♖d8 12 ♕b5+ ♖d7 13 ♖d1 ♕b6 = Sher) 9...exd5 (I don't see anything especially wrong with 9...♘d4 10 ♕d1 c5, which is also suggested by Sher) 10 cxd5 ♕e7+ 11 ♗e3 ♘d4 (Mortensen-Sher, Vejle 1994) 12 ♕d1 ♘f5 13 ♗b5+ ♘d7 14 ♕f3 ♘xe3 15 fxe3 0-0-0 16 0-0 ♘e5 17 ♕f4 ±.

b) 7 ♘ge2!? ♗e7 (Sher suggests 7...♗d6!?) 8 ♘f4 0-0 9 ♗e2 ♗d6 10 0-0 e5 11 ♘fd5 ♗xd5 12 cxd5 exd4 13 ♕xd4 ♘c6 14 ♕d1 ♘e7 15 ♗f3 ± Glek-Budnikov, Douai 1993.

c) 7 f3!? ♗e7 8 ♗e3 ♕d7 9 ♘h3 a6!? 10 ♘f4 b5 11 ♘d3 bxc4 12 ♘e5 ♕d6 13 ♘xc4 ♕b4 14 a3 ♕b7 15 ♕d2 ♗d5 = Leyva-Camacho, Adelquis Remon 1997.

5...♗c6 6 ♗d3 *(D)*

Or:

a) If 6 ♘eg5, the simplest reply is 6...♗d6! (6...♘d7 may be feasible but it tempts White to sacrifice on f7). Then:

a1) 7 ♗c4 h6 8 ♘xe6 fxe6 9 ♗xe6 ♕f6 10 d5 ♗d7 11 ♘d4 is a dubious sacrifice which was easily repelled in Aronian-Turner, Hastings 2000/1: 11...♕e5+ 12 ♗e3 ♘f6 13 ♕d3 ♘xd5 14 ♕g6+ ♔d8 15 0-0-0 ♘xe3 16 fxe3 ♗e8 −+.

a2) 7 ♗d3 h6 8 ♘e4 ♗xe4 9 ♗xe4 c6 10 ♕e2 ♘f6 11 ♗d3 ♘bd7 = Anand-Karpov, Linares 1993. Black is two tempi better than Line D1 and should not have much to worry about. The only difference is that here Black's h-pawn is on h6; this is hardly that significant.

b) It remains to point out that if White wants to play the line *6 ♗d3 ♘d7 7 0-0 ♘gf6 8 ♘ed2* and wants to avoid *6...♗xe4*, then 6 ♘ed2!? is a feasible move-order which most likely achieves its goal after, for example, 6...♘f6 7 ♗d3 ♘bd7 8 0-0.

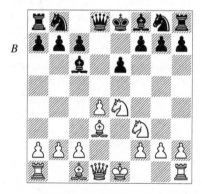

Now:

D1: 6...♗xe4 13
D2: 6...♘d7 14

D1)

6...♗xe4

Is it really worth spending three moves with this bishop only to exchange it for a knight? Well, to be honest I find it hard to believe since White now possesses the bishop-pair, the position is open, and more importantly White's position is very solid. However, Black argues that his position is also free of weakness and it will not crack just like that. Indeed, White will need to take some risks if he is to make inroads, and this is liable to give Black counterchances.

7 ♗xe4 c6 (D)

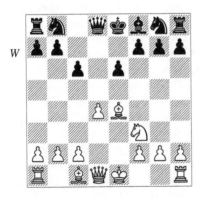

W

8 0-0

White has tried many slightly different set-ups but this appears the most logical since castling queenside never really enters into White's plans. The only reasonably important alternative consists of White playing 8 c3 ♘f6 9 ♗c2, which has the advantage that White avoids blocking the d-file with the bishop and that White might seek to set up a battery towards the black kingside by playing ♕d3 at some point. The drawback of this set-up is that it does little to strengthen White's control of the centre, and thus Black may get a chance to break with ...c5 later. After 9...♘bd7 10 0-0, Black has a choice of two different set-ups:

a) 10...g6!? 11 ♗f4 ♗g7 12 ♕e2 0-0 13 ♗d6 ♖e8 14 ♘e5 ♗f8 15 ♗xf8 ♔xf8 16 f4 ♕b6 (16...a5 is probably better) 17 b4! and White enjoyed a promising initiative in M.Schlosser-Dizdarević, Strasbourg ECC 1994.

b) 10...♗d6 11 ♖e1 ♕c7 and then:

b1) 12 ♕e2 0-0 (12...♗f4!? 13 ♗xf4 ♕xf4 14 ♘e5 ♘xe5 15 dxe5 ♘d5 16 a4 ± Xie Jun-Ivkov, Vienna (Ladies vs Veterans) 1993) 13 ♘e5 c5 14 ♘xd7 ♘xd7 15 dxc5 ♗xh2+ 16 ♔h1 ♗e5 17 ♗e3 g6! 18 ♗a4 ♗g7 19 ♗xd7 ♕xd7 with equality, Cu.Hansen-Rozentalis, Århus 1997.

b2) 12 ♗g5!? 0-0 (12...♗f4 is again interesting; White can play to occupy e5, as in Xie Jun-Ivkov above, or he can try 13 ♗h4 0-0 14 ♕d3, but then 14...♖fe8 looks alright for Black, with the idea of 15 ♘e5 ♘xe5 16 dxe5 ♗xe5 17 ♗xf6 ♗xf6 18 ♕xh7+ ♔f8 =) 13 ♕d3 ♖ad8 14 ♖ad1 ♖fe8 15 a3!? b5 (15...c5?! is premature in view of 16 ♗a4!) 16 ♗b1 a6 17 ♗h4!? g6 18 ♕e2 ♗e7 19 ♗g3 ♕b7 20 h3 ♘d5 21 ♗a2 ♗f8 22 c4! bxc4 23 ♗xc4 a5

24 ♖c1! ± Ponomariov-Rozentalis, Belfort 1998.

8...♘f6 9 ♗d3 ♘bd7

This is natural and flexible. Another interesting idea is 9...g6 (fianchettoing the bishop is normal in these positions but usually only after Black has developed the bishop to e7 or d6 and then prepared the fianchetto by ...0-0, ...♖e8, ...♗f8, ...g6, etc.; here Black hopes to gain time by immediately developing the bishop on g7) 10 b3 ♗g7 11 ♗a3 ♗f8 12 ♗b2 (strategically, Black would be quite content to exchange minor pieces, so White avoids the exchange and even gains a tempo with the manoeuvre) 12...♗g7 13 c4 0-0 14 ♕e2 ♘bd7 15 ♖ad1 ♖e8 16 ♗b1, when White has a typical slight advantage in the form of a solid position with two bishops and more space, Donchev-L.B.Hansen, Thessaloniki OL 1988.

10 c4 ♗d6

Or 10...♗e7 11 ♗f4! with a very good position for White. Black is simply too passive and soon ran into trouble in Arakhamia-L.B.Hansen, Biel 1991: 11...0-0 12 ♗c2 ♕a5 13 ♕d3 ♕h5 14 ♖fe1 ♖ad8 15 h3 ♖fe8 16 ♘e5 ±.

11 b3 0-0 12 ♗b2 a5 13 a3 ♕c7 14 ♕e2 ♖fe8 15 ♖fe1 ♗f8 16 ♖ad1

± Jansa-Voloshin, Ceske Budejovice 1993.

D2)

6...♘d7 (D)

This is somewhat more flexible than 6...♗xe4 as it is very likely that Black

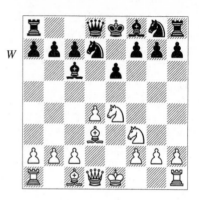

will at least get a second chance to exchange his bishop for one of White's knights.

7 0-0

A rather more aggressive set-up is represented by 7 c4, when in the event of 7...♗xe4 8 ♗xe4, White will be able to retreat his bishop all the way to c2, with a favourable version of Line D1. Hence, Black usually continues 7...♘gf6 8 ♘c3 (another point behind White's last move) 8...♗xf3 9 ♕xf3 and then:

a) 9...c6 10 0-0 ♗e7 11 ♖e1 0-0 12 ♗f4 ♖e8 13 ♖ad1 ♘b6 14 b3 a5 15 a4 g6 16 ♗c2 ± Kudrin-Naumkin, Kusadasi 1990.

b) 9...c5 10 d5!? ♘e5 11 ♕e2 ♗d6 12 ♗g5 h6 13 ♗h4 g5 14 ♗g3 ♘xd3+ 15 ♕xd3 exd5 16 ♘xd5 ♘xd5 17 0-0-0! 0-0 18 ♕xd5 ♗xg3 19 hxg3 ± E.Berg-Rustemov, Bydgoszcz 2000.

7...♘gf6 8 ♘g3

I am of the opinion that White's choice here is largely a matter of taste. White should move the knight, and exchanging on f6 eases Black's game considerably, but moving it to g5, d2 or g3 also makes sense. Thus:

a) 8 ♘eg5 and now:

a1) 8...♗xf3 9 ♕xf3 c6 10 ♖e1 ♗e7 11 ♕h3 gives White a huge initiative and no real weaknesses. It is no surprise that Black has fared badly here: 11...♘f8 12 c3 ♕c7 13 f4! ♘d5 (or 13...h6 14 f5 ♖g8 15 fxe6! hxg5 16 exf7+ ♔xf7 17 ♘c4+ ♔e8 18 ♗xg5 +− Pavasović-Steiner, Kranj 1999) 14 f5 ♘f4 15 ♗xf4 ♕xf4 16 fxe6! ♕xg5 17 exf7+ ♔xf7 18 ♖e5 ♕h4 19 ♖f1+ 1-0 Rajlich-Franchini, Budapest 2000.

a2) 8...♗e7 invites a tempting but not totally clear sacrifice: 9 ♘xf7 (if 9 ♖e1 h6 10 ♘h3, even 10...g5 comes into consideration) 9...♔xf7 10 ♘g5+ ♔g8 11 ♘xe6 ♕c8 12 ♖e1 (12 ♕e2 ♗d6 13 ♗c4 ♘b6 14 ♗b3 ♗a4 15 c4 ♗xb3 16 axb3 also looked like reasonable compensation in Nataf-K.Arkell, Hastings 1995) 12...♗d6 13 ♗f5!? ♗d5 14 ♗g5 ♕b8 15 ♕d3 b5 16 ♕h3 h6 17 ♗h4 with strong pressure as compensation for the piece, Winsnes-Bus, Gothenburg 1993.

a3) 8...h6?! 9 ♘xe6 fxe6 10 ♗g6+ ♔e7 11 ♖e1 is another interesting piece sacrifice but here I would be very willing to take White's side. Levačić-Lupu, Cannes 1999 continued 11...♗xf3 (11...♘b6!?) 12 ♕xf3 ♘b6 13 ♕xb7 ♕c8 14 ♕f3 ±.

a4) 8...♗d6 (this looks the most solid but Black still has a few problems to solve) 9 ♖e1 h6 (9...0-0 10 ♘e5 ± shouldn't be allowed) 10 ♘h3 ♗xf3 11 ♕xf3 c6 12 ♘f4 *(D)* and then:

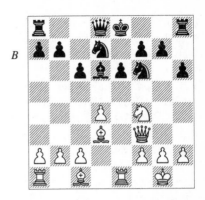

B

a41) 12...0-0 13 ♘h5! ♖e8 (alternatively, 13...♘xh5 14 ♕xh5 ♘f6 15 ♕h3! ♖e8! 16 ♗d2 ♕b6 17 ♕h4 ±) and here:

a411) 14 ♘xf6+ ♘xf6 15 ♗d2 e5 16 dxe5 ♗xe5 17 g3 ♕d5 18 ♕xd5 ♘xd5 19 ♖ab1 and White is slightly better, Bologan-C.Bauer, Bundesliga 1998/9.

a412) 14 ♗d2 and now:

a4121) 14...e5? is too risky: 15 ♘xg7! e4 (15...♔xg7 16 ♕g3+ ♔h8 17 ♗xh6 ♘h5 18 ♕h3 ♘df6 19 ♗g5!? ♔g8 and now both 20 ♕h4! and 20 g4!? should be winning for White) 16 ♕h3 (Korchnoi mentions the beautiful 16 ♖xe4! ♔xg7 {or 16...♖xe4 17 ♘f5 +−} 17 ♗xh6+!! ♔xh6 18 ♕e3+! ♔g7 19 ♕g5+ ♔f8 20 ♕h6+ ♔g8 21 ♖h4 and White will mate in a few moves) 16...♔xg7 17 ♕xh6+ ♔g8 18 ♗c4 ♖e7 19 ♕g6+ ♔h8 20 ♕h6+ ♔g8 (Korchnoi-Dreev, Brno 1992) 21 ♗b4!! ♗xb4 22 ♖e3 ♗d6 23 ♖h3 +− Dreev.

a4122) 14...♘xh5, with similar play to *13...♘xh5*, is better.

a42) 12...♕a5 13 c3 0-0-0 14 ♗f1?!
e5 15 dxe5 ♘xe5 16 ♕h3+ ♔b8 was
comfortable for Black in Rotshtein-
S.Arkell, Olot 1993.

b) 8 ♘ed2!? ♗e7 9 ♖e1 0-0 10
♘c4 b6 11 ♘ce5 (11 a4 a5 12 c3 ♗b7
13 ♗g5 ♘d5 14 ♗d2 c5 15 dxc5 ♘xc5
16 ♗c2 ♕c7 = J.Polgar-Aung Aung,
Istanbul OL 2000) 11...♗b7 (11...♘xe5
12 dxe5 ♘d7 13 ♘d4 ♗b7 14 ♕g4 ±
Smirin-Chernin, Moscow PCA rpd
1994) 12 ♗b5 ♘b8 13 ♕e2 a6 14 ♗d3
♘c6 15 c3 ♘xe5 16 dxe5 ♘d7 17 ♗f4
♘c5 18 ♗c2 ± Avrukh-Kelečević,
Biel 2000.

8...♗e7 (D)

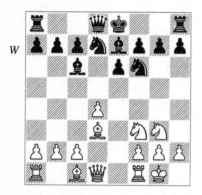

9 ♖e1

Or 9 b3 0-0 10 ♗b2 a5 11 c4! (11 a3
b5! 12 ♖e1 b4 13 a4 ♗b7 14 ♘d2 c5
was fine for Black in Adams-Dreev,

Manila OL 1992) 11...a4 12 ♘e5 axb3
(12...♘xe5 13 dxe5 ♘d7 14 ♕c2, intending ♖ad1, is better for White –
Bologan) 13 ♘xc6 bxc6 14 ♕xb3 c5
15 d5! exd5 16 cxd5 ♗d6 17 ♗b5 ♖b8
18 a4 ♘b6 19 ♖ad1 ♘bxd5 20 ♘e4!
♘xe4 21 ♕xd5 ♘g5 22 ♖fe1 ± Bolo-
gan-Kramnik, Khalkidhiki 1992.

9...0-0 10 c3 ♖e8

10...♗xf3 11 ♕xf3 c6 12 ♗f4 ♖e8
13 ♖ad1 ♘f8 14 a3 ♘g6 15 ♗c1 ♕c7
16 ♘e4!? ♘xe4 17 ♗xe4 ♖ad8 18 g3
♖d7 19 h4 was better for White in
Leko-Seirawan, Istanbul OL 2000.

**11 ♗f4 a5 12 ♕e2 ♗f8 13 ♖ad1
♗xf3 14 ♕xf3 c6 15 h4 ♕b6** (D)

15...♘d5 16 ♗g5 ♗e7 17 ♕g4 ♘5f6
18 ♕h3 ± I.Sokolov.

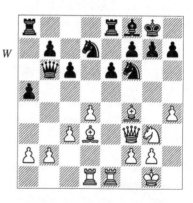

16 ♖e2 c5 17 dxc5 ♘xc5 18 ♗c2
± I.Sokolov-Suba, Antwerp 1996.

2 Rubinstein Variation: 4...♞d7

1 e4 e6 2 d4 d5 3 ♘c3 dxe4 4 ♘xe4 ♘d7 *(D)*

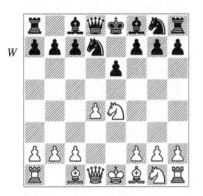

This is one of the most solid lines of the French. It has the advantage that the plans for Black are very clear-cut, but it is very difficult to win with it. However, used as a counter-attacking weapon it is not a bad choice, as may be seen from the fact that several top players have taken it up recently.

We shall consider three replies for White:

A: 5 g3   17
B: 5 ♘f3   19
C: 5 ♗d3   30

Lines B and C are the most common and may lead to very similar positions but we shall distinguish between White castling kingside and White castling queenside. Line C is the more aggressive, and generally implies that White intends to castle queenside.

A)

5 g3

The last couple of years have seen an increased interest in this quiet move.

5...♘gf6

The other option is 5...♗e7 6 ♗g2 ♘gf6 7 ♘xf6+ ♗xf6, which has the advantage that the bishop supports an ...e5 advance. In this type of position, Black should try to restrict White's g2-bishop but this is more easily said than done. The logical continuation is 8 ♘f3 0-0 9 0-0 e5 10 ♗e3 exd4 11 ♗xd4. Now there is a lot to be said for the solid 11...c6 but White can attempt to initiate some queenside pressure with 12 a4. Instead, the active 11...c5 12 ♗xf6 ♘xf6 13 ♕xd8 ♖xd8 14 ♘e5 is probably satisfactory for Black if he plays 14...♖b8. 14...g6 15 ♘d3 ♗f5, as in Al.Ivanov-Christiansen, USA Ch (Chandler) 1997, may also be OK for Black, since 16 ♘xc5 ♖ac8 17 ♘xb7

♖d2 offers Black a fair amount of activity to compensate for the two-pawn deficit.

6 ♘xf6+ *(D)*

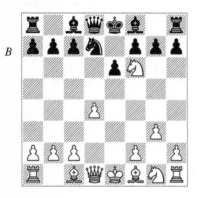

6...♘xf6

6...♕xf6 is a different strategy, as Black goes for a more or less symmetrical pawn-structure by aiming to exchange his e-pawn for White's d-pawn. 7 ♗g2 ♗d6 (7...e5?! is premature, owing to 8 ♕e2! ♕e7 9 dxe5 ♕xe5 10 ♗f4 ♕xe2+ 11 ♘xe2 c6 12 0-0-0 ♗c5 13 ♘d4 and White was better in Ki.Georgiev-Kurajica, Sarajevo 1998) 8 ♘e2 e5 9 0-0 0-0 10 ♘c3 (10 ♗e3!? – Beliavsky) 10...exd4 (10...♕e7 11 ♘e4 ♘b6 12 ♘xd6 cxd6 is given as equal by Beliavsky but I would definitely prefer White; e.g., 13 a4 followed by a5 or just b3 looks good) 11 ♘e4 ♕g6 12 ♕xd4 ♗e5 13 ♕e3 and after 13...♘f6 14 f4! ♘g4 15 ♕d3 ♕b6+ 16 ♔h1 ♗d4 17 f5! White was better in Beliavsky-Vaganian, Tilburg 1993, owing to the possibility of a kingside attack. However, I suspect

that Black should be doing OK with 13...♕b6!? instead.

7 ♗g2

White can maybe avoid the idea mentioned in the next note by playing 7 ♘f3!? before ♗g2.

7...c5

This is invariably played, but perhaps is not Black's best. Korchnoi recommends 7...e5. This needs some tests but 8 ♘f3 exd4 9 ♕xd4 ♕xd4 10 ♘xd4 doesn't seem to offer White much. Nor does 8 dxe5 ♕xd1+ 9 ♔xd1 ♘g4 10 ♘h3 ♘xe5 11 ♗f4 ♗g4+! 12 ♔c1 ♗f3!.

8 ♘f3 ♕b6

Or 8...cxd4 9 ♕xd4 ♕xd4 10 ♘xd4 ♗c5 11 ♘b3, and now:

a) After 11...♗d6 12 0-0 ♔e7 White obtains unpleasant queenside pressure with 13 ♘a5!. After 13...♖b8 14 ♗e3, 14...♗c7? 15 ♗xa7 ♖a8 16 ♗c5+ left White a pawn up in Palac-Neubauer, Baden 1999. Finkel gives 14...♘d7 as Black's best, with "a chance to keep fighting" but 15 ♘c4! ♗c5 16 ♗f4 ♖a8 17 ♖ad1 is also very bad for Black.

b) 11...♗b6 is best. I have a feeling that White should still be slightly better somehow but it is not totally clear how he should proceed. After 12 ♔e2?! (12 0-0 0-0 13 ♗f4 looks more natural) 12...e5 13 ♖e1 0-0 14 ♘d2 ♘g4 15 ♘e4 ♗e6 Black was doing well in Hertneck-Luther, Bad Lauterberg 1991.

9 0-0 ♗d7 10 a4!? ♘c6

White might also claim a slight advantage after 10...♖d8 11 a5 ♕c7 12

♗f4 ♗d6 13 ♗xd6 ♕xd6 14 dxc5
♕xc5 15 ♕d4.

**11 a5 ♕c7 12 a6 ♖d8 13 c3 b5 14
♕e2 c4 15 b3! ♗d5**

Black may have underestimated
White's last move; instead 15...cxb3
16 ♘e5! ♗xg2 17 ♕xb5+ ♘d7 18
♔xg2 ♖b8 19 ♕a4! f6 (19...b2? 20
♗xb2 ♖xb2 21 ♖fb1 +–) 20 ♘xd7
♕xd7 21 ♗f4 ♖b6 22 ♖fb1 ♗e7 23
♗e3 gives White a clear advantage.

**16 ♘e5 ♗e7 17 bxc4 bxc4 18 ♗f4
♕c8 19 ♖fb1**

± Macieja-Speelman, New Delhi
FIDE 2000.

B)

5 ♘f3 ♘gf6 (D)

5...♗e7 6 ♗d3 and now:

a) 6...♘gf6 – 5...♘gf6 6 ♗d3 ♗e7
±.

b) Lately Black has also experimented with 6...b6 but 7 ♗b5 is good
for White. Black's best is then 7...♘f6
8 ♘xf6+ (8 ♘e5!?) 8...gxf6 with just a
slight disadvantage. Instead, 7...♗b7
is virtually refuted by 8 ♘e5! ♗xe4
9 ♗xd7+ ♔f8 10 ♕h5 g6 11 ♗h6+
♘xh6 12 ♕xh6+ ♔g8 13 ♕f4 ♗f5 14
g4 g5 15 ♕f3 ♗g6 16 ♗xe6! fxe6 17
♘c6 ♕d7 18 ♘xe7+ ♔g7 19 ♘xg6
hxg6 20 0-0-0 and White was a pawn
up in Gaprindashvili-Shengelia, Alushta 2000.

Now:

B1: 6 ♗d3   19
B2: 6 ♘xf6+   21

Other moves:

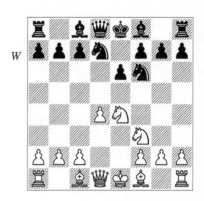

a) 6 ♗g5 – 3...♘f6 4 ♗g5 dxe4 5
♘xe4 ♘bd7 6 ♘f3 (Chapter 3).

b) 6 ♘g3 is seen occasionally when
White wants to avoid exchanges at all
costs. Nevertheless, White can hope
for no real advantage after this; e.g.,
6...c5 7 dxc5 ♗xc5 8 ♗d3 0-0 9 0-0 b6
10 ♕e2 ♗b7 11 c3 ♕c7 with a comfortable position for Black, Meštro-
vić-Kosić, Budapest 1999.

B1)

6 ♗d3 c5

In my opinion, this is Black's most
natural move. It links well with the
more established Line B22, to which
the game would now transpose after 7
♘xf6+ ♘xf6. Alternatives for Black
on move 6 give White good chances of
an advantage:

a) 6...b6 7 ♘xf6+ ♘xf6 8 ♕e2 – 6
♘xf6+ ♘xf6 7 ♗d3 b6 8 ♕e2 ±.

b) 6...♘xe4 7 ♗xe4 ♘f6 8 ♗g5
and now:

b1) 8...♗e7 9 ♗xf6! gxf6 (9...♗xf6
and now 10 c3 ♕d6 11 ♕e2 0-0 12
0-0-0!? is slightly better for White,

Smyslov-Rudnev, USSR 1938, or 10 ♕d3 ±) 10 ♕e2 c6 (Anand regards this as dubious and prefers 10...♕d6) 11 0-0! ♕b6 12 c4 ♗d7 13 c5 ♕c7 14 ♖fd1 h5 15 ♘d2 ± Anand-Vaganian, Riga Tal mem 1995.

b2) 8...♕d6!? 9 ♗xf6 gxf6 10 c3! ♗d7 (White is also better after 10...f5 11 ♗c2 ♗g7 12 ♕e2, but this is clearly the lesser evil) 11 ♘d2 ♗c6 12 ♕f3 ♗e7 13 ♘c4 ♕d7 14 ♗xc6 ♕xc6 15 ♕xc6+ bxc6 16 b4 ± Kharlov-Zakharevich, Novgorod 1999.

c) 6...♗e7 and then:

c1) 7 ♘xf6+ ♗xf6 8 ♕e2 ♕e7 (or 8...c5 9 d5 ♘b6 10 ♗b5+ ♔f8 11 dxe6 ♗xe6 12 a4 a6 13 ♗d3 ♕c7 14 0-0 ± Timman-Granda, Amsterdam 1995) 9 0-0 c5 10 c3 0-0 11 ♗f4 cxd4 12 cxd4 ♘b6 13 ♗e5 and White is slightly better, Dominguez-Rod.Perez, Villa Clara 2000.

c2) 7 ♕e2 ♘xe4 8 ♗xe4 c5 9 0-0 0-0 10 ♖d1 ♕c7 11 c3 and then:

c21) 11...♘f6 12 ♗g5! ± Yermolinsky-Seirawan, Merrillville 1997.

c22) 11...cxd4 12 cxd4!? (or 12 ♘xd4 ♘f6 13 ♗c2 ±) 12...♘f6 13 ♗g5 ♗d7 14 ♖ac1 ♕b6 and now White should play 15 d5 rather than 15 ♘e5 ♗b5 16 ♕f3 ♖ad8! with counterplay, Kudrin-Christiansen, USA Ch (Salt Lake City) 1999.

7 0-0 *(D)*

Or:

a) Black equalizes easily after 7 dxc5 ♘xe4 8 ♗xe4 ♘xc5.

b) 7 ♘xf6+ ♘xf6 – *6 ♘xf6+ ♘xf6 7 ♗d3 c5*.

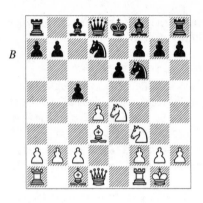

7...cxd4

With 7...♘xe4 8 ♗xe4 ♘f6 Black hopes for a transposition to *6 ♘xf6+ ♘xf6 7 ♗d3 c5 8 0-0 cxd4 9 ♘xd4 =*, after 9 ♗d3. However, 9 ♗g5 cxd4 gives White the additional possibility 10 ♕e2!? (10 ♘xd4 – *7...cxd4 8 ♘xd4 ♘xe4 9 ♗xe4 ♘f6 10 ♗g5*) 10...♗e7 11 ♖ad1, which looks promising for White. Now, several games have continued 11...♘xe4 (11...♕b6 12 ♖xd4 ♕xb2 13 ♖fd1 0-0 14 ♘e5 gives White a strong attack) 12 ♖xd4! ♕xd4 (after 12...♗d7 13 ♕xe4 ♕c7 14 ♗xe7 ♗c6 15 ♖c4! White is clearly better) 13 ♘xd4 ♘xg5, and now:

a) 14 f4!? 0-0 15 fxg5 ♗xg5 16 ♘f3 ♗d8 17 ♕e4, Rublevsky-Zakharevich, Russian Clubs Cup (Maikop) 1998, and now 17...♖b8 looks like a reasonable equalizing attempt.

b) 14 h4 e5 15 ♕xe5 ♘e6 16 ♘f5 f6 17 ♕b5+ ♔f7 18 ♘xe7 ♔xe7 19 f4 was unclear or perhaps even slightly better for White in Shirov-Van Wely, Monaco Amber rpd 2001.

8 ♘xd4 ♘xe4

This is a natural liquidation but Black should seriously consider playing 8...♗e7 first.

9 ♗xe4 ♘f6 10 ♗g5 ♗e7

Another option is 10...♗c5 11 ♘b3, and then:

a) 11...♗e7 12 ♕xd8+ ♗xd8 13 ♗f3 0-0 14 ♖ad1 ♗c7 15 ♘c5 is much better for White.

b) 11...♗d6 12 ♗xf6 gxf6 13 ♕h5 f5 14 ♗f3 (14 ♗xf5? exf5 15 ♖fe1+ ♗e7 was insufficient for White in Morozevich-Zakharevich, Novgorod 1997) 14...♕c7 15 ♖ad1 ±.

11 ♗f3!

Most players would probably try to preserve the bishop on the b1-h7 diagonal for attacking purposes but it is much better on this diagonal, where it hinders Black's development.

11...0-0 12 ♖e1 ♕c7 13 c3 a6 14 ♗h4!

± Shirov-Anand, Wijk aan Zee 2001.

B2)

6 ♘xf6+ ♘xf6 (D)

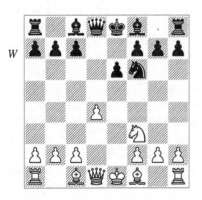

Now:

B21: 7 ♗g5   21
B22: 7 ♗d3   25

7 c3 is also worth mentioning. It is a solid set-up which promises White reasonable chances of a slight edge; e.g.:

a) 7...h6!? 8 ♗d3 ♗d6 9 ♕e2 b6 10 ♘e5 ♗b7 11 ♗b5+ ♔f8 12 0-0 g6 13 ♖e1 ♔g7 14 ♗f4 ♘h5 15 ♗d2 ♘f6 16 ♖ad1 a6 17 ♗d3 and White was better in Adams-Nogueiras, Lucerne Wcht 1997.

b) 7...c5 8 ♗e3 ♕c7 (8...cxd4 9 ♗xd4 ♗e7 10 ♗d3 0-0 11 ♕e2 ♕c7 12 0-0 ♖d8 13 ♖ad1 ♗d7 14 ♘e5 ♗e8 and Black is close to equality, Sadvakasov-Mirzoev, Dubai 1999) 9 ♘e5 a6 10 ♕a4+ ♘d7 11 0-0-0 cxd4 12 ♗xd4 ♗d6 13 ♘xd7 ♗xd7 14 ♕b3 0-0 = Dvoirys-Zakharevich, St Petersburg 1998.

B21)

7 ♗g5

This is also often reached via the Burn move-order *3...♘f6 4 ♗g5 dxe4 5 ♘xe4 ♘bd7 6 ♘xf6+ ♘xf6 7 ♘f3*. The move-order is frequently chosen if Black does not fancy Line B22 (7 ♗d3), but of course Black must then also reckon with *4 e5*.

7...h6

This move makes White decide immediately where he wants his bishop. This has some specific advantages as it helps Black decide on a set-up afterwards and is also a useful move in itself if White replies 8 ♗h4. The move ...c5 is a vital part of Black's plans.

Otherwise, 7...♗e7 is feasible but slightly passive. White can play 8 ♗d3 – 7 ♗d3 ♗e7 8 ♗g5 ±.

A more serious alternative is 7...c5 (D):

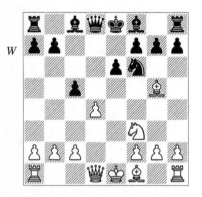

This has especially been a preference of Korchnoi's, and may of course lead to similar positions to those in the main line. Now:

a) 8 dxc5 ♗xc5 (8...♕a5+ 9 c3 ♕xc5 is also sensible) 9 ♕xd8+ ♔xd8 10 ♘e5 ♔e7 11 ♘d3 ♗d6 12 ♗e2 ♗d7 13 ♗f3 ♖ac8 14 0-0-0 ♗c6 15 ♗xc6 ♖xc6 = Wehmeier-Luther, Lippstadt 1996.

b) 8 c3 ♗e7 9 ♗b5+ ♗d7 10 ♗xd7+ ♘xd7 11 ♗xe7 ♕xe7 12 0-0 0-0 13 ♖e1 ♖fd8 14 ♕e2 cxd4 15 ♘xd4 ♘c5 16 ♖ad1 g6 = Thorhallsson-Morozevich, New York 1997.

c) 8 ♗e2 cxd4 (maybe 8...♗d7 is simplest, intending only to capture on d4 after White has castled kingside) 9 ♕xd4 ♕xd4 10 ♘xd4 ♗d7 11 0-0-0 ♗c5 12 ♘b5 0-0-0 (12...♔e7 looks equal) 13 ♘d6+ ♗xd6 14 ♖xd6 ♗c6 15 ♖xd8+ ♖xd8 16 f3 ± Nouro-Kytoniemi, Tampere 1998.

d) 8 ♗c4 and then:

d1) 8...♕a5+!? 9 c3 (9 ♗d2 ♕b6 10 ♗c3 cxd4 11 ♘xd4 ♗d7 12 ♕d3 ♗b4 offered Black easy equality in Lanka-Luther, Bundesliga 1998/9) 9...♗e7 10 0-0 0-0 11 ♖e1 and then:

d11) 11...♖d8 12 ♖e5!? (a slightly unorthodox deployment of the rook but in some lines it may join in with a kingside attack) 12...♕b6 13 ♕e2 h6 (13...cxd4 14 ♘xd4 h6 15 ♗h4 ♘d5 16 ♗xe7 ♘xe7 17 ♖e1 ♗d7 18 ♗d3 ♘c6 19 ♘xc6 ♗xc6 left Black close to equality in Shirov-Topalov, Monte Carlo Amber rpd 1997) 14 ♗xf6 gxf6 15 ♖h5 ♗f8 16 dxc5 ♕c7 17 ♖e1 ♗g7 18 h3 b6 and Black has enough compensation for the pawn, Morozevich-Korchnoi, Wijk aan Zee 2000; Morozevich offered a draw only a few moves later.

d12) 11...cxd4 12 ♕xd4 (12 cxd4 ♖d8 gives Black a fairly solid IQP type of position) 12...h6 13 ♗f4 ♖d8 14 ♕e5 ♕xe5 15 ♘xe5 g5!? (an active way of solving the problem of the light-squared bishop; 15...♗d7 looks solid but of course gives White the possibility of exchanging it) 16 ♗e3 ♘d7! 17 ♘f3 b6 18 ♗b5 ♗b7 with approximately equal chances, Van den Doel-Luther, Venlo 2000.

d2) 8...cxd4 9 0-0. White temporarily sacrifices a pawn for rapid development. Now:

d21) 9...♗c5 attempts to hold on to the pawn but in doing so Black wastes valuable time and White soon develops a strong initiative: 10 ♕e2 ♕b6 11 ♖ad1 ♗d7 12 ♘e5 ♖c8 13 c3! h6 14 ♗h4!? (14 ♗xf6!? gxf6 15 ♘xd7 ♔xd7 16 b4 ♗d6 17 ♖xd4 ±) 14...a6 15 cxd4 ♗xd4 16 ♕d3 (a simpler line is 16 ♘xd7 ♘xd7 17 ♗xe6! ♕xe6 18 ♕xe6+ fxe6 19 ♖xd4 ±) 16...♗xe5 17 ♗xf6 ♗xh2+ 18 ♔h1! ♕c7 19 ♗c3 ♗f4 20 ♕d4 (Nataf-Gretarsson, Bermuda 1999) and now 20...♖g8 leaves things unclear.

d22) 9...♗e7 10 ♕e2 h6 11 ♗f4 0-0 12 ♖ad1 ♗d7 13 ♖xd4 ± Tal-Portisch, Bled Ct (4) 1965 (and others).

d3) 8...a6!?, with similar ideas as in the main line, should definitely be considered.

e) 8 ♗b5+ ♗d7 9 ♗xd7+ ♕xd7 10 ♕e2! *(D)* and now:

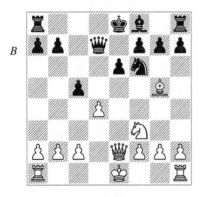

e1) 10...0-0-0?! (this move looks a bit risky) 11 ♖d1 ♕c7 12 0-0 cxd4? (12...♗d6 is better) 13 ♘xd4 a6 14 ♘xe6! fxe6 15 ♕xe6+ ♖d7 16 ♗xf6 gxf6 17 ♖d4 ♗c5 18 ♖c4 ± Benjamin-Seirawan, USA Ch (Seattle) 2000.

e2) 10...cxd4 11 0-0-0 ♗c5 12 ♕e5 ♖c8! 13 ♘xd4 (13 ♗xf6 gxf6 14 ♕xf6 ♖g8 gives Black excellent compensation with not only g2 attacked but also ...♕a4 lurking) 13...♕c7 14 ♕xc7 ♖xc7 15 f3 a6 16 ♖he1 0-0 17 ♗f4 ½-½ Almasi-Ehlvest, Biel 1996.

e3) 10...♗e7 and now:

e31) 11 0-0-0 0-0 and then:

e311) 12 dxc5 ♕a4!? (12...♕c6, as in the main line, should also be considered) 13 ♔b1 ♗xc5 14 ♗xf6 gxf6 (a fairly typical structure; as long as Black is careful he shouldn't be in any danger as his bishop is good and he can take control of the d-file) 15 ♘e1 ♖fd8 16 ♘d3 ♗f8 17 f4 ♖d5 = Leko-Korchnoi, Vienna 1996.

e312) 12 ♖he1 ♕a4 (12...♖fd8 is Timman's suggestion, with the idea that 13 d5?! ♘xd5 14 ♖xd5 ♕xd5 15 ♗xe7 ♕xa2! 16 ♗xd8 ♕a1+ 17 ♔d2 ♖xd8+ 18 ♔e3 ♕xb2 gives Black a strong attack) 13 ♔b1 ♖fd8 14 dxc5 ♗xc5 15 ♖xd8+ ♖xd8 16 ♘e5 ♗e7 17 f3 h6 18 ♗c1 ♘d5 19 c4 ♘b4 20 b3 ♕a6 21 a3 ♘c6 = Van der Wiel-Van der Sterren, Rotterdam 2000.

e313) 12 ♔b1 ♕c7! 13 d5!? (13 dxc5 ♕xc5 14 ♘e5 ♖fd8 15 ♗xf6 ♗xf6 16 ♘d7, Timman-Korchnoi, Lucerne Wcht 1989, 16...♕e7! 17 ♕b5 a6! 18 ♘xf6+ ♕xf6 19 ♕b6 ♕e7 = Timman) 13...exd5! 14 ♖he1 ♗d8 15 ♗xf6 ♗xf6 16 ♖xd5 c4!? 17 c3 ♕c6 18 ♖ed1 ♖fe8 19 ♕c2 ♖e6 = Nisipeanu-Rogozenko, Bucharest 1998.

e32) 11 dxc5 and then:

e321) 11...♗xc5 12 ♘e5! ♕a4? (after 12...♕d5, 13 ♖d1! ♕e4 probably holds, so White should prefer 13 0-0 0-0 – 11...0-0 12 ♘e5 ♕d5 13 0-0 ♗c5 ±) 13 0-0 0-0 14 ♗xf6 gxf6 15 ♕f3! f5 (or 15...fxe5 16 ♕g3+ ♔h8 17 ♕xe5+ f6 18 ♕xc5 ±) 16 ♖ad1 ± Hraček-Slobodjan, Koszalin 1999.

e322) 11...0-0 12 ♘e5 ♕d5 13 0-0 ♗xc5 14 ♖fe1! ♘d7 15 ♘f3 ± Leko-Korchnoi, Wijk aan Zee 2000.

We now return to 7...h6 (D):

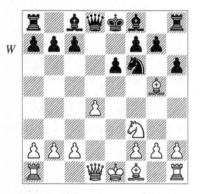

8 ♗h4

This is White's most common but other moves also come into consideration:

a) 8 ♗xf6 ♕xf6 9 ♗b5+!? c6 10 ♗d3 ♗d6 11 ♕e2 ♗d7!? 12 ♘e5 0-0-0 13 0-0 c5 14 c3 ♔b8 15 ♕e3 ♗c8 = Hraček-Lobron, Bad Wiessee 1999.

b) 8 ♗e3!? and then:

b1) 8...♗d6 9 ♗d3 ♕e7 10 0-0 0-0 11 ♖e1 b6 12 c4 ♗b7 13 d5 ♖ae8! 14 h3 ½-½ Z.Almasi-Hübner, Baden 1999.

b2) 8...a6!? 9 ♘e5 b6 10 c3 ♗b7 11 ♕a4+ ♘d7 12 c4 ♗d6 13 0-0-0 ♕e7 14 f4 ♗xe5 15 dxe5 0-0-0 16 ♗e2 g5! with counterplay for Black, Zhang Zhong-M.Gurevich, Cap d'Agde 2000.

8...c5

Another move is 8...♗e7 but this is passive and White has several plausible set-ups. For example, 9 ♗d3 – 7 ♗d3 ♗e7 8 ♗g5 h6 9 ♗h4 ±.

9 ♗b5+

This check is the most common reply to 7...c5 but with the insertion of ...h6 and ♗h4, White has frequently tried other options:

a) 9 c3 cxd4 10 ♘xd4 ♗e7 11 ♗b5+ ♗d7 12 ♕b3 ♗xb5 13 ♕xb5+ ♕d7 = Sax-Psakhis, Manila OL 1992.

b) 9 ♗d3 cxd4 10 ♘xd4 ♗e7 11 0-0 0-0 12 ♗g3 ♗d7 13 c3 ♕b6 14 ♕e2 ♗d6 = Ponomariov-Psakhis, Ohrid Ech 2001.

c) 9 ♗e2!? (the idea of this is that White wants his bishop to appear on f3 after Black exchanges on d4) 9...cxd4 (9...♗e7 should be considered; then 10 dxc5 ♕a5+ 11 c3 ♕xc5 12 ♕b3 0-0 13 0-0 b6 was equal in Dutreeuw-Yanovsky, Werfen 1992; 9...♗d7 also deserves attention) 10 ♕xd4 ♕xd4 11 ♘xd4 ♗d7!? 12 ♘b5 (12 ♗f3 0-0-0 =) 12...♖c8 13 0-0-0 a6 14 ♘d6+ ♗xd6 15 ♖xd6 g5 16 ♗g3 ♘e4 17 ♖d4 ♘xg3 18 hxg3 ♔e7 with equality, Galkin-Bareev, Russian Cht (Tomsk) 2001.

d) 9 ♗c4 a6! 10 0-0 ♗e7 and now:

d1) 11 a4 0-0 12 ♕e2 cxd4 13 ♖ad1 ♕b6 14 b3!? ♗d7 15 ♘xd4 ♖fe8 16

♘f3 ♖ed8! 17 ♘e5 ♗e8 = Bologan-M.Gurevich, Saint-Pierre 2000.

d2) 11 dxc5 ♕xd1 12 ♖axd1 ♗xc5 13 a4 ♔e7 14 ♖fe1 ♗d7 15 ♗b3 ♖hd8 16 ♘e5 ♗e8 = Svidler-M.Gurevich, Frankfurt rpd 2000.

d3) 11 ♗b3!? cxd4 12 ♘xd4 0-0 13 ♖e1 ± Nataf.

9...♗d7 10 ♗xd7+ ♕xd7 11 ♕e2 ♗e7 *(D)*

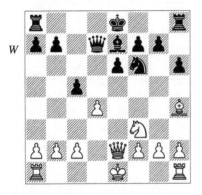

Obviously this needs to be compared with *7...c5 8 ♗b5+ ♗d7 9 ♗xd7+ ♕xd7 10 ♕e2! ♗e7*. The only difference is the insertion of the moves ...h6 and ♗h4, which is probably to Black's advantage. The bishop is stuck away on the kingside and sometimes Black might even have aggressive ideas with ...g5. The problem is the usual one: ...h6 may turn out to be a weakening of Black's kingside.

12 0-0-0 0-0 13 dxc5

In Chandler-Vaganian, Bundesliga 1995/6, White tried to go straight for the king with 13 g4 but this turned out to be a rather random thrust, and by

13...♘d5 14 ♗xe7 ♕xe7 15 ♔b1 b5! 16 dxc5 ♕xc5 17 ♘e5 ♖ad8 18 ♘d3 ♕c4 19 ♕e5 ♖c8 20 c3 ♖fd8 Black gradually took over the initiative.

13...♕c6!

Probably better than 13...♕a4 14 ♔b1 ♖fd8 15 a3 ♗xc5 16 ♗xf6 gxf6, which should be equal, but White has some chances due to his better pawn-structure and the combination of queen + knight vs queen + bishop, Benjamin-Psakhis, New York 1992.

14 ♔b1 ♖fd8 15 ♖he1

15 ♘e5 ♕xc5 16 ♗xf6 ♗xf6 17 ♘d7 ♕e7 18 ♕b5 a6 is equal according to Anand. Note the trap 19 ♕xb7? ♖db8 –+.

15...♕xc5

= Anand-Ivanchuk, Linares (2) 1992.

B22)
7 ♗d3 *(D)*

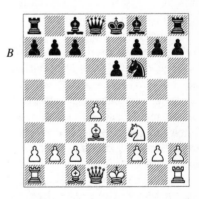

7...c5

This direct attack on White's centre is best. Other moves lead to a more passive position:

a) 7...b6?! 8 ♕e2 ♗b7 9 ♗g5 ♗e7 10 0-0-0 ♕d6 (10...0-0 is feasible but also very pleasant for White; e.g., 11 h4 ♕d5 12 ♔b1 ♖fd8 13 c4 ♕d6 14 ♖he1 ± Bronstein-Kan, Moscow Ch 1947) 11 ♘e5 0-0 12 ♔b1 ♖ad8, Top-alov-Vaganian, Novgorod 1995, and now Dolmatov suggests that 13 ♗f4 causes trouble for Black after 13...♘d5 14 ♗g3 or 13...♕d5 14 c4 ♕xd4 15 ♗xh7+ ♔xh7 16 ♖xd4 ♖xd4 17 ♗e3.

b) 7...♗e7 with two promising options for White:

b1) 8 ♗g5 h6 9 ♗h4 c5 10 dxc5 ♕a5+ 11 c3 ♕xc5 12 ♕e2 ♗d7 13 ♘e5 ♗c6 14 0-0-0 0-0 15 f4 ♖ad8 16 ♖he1 ± Kupreichik-Savon, USSR Ch (Leningrad) 1974.

b2) 8 ♕e2 0-0 9 ♗g5 c5 10 0-0-0 (10 dxc5 is of course also possible) 10...♕a5 11 ♔b1 cxd4 12 h4 ♗d7 13 ♘xd4 ♗c6 14 ♘xc6 bxc6 15 ♗d2!? ♕b6 16 c4 ♖fb8 17 ♗c3 ± Nunn-Skembris, Paris 1983.

8 dxc5

This is White's most common continuation but 8 0-0 cxd4 9 ♘xd4 is also interesting. Then I believe Black's best is 9...♗c5 *(D)* (rather than the slightly passive but, I admit, solid 9...♗e7), when the question is whether White should keep his knight centralized on d4 or retreat it to b3:

a) 10 ♘b3 ♗d6 11 ♕f3 (11 ♗g5 h6 12 ♗h4 ♕c7 13 ♗g3 ♗xg3 14 hxg3 0-0 15 ♕e2 e5! is comfortable for Black, Suetin-Speelman, London Lloyds Bank 1991) 11...♕c7 12 h3 ♗d7 13 ♘d4 (this is almost identical

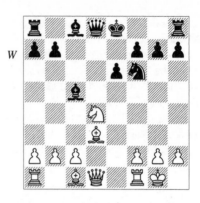

to a line in the French Tarrasch arising from *3 ♘d2 c5 4 exd5 ♕xd5*, although in those positions White's bishop is usually on b3) 13...♗e5!? 14 ♘b5 ♕b8 15 ♖e1 a6 16 ♘c3 ♗c6 ∓ Kuzmin-Chernin, Irkutsk 1983.

b) 10 ♗e3 ♗b6 (I tried recently 10...♕e7, but now I think the queen is not so well placed there; after 11 c3 0-0, I expected 12 ♖e1 ±, but 12 ♕f3 ♘d5 13 ♗d2 ♗xd4 14 cxd4 ♗d7 was fine for Black in Asrian-S.Pedersen, Istanbul OL 2000) and now:

b1) 11 c3 0-0 12 ♖e1 (Beliavsky-Ehlvest, Erevan OL 1996) 12...♘d5 13 ♗d2 ♗xd4 14 cxd4 ♗d7 = Beliavsky.

b2) 11 ♗b5+ ♗d7 12 ♕e2 0-0 (12...♗xb5!?) 13 ♖ad1 ♘d5 14 ♗xd7 ♕xd7 15 ♗c1 ♖fe8 16 c4 ♘f6 (Nadyr-khanov-Supatashvili, Cherkessk 1997) 17 ♗e3 ±.

c) 10 c3 0-0 11 ♗g5 h6 12 ♗h4 ♗xd4!? (even with White's bishop on h4, as compared to d2 in 'a' and 'b' above, this exchange seems to solve Black's problems) 13 cxd4 ♗d7 14

♖e1 ♗c6 15 ♖e5! ♕e7 16 ♗c2 (Nogueiras suggests 16 ♕d2 ♖fd8 17 ♖ae1
♖d5 18 ♗c4 instead, presumably with
a roughly equal position after 18...♖xe5
19 ♖xe5) 16...♖fd8 17 ♕d3 ♖ac8.
Black has a comfortable position with
play against the IQP, Arencibia-No-
gueiras, Cienfuegos 1997.

8...♗xc5 9 ♕e2 *(D)*

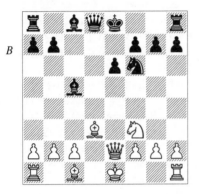

9...0-0

9...♕c7 may lead to positions similar to those considered later but has
the advantage of avoiding some of the
sharper lines (for example, *9...0-0 10
♗g5 h6 11 h4*). However, there is also
a drawback in that White now can play
a set-up with ♗d2 and 0-0-0. Let us
see:

a) 10 0-0 0-0 – *9...0-0 10 0-0 ♕c7*
±/=.

b) 10 ♗g5 ♗b4+!? 11 ♘d2 (11 c3
♗xc3+ 12 bxc3 ♕xc3+ 13 ♕d2 ♕xa1+
14 ♔e2 ♕xh1 15 ♗xf6 gxf6 16 ♗b5+
♔f8 17 ♕b4+ ♔g7 18 ♕g4+ ♔f8 19
♕b4+ = Cifuentes) 11...h6 12 ♗h4
♕f4 (12...♗d7!?) 13 ♗g3 ♕xd2+ 14

♕xd2 ♗xd2+ 15 ♔xd2 ♗d7 16 ♖ad1
0-0-0 17 ♔c1 ♗c6 18 f3, Nijboer-Ci-
fuentes, Dutch Ch (Rotterdam) 1997,
and now Cifuentes suggests 18...♘d5
=.

c) 10 ♗d2 0-0 11 0-0-0 b6 12 ♘e5
♗b7 13 f4. This set-up for White is in
my opinion the only one that chal-
lenges 9...♕c7. Now:

c1) 13...♘d5 14 ♖hf1 ♘b4 (Fedorov suggests 14...♖ac8) 15 ♗xb4 ♗xb4
16 g4 and White's attacking chances
should be preferred. The game Fedorov-Dashchian, Moscow 1998 continued 16...♖ad8 17 g5 ♗d6 18 h4
♗xe5 19 fxe5 ♖d5 20 ♖de1 ♖c8 21
♖f4 ♕d7?! (21...♖cd8!?) 22 ♔b1 ♖cc5
23 ♖ef1 ♖xe5 24 ♕f2 ♖c7 25 ♕g3
♕d6 26 h5 ♖d5 27 g6 f5 28 h6 and
White's attack crashed through. A
rather lengthy line and, I admit, there
is plenty of room for improvements
for Black along this road, but this was
just to give you an idea of how to handle this type of position from White's
point of view.

c2) 13...♖fd8 14 ♔b1 ♖ac8 15
♖hf1 ♘d5 and now 16 a3 (Glek-No-
gueiras, Linares 1996) should be answered by 16...b5! with counterplay.
The main idea is 17 ♗xb5 ♗xa3!.
However, judging from the game
Fedorov-Dashchian above there is no
need for White to prevent ...♘b4, so
16 g4 ♘b4 17 ♗xb4 ♗xb4 18 g5 is the
way to play it.

10 0-0

10 ♗d2 e5! is just *10 ♗g5 h6 11
♗d2* with the h-pawn on h7 instead of

h6. This should not make any major differences, but 10 ♗g5 *(D)* is a sharp alternative, intending to castle queenside. Then:

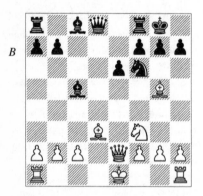

a) 10...♕a5+ 11 c3 (11 ♗d2 ♕c7 – 9...♕c7 10 ♗d2 0-0 ±) 11...♗e7 (another idea is 11...♕c7!?) 12 ♘e5 h6 13 ♗h4 ♖d8 14 0-0 ♕c7 15 ♖ad1 gives White a typical slight advantage, Karpov-Speelman, Reykjavik 1991 (and others).

b) 10...h6. If White had time to attack on the kingside, such a move could be a fatal weakness as White can more easily break up the kingside with g4-g5. However, Black seems to have sufficient counterplay to distract White from this plan. We have:

b1) 11 ♗h4 ♕a5+ 12 c3 (12 ♔f1 is an original attempt to pursue the above-mentioned plan at the cost of weakening the king's position: after 12...♗e7 13 g4 ♖d8 14 g5 hxg5 15 ♗xg5 e5! Black had good counterplay in Grishchuk-Gaprindashvili, Ubeda 1999) 12...♘d5 (this is the main

difference compared with 'a' above; the f4-square is weakened) 13 ♕d2 (13 b4? ♕a3!) 13...♗e7 14 ♗xe7 ♘xe7 15 0-0 ♕c7 = Smirin-Yudasin, Israel 1995.

b2) 11 ♗d2 e5! (this actually makes me wonder if Black could play ...e5!? on his last move) 12 0-0-0 (12 ♘xe5 ♖e8 13 ♗c4? ♗xf2+! 14 ♔xf2 ♖xe5 –+ Kholmov) 12...♖e8 13 ♗c3 ♕b6 14 ♘xe5 ♗e6, and Black had excellent compensation for the pawn in Fedorov-Supatashvili, Ekaterinburg 1997.

b3) 11 h4!? ♕a5+ 12 ♗d2 ♕b6 13 0-0-0 (13 0-0 was played in Ponomariov-Speelman, Pamplona 1996/7 but I just cannot believe it should be any good; perhaps even 13...♕xb2 is feasible and 13...e5!?, as Speelman chose, is not bad either) 13...♘g4 14 ♖df1 and then:

b31) 14...♘xf2?! 15 ♖xf2 ♗xf2 16 g4! is actually very dangerous for Black, Sermek-Golubović, Medulin 1997.

b32) 14...♗xf2 15 ♘h2! ♘xh2 16 ♖xh2 is also far from clear according to Zakharevich, because g4-g5 again comes quickly.

b33) 14...♗d7! is safest as Black quickly develops counterplay on the queenside, while the pressure against f2 remains and makes White's position somewhat cramped. A draw was agreed here in Goloshchapov-Zakharevich, Ekaterinburg 1999.

We now return to 10 0-0 *(D)*:

10...b6

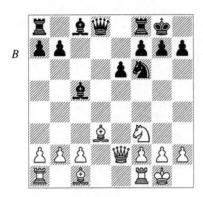

Other moves:

a) 10...h6 is a viable alternative as it deprives White of a ♗g5 set-up. Hence, another piece configuration is required, and the most logical is 11 b3 b6 12 ♗b2 ♗b7 13 ♖ad1 ♕e7 14 ♘e5 ♖ad8 15 ♖fe1 ♖d5 with approximately equal chances. The continuation of Bauer-Rausis, Enghien les Bains 1999 was entertaining though: 16 ♗c4 (16 c4!?) 16...♘e4!? (a very creative solution) 17 ♘g4 (17 ♗xd5? ♗xf2+ 18 ♔h1 exd5 is obviously too dangerous for White) 17...♘xf2!? (17...♖xd1 18 ♖xd1 ♕g5 and 17...♖g5!? are less risky options, while 17...♖f5! looks strong) 18 ♘xf2 ♖g5 19 g4 ♕c7 20 ♗d4 ♕c6 21 ♘e4 ♖e5 with a complete mess.

b) 10...♕c7 11 ♘e5 (11 ♗g5 b6 and now 12 ♖ad1 ♗b7 – *10...b6 11 ♗g5 ♗b7 12 ♖ad1 ♕c7 ±/=*, while 12 ♗xf6 gxf6 13 ♕e4 f5 14 ♕xa8? ♗b7 15 ♕xf8+ ♔xf8 is very good for Black) 11...b6 12 ♗f4 ♗b7 13 ♖ad1 ♖ad8 14 ♗g3 ♕c8!? 15 ♗h4 ♗e7 16 ♖fe1 ♕c5 17 c4 ♗a8 18 b3 ♕c7 19

♗b1 ♕b7 20 ♘f3 ♖fe8 with an equal position, Herrera-Supatashvili, Erevan OL 1996.

11 ♗g5 ♗b7 12 ♖ad1 ♕c7 13 ♗xf6

This gives White a structural plus but is not very dangerous for Black. However, it seems the only way to play for an advantage. 13 ♘e5 ♖fd8 is the alternative but doesn't promise White anything. In Ginzburg-Hoffmann, Argentinean Ch (Buenos Aires) 1998 Black even got a good position after 14 ♔h1?! h6 15 ♗h4 ♗d4!, and 14 ♗xf6 gxf6 15 ♕g4+ ♔f8 16 ♘f3 f5 (I would be tempted to play for more, with 16...♗e7!?) 17 ♕h5 ♗xf3 18 ♕xf3 ♔g7 was only level in Donev-Dobosz, Goetzis 1997.

13...gxf6 (D)

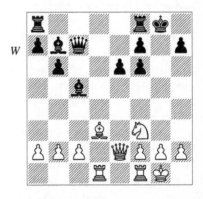

14 ♗e4

Ideally, White now hopes to reach a queen + knight vs queen + bishop ending. Hence, besides the exchange of bishops White also attempts to exchange all the rooks.

14...♗xe4

In my opinion this is the most accurate as it makes it more difficult for White to trade both pairs of rooks.

15 ♕xe4 ♖fd8

15...♖ad8 16 g3 ♖d7 is another set-up, perhaps a more accurate one, which leads to equal chances. Black is ready to fight for the d-file without being forced to exchange both pairs of rooks.

16 c3

16 g3 is an alternative:

a) 16...f5 17 ♕e2 ♗e7 18 c3 ♗f6 19 ♖xd8+ ♖xd8 20 ♖d1 ♖xd1+ 21 ♕xd1 ♕c4 22 a3 b5 23 ♘e1 a5 24 ♘d3 was Tiviakov-Speelman, Beijing 1997. Although White's advantage is minimal after 24...♔g7, this is exactly the sort of endgame where Black can run into trouble if he is not careful. Speelman, by the way an expert in this endgame, went wrong with 24...e5? which only served to weaken Black's central pawns. In general I would prefer to keep the pawns back for as long as possible (though it may at some point be necessary to advance them in order to create counterplay), keeping Black's position very compact.

b) Hence, as suggested by Tiviakov, Black should maybe turn to the plan of fighting for the d-file by 16...♖ac8, intending ...♖d7 followed by ...♖cd8.

16...b5!?

A small sign of Black being ambitious, perhaps?

17 g3 a5 18 ♔g2 b4

Bauer-Speelman, Escaldes Z 1998. Black has good counterplay on the queenside and even went on to obtain some winning chances by advancing his pawns to a4 and b3, after White had played c4.

C)

5 ♗d3 ♘gf6 6 ♕e2 (D)

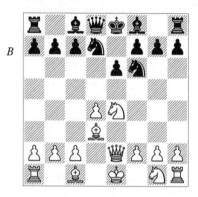

B

This is a modern line, which is similar to Line B22 but it is designed for a sharper set-up with queenside castling.

6...c5

Since White intends to castle queenside and as he is well positioned for a possible attack on the kingside, Black should do whatever he can to interfere with White's development. The ...c5 thrust is the most logical. Note that after 6...♘xe4 7 ♗xe4 ♘f6 (7...c5 8 d5! exd5 9 ♗xd5+ ♕e7 10 ♗e3 ±) White can snatch a pawn with 8 ♗xb7!. Then there are two options for Black but both are insufficient:

a) 8...♖b8 9 ♗xc8 ♕xc8 10 ♘f3 c5 11 0-0 cxd4 12 ♘xd4 ♗c5 13 ♘b3 ± Potkin-Biriukov, Moscow 1997.

b) 8...♗xb7 9 ♕b5+ ♘d7 10 ♕xb7 ♗d6 11 ♘f3 0-0 12 0-0 e5 13 ♗g5

♕c8 14 ♕xc8 ♖fxc8 15 ♖ae1 f6 16
♗c1 c5 17 dxe5 ♘xe5 18 ♘xe5 ♗xe5
19 c3 c4 20 ♖d1 +– Kobaliya-Khol-
mov, Moscow 1996.

7 ♘xf6+

One point worth noting is that 7
dxc5 ♘xe4 8 ♗xe4 ♘xc5 gives Black
a comfortable position. If instead 7
♘f3 then Black equalizes easily with
7...cxd4 8 ♘xd4 ♘xe4 9 ♕xe4 ♘c5
10 ♗b5+ ♗d7.

7...♘xf6

In Fedorov-Goldshtein, Perm 1997
Black actually got away with 7...♕xf6
8 ♘f3 h6 9 d5 ♗d6 10 dxe6 fxe6 11
0-0 0-0 12 ♖e1 ♘b6, and later won the
game, but I am pretty sure Fedorov
would not mind repeating this. White
stands clearly better.

8 dxc5

8 ♗g5?! cxd4 9 0-0-0 is a rather
speculative pawn sacrifice that I don't
trust for White. In Sulskis-Zakhare-
vich, St Petersburg 1998, Black found
a safe defensive set-up: 9...♗d7! 10
♘f3 ♕a5 11 ♗xf6 gxf6 12 ♔b1 ♗c5
13 ♘d2 ♕c7 14 g3 ♗c6 15 ♗b5 0-0-0
16 ♗xc6 ♕xc6 17 f4 ♖d5 18 ♖hf1
♖hd8 and White did not seem to have
quite enough for the pawn.

8...♗xc5 *(D)*

9 ♗g5

Or:

a) 9 ♘f3 – 5 ♘f3 ♘gf6 6 ♘xf6+
♘xf6 7 ♗d3 c5 8 dxc5 ♗xc5 9 ♕e2
±/=.

b) 9 ♗d2 is another way to prepare
queenside castling. Actually, in view
of Van Wely's idea of meeting *9 ♗g5*

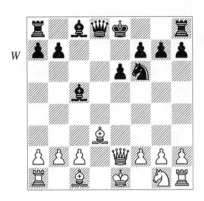

with *9...h6!?*, this should perhaps be
White's preference. Sometimes the
bishop may take up an attacking position on c3. Black can transpose to the
main lines with ...♕b6 or ...♕c7 here
or on the next move, but White can
have some fun if Black becomes
greedy with 9...0-0 10 0-0-0 ♕d5.
There are many reasons to prefer castling to ♘f3 but this double attack is of
course a logical way to try to punish
White for changing the move-order.
We all know, though, that going
pawn-grabbing in the opening can be
a very risky business. White has:

b1) 11 ♔b1 and now:

b11) 11...♕xg2? 12 ♘f3 ♕xf2 13
♕e5 ♕xf3 14 ♕xc5 b6 15 ♕g5 h6 16
♕h4 ♕h5 17 ♕g3 ♔h8 18 ♖hg1 ♖g8
19 ♖df1 ♗b7 20 ♗c3 gave White a
devastating attack in Ivanišević-Sup-
atashvili, Panormo Z 1998.

b12) 11...e5! is the correct way to
proceed; e.g., 12 ♗b4 ♕c6 13 ♗b5
♕b6 14 ♗xc5 ♕xc5 is fine for Black.

b2) 11 ♗c3 gives Black the choice
of which pawn to go for:

b21) 11...♕xg2 allows White to regain material with 12 ♘f3 ♕xf2 13 ♕xf2 ♗xf2 14 ♗b4. The resulting position is slightly better for White due to his modest initiative.

b22) 11...♕xa2 (D) and then:

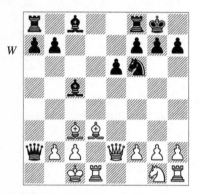

b221) White can force a draw with 12 ♗xf6 gxf6 13 ♕h5 ♕a1+ 14 ♔d2 ♕a5+ 15 ♔e2 f5 16 ♕g5+ ♔h8 17 ♕f6+ ♔g8 18 ♕g5+, etc. Going for more in this line looks risky.

b222) 12 ♘f3 might be dangerous for Black. Black is not really threatening anything on the queenside, while White simply adds to his attack on the kingside. A sample line is 12...♘d5 13 ♗xh7+! ♔h8 (13...♔xh7 14 ♕e4+ f5 15 ♕h4+ ♔g8 16 ♘g5 ♖f7 17 ♖xd5! ♕xd5 18 ♖d1 +−) 14 ♗e5 ♘xc3 15 ♗d3, when 15...♔g8 16 ♕h5 g6 17 ♗xg6 ♕a1+ 18 ♔d2 ♖d8+ 19 ♔xc3 ♕a5+ 20 ♔b3 wins for White, but 15...♕d5 is probably a better defence for Black, though 16 ♕xc3 is at any rate dangerous. Also, in the event of 12...h6, with the idea of preventing

♘g5 and ruling out possible bishop sacrifices, White's attack is dangerous. Even just catapulting the g-pawn ahead is interesting since it takes ages for Black to open the queenside; e.g., 13 g4 ♘d5 14 g5 ♘xc3 15 bxc3 hxg5 16 ♘xg5 g6 17 ♖dg1 with a fantastic attack.

b23) 11...♕g5+?! 12 ♔b1 ♘d5 13 ♗e5 ♕xg2?! (this is horribly risky, but 13...f6 14 ♗g3 is just better for White, so there is really no sensible way back) 14 ♕h5 f5 (14...g6 is perhaps better but I am sure 15 ♕h6 f6 16 ♘h3! soon crashes through) 15 ♘f3 ♕g4?! 16 ♖hg1! ♕xh5 (16...♘f4 17 ♕h4 ♘g2 18 ♖xg2 ♕xg2 19 ♖g1 +−; 16...♘f6 17 ♗xf6 ♕xh5 18 ♖xg7+ ♔h8 19 ♖dg1 and Black is mated) 17 ♖xg7+ ♔h8 (Sadler-Miles, British Ch (Hove) 1997) and now 18 ♖dg1! forces a quick mate.

We now return to 9 ♗g5 (D):

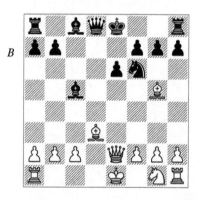

9...♕a5+

This move, forcing White's bishop back to d2, has been played almost invariably, but recently Van Wely came up with another idea for Black: 9...h6!? (this simple move has gone unnoticed for a long time) 10 ♗b5+ (White doesn't get anything from exchanging on f6, while 10 ♗h4 ♕d4! is irritating and if 10 ♗d2, Black cannot complain about having his pawn on h6) 10...♗d7 11 ♗xd7+ (11 ♗xf6?! ♕a5+ 12 ♗c3 ♕xb5 ∓) 11...♕xd7 12 ♗xf6 gxf6 13 ♖d1 ♕c6 14 ♘f3 0-0 15 0-0 ♖fd8 16 c3 b5, and Black has roughly equalized, Fedorov-Van Wely, Istanbul OL 2000.

10 ♗d2 ♕b6

Alternatively, 10...♕c7 11 ♘f3 – *5 ♘f3 ♘gf6 6 ♘xf6+ ♘xf6 7 ♗d3 c5 8 dxc5 ♗xc5 9 ♕e2 ♕c7 10 ♗d2 ±.*

On b6, the queen attacks b2 and f2 simultaneously. Particularly the attack on f2 is somewhat awkward for White but if it turns out to be ineffective, the queen will not be so well placed on b6.

11 0-0-0 ♗d7 *(D)*

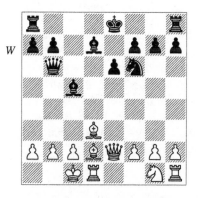

This position has occurred several times, with Black scoring quite well, but

it seems to me that White's problems have stemmed from an excessive concern for the f2-pawn. Now:

a) 12 ♘h3 (White develops and defends f2, but the knight is not well placed on h3) 12...h6 13 ♕e1?! (this is just a bad move; White should play 13 ♗c3 immediately but Black has no problems after 13...0-0-0) 13...a5! 14 ♗c3 ♗b4 15 a3 ♗xc3 16 ♕xc3 ♖c8 17 ♕e5 0-0 and Black is already a tiny bit better, Asrian-Feoktistov, St Petersburg 1999.

b) 12 f4 0-0-0 13 ♘f3 ♘g4 14 ♘g5 f5! 15 ♘f7 ♘f2 16 ♘xh8 ♖xh8 17 ♔b1 ♖e8 18 ♗c3 ♘xh1 19 ♖xh1 ♗d4 20 ♗xd4 ♕xd4 = Lastin-Feoktistov, Voronezh 1998.

c) 12 ♘f3! is the only critical test, simply ignoring the attack on f2. After 12...♘g4 13 ♗e1, Black has a difficult choice:

c1) 13...♘xf2 14 ♗xf2 ♗xf2 15 ♔b1 ♗c6 16 ♖hf1 ♗c5 17 ♘g5 gives White a strong attack.

c2) 13...♗xf2 14 ♘d2!? ♗xe1 15 ♘c4 is even worse for Black.

c3) 13...0-0-0 14 ♘g5 f5 (another possibility is 14...♘h6!?) 15 ♘f7 ♗xf2 16 ♘xh8 ♖xh8 17 h3 ♗d4 18 c3 ♗e3+ 19 ♗d2 with an advantage for White.

c4) 13...h6 prepares ...♘xf2 without having to worry about ♘g5 ideas as in 'c1' above, and is perhaps Black's best; e.g., 14 ♖f1 ♗c6 15 h3 ♘f6 (15...♗xf3 16 gxf3 ♘f6 17 ♖g1 gives White a strong initiative) 16 ♗c3 0-0-0 with a fairly balanced game.

3 Burn Variation: 5...♘bd7

1 e4 e6 2 d4 d5 3 ♘c3 ♘f6 4 ♗g5 dxe4 5 ♘xe4 ♘bd7 *(D)*

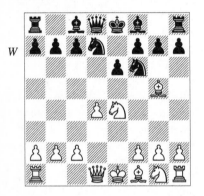

The Burn Variation with 5...♘bd7 is closely related to the lines of the Rubinstein Variation that we looked at in the previous chapter. Indeed, the lines we are going to examine here often arise from a Rubinstein move-order; e.g., *3...dxe4 4 ♘xe4 ♘d7 5 ♘f3 ♘gf6 6 ♗g5 ♗e7*. The positions arising are often slightly in White's favour but Black can obtain good counterchances if White over-presses.

6 ♘f3 *(D)*

6 ♘xf6+ ♘xf6 7 ♗d3 h6 8 ♗h4 will transpose to the Rubinstein Variation:

a) 8...♗e7 9 ♘f3 – *3...dxe4 4 ♘xe4 ♘d7 5 ♘f3 ♘gf6 6 ♘xf6+ ♘xf6 7 ♗d3 ♗e7 8 ♗g5 h6 9 ♗h4* ±.

b) 8...c5 9 ♘f3 – *3...dxe4 4 ♘xe4 ♘d7 5 ♘f3 ♘gf6 6 ♘xf6+ ♘xf6 7 ♗g5 h6 8 ♗h4 c5 9 ♗d3* =.

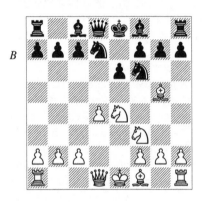

Now we look at:

A: 6...h6   34
B: 6...♗e7   35

A)

6...h6 7 ♗h4

7 ♗xf6 is tame: 7...♘xf6 8 ♗d3 ♗e7 9 0-0 ♘e4 10 ♗xe4 0-0 11 c3 c5 12 dxc5 ♗xc5 13 ♕xd8 ♖xd8 14 ♖ad1 ♗e7 = Malaniuk-Psakhis, Polanica Zdroj 1997.

7...♗e7

7...c5 is also feasible:

a) 8 ♘xf6+ ♘xf6 – *3...dxe4 4 ♘xe4 ♘d7 5 ♘f3 ♘gf6 6 ♘xf6+ ♘xf6 7 ♗g5 h6 8 ♗h4 c5*.

b) 8 ♘xc5 ♘xc5 9 dxc5 ♕a5+ 10 c3 ♕xc5 11 ♗d3 ♗e7 12 ♕e2 0-0 13 0-0 ♖d8 14 ♘e5 ♗d7 15 ♖fe1 ♗e8 = Gurcan-Antić, Erevan Z 2000.

c) 8 ♗xf6 ♘xf6 9 ♘xc5 ♗xc5 10 dxc5 ♕a5+ 11 ♕d2 ♕xc5 12 0-0-0 0-0 = Dolmatov-Psakhis, Haifa 1995.

8 ♘xf6+ ♗xf6 9 ♗xf6 ♕xf6

9...♘xf6 is also natural but is more common when Black hasn't played ...h6 (see Line B2).

10 ♕d2 0-0

Or 10...c5 11 0-0-0 0-0 12 ♕e3 cxd4 (12...b6 13 ♗b5! is good for White) 13 ♖xd4 e5 14 ♖e4 ♖d8, Hector-Korchnoi, Hamburg 1995, and now 15 ♗e2 or 15 ♗d3 is very good for White.

11 ♕e3

11 0-0-0 e5 =.

11...♖d8 12 0-0-0 b6 13 ♗d3 ♗b7 14 ♗e4 ♗xe4 15 ♕xe4 c5

The game is equal, Hector-Speelman, Roskilde 1998.

B)

6...♗e7 7 ♘xf6+ ♗xf6 (D)

Again, 7...♘xf6 is a rather passive line of the Rubinstein Variation – *3...dxe4 4 ♘xe4 ♘d7 5 ♘f3 ♘gf6 6 ♘xf6+ ♘xf6 7 ♗g5 ♗e7 ±.*

Now play divides into:

B1: 8 ♕d2   35
B2: 8 ♗xf6   36
B3: 8 h4   38

B1)

8 ♕d2 ♗xg5

This diverts White's knight, and thus looks like Black's best option, although

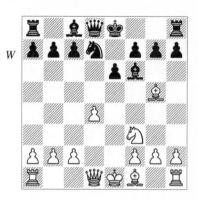

W

8...0-0 9 0-0-0 ♗xg5 leads to the same thing.

9 ♘xg5

Recapturing with the queen is without prospects as the resulting ending is completely equal; e.g., 9 ♕xg5 ♕xg5 10 ♘xg5 ♘f6 11 g3 h6 12 ♘f3 b6 13 ♗b5+ ♗d7 14 ♗xd7+ ♘xd7 15 0-0-0 0-0-0 16 ♖he1 c6 = Forgacs-Rubinstein, San Sebastian 1912.

9...♘f6 10 0-0-0 (D)

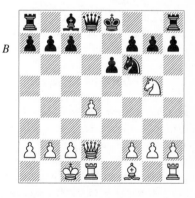

B

10...0-0

This is very logical, of course. Black usually does best not to play ...h6 in this line, as White's knight is only going to be better placed after ♘f3-e5. Furthermore, ...h6 would weaken the kingside, since White may be able to build up an attack with g4-g5. Apart from castling, Black could consider 10...♗d7, intending to place the bishop on the a8-h1 diagonal as soon as possible. However, the bishop is probably not that well placed on c6, since White can attack it with 11 ♘f3, intending ♘e5. Then Inkiov-Lobron, Novi Sad OL 1990 continued 11...♕e7 12 ♘e5 0-0 13 ♗d3 ♖fd8 14 g4 ♗e8 15 g5 ♘d7 16 ♘g4, and White had promising attacking chances.

11 ♗e2 ♕d6!?

Another idea that seems to equalize is 11...b6 12 ♗f3 ♖b8 13 ♖he1 ♗b7 14 ♗xb7 ♖xb7, as in Ochoa-Korchnoi, Barcelona 1992. Black's rook is temporarily misplaced but it can rapidly be reactivated.

12 ♗f3 ♗d7!?

12...♖b8 13 ♘e4 ♘xe4 14 ♗xe4 ♗d7 15 ♕e3 ♗c6 16 f3 ♖fd8 is also fine for Black, Karpov-Bareev, Tilburg 1991.

13 ♗xb7 ♖ab8 14 ♗f3 ♗c6!

Black has sacrificed a pawn to open the b-file against White's king. Now the intention is to exchange the light-squared bishops, so the knight can join the attack via d5. J.Polgar-Shirov, Merida 2000 continued 15 ♖he1 h6 16 ♗xc6 ♕xc6 17 ♘f3 ♘d5! (threatening ...♕a4) 18 ♕a5 (18 ♕d3 looks like a more critical test, but Black appears to have good compensation for the

pawn after 18...♘b4 19 ♕b3 ♕a6 20 ♔b1 ♘d5 21 ♕d3 ♕a5 22 ♔a1 c5!?) 18...♖b6 19 ♘e5 ♕b7 20 ♕a3 ♖a6 21 ♕b3 ♖b6 ½-½.

B2)

8 ♗xf6 ♘xf6 (D)

8...♕xf6 is also possible. After 9 ♗d3 0-0 10 0-0 e5 11 ♖e1 exd4 12 ♘xd4 White was only very slightly better in Pilnik-Ståhlberg, Beverwijk 1963. Recently, the idea of recapturing with the queen on f6 has become more popular, but only after 6...h6, and the type of position is examined more closely in Line A and Line B31. These days, White would probably choose 9 ♕d2 or 9 ♗c4.

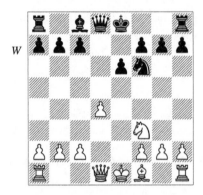

9 ♗d3

This is the most common. White anticipates that Black will castle kingside, and thus develops his bishop so it points at h7. Another idea is 9 ♗c4, which in some lines might usefully prevent ...♕d5. Now the most logical course is 9...0-0 10 ♕e2 b6 11 0-0-0

♗b7, when White has tried two alternatives:

a) 12 ♘e5 ♕e7 (I suppose very few players would dare to take on g2) 13 ♖hg1 c5 14 g4 cxd4 (14...♖fd8 could be an improvement, after which playing by analogy to Svidler's idea 15 g5 ♘d7 16 g6 fails to 16...hxg6 17 ♘xg6 fxg6 18 ♗xe6+ ♔f8!) 15 g5 ♘d7 16 g6! ♘xe5 (after 16...hxg6, 17 ♘xg6 fxg6 18 ♗xe6+ ♖f7 does not look clear, but 17 ♘xd7 ♕xd7 18 ♖xg6! is good for White) 17 gxh7+ ♔h8 18 ♕xe5 ♕f6 19 ♕xf6 gxf6 20 ♖xd4 +– Svidler-Luther, Frankfurt rpd 1999.

b) 12 ♖he1 a6 13 ♔b1 ♕d6 14 g3 (14 ♘e5 looks more natural, when I don't believe Black can actually take on g2) 14...b5 15 ♗d3 ♗xf3 16 ♕xf3 ♖fd8 17 ♖e5 ♖ab8 18 ♖c5 ♖b6 19 g4 ♘d5 = Degraeve-Komarov, Sremić Krsko ECC 1998.

9...0-0

9...c5 is an alternative, but then Unzicker thinks White is better after 10 ♕d2 cxd4 11 ♕b4! ♕e7 (11...♘d5 12 ♕xd4 0-0 13 0-0-0 ± Spassky-Unzicker, Bad Kissingen 1980) 12 ♗b5+ ♗d7 13 ♗xd7+ ♕xd7. I suppose that White then castles queenside and indeed looks minutely better.

10 ♕d2

Aiming to castle queenside looks like the most serious try for an advantage. 10 0-0 b6 11 ♕e2 ♗b7 12 ♖ad1 has been played a few times but after 12...♕e7 the position is just equal.

10...b6 11 0-0-0 ♗b7 12 ♘e5 ♕d5 13 c4 ♕d6

13...♕xg2? loses to 14 ♖hg1 ♕xh2 15 ♖xg7+ ♔xg7 16 ♕g5+ ♔h8 17 ♕xf6+ ♔g8 18 ♘g4 +–, but 13...♕a5!? is an idea that has been played by Speelman in a similar position and deserves attention here as well.

14 ♖he1 c5 15 ♕f4 cxd4 16 ♖e3!? *(D)*

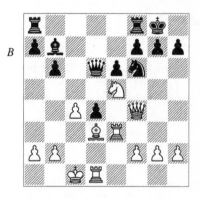

An inventive idea to bring more ammunition into the attack. Obviously, Black cannot take the rook, owing to ♗xh7+.

16...♖ac8 17 ♖h3

17 ♖g3 ♘h5! 18 ♕h6 f5 19 ♕xh5 ♕xe5 ∓ M.Gurevich.

17...♖c5?

Kasparov has given 17...b5 18 ♖e1 ♖xc4+ 19 ♔b1 ♕b4 20 ♖e2 and now 20...♖c3. This looks very unconvincing in view of 21 ♘d7!, which appears virtually decisive. Perhaps he meant 20...♖c7!, which looks good.

18 ♖e1

White now intends to continue with ♗xh7+, which would be incorrect if played immediately: 18 ♗xh7+? ♘xh7

19 ♕h4 ♗e4! 20 ♕xe4 ♘g5 and Black wins.

18...♗xg2 19 ♖g3 ♖xe5 20 ♖xe5 ♘h5 21 ♕h6! f5 22 ♕xh5 ♕xe5 23 ♖xg2 ♕f4+ 24 ♔d1!

Black has insufficient compensation for the sacrificed piece, Gelfand-M.Gurevich, Reggio Emilia 1991.

B3)

8 h4 *(D)*

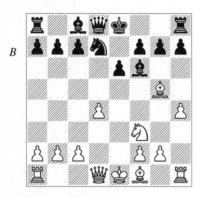

Now:

B31: 8...h6   38
B32: 8...0-0   39

Black can also play 8...c5 9 ♕d2 cxd4 10 0-0-0, and now:

a) 10...e5?! is probably too risky; Timman-Korchnoi, Tilburg 1991 continued 11 ♖e1 0-0 12 ♘xe5 ♖e8? (12...♘xe5 13 ♖xe5 ♗e6 is safer, with only a slight advantage to White) 13 ♘xf7! ♖xe1+ 14 ♕xe1 ♔xf7 15 ♗c4+ ♔f8 16 ♕e6 +–.

b) 10...0-0 11 ♘xd4 ♕b6 (alternatively, 11...♘b6 12 ♘f3 ♕xd2+ 13

♖xd2 ♗d7 14 ♗xf6 gxf6 15 ♗e2 ♖fc8 16 ♖hd1 ♖c7 17 b3 with an edge for White, Čabrilo-Draško, Subotica 1992) 12 g4!? ♖d8 13 ♗g2 ± Rõtšagov-Lamprecht, Groningen open 1997.

B31)

8...h6 9 ♗xf6 *(D)*

9 ♗e3 is unlikely to worry Black. The game Hjartarson-Speelman, Copenhagen 1996 continued 9...♕e7 10 c3 (passive, but 10 ♕d2 e5 is also fine for Black) 10...e5 11 d5 ♘b6 12 ♕b3 0-0 13 ♘d2 ♖d8 14 c4 e4! 15 ♕c2 c6 16 dxc6 bxc6 ∓.

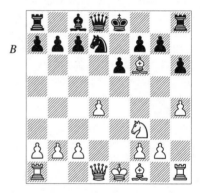

9...♕xf6

This position is also examined in Line A, only with White's h-pawn still on h2. 9...♘xf6 is seen less frequently. The inclusion of 8 h4 h6 compared to Line A2 is going to favour White since g4-g5 gains in strength because Black has weakened his kingside with ...h6. Anand-Korchnoi, Wijk aan Zee 2000 lasted less than 20 moves but Black is not in such bad shape as that suggests:

10 ♕d2 b6?! (this is probably inaccurate; Black should first play 10...0-0, or 10...c5) 11 0-0-0 (11 ♗b5+! ♗d7 12 ♗d3 ♗c6 13 ♘e5 gains White a tempo over the main line, as Black will have to play ...♗b7 and ...c5) 11...♗b7 12 ♘e5 0-0 13 ♗d3 c5 14 dxc5 ♕c7 (14...bxc5 is better) 15 ♖he1 ♗xg2? (15...bxc5 is essential, when Black is actually doing alright after 16 g4 c4 17 ♗xc4 ♘xg4 18 ♕d7 ♖ac8!; instead 16 f4 looks a little better for White) 16 ♖e2! ♔h8 17 ♖g1 ♗d5 18 ♕f4 ♕xc5 19 ♖e3 1-0. The problem is 19...♖ac8 20 ♖eg3 ♘h5 21 ♕xh6+! gxh6 22 ♖g8+ ♖xg8 23 ♘xf7# – a spectacular finish!

10 ♕d2 0-0

10...c5 is also possible. See Line A for this type of position.

11 0-0-0

White should also consider 11 ♕e3 to stop ...e5. Again, this should be compared with Line A but I think that the extra move, h4, is certainly not a disadvantage and might even sometimes help White to get in the advance g4-g5.

11...e5 12 dxe5

12 ♖e1 exd4 13 ♕xd4 ♕xd4 14 ♘xd4 ♘b6 15 ♘b5 c6 16 ♘d6 ♖d8 17 ♗d3 ♔f8 18 ♘xc8 ♖axc8 gives White only a symbolic advantage, Leko-Korchnoi, Tilburg 1998.

12...♘xe5 13 ♘xe5 ♕xe5 14 ♗c4 ♗e6! 15 ♖de1 ♕c5 16 ♗xe6 fxe6 17 f3 ♖ad8 18 ♕e3 ♕xe3+ 19 ♖xe3 ♔f7

The endgame is equal, Degraeve-Speelman, Istanbul OL 2000.

B32)
8...0-0 *(D)*

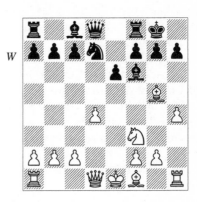

9 ♗d3

This seems to be White's most dangerous move. The forthcoming attacking scheme is attributed to Kasparov, due to a fine win against Shirov in Frankfurt 2000, but he wasn't the first to play it.

a) In Topalov-Anand, Monaco Amber rpd 2000, White tried to prevent ...e5 with another idea but had no more than equal play after 9 ♗xf6 ♕xf6 10 ♕e2!? b6 11 ♕e4 ♖b8 12 ♗d3 g6 13 ♘e5 c5 14 ♗b5 ♘xe5 15 ♕xe5 ♕xe5+ 16 dxe5 ♗b7 =.

b) 9 ♕d2 e5! seems to give Black a satisfactory game; for example:

b1) 10 ♗xf6 ♕xf6 11 0-0-0 h6 – *8...h6 9 ♗xf6 ♕xf6 10 ♕d2 0-0 11 0-0-0 e5.*

b2) 10 dxe5 ♘xe5 11 ♘xe5 ♕xd2+ 12 ♗xd2 ♗xe5 13 0-0-0 =.

b3) 10 0-0-0 e4 (10...h6? 11 dxe5!) 11 ♗xf6 ♘xf6 12 ♘e5 ♗e6 and now 13 ♔b1 c5! led to equality in the game

Anand-Korchnoi, Tilburg 1991. Korchnoi suggests 13 c4 as a possible improvement, with the idea 13...c5 14 d5 ♕d6 15 ♗g5! followed by f4. Maybe 13...♕d6 is more accurate.

9...c5 10 ♕e2!?

This is the idea. 10 c3 cxd4 11 cxd4 h6 (or 11...e5) is fine for Black.

With the text-move, White wants to play ♕e4, which forces ...g6. Later this may give White an opportunity to open the h-file with h5.

10...cxd4 11 ♕e4 g6 12 0-0-0 e5 *(D)*

12...♕a5 13 ♗xf6 ♘xf6 14 ♕xd4 ♘h5 15 a3 ♖d8 16 ♕e3 was comfortable for White in Kasparov-Shirov, Frankfurt rpd 2000.

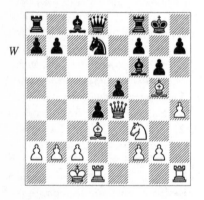

13 ♗xf6

Another very logical continuation is 13 ♖he1 ♖e8, when White has two options:

a) 14 ♗c4 ♘c5 (14...♘b6!?) 15 ♗xf6 ♕xf6 16 ♕d5 ♘d7 17 ♖xd4 ♘b6 18 ♖xe5 ♘xd5 (18...♗e6 19 ♕e4 ♘xc4 20 ♖xc4 ±) 19 ♖xe8+ ♔g7 20 ♗xd5 ♗g4 21 ♖xa8 ♗xf3 22 c3 ♗xd5 23 ♖xd5 ♕xf2 24 ♖d2 with equality.

b) 14 ♕d5!? ♖e6 15 ♗b5 (15 ♗c4!? is also possible) 15...♕a5 16 ♗c4 ♕xd5 (maybe 16...♕c7 17 ♗b3 ♘c5 18 ♗xf6 ♘xb3+ 19 axb3 ♖xf6 with the idea that 20 ♖xe5 is answered by 20...♗e6 21 ♕xd4 ♗xb3) 17 ♗xd5 ♖d6 18 ♗b3 ♔g7 19 ♗xf6+ ♖xf6 20 ♘xe5 ♘xe5 21 ♖xe5 ♖xf2 22 ♖xd4 gave White an edge in Nataf-P.Schlosser, French Cht (Mulhouse) 2001.

13...♕xf6 14 ♗b5 *(D)*

14 h5 doesn't impress in view of 14...♖e8 intending ...♘c5.

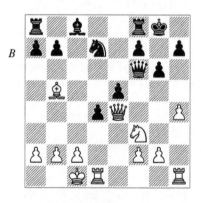

14...♖d8 15 ♖he1 a6 16 ♗xd7 ♗xd7 17 ♕xe5 ♕xe5 18 ♖xe5 ♗c6 = Balashov-Kruppa, Elista 2000.

4 Burn Variation: 6...gxf6

1 e4 e6 2 d4 d5 3 ♘c3 ♞f6 4 ♗g5 dxe4 5 ♘xe4 ♗e7 6 ♗xf6 gxf6 *(D)*

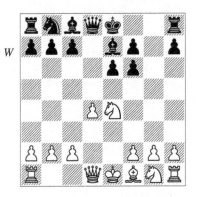

This anti-positional move usually leads to sharper positions than the bishop capture but Black can handle it in several different ways, which says something about its flexibility. In many lines Black plays ...f5, which drives White's knight away from its central post and frees f6 for a bishop or a knight. The question is when is the right time for such an idea. Usually Black also aims to fianchetto his light-squared bishop, which gives him a good dynamic positions with thrusts like ...f5 and ...c5 in the air. Black's worst problem is the lonely h-pawn, and if or when he plays ...f5, this will leave some dark-squared weaknesses.

We shall look at four main continuations for White:

A: 7 ♗c4   41
B: 7 g3   42
C: 7 ♕d3   45
D: 7 ♘f3   46

A)

7 ♗c4 ♘d7

This seems the most flexible. Otherwise:

a) What puzzles me is that the supposed idea behind White's last move, namely to meet 7...b6 with 8 d5 (8 ♘f3 – *7 ♘f3 b6 8 ♗c4*), looks far from convincing after 8...♗b7 9 ♗b5+ (White should try 9 ♕g4!?) 9...♔f8. In Iskov-A.Poulsen, Copenhagen 1974 White was successful with 10 ♕h5 ♕xd5 11 ♕h6+ ♔g8 12 ♗d3 but this looks very speculative. I think 10 ♘c3 ♗xd5 11 ♘xd5 ♕xd5 12 ♕xd5 exd5 13 0-0-0 c6 14 ♗e2 is better, with some compensation, but it probably doesn't suffice to give White a real advantage.

b) 7...a6 8 a4 ♘d7 (here, on 8...b6 White really should discard the thought of playing 9 d5 and instead aim with 9 ♘f3! for a highly improved version of Line D3) 9 ♘f3 c5 10 0-0 ♘b6 (Leko disapproves of this and instead suggests

10...cxd4) 11 ♗e2 cxd4 12 ♘xd4 e5 13 ♘b3 f5 14 ♕xd8+ ♔xd8 15 a5!? ♘d7 16 ♘ed2! ♘c5 17 ♘c4 ♘xb3 18 cxb3 ± Leko-Bunzmann, Hamburg (2) 1999.

c) 7...f5. It is often difficult to decide which is the best reaction to ...f5 in this type of position. Here White's replies are limited to 8 ♘c3 and 8 ♘g3, whereas in other lines White has the additional possibility of putting the knight on d2. I believe the right move in this particular position is 8 ♘g3. Then 8...♕d6 (8...♘d7 9 ♘f3 – 7...♘d7 8 ♘f3 f5 9 ♘g3 ±; 8...♖g8 9 ♘f3 ♘d7 10 ♕e2 ♘b6 11 ♗b3 ♘d5 12 0-0-0 ± Minasian-Savchenko, Belgrade 1989) 9 c3 ♘c6 10 ♘f3 ♗d7 11 ♕e2 0-0-0 12 0-0-0 ♘a5 13 ♗d3 ♘c6 14 ♔b1 ± Vogt-Alienkin, Chemnitz 1998.

8 ♘f3 c5 (D)

Or 8...f5 9 ♘g3 ♘b6 (9...c5 can be met by 10 d5 ♘b6 11 ♗b5+ ± or simply 10 0-0 ±) 10 ♗b3 c5 11 ♕e2 ♕c7 12 c3 c4 13 ♗c2 ♗d7 14 ♘e5 ♗c6 15 ♖g1 ♗d5 16 0-0-0 ♖g8 17 ♔b1 ± Al Modiahki-Sakaev, Duisburg U-18 Wch 1992.

9 0-0

9 d5 ♘b6 10 ♗b5+ ♗d7 11 ♕e2 (11 ♗xd7+ ♕xd7 12 dxe6 ♕xe6 13 ♕e2 0-0-0 looks fine for Black despite his inferior pawn-structure) 11...♗xb5 (not 11...exd5? 12 ♘xf6+ ±, but the alternative 11...♘xd5!? 12 0-0-0 ♗xb5 13 ♕xb5+ ♔f8 may be playable, because 14 c4? can be met by 14...♕b6 and 14 ♕xb7 ♖b8 offers Black good

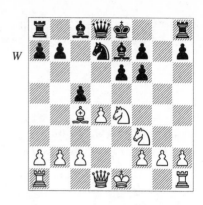

prospects of counterplay) 12 ♕xb5+ ♕d7 13 ♕xd7+ ♔xd7 14 dxe6+ fxe6 15 0-0-0+ ♔c7 (Tseshkovsky-Bronstein, Moscow 1981) 16 ♘c3 ♖ad8 17 ♖de1! is good for White (Dolmatov).

9...0-0

9...cxd4 10 ♘xd4 ♘e5 11 ♗b5+ ♗d7 12 ♕e2 also looks promising for White.

10 ♖e1 ♘b6

Perhaps this is the right moment for 10...cxd4. Then after 11 ♘xd4 Black has the option of placing his knight more actively on e5.

11 ♗f1 cxd4 12 ♘xd4 ♔h8 13 c3! e5 14 ♕h5 ♘d5

Shirov-Short, Las Vegas FIDE 1999. Now Shirov won a fantastic game with the imaginative 15 ♖ad1? exd4 16 ♖xd4 but objectively White doesn't have sufficient compensation for the piece. Much stronger (and safer) would have been 15 ♘e2! ♕c7 16 ♖ad1 ♗e6 17 c4! (Shirov), when White is better.

B)

7 g3 (D)

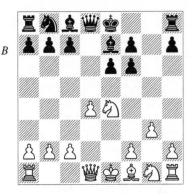

B

This move aims for a natural fianchetto set-up, and used to be a Fischer favourite.

7...f5

Black prefers to play this sooner rather than later. It is best to do it now before White gets the option of placing the knight more ideally. An example: 7...♗d7 8 ♘f3 ♗c6 9 ♕e2 f5 10 ♘ed2 ♗f6 11 c3 ♕e7 12 ♗g2 ♘d7 13 0-0 ± Fischer-Minev, Havana OL 1966.

8 ♘c3 ♗f6 9 ♘ge2

There has been some debate about where the knight is best placed. Some players argue that the knight is much better placed on f3, but I don't agree. 9 ♘f3 b6 (9...♘c6!? and 9...c5 may also be OK) 10 ♗g2 ♗b7 11 0-0 0-0 12 ♖e1 ♘d7 (Zurakhov-Boleslavsky, USSR Ch (Leningrad) 1956) doesn't look like a particular problem for Black if he gets in ...c5, which White seems unable to prevent.

9...♘c6 10 d5 exd5

This leads to a complex position. 10...♘b4!? 11 ♗g2 (11 dxe6? ♕xd1+

12 ♖xd1 ♗xe6 ∓ D.Pedersen-Kacheishvili, Golden Sands 2000) 11...c6! 12 dxc6 ♕xd1+ 13 ♖xd1 ♘xc6 14 ♘b5 ♔e7 = Iordachescu-Itkis, Kishinev 1996 looks like a safe alternative.

11 ♘xd5

11 ♕xd5 is seen much less often but is not necessarily any worse. Petrosian and Suetin give 11...♗e6. They continue 12 ♕b5 0-0 13 ♕xb7 ♘a5 with compensation for Black, which looks quite right, but 12 ♕c5!, as in Arapović-Pytel, Martigny 1988, is stronger, perhaps with a slight edge for White. I am also uncertain about Petrosian and Suetin's other suggestion, 11...♗xc3+ 12 ♘xc3 ♕e7+ 13 ♗e2 ♗e6, when Black has some temporary piece activity but his structure is weakened.

11...♗xb2 12 ♗g2! 0-0 13 0-0

13 ♖b1 is a logical alternative if only to avoid the risk of losing the exchange.

13...♗h8

This has been considered Black's best since Fischer-Petrosian, Buenos Aires Ct (3) 1971, but matters are not so clear. The bishop often returns to g7 later, so the question is what happens if the bishop goes to g7 immediately. We shall have a brief look at this, and Black's other alternatives:

a) 13...♗xa1 14 ♕xa1 f6 has to some extent been ignored. Petrosian and Suetin only give 15 ♘ef4 ♘e5 16 ♖d1 c6 '∓', but I am very sceptical of this assessment.

b) 13...♗e5 14 ♖b1 ♖b8 15 ♕c1! ♗e6 16 ♖d1 ♗xd5 17 ♖xd5 ♕f6 18

♖db5 ± Nadanian-Khachian, Armenia 1993.

c) 13...♗g7 14 ♘ef4 ♘e7! (14...♘e5 15 ♘h5 is of course a disadvantage of 13...♗g7 compared to 13...♗h8) 15 ♖b1 ♘xd5 16 ♕xd5 c6 17 ♕f3 ♕c7 18 ♖fe1 ♗d7 19 ♘h5 ♖ae8 = Rezaei-Vakhidov, Udaipur 2000.

14 ♘ef4 (D)

14 ♖b1 ♘e5 15 ♘ef4 c6 16 ♘e3 gave White compensation for the pawn in Kogan-Zifroni, Tel-Aviv 1996. This type of position would be likely to occur if White played the safe 13 ♖b1 instead of 13 0-0.

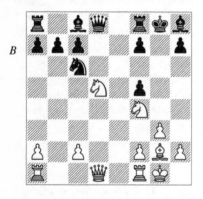

B

14...♘e5 15 ♕h5

This is a dangerous idea (White prepares ♘h3-g5) which would of course be much less effective if Black's bishop were on g7 instead of on h8.

15...♘g6

15...c6 might be better, since 16 ♘h3? can be met by 16...♘g4!. 16 ♘e3 is necessary, but doesn't look too menacing.

16 ♘h3!?

16 ♖ad1 c6 17 ♘e3 ♕f6 was played in Fischer-Petrosian, Buenos Aires Ct (3) 1971, leading to chances for both sides.

16...♗g7 17 ♘g5 h6 18 ♘xf7 (D)

Retreating White's knight certainly doesn't leave a big impression, so this is a virtually forced consequence of White's 16th and 17th moves.

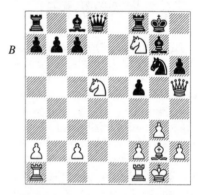

B

18...♖xf7!

Only so! 18...♔xf7? 19 ♘f4 ♕g5 20 ♗d5+ ♔f6 21 h4! ♘xh4? allowed a beautiful finish in Nadanian-Varlamov, corr. 1992-3: 22 ♕d1!! c5 23 ♕d3 1-0. That Black is completely lost isn't difficult to work out in a correspondence game; e.g., 23...♘g6 24 ♕c3+ ♘e5 25 ♖ae1 ♖e8 26 ♖xe5 ♖xe5 27 ♖e1 ♔e7 28 ♖xe5+ ♗xe5 29 ♕xe5+ ♔d7 30 ♗e6+ ♔c6 31 ♕d5+ ♔b6 32 ♕d6+ ♔b5 33 c4+ ♔a4 34 ♕xc5 +−.

19 ♕xg6 ♕g5! 20 ♕xg5 hxg5 21 ♖ae1 ♔f8! 22 ♖e2 c6 23 ♖fe1 ♗d7 24 ♘c7 ♖d8

= Nadanian-Altounian, Armenia 1994.

C)
7 ♕d3 *(D)*

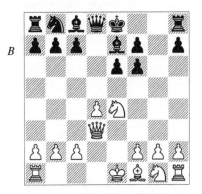

A fairly recent attempt to sharpen the position.

7...b6

This is the most common. Black continues his development in the usual way by fianchettoing his light-squared bishop. He may also take into account White's plan and try to take measures against White's coming ♕g3 idea; e.g., 7...♘d7 8 0-0-0 and then:

a) 8...f5 9 ♘c3 c6 10 ♘f3 (the more aggressive 10 g4!? was seen in Velimirović-Andersson, Bar 1997: 10...fxg4 11 h3 gxh3 12 ♗xh3 ♕c7 13 ♘f3 b6 14 ♔b1 ♗b7 15 ♘e5! ♖f8! 16 f4 0-0-0 17 ♕xh7 ♘xe5 18 dxe5 ♔b8 with approximately equal chances) 10...♕c7 11 ♕e3! ♖g8 12 ♔b1 ♘f6 13 h3! (White prepares to play ♘e5; the immediate 13 ♘e5 is less precise due to 13...♘g4! 14 ♘xg4 ♖xg4 15 h3 ♖g7 followed by ...♗d7 and 0-0-0 with an equal position) 13...b5!? 14 ♘e5 b4 15 ♘a4 ♘d5 16 ♕b3! ♖b8 17 g4 ±

Scherbakov-Kiriakov, Ekaterinburg 1999.

b) 8...c6!? 9 ♕g3 ♘f8 (9...f5 10 ♘d6+ ♔f8 11 ♘f3 ♖g8 12 ♕f4 ♖g4 13 ♕h6+ ♔g8 14 ♘c4 ±) 10 ♘f3 (10 ♕g7 ♘g6) 10...♘g6 is given by Scherbakov as 'unclear'. This evaluation should probably be interpreted as 'roughly equal'.

8 0-0-0 ♗b7 *(D)*

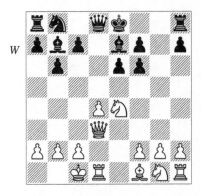

9 ♘c3 c6 10 ♕g3!? *(D)*

White is threatening simply to pick up a pawn by ♕g7 and hence forces some sort of concession from Black. Alternatively, 10 f4 f5!? (10...♕c7 11 f5! ±) 11 g4!? is a violent attempt to exploit White's slight lead in development. Then after 11...fxg4 (11...♕c7 12 gxf5 ♕xf4+ 13 ♔b1 ♕xf5 14 ♕xf5 exf5 15 ♗h3 gives White the initiative – M.Gurevich) 12 f5 ♕d6!? (12...exf5 13 ♕xf5 ♕d7 14 ♕e5 gives White good compensation – M.Gurevich) 13 fxe6 fxe6 (13...♕xe6 14 d5 cxd5 15 ♗g2 looks very dangerous for Black), we have:

a) 14 ♕e4 ♘d7 15 ♕xg4 ♘f6 16 ♕h3 0-0-0 17 ♗c4 ♔b8! 18 ♗xe6 ♕f4+ 19 ♔b1 ♖xd4 20 ♖f1 and a draw was agreed here in Goloshchapov-Kiriakov, Ekaterinburg 1999.

b) 14 h3!? ♘d7!? (14...gxh3 is risky in view of 15 ♗e2! intending ♗h5+) 15 hxg4 0-0-0 16 ♖xh7 ♖xh7 17 ♕xh7 ♘f6 = Magem-M.Gurevich, Gonfreville 1999.

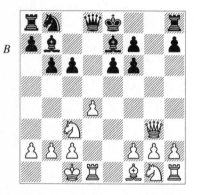

At this point Black has three options:

a) 10...♔f8 and now 11 ♕h3 h6 12 ♗c4 ♕d6 13 ♘ge2 b5 14 ♘e4 ♕c7 15 ♗b3 ♘d7 was fine for Black in Rainfray-Touzane, France 1999 but White should adopt a similar set-up as in 'b' below, by 11 ♘f3 or 11 h4!?.

b) 10...f5 11 ♘f3 ♘d7 12 ♗c4 ♔f8 (12...♘f6 13 ♘e5 ♖g8 14 ♕h3 b5 15 ♗b3 ♗b4 16 ♖he1 ♘d5 17 ♗xd5 cxd5 18 ♖e3 ± Magem-Herraiz Hidalgo, Cordoba 1995) 13 h4 ♖g8 14 ♕f4 b5 (14...♖xg2 15 ♖dg1 ♖xg1+ 16 ♖xg1 gives White excellent compensation) 15 ♗b3 a5 16 a4 b4 17 ♘e2

♖g4 18 ♕h6+ ♔g8 19 ♔b1 ± Pinski-Belov, Polanica Zdroj 2000.

c) 10...♗f8 11 ♘f3 (perhaps 11 ♗c4 ♘d7 12 ♘ge2 ♕b8 13 f4 is a better chance to gain an advantage) 11...♘d7 12 ♗c4 ♕b8 13 ♕h4 h5!? 14 ♖he1, Reinderman-de la Riva, Buenos Aires 1992, and now 14...♗e7 15 ♘e4 ♕c7 looks fine for Black.

D)

7 ♘f3 (D)

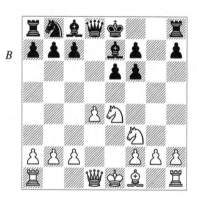

Now:

D1: 7...f5	46
D2: 7...♘d7	50
D3: 7...b6	51
D4: 7...a6	53

D1)

7...f5

This is an ambitious move, quickly leading to a very sharp position and certainly very different in character from the quiet 7...b6 lines. There is a resemblance, though, to the Morozevich variation, 7...a6.

8 ♘c3

It is not easy to decide on which is best, this or 8 ♘g3, but there is a majority of preference for the text-move, most likely because it supports d5 as a reply to ...c5. The alternatives:

a) 8 ♘ed2 is not very popular, as it is too slow. Black equalizes comfortably; e.g., 8...c5 9 ♗b5+ ♗d7 10 ♕e2 ♗xb5 11 ♕xb5+ ♕d7 12 ♕xd7+ ♘xd7 = Waschk-Steckner, Germany 1991/2.

b) 8 ♘g3 c5 and then:

b1) 9 dxc5 ♕xd1+ 10 ♖xd1 ♗xc5 11 ♘e5 ♔e7 12 ♗c4 ♘d7 13 ♘d3 ♗d6 14 0-0 ♖d8 15 ♖fe1 ♔f8 16 ♘h5 ♘b6 17 ♗b3 ♗d7 18 ♘e5 ♗e8 = Bakre-Bunzmann, Paks 1998.

b2) 9 ♗b5+ ♗d7 10 ♗xd7+ ♕xd7 and then:

b21) 11 0-0 ♘c6 12 dxc5 ♕xd1 13 ♖axd1 ♗xc5 14 c3 ♗e7 15 ♖fe1 ♖d8 16 ♖xd8+ ♔xd8 = Van der Wiel-Sielecki, Breda 2000.

b22) 11 d5!? (with this interesting positional sacrifice, White intends to leave Black with vulnerable f-pawns) 11...exd5 12 ♕d3 (White cannot count on any advantage after 12 ♘e5 ♕e6 13 f4 ♘c6 14 0-0; e.g., 14...♘xe5 15 fxe5 0-0-0 = Van der Wiel-Kuijf, Dutch Ch (Hilversum) 1990) 12...♘c6 13 0-0-0 (13 ♕xf5 ♕e6+ =) 13...f4 14 ♘h5 0-0-0! (a strong improvement over 14...♖g4? 15 ♕xd5 ♖d8 16 ♕f5! ± Savchenko-Shabalov, Tbilisi jr 1989) 15 ♘xf4 ♘b4! 16 ♕a3 c4 (16...♕g4 17 g3 ♗d6! is also good) 17 ♘e5 ♕c7 18 ♕h3+ ♔b8 ∓ V.Ivanov-Danielian, USSR 1991.

b3) 9 ♕d2 cxd4 10 0-0-0 ♘c6 11 ♗b5 a6! (much stronger than 11...♗d7 12 ♘xd4 ±) 12 ♗xc6+ bxc6 13 ♘h5 (13 ♘xd4 c5 ∓ A.Horvath-Bunzmann, Paks 1998) 13...♖g8 14 ♔b1 ♖g6 15 ♘f4 ♖g8 = Galkin-Kiriakov, Groningen open 1997.

8...♗f6 *(D)*

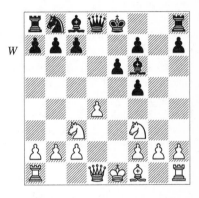

9 ♕d2

There are several other moves available to White, but this is by a large margin the most common and natural. One other idea worth mentioning is 9 ♗d3 0-0 (9...♘c6 10 ♗b5 transposes to a line which may also arise from *9 ♗c4 ♘c6*; then 10...♕d6 11 ♕d2 ♗d7 12 ♕h6!? ♕e7 13 0-0-0 0-0-0 was approximately equal in Rohde-Speelman, London 1984) 10 ♘e2 c5 11 ♕d2 (11 c3!?) 11...cxd4 12 g4!? (the main idea of White's set-up, and a very dangerous one) 12...♔h8! 13 gxf5 exf5 14 ♖g1 ♘c6, Zso.Polgar-Rabinovich, Tel-Aviv 1998, and now 15 0-0-0 seems the most precise, with reasonable compensation for the pawn.

9...c5

This quick attack on White's centre is the main idea of the 7...f5 variation. It is usually a favourable trade for Black to exchange his c-pawn for White's d-pawn, because White's control of the centre is then decreased. White's set-up is therefore aimed at preventing this exchange.

10 d5

Clearly the most critical. Other moves shouldn't worry Black:

a) 10 ♗b5+ ♗d7 11 ♗xd7+ (after 11 dxc5 a6 12 ♗xd7+ ♘xd7 Black regains the pawn with an equal position) 11...♘xd7 12 0-0-0 ♕a5 13 ♔b1 0-0-0 14 ♘e2 ♕xd2 15 ♖xd2 cxd4 16 ♘exd4 ♘c5 =/∓ Velička-Kiriakov, Pardubice 1995.

b) 10 0-0-0 cxd4 11 ♗b5+!? ♔e7! 12 ♘xd4 ♕xd4 13 ♕xd4 ♗xd4 14 ♖xd4 a6 15 ♗e2 ♘c6 16 ♖h4 ♘e5! = Tseshkovsky-Volkov, Novgorod 1995.

c) 10 dxc5 ♕xd2+ 11 ♘xd2 ♔e7 12 ♘b3 ♗d7 13 0-0-0 ♗xc3 14 bxc3 a5 (14...♗c6 also seems fine for Black; it is not very likely that White is going to make any use of his tripled c-pawns) 15 ♗d3 a4 16 ♘d4 ♖a5 17 ♔d2 ♖c8 18 ♖b1 ♖c7 19 ♖he1 ♔f6 = Gaponenko-Kiriakov, Groningen 1995.

10...0-0

10...exd5 11 ♕e3+ ♗e6 12 ♕xc5 was good for White in Arnason-Skembris, Thessaloniki OL 1988.

11 0-0-0 e5 (*D*)

This rather decides the outlook of the centre. Black dreams of being able to activate his pieces with ...e4 and

...♘d7-e5. This may look impressive but also has certain drawbacks, for the centre is very vulnerable and can be broken up by f3 or g4. A sensible-looking alternative is 11...♗g7, which makes room for ...♕f6 and keeps open the question of how to handle the central tension. Then after 12 ♕e3!? ♕b6 13 ♘e5 exd5!? (Black is running out of reasonable moves and has to embark on a risky opening of the centre) 14 ♘xd5 ♕e6 15 f4 ♘d7!? a complicated game arose in Landenbergue-Luther, Ptuj Z 1995.

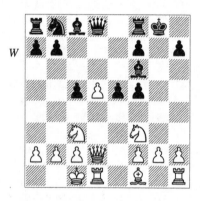

12 h4

This is the most common. It is very useful for White to have ♘g5 available as a reply to ...e4. However, a recent game suggests that White can perhaps consider playing even more directly: 12 ♔b1!? ♘d7 (12...♗g7!?) 13 g4! e4 14 ♘g1 fxg4 (perhaps 14...♗xc3!? 15 ♕xc3 fxg4, intending to meet 16 h3 with 16...♕h4, is better) 15 ♘xe4 ♗g7 16 h3 ♕b6 17 c3 ♘e5 (17...♖e8!?) 18 hxg4 ♗xg4 19 ♖e1 ♖fe8 leading to an unclear position, Saulin-Kiriakov, Moscow 1999.

12...♘d7 *(D)*

Black prepares ...e4 followed by ...♘e5. Another option is keep the position flexible with 12...♗g7. Then after 13 d6! (13 ♔b1 is feasible but the text is obviously critical; White creates a square on d5 for his knight but also gives one away on c6, making ...♘c6-d4 possible for Black) there are:

a) 13...♗d7 14 ♘d5 ♘c6 is untested but perhaps worth a try.

b) 13...♗e6 14 ♘g5 ♘c6 15 g4! ♘d4 (15...fxg4? 16 ♕d3 +−) 16 gxf5 ♗xf5 17 ♗d3 ♕d7 18 ♗xf5 ♕xf5 19 ♘d5 ± Klovans-Dizdar, Groningen 1991.

c) 13...e4!? 14 ♘g5 ♘d7 (14...h6?! looks much too risky in view of 15 ♘h3 ♕xh4 16 g3 ♕f6 17 ♘f4) 15 f3 h6 16 ♘d5!? ♖e8 (16...♘f6? 17 ♘e7+ ♔h8 18 ♗c4! gives White a winning attack) 17 ♘xf7!? (this forces Black to play very precisely, but 17 ♘e7+ ♖xe7 18 dxe7 ♕xe7 19 ♘h3 is objectively better; then Black does not seem to have fully adequate compensation) 17...♔xf7 18 ♘c7 ♘b6! 19 ♘xa8 e3 20 ♕d3 c4!? 21 ♕a3 e2 22 ♗xe2 ♖xe2 23 ♘xb6 axb6 (Vokarev-Kiriakov, Moscow 1999). With a series of strong and active defensive moves, Black has nearly equalized but not quite. Vokarev points out that White can maintain some advantage with 24 ♖he1 ♖xe1 25 ♖xe1 ♗e6 26 ♖d1 ♕d7 27 ♕e3, as the passed d-pawn greatly reduces the power of Black's bishops.

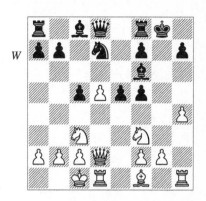

13 d6

13 ♖g1 (intending g4, but actually the rook doesn't appear very useful on g1 as long as g4 is prevented) 13...e4 14 ♘g5 ♘e5 15 ♗e2 (15 f3 h6 16 ♘h3 ♗g7 17 fxe4 ♕xh4 is unclear according to Sakaev) 15...h6 16 ♘h3 ♗g7 17 ♘f4 and now:

a) 17...b5!? 18 g4 b4 19 ♘a4 fxg4 20 ♘h5 (M.Pavlović-Sakaev, Yugoslavia 1998) and now 20...♕d6 is safest, when Black is perhaps slightly better.

b) Sakaev prefers 17...♕xh4!, giving 18 g4 fxg4 19 ♘xe4 ♗f5 20 ♖h1 ♕d8 21 ♘g3 ♗g6 ∓, but 18 f3!? looks more dangerous to me.

13...♘b6

In this case the 13...e4 14 ♘g5 ♘e5 idea would be less good due to 15 f3! (± Sakaev).

14 ♕e3 e4 15 ♘g5 ♗d7

A vital idea in Black's defence is the move ...♗d4, but here it appears inaccurate: 15...♗d4?! 16 ♕g3 ♔h8 17 ♘b5 ±.

16 g4! ♗d4 17 ♖xd4!? cxd4 18 ♕xd4 f6 19 ♗c4+ ♘xc4 20 ♕xc4+

♔g7 21 ♘e6+ ♗xe6 22 ♕xe6 ♖e8! 23 ♕xf5 ♖e5 24 ♕f4 ♕xd6

The position is dynamically equal, Lau-Sakaev, Dortmund 1991.

D2)

7...♘d7 (D)

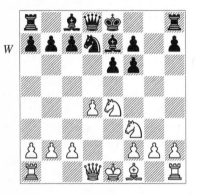

This flexible move may transpose to other lines. In the first place Black wants to play ...c5, but after seeing White's reply Black might also consider other set-ups. Short has experimented with the ...c5 idea, but to be honest I don't really like it. White can react with d5 but can also just maintain the tension, seeking an advantage in development and the better pawn-structure.

8 ♕d2

Other moves:

a) 8 ♗c4 – 7 ♗c4 ♘d7 8 ♘f3 ±/=.

b) 8 g3!? c5 (8...b6!?) 9 ♗g2 (9 d5!? is worth considering but clearly White would rather have ♕d2 substituted for g3) 9...♕b6 10 0-0 cxd4 (grabbing the pawn with 10...♕xb2 is probably too risky) 11 ♘xd4 (11 ♕xd4 ♕xd4 12 ♘xd4 a6 13 ♖ad1 ±) 11...0-0 12 ♘c3 ♘e5 13 ♘b3 ♗d7 14 ♕h5 f5 = Sutovsky-Short, Bugojno ECC 1999.

8...c5

8...b6!? is not a stupid idea since against an immediate 7...b6 (Line D3) White usually puts his queen on e2 to protect the e4-knight and support a bishop exchange with ♗a6. White has tried two moves:

a) 9 ♗b5 ♗b7 10 ♕f4 c6 11 ♗d3 ♕b8 12 ♕h6 ♕c7 13 ♕g7 ♖f8 14 ♕g3 0-0-0 was fine for Black in Røyset-Djurhuus, Norwegian Cht 1997.

b) 9 d5 f5 (maybe 9...♗b7 10 ♗c4 exd5 11 ♗xd5 ♗xd5 12 ♕xd5 ♘e5 13 0-0-0 ♕xd5 14 ♖xd5 c6 15 ♖d2 ♘xf3 16 gxf3 ♖d8, and Black should hold) 10 dxe6 (I like 10 ♘c3!, as in the note to White's 9th move) 10...fxe4 11 exf7+ ♔xf7 12 ♕d5+ ♔g7 13 ♕xa8 ♘c5 gave Black excellent compensation in Stisis-Zifroni, Israeli Cht 1996.

9 0-0-0

9 d5!? looks like a much more serious test of Black's position. 9...f5 and now:

a) 10 dxe6 fxe4 11 exd7+ ♕xd7 12 ♕xd7+ ♗xd7 13 ♘e5 ♗e6 14 ♗b5+ ♔f8 was fine for Black in Sack-Bednarski, Hamburg 1981.

b) White should consider 10 ♘c3, after which it is far from clear how Black should react:

b1) 10...♗f6 11 0-0-0 0-0 12 ♕e3 ±.

b2) 10...♘b6 11 0-0-0 exd5 (11...0-0 12 d6 ♗f6 13 ♕e3 ±) 12 ♗b5+ ♗d7

13 ♗xd7+ ♕xd7 14 ♘xd5 ♘xd5 15 ♕xd5 ♕xd5 16 ♖xd5 ±.

b3) 10...♘f6 11 ♗b5+ ♗d7 12 d6 ♗f8 13 0-0-0 ♗g7 14 ♕e3 also looks good for White; e.g., 14...♕b6 15 ♕g5 0-0 16 ♗xd7 ♘xd7 17 g4 with good attacking chances for White.

9...cxd4 10 ♕xd4 ♕b6 11 ♕a4

11 ♘d6+!? ♗xd6 12 ♕xd6 ♕xd6 13 ♖xd6 ♔e7 14 ♖d4 is slightly better for White.

11...a6 12 ♗e2 ♕c7 13 ♕d4 b5 14 ♘d6+ ♗xd6 15 ♕xd6 ♕xd6 16 ♖xd6 ♗b7 17 ♖hd1 ♘c5 18 ♘e1!

White has a slight advantage, J.Polgar-Short, Pamplona 1999/00.

D3)

7...b6 (D)

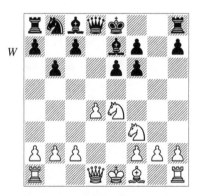

This usually gives Black a slightly passive but very solid position. Black wants to play ...♗b7 and prepare to castle queenside. Later he will think about how to gain more space, often with ...f5 and/or ...c5.

8 ♗d3

Not long ago it was thought to be clever for White to throw in 8 ♗b5+ c6 and only then retreat the bishop. We now know that this isn't very useful since Black wants to play ...c6 anyway. I have actually done this myself recently, and even though it doesn't matter that much, White is effectively going to be a tempo down on the main lines.

If White plans to exchange bishops with ♗a6 later, it might be worth placing the bishop on c4 instead of on d3. This would rule out Black's option of 9...♕d5 in the main line, but of course then White wouldn't be able to play ideas with a quick c4. Hence we shall consider ideas where White exchanges bishops here plus a few other, quite dangerous, concepts. 8 ♗c4 ♗b7 9 ♕e2 c6 and now:

a) 10 0-0-0 ♕c7 11 ♖he1 ♘d7 and then:

a1) 12 g3 0-0-0 13 c3 ♔b8 14 ♗b3 ♖he8 (14...♖hg8, intending ...f5, looks like a better idea) 15 ♔b1 ♗f8 16 ♘h4 h6 17 f4 f5 18 ♘f2 ♘f6 19 ♘f3 ♗d6 20 ♘e5 and White was better in de Firmian-Knaak, Bundesliga 2000/1. Note White's concept of slowly improving his position before playing f4 to provoke ...f5 and then clamping down on the e5-square.

a2) 12 ♘c3!? 0-0-0 13 d5 cxd5 14 ♗xd5 ♘c5 15 ♗xb7+ ♕xb7 16 ♕c4 a6!? 17 ♕f4 b5 with counterplay for Black, Smikovsky-Kiriakov, St Petersburg 2000.

a3) 12 ♔b1 0-0-0 13 ♗a6 and then:

a31) 13...♗xa6 (it is probably a matter of taste, but it seems that Andersson has decided that Black's king is better on b8 than it is on b7, which explains this capture instead of the alternatives 13...♖he8 or 13...♖hg8) 14 ♕xa6+ ♔b8 15 ♕e2 ♖dg8!? (an interesting idea instead of the more common 15...♖hg8) 16 g3 f5 17 ♘ed2 h5 18 ♘c4 h4 19 ♖d3 hxg3 20 hxg3 ♖d8 21 ♖ed1 ♗f6 and Black was very solid in Z.Almasi-Knaak, Bundesliga 1997/8.

a32) 13...b5!? (a recent attempt to sharpen the position) 14 ♗xb7+ ♔xb7 15 c4 bxc4 16 ♕xc4 ♘b6 17 ♕b3 ♔a8 18 ♖c1 ♖b8 19 ♕c2 ♖hc8 20 ♖e3 ♘d5 21 ♖b3 ♖xb3 22 ♕xb3 ♕f4 with counterplay, Sziebert-Radjabov, Budapest 2000.

b) 10 0-0 ♕c7 11 ♘g3!? is a new idea that we will certainly see more of. 11...♘d7 (11...h5 12 ♘h4 ♘d7 13 ♘gf5 exf5 14 ♘xf5 ♘f8 15 ♖fe1 is just a different route to the main line after 11...♘d7) 12 ♘f5! exf5 13 ♖fe1 ♘f8 14 ♘h4 ♘g6 15 ♘xf5 h5 16 ♕f3 ♔f8 17 ♘xe7 ♘xe7 18 ♕xf6 and now Black has tried to defend in two different ways:

b1) 18...♘g6 19 ♖e5!? ♖h7 20 ♖g5 ♖g7 21 ♖e1 was Sutovsky-Volkov, Isle of Man 2000, and now Sutovsky gives 21...♕d7! (intending ...♖e8) 22 ♖ee5 ♖e8 23 ♖xg6 ♖xg6 24 ♕h8+ ♖g8 25 ♕h6+ ♖g7, when White has nothing better than a perpetual check.

b2) 18...♖h7 19 ♖e5 ♘g8 20 ♕f4 ♕d7, Iordachescu-Itkis, Romania 2000, and now Iordachescu thinks White

should try 21 ♗e6! ♕d8 and here either 22 ♖xh5 or 22 ♖ae1. I would prefer the latter, which threatens 23 ♖f5.

8...♗b7 9 ♕e2 ♘d7 (D)

Volkov has tried 9...♕d5 on a number of occasions but if White simply castles kingside, this looks a bit out of place; e.g., 10 0-0 (10 c4 ♕a5+ 11 ♘c3 ♗b4, with counterplay, is one of Black's ideas) 10...♘d7 11 ♖fe1 0-0-0 12 a4 and White was better in J.Polgar-Volkov, Batumi Echt 1999.

Andersson has come up with a new concept recently in 9...♘c6 10 c3 ♖g8 11 0-0 ♕d7 12 a4 a5 13 ♖fe1 0-0-0 14 ♗a6 ½-½ Ivanović-Andersson, Belgrade 2000. Obviously this needs further tests but personally I doubt that this will establish itself as a real option for Black.

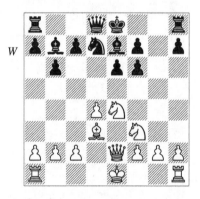

10 0-0

This is sensible and seems to give White a pleasant position by just making quiet space-gaining and solidifying moves. The alternative is 10 0-0-0 c6 11 ♔b1 ♕c7 12 c4 0-0-0, and then:

a) 13 d5? is unconvincing in view of 13...cxd5! 14 cxd5 ♗xd5 15 ♖c1 ♘c5, when, surprisingly, White cannot exploit the pin; e.g., 16 b4 (16 ♘xc5 bxc5 is safe for Black) 16...♘xd3! 17 ♖xc7+ ♔xc7 with terrific compensation for Black, Golubev-Itkis, Romania 2000.

b) 13 ♘c3 ♔b8 14 a3 ♖he8 15 ♖he1 ♘f8 16 g3 f5 17 ♗c2 ♘g6 18 h4 h5 19 ♖d2 ♗f6 = Peptan-Züger, Biel 1996.

10...c6 11 c4 ♕c7 12 ♘c3 0-0-0 13 ♖fd1 ♔b8 14 a3 ♘f8 15 b4 ♘g6 16 ♕e3

± Leko-Bunzmann, Hamburg (6) 1999.

D4)

7...a6 *(D)*

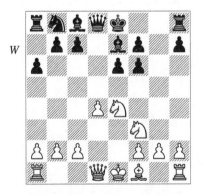

Morozevich's pet variation. Black mainly aims for a more aggressive set-up with ...b5, rather than the more conventional, albeit more solid, ...b6.

8 g3!?

White has tried a great many things at this juncture but this well-justified positional approach casts some doubt on the correctness of Black's concept. White simply prepares to set up a counterpart to Black's light-squared bishop, which is going to appear on the a8-h1 diagonal in a few moves. Before we proceed, we shall take a look at White's alternatives:

a) 8 c3?! f5 9 ♘c5 0-0 10 ♗c4 b5 11 ♗b3 ♗xc5 12 dxc5 ♗b7 13 ♘d4 ♕f6 ∓ Svidler-Morozevich, British League (4NCL) 2000/1.

b) 8 ♕d2 b5 9 0-0-0 (9 ♕h6 ♗b7 10 ♗d3 ♘d7 11 ♘g3?! f5 12 ♘h5 ♗f8 13 ♕e3 ♘f6 ∓ Sutovsky-Morozevich, Pamplona 1998/9) 9...♗b7 10 ♗d3 ♘d7 11 ♔b1 ♗d5 12 ♕h6 c6 13 ♕g7 ♖f8 14 ♕xh7 f5 15 ♘c3 ♘f6 16 ♕h3 ♘g4 with counterplay, Klovans-P.H.Nielsen, Istanbul OL 2000.

c) 8 ♗c4 b5 9 ♗b3 ♘c6!? 10 c3 ♗b7 11 ♕e2 ♘a5 12 ♗c2 ♕d5 = Lehto-Manninen, Finnish Cht 1999.

d) 8 ♗d3 ♘d7 9 ♕e2 b5 10 0-0-0 ♗b7 11 ♖he1 ♗d5 12 ♔b1 c6 13 c4 bxc4 14 ♗xc4 a5 with counterplay, Govedarica-Zontakh, Belgrade 2000.

e) 8 c4 (this is clearly the most critical of White's alternatives) 8...f5 9 ♘c3 ♗f6 10 ♕d2 c5 11 d5 0-0 12 0-0-0 is the same as Line D1 with the exception that White has his c-pawn on c4 instead of c2 and that Black's a-pawn is on a6 instead of a7. This gives Black the opportunity of countering with ...b5. Black has two options:

e1) 12...♗g7 13 h4! exd5 (risky) 14 ♘xd5 ♘c6 15 h5 h6 16 ♖h3 f4 17 ♖h4 ± Shirov-Morozevich, Astana 2001.

e2) 12...e5 13 h4 b5! 14 d6 ♗e6 (improving over 14...♘c6? 15 d7! ♗b7 16 ♕d6 e4 17 ♘d5 ♗g7 18 ♘g5 with a large advantage to White, Shirov-Topalov, Sarajevo 2000) 15 ♘d5 (15 g4!? looks more dangerous) 15...♗xd5 16 ♕xd5 ♘d7 17 ♘d2 ♗g7 18 ♖h3 ♕f6 with counterplay, Belotti-Radjabov, St Vincent 2001.

8...b5

Or:

a) 8...f5 9 ♘c3 ♗f6 has a lot in common with other lines of the ...gxf6 Burn Variation. Compared with Line D1, for example, Black has played ...a6 and White g3. White has two logical ways to continue:

a1) 10 ♕d2 c5 11 d5 0-0 12 0-0-0 b5 takes advantage of the extra ...a6 Black has in comparison with Line D1, while g3 seems of little significance. Then Black was fine after 13 dxe6 ♕xd2+ 14 ♘xd2 fxe6 15 ♗g2 ♖a7 in de la Villa-Short, Pamplona 1999/00.

a2) 10 ♗g2 is stronger. Then:

a21) 10...c5 11 d5 ♕b6 (11...♗xc3+ 12 bxc3 exd5 looks very risky but I don't think there is an immediate refutation) 12 ♖b1 0-0 13 0-0 ♖d8 and now in Glek-Short, Oz.com qualifier blitz 2000, 14 ♖e1?! allowed 14...♘c6 followed by ...♘d4. Glek later found out that 14 ♕c1 ♘d7 15 ♖d1 ♘f8 16 ♕h6 ♗g7 17 ♕h5 h6 18 ♘d2 would have been very good for White.

a22) 10...♘c6!? appears better. 11 d5? is not good in view of 11...♘b4, so to protect d4 White has to play the slightly passive 11 ♘e2. All the same, this has some positive sides too, since the knight can later go to f4. Then 11...♕d6 12 c3 ♗d7 13 ♘f4 ♖g8 is an idea for Black, vacating h8 for the bishop in the event of ♘h5 coming. Black then wants to castle queenside, and, depending on White's reply, follow up with a quick ...e5 or ...♘e7 and ...♗c6.

b) Recently, Morozevich has also tried 8...♘c6:

b1) 9 ♗g2 e5 10 d5 ♘b4 11 ♘c3 c6 12 dxc6 ♕xd1+ 13 ♖xd1 bxc6 14 a3 ♘d5! 15 ♘xd5 cxd5 16 ♖xd5 0-0 17 0-0 ♗e6 18 ♖d2 ♖ab8 19 b4 a5 20 bxa5 ♖b5 21 ♘h4 ♖xa5 22 ♗e4 ½-½ Milos-Morozevich, Istanbul OL 2000. Black obviously had enough play for the pawn in this game.

b2) I am not sure how Morozevich would have reacted to 9 c3!?, which tries to exploit the oddly-placed knight on c6.

9 ♗g2 ♗b7 10 ♕e2 (D)

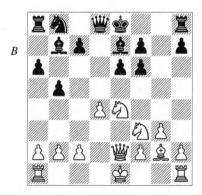

10...♘d7 (D)

10...♗d5 11 ♘c3 has caused Black some problems. Then:

a) 11...♗b4!? 12 ♕e3 c6, intending ...♗xc3 and ...♘d7 with a solid but perhaps uninspiring position, should be tested.

b) Black has usually chosen 11...c6:

b1) 12 0-0-0 ♘d7 13 ♔b1 and now 13...♘b6 14 ♖he1 ♕c7 15 ♘h4! h5 16 f4 f5 17 ♘f3 was better for White in Leko-Morozevich, Frankfurt rpd 1999 but it should be possible to improve on Black's play in this line. For example, 13...♗c4 14 ♕e3 b4, or perhaps even just 13...b4.

b2) 12 ♘xd5 cxd5 13 c3 ♘c6 14 a4 was played two rounds later in Lutz-Morozevich, Frankfurt rpd 1999, and looks like a more serious test of Black's position. The game continued 14...0-0 15 0-0 ♕b6 (15...b4 16 c4 dxc4 17 ♕xc4 also looks good for White) 16 b4! ♖fc8 17 ♖fd1 ♘a7 18 a5 ♕d8 19 ♖d3 with a definite advantage for White.

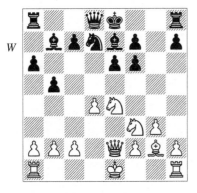

11 0-0 0-0

I was toying with the idea of delaying this, but after 11...♗d5 12 ♖fd1 c6 13 c3 ♕c7 14 b3 White manages to play c4.

12 ♖fd1!

An improvement over J.Polgar-Morozevich, Wijk aan Zee 2000, where Black obtained good counterplay after 12 ♖ad1 ♗d5 13 ♖fe1 ♔h8!? 14 ♘fd2 c6 15 c4 bxc4 16 ♘xc4 a5!. Positionally, White is better at the moment but Black has the more promising dynamic possibilities.

12...f5 13 ♘ed2 ♗d5 (D)

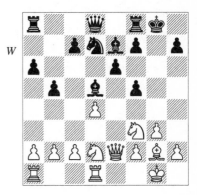

14 c3

White is now preparing b3 followed by c4. The immediate 14 b3 could be met by 14...b4.

14...c5 15 dxc5 ♘xc5 16 ♘f1 ♕c7 17 ♖xd5!

Kasparov is a true master of attacking positional exchange sacrifices. Of course, Black would have no problems if he could keep his light-squared bishop. Now the pride of his position is gone and his pawn-structure shattered.

17...exd5 18 ♘e3 ♗f6 19 ♘d4 ♗xd4 20 cxd4 ♘e4 *(D)*

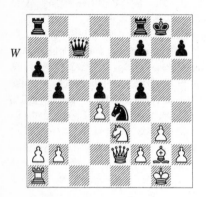

Now:

a) 21 ♘xd5 ♕d6 22 ♘e3 ♕f6 occurred in Kasparov-M.Gurevich, Sarajevo 2000. At this point White should,

objectively, go for 23 ♘xf5 ♕xf5 24 ♗xe4 ♖ae8 25 ♖e1 ♕d7 26 ♕h5 f5 27 ♗d5+ ♚h8 28 ♖xe8 ♕xe8 (28...♖xe8 29 ♗f3 ♖e1+ 30 ♚g2) 29 ♕d1 f4 30 ♚g2 ♕d7 31 ♗f3 ♕f7 32 d5 ♕f6 33 ♕e2 with an edge for White (Kasparov). This is probably not enough to win, as it is not clear how White is ever going to make use of the d-pawn, and I don't see how White can create enough other threats.

Kasparov also considers two alternatives for White, which he considers more promising:

b) 21 ♗h3! (his exclamation mark) 21...♖fe8 22 ♗xf5 ♘f6 23 ♕d1 ♕d6 24 ♖c1 with an initiative.

c) 21 ♘xf5 ♚h8 22 ♗xe4 dxe4 23 ♕xe4 ±.

5 Burn Variation: 6...♗xf6

1 e4 e6 2 d4 d5 3 ♘c3 ♘f6 4 ♗g5 dxe4 5 ♘xe4 ♗e7 6 ♗xf6 ♗xf6 *(D)*

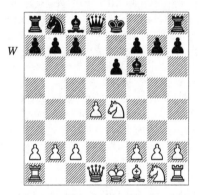

At the time of writing, at elite level, this is an immensely popular line of the Burn Variation. The positions arising lead to interesting strategic battles where White gets a chance for a kingside attack if Black doesn't play actively enough. On the other hand, if Black does manage to create counterplay, his chances are excellent.

7 ♘f3

Now we look at:

A: 7...0-0   58
B: 7...♘d7   61

The two might transpose to each other but there are a few important differences with respect to the move-order. While the first is very natural and preserves the option of developing the knight to c6, the latter is probably better designed to counter white set-ups with 8 ♗c4 or 8 ♕d3!?.

A few alternatives for Black are:

a) 7...b6 is of course a common set-up but it is rarely seen at this point. White has a pleasant choice:

a1) 8 ♗d3 followed by ♕e2 and 0-0-0 is a good set-up for White.

a2) 8 ♕d2 ♗b7 9 ♗b5+ c6 10 ♗e2 ♗e7 11 ♕f4 ♘d7 12 0-0-0 ♕b8 13 ♘e5 and now 13...0-0 14 ♕g3 gave White the better position in Eliskases-Spielmann, Semmering (8) 1936, but here it might be worth investigating 13...f6 14 ♘d3 f5, when Black becomes very active at the expense of weakening his pawn-structure.

b) 7...♗d7 8 ♕d2 (White has tried a number of other set-ups but I like Spassky's idea) 8...♗c6 9 ♘xf6+ ♕xf6 (9...gxf6 10 ♗e2 ♕d6 11 c4! is good for White according to Dolmatov and Dvoretsky; 11...♘d7 is met by 12 ♖d1 intending d5, and 11...♖g8 12 0-0 ♘d7 13 ♖fd1 again intends d5 ±) 10 ♘e5 0-0 11 0-0-0 ♖d8 12 ♕e3 ♗e8 13 g3 ♘d7 14 ♗g2 c6 15 f4 ♕e7 16 h4 favours White, Spassky-Donner, Leiden 1970.

A)

7...0-0 *(D)*

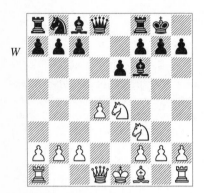

Now:

A1: 8 c3   58
A2: 8 ♕d2   59
A3: 8 ♕d3!?   60
A4: 8 ♗c4   60

A1)

8 c3

This is quite a logical set-up. White reinforces his d-pawn and prepares to set up a battery with queen and bishop on the b1-h7 diagonal. However, this is a little slow and Black has no problems if he prepares to play a quick ...e5.

8...♘d7 9 ♕c2

Or 9 ♗d3 e5 10 ♘xf6+ ♕xf6 11 0-0 exd4 12 ♘xd4 ♘e5 13 ♗e4 g6 14 ♕b3 c6 15 ♖fe1 ♘d7 16 ♕a3 ♖d8 = Groszpeter-Chernin, Hungarian Cht 1996.

9...e5 10 0-0-0 *(D)*

The tedious 10 dxe5 is of course not to be feared but 10 d5 is an obvious

alternative. Then 10...♗e7 (10...g6!?) 11 0-0-0 ♗d6 is the critical reply:

a) 12 ♗d3 g6 13 h4 f5 14 ♘xd6 cxd6 15 ♘g5 ♘f6 16 ♗c4 ♕e7 17 ♕b3 ♖b8 18 ♕a3 b5 19 ♗b3 ♕c7 20 ♔b1 ♕b6 ∓ Gdanski-Hedman, Stockholm 2000.

b) 12 h4 ♘f6 13 ♘fg5 g6 14 f3 (14 h5!? ♘xe4 15 ♘xe4 f5 16 ♘xd6 cxd6 17 hxg6 ♕g5+ 18 ♔b1 hxg6 looks alright for Black) 14...♘h5 15 g4 ♘f4 16 h5 f5 17 hxg6 fxe4 18 ♘xh7 ♖f6! 19 ♘g5 ♘xg6 20 ♘xe4!? (20 ♕xe4 ♘f8 21 ♖h5 ♖h6! 22 ♘e6 ♗xe6 23 dxe6 ♖xh5 24 gxh5 ♕g5+ 25 ♔b1 ♖b8! ∓ Minasian-Dreev, St Petersburg 1993) 20...♖f7 (20...♖xf3? 21 ♖h6 ♘f8 22 ♕h2 ♖f4 23 ♖h8+ ♔g7 24 ♕h6+ ♔f7 25 ♕h5+ and White wins after 25...♔e7 26 ♖g8! +− or 25...♔g7 26 g5 +−) 21 ♖h6 ♖g7 22 ♕h2 ♕f8!? with a messy position, Hector-M.Gurevich, Antwerp 1994.

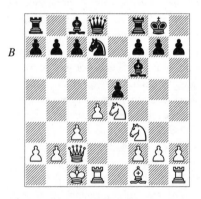

10...exd4 11 ♘xd4 *(D)*

11 ♘xf6+?! ♕xf6 12 ♖xd4 ♘c5 13 ♗c4 ♗f5 14 ♕d2 (Ljubojević-Dreev,

Linares 1995) 14...♘e6 15 ♖d7 ♘g5! 16 ♖xc7 ♘xf3 17 gxf3 ♗g6 intending ...♕f5 ∓ (Dreev).

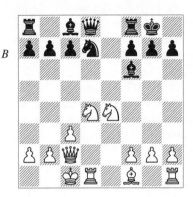

11...♗xd4

A sensible alternative is 11...♕e7 12 ♗d3 h6 13 ♖he1 ♘c5 14 ♘xf6+ ♕xf6 15 ♗f5, when 15...♗xf5?! 16 ♕xf5 ♕xf5 17 ♘xf5 ♖fe8 18 ♔c2 ♔f8 19 b4 gave White an edge in Hübner-Chernin, Groningen PCA 1993, but Chernin recommends 15...g6 16 ♗xc8 ♖axc8 =.

12 ♖xd4 ♕e7 13 h4 ♘e5 14 ♘g5 g6 15 ♕e2 f6 16 ♘f3

Now 16...♗f5 17 ♘xe5 fxe5 was Glek-Lputian, Dortmund 1992, when Glek gives 18 ♕e3 ±. I think Black should have few problems if he plays 16...♘c6!? 17 ♕xe7 ♘xe7 18 h5 g5.

A2)

8 ♕d2 b6 *(D)*

Or:

a) 8...♘d7 – *7...♘d7 8 ♕d2 0-0.*

b) 8...♗e7 9 ♗c4 b6 10 0-0-0 ♗b7 11 ♖he1 ♘c6 12 ♕e2 ♘b4 13 ♘e5 c6

14 a3 ♘d5 15 ♗b3 ♕c7 16 c4 ♘f6 17 ♘xf6+ ♗xf6 18 c5! ± Kindermann-Lautier, Baden-Baden 1992.

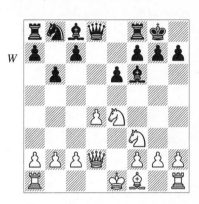

9 ♘xf6+!

Simple and strong. 9 0-0-0 ♗b7 is more common but we will discuss this type of position in Line B, and the text-move is just good for White.

9...♕xf6 10 ♗d3 ♗b7

10...h6 11 ♗e4 c6 12 0-0-0 intending g4-g5 is very good for White.

11 ♘g5 h6

Black has more often gone for the text-move, sacrificing an exchange in the hope of obtaining some counter-play, than 11...g6, which invites White to open the h-file with h4-h5. For example, 12 0-0-0 ♘d7 (12...♖d8 13 ♗e4!? ♘c6 14 ♕e3 ± Macieja) 13 h4 h6 14 ♘e4 ♕xd4 15 ♕xh6 ♕g7 16 ♕e3 was very good for White in Yudasin-Dreev, Lyons 1994.

12 ♘h7 ♕xd4 13 ♘xf8 ♔xf8 14 c3 ♕e5+

Nor does 14...♕h4 give Black full compensation: 15 g3 ♕f6 16 ♖f1 ♘d7

17 f4! ♘c5 18 0-0-0 ♗d5 19 c4 ♘xd3+ 20 ♕xd3 ± Kindermann-Bareev, Pardubice 1994.

15 ♗e2 ♘c6 16 0-0 ♖d8 17 ♕e1 ± Z.Almasi-Dreev, Tilburg 1994.

A3)

8 ♕d3 (D)

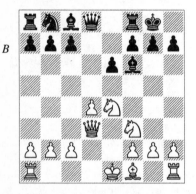

This is not a completely new move but it has been developed significantly in the last few years. One idea is that White can quickly develop an attack against h7.

8...♘d7 9 0-0-0 b6 10 h4

Another idea is to put a knight on e5 by 10 ♕e3 ♗b7 11 ♘e5 but 11...♗e7 12 ♗b5 ♘f6 seems to solve Black's problems; e.g.:

a) 13 ♘xf6+ ♗xf6 14 ♘d7 c6!? is fine for Black.

b) 13 ♗c6 ♘d5 14 ♕g3 ♗xc6 15 ♘xc6 ♕e8 16 ♘xe7+ ♕xe7 = Senff-Arnold, Paks 2000.

10...♗b7 11 ♘fg5

11 ♘eg5 g6 12 ♕e3 h6 13 ♘e4 ♗g7 14 ♗d3 c5! and Black equalized

without any problems in J.Polgar-Bareev, Madrid 1994.

11...♗xg5+ 12 hxg5

12 ♘xg5 ♘f6 is just equal, so White sacrifices a pawn to open the h-file.

12...♗xe4 13 ♕xe4 ♕xg5+ 14 ♔b1 ♘f6 15 ♕c6 ♕f4 16 ♗d3 ♖ad8 17 c3 ♖d5

Milos-Shirov, Las Vegas FIDE rpd 1999. Black is a pawn up but White has some compensation due to the semi-open h-file, and this roughly balances the position.

A4)

8 ♗c4

Most of the top players seem to have decided that this fashionable continuation is the critical test of 7...0-0. One point is that against a ...b6 set-up White gets his queen on e2.

8...♘c6

By immediately attacking d4, Black prevents a white set-up with the queen on e2 and the knight also supports an ...e5 advance. The disadvantage is of course that the knight is somewhat clumsily placed on c6. There are a few alternatives:

a) 8...b6 9 ♕e2 ♗b7 10 0-0-0 ♗d5!? (10...♘d7 11 ♘e5 ±) 11 ♘e5!? ♗xe5 12 dxe5 ♘c6 13 f4 ♗xc4 14 ♕xc4 ♘a5 (D.Gross-I.Almasi, Budapest 1999) 15 ♕a4 ♕e8 16 ♕xe8 ♖fxe8 17 ♖d7 ± I.Almasi.

b) 8...♘d7 9 ♕e2 ♗e7!? 10 0-0-0 c6 11 h4 b5 12 ♗d3 ♕c7 13 ♔b1 ♘f6 14 ♘xf6+ ♗xf6 15 ♕e4 g6 16 h5 gave White a strong attack in the game

Topalov-Kramnik, Monaco Amber blindfold 1997.

9 c3 e5 10 d5 *(D)*

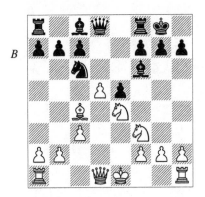

10...♘b8

Two other knight moves also come into consideration:

a) 10...♘a5 11 ♗d3 b6 12 h4 ± Baklan-Goloshchapov, Ordzhonikidze Z 2000.

b) 10...♘e7!? 11 ♘xf6+ gxf6 12 ♘h4 (12 ♕d2 ♔h8 13 0-0-0 ♗g4 14 ♗e2 ♕d6 led to an equal position in Anand-Shirov, Sydney Olympic exh rpd (2) 2000) 12...♘g6 13 ♕h5 ♕d7!? 14 h3! ± Short-M.Gurevich, British League (4NCL) 1999/00.

11 ♕e2 ♗f5 12 ♗d3!?

A recent refinement. Otherwise:

a) 12 0-0 ♗xe4 13 ♕xe4 ♕d6 led to easy equality for Black in Sutovsky-Psakhis, Pula Z 2000.

b) 12 0-0-0 ♘d7 (the continuation 12...♗xe4 13 ♕xe4 ♕d6 still deserves attention, even though the position is of course sharpened by White castling queenside) 13 ♘g3 and now:

b1) 13...♗g6 14 ♗d3! ♗xd3 15 ♕xd3 ♘c5 16 ♕e3 b6 17 h4 ♖e8 18 ♘e4 ♘xe4 19 ♕xe4 gave White a substantial advantage in Leko-Khalifman, Budapest (4) 1999.

b2) 13...♗g4 14 h3 ♗xf3 15 ♕xf3 ♘b6 16 ♗b3 a5 with counterplay.

b3) 13...♗g5+!? 14 ♘xg5 ♕xg5+ 15 ♕e3 ♕xe3+ 16 fxe3 ♗g4 (another possibility is 16...♗g6!?) 17 ♖d2 ♘b6 18 ♗b3 a5 is roughly equal.

c) 12 ♘g3!? ♗g4!? 13 h3 ♗xf3 14 ♕xf3 ♘d7 (14...g6!?) 15 ♘e4 ♗e7 16 0-0-0 ♗d6 17 g4 ± Leko-Shirov, Frankfurt rpd 2000.

12...♗xe4

Something like 12...♘d7 13 0-0-0 a5 14 d6 also looks better for White. Short suggests 12...♗e7 13 0-0-0!? ♕xd5 14 g4, when 14...♗g6 15 h4 ♘c6 16 ♔b1 ♖ad8 17 h5 ♗xe4 18 ♗xe4 ♕e6 looks unclear.

13 ♗xe4 ♘d7 14 0-0-0 ♗e7 15 g4 ♗d6 16 ♔b1 ♖b8 17 h4

White's attack is more promising, Short-M.Gurevich, Shenyang FIDE WCup 2000.

B)

7...♘d7 *(D)*

Now there are two main lines:
B1: 8 ♗c4   62
B2: 8 ♕d2   63

Other moves:

a) 8 ♕d3. Here Black might just transpose to Line A3 with 8...0-0, but he can profitably delay this; e.g., 8...b6 9 0-0-0 ♗b7 10 h4 ♗e7 11 ♔b1 ♘f6 =

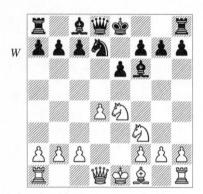

Morozevich-M.Gurevich, Cannes rpd 2001.

b) 8 ♕e2 is probably going to be further developed in the near future. It is not a new move: it was used by Bogoljubow in his 1929 World Championship match against Alekhine, but only recently has it reappeared in a couple of top-level encounters. 8...0-0 9 0-0-0 b6 (9...♗e7!? was Alekhine's preference, with which he equalized after 10 ♔b1 b6 11 g4 ♗b7 12 ♖g1 c5 in Bogoljubow-Alekhine, Wiesbaden Wch (24) 1929) 10 ♘e5!? ♗xe5 11 dxe5 ♕e7 12 f4 ♗b7 13 ♕e3 ♖ad8 14 ♗d3 ♗xe4 15 ♗xe4 ♘c5 16 ♗c6 ± Bologan-Bareev, Enghien les Bains 2001.

c) 8 ♗d3 c5 (8...0-0 9 c3 – 7...0-0 8 c3 ♘d7 9 ♗d3 =) 9 dxc5 (9 ♘xf6+ ♘xf6 – 5...♘bd7 6 ♘f3 ♗e7 7 ♘xf6+ ♗xf6 8 ♗xf6 ♘xf6 9 ♗d3 c5 ±/=) 9...♘xc5 10 ♗b5+ ♔e7 11 ♕xd8+ ♖xd8 12 ♘xc5 ♖d5 =.

B1)

8 ♗c4 (D)

Against 7...♘d7 this trendy set-up has less sting. Now Black can try a set-up akin to Morozevich's *6...gxf6 7 ♘f3 a6*.

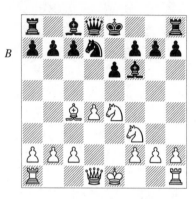

8...a6! 9 ♕e2 b5 10 ♗d5

10 ♗b3 0-0 11 0-0-0 ♗b7 12 d5 was Kindermann-Roth, Vienna 1996, and now 12...exd5 13 ♗xd5 c6 14 ♗b3 ♕c7 doesn't look bad for Black.

10...♖b8 11 0-0-0 0-0 12 ♗c6

Or 12 ♘xf6+ ♕xf6 (12...♘xf6 13 ♗c6 ♖b6 14 ♘e5 ♘d5 also looks OK for Black) 13 ♗c6 ♖b6 14 ♗xd7 ♗xd7 15 ♘e5 ♖d8 followed by ...♗c6-d5 = Milos-Bareev, Shenyang FIDE WCup 2000.

12...♖b6 13 d5 exd5 14 ♗xd5

On the face of it White might look a little better since Black has still not completed his development and White's pieces are (temporarily) more active. However, Black doesn't really have anything to worry about.

14...c6 15 ♗b3 c5!

This is the move that solves Black's problems.

16 ♗d5

The point of Black's last move is that 16 ♘xc5?! is met by 16...♗xb2+! 17 ♔xb2 ♕f6+ followed by ...♘xc5.

16...♕c7 17 ♖he1 ♗d8!

Another fine move. This makes room for ...♘f6.

18 ♘eg5 ♗xg5+ 19 ♘xg5 ♘f6

The game is equal, Svidler-M.Gurevich, Esbjerg 2000.

B2)

8 ♕d2 *(D)*

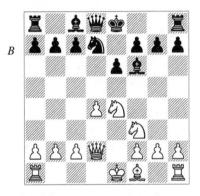

8...0-0

The immediate 8...b6 is now rarely seen, mainly owing to 9 ♗b5 ♗b7 10 ♘xf6+, when Black is forced to play 10...gxf6, when White has a pleasant choice:

a) 11 0-0-0 ♕e7 12 d5! 0-0-0 13 ♕e2 ♘e5 14 ♘xe5 fxe5 15 ♕xe5 ♕c5 16 ♗e2 ♗xd5 17 ♗a6+ ♗b7 18 ♗xb7+ ♔xb7 19 ♕xc5 bxc5 20 ♖he1 ± Tal-Pachman, Portorož IZ 1958.

b) 11 ♕c3!? ♕e7 12 ♕xc7 ♕b4+ (12...♗xf3 13 ♗xd7+ ♕xd7 14 ♕xd7+ ♔xd7 15 gxf3 ±) 13 c3 ♕xb5 14 ♕xb7 ♕xb2 15 0-0 ♖d8 16 c4 and White was better in L.Steiner-Ståhlberg, Saltsjöbaden IZ 1948.

9 0-0-0 *(D)*

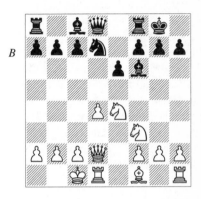

Now:

B21)

9...♗e7

This retreat makes room for ...♘f6 and assists a possible ...c5.

10 ♕c3!?

The result of Kasparov's labour on this line. White discourages ...c5 ideas and frees the d-file for his rook. There are a number of other interesting ideas for White:

a) 10 h4!? b6 11 ♗c4 ♗b7 is a type of position that occurs more frequently in Line B22. Hraček-Sakalauskas, Istanbul OL 2000 continued 12 ♖he1 ♘f6 13 ♘xf6+ ♗xf6 14 ♕f4 ♗d5 15 ♗d3 ♕d6 16 ♘e5 ♖fd8 with roughly equal chances.

b) 10 ♕e3 c5! 11 dxc5 ♕c7 12 ♗d3 ♗xc5! 13 ♘xc5 ♘xc5 = Bezgodov-Sakaev, Russian Ch (Moscow) 1999.

c) 10 ♗c4 and then:

c1) 10...♘f6 11 ♖he1 ♘d5?! (this seems like a dubious idea; 11...♘xe4 12 ♖xe4 b5!? is suggested by Ftačnik) 12 ♘e5 f5 13 ♗xd5! (this had probably been underestimated by Bareev) 13...exd5 (13...♕xd5 14 c4! ♕d8 15 ♘c3 is good for White, and 13...fxe4 14 ♗xe4 ♗g5 15 ♖e3 gives White more than adequate compensation) 14 ♘c5 ♗g5 15 f4 ♗f6 16 h3 ♕d6 17 ♘cd3 b6 18 g4 ± Shirov-Bareev, New Delhi FIDE 2000.

c2) 10...c5!? 11 dxc5 (11 d5 ♘b6!) 11...♕c7 12 ♖he1 ♘xc5 13 ♘xc5 ♕xc5 14 ♗d3 ♗f6 15 ♕e2 g6 16 h4 ♖d8 17 ♗b5 ♗xb2+ 18 ♔xb2 ½-½ Z.Almasi-Dizdar, Makarska Tucepi 1995.

10...♘f6

10...b6 is a logical alternative, suggested by Bareev. White might then try something like 11 ♘e5 ♗b7 12 ♘c6 ♕e8 13 f3!?, threatening ♘xe7+.

11 ♘xf6+ ♗xf6 12 ♗d3 ♕d6 13 ♔b1 ♖d8 14 h4 a5 15 ♕e1!? ♗d7 16 ♘g5 h6 17 ♗h7+ ♔f8 18 ♘e4 ♕e7 19 ♘xf6 ♕xf6 20 ♗e4

± Kasparov-Bareev, Sarajevo 2000.

B22)

9...b6 (D)
10 ♗c4

White prepares to open the centre with d5. Other moves are not dangerous:

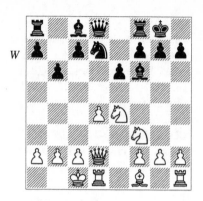

a) 10 d5 ♘c5! 11 ♘xc5 bxc5 12 ♗c4 e5 (12...♖b8 13 c3 e5 can also be considered) 13 ♕a5 ♕d6 14 ♘d2 ½-½ Wahls-M.Gurevich, Munich 1992. It is clear that White is better structurally but Black's two bishops and counterplay on the b-file clearly compensate for that.

b) 10 ♕e3 ♗b7 11 ♗d3 ♗e7 12 ♘e5 f5! 13 ♘c3 ♘xe5 14 ♕xe5 ♗d6 15 ♕xe6+ ½-½ Leko-Akopian, Dortmund 2000.

c) 10 ♕f4 ♗b7 gives White more choice as to how to utilize his bishop. For example, it might be developed to d3, which appears more aggressive because it points towards the black king. However, this isn't considered very dangerous and Black can solve his problems after 11 ♗d3 (11 ♗c4 – 10 ♗c4 ♗b7 11 ♕f4) 11...♗e7 12 h4:

c1) 12...♘f6 13 c4 (13 ♘eg5 ♗xf3 14 ♘xf3 ♕d6 15 ♘e5 c5 16 dxc5 ♕xc5 17 ♖he1 ♖ac8 18 ♔b1 ♖fd8 19 g4 ♗d6 = Nunn-M.Gurevich, Belgrade 1991) 13...c5 14 dxc5 ♕b8! 15 ♕xb8 ♖fxb8 16 ♘xf6+ ♗xf6 17 cxb6 axb6

18 ♔b1 ♗xf3 19 gxf3 h5! = Fressinet-Tukmakov, Solin/Split 2000.

c2) 12...♕b8!? 13 ♘e5 c5 14 ♘g5 (14 g3 ♘xe5 15 dxe5 f5! ∓ Kharlov-Dreev, St Petersburg 1993) 14...♘f6 15 c3 cxd4 16 cxd4 ♗d5 17 ♔b1 with an unclear position, Zso.Polgar-Furlan, Ljubljana 1994.

10...♗b7 *(D)*

10...c6 has mainly been used by Dreev. It is slightly passive, so White should be able to get an advantage:

a) 11 ♕e3!? ♕c7 12 ♘xf6+ ♘xf6 13 ♘e5 (White's plan is very simple: he intends to support the e5-knight with f4 and possibly try to build up a kingside attack) 13...a5 14 c3 a4 15 a3 ♖a5 16 ♗a2 c5 17 ♖he1 ♗b7 18 f4 ± Kindermann-Dreev, Nussloch 1996.

b) 11 ♕f4 ♗b7 12 h4 ♗e7?! (12...♕b8! 13 ♘xf6+ ♘xf6 14 ♘e5 c5 15 dxc5 ♕c7! is better) 13 ♘e5 ♕c7 14 ♕g3 ♘xe5 15 dxe5 b5 16 ♗e2 ♖ad8 17 ♘d6 ± Golubev-Willemze, Dieren 1999.

c) 11 g4! (of course this only comes into consideration because Black has closed the a8-h1 diagonal) 11...♗e7 12 g5 ♗b7 13 ♕f4 ♕b8 (13...c5 14 d5 is also good for White) 14 ♕h4 (this is primitive but perhaps lethal; the direct threat is 15 ♖hg1 with the idea of ♘f6+) 14...c5 15 d5 ♘e5? (a mistake, but Black's position was difficult in any case) 16 ♘xe5 ♕xe5 17 ♖he1 ♕f5 18 ♗d3 h6 19 f4 1-0 Velimirović-Cosma, Nikšić 1994. 19...♕xd5 20 ♘f6+! ♗xf6 21 gxf6 is hopeless for Black.

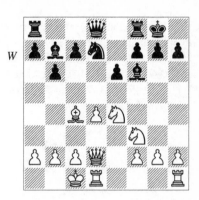

11 ♕f4 *(D)*

Sensible; White centralizes his queen and prepares d5. Other moves:

a) 11 ♖he1 ♗d5 and then:

a1) 12 ♗xd5 exd5 13 ♘xf6+ ♘xf6 14 ♕f4 ♘e4 15 ♘e5 f6 16 ♘d3 ♕d7 with equality, Finkel-M.Gurevich, Belgrade 1999.

a2) 12 ♕d3 c6 13 ♗b3 b5! 14 ♗xd5 cxd5 15 ♘xf6+ ♘xf6 16 ♕xb5 ♖b8 17 ♕a4 ♘e4 18 ♖e2 ♕b6 gives Black excellent compensation, Wedberg-P.H.Nielsen, Reykjavik 2000.

a3) 12 ♗d3 c5 13 c4 ♗b7 14 dxc5 ♕e7!? 15 ♘xf6+ ♘xf6 16 cxb6 axb6 17 ♔b1 ♖a5 and Black had reasonable compensation in A.David-M.Gurevich, Amsterdam 2000.

b) 11 d5!? b5! 12 ♗b3 (12 ♗xb5 exd5 13 ♘xf6+ ♘xf6 looks fine for Black) and now:

b1) 12...c5!? 13 ♘d6 (or 13 dxe6 ♗xe4 14 exf7+ ♔h8 15 ♕xd7 ♕xd7 16 ♖xd7 ♗xf3 17 gxf3 c4 ∓ M.Gurevich) 13...♗xd5 14 ♗xd5 exd5 15 ♕xd5 ♘b6!? 16 ♕e4! ♘a4 (16...♕d7!?) 17 ♘e5 ♕b6 18 ♕d5 ♖ad8 leading to a complicated game, Van den Doel-M.Gurevich, Hoogeveen 1999.

b2) 12...♘b6 13 ♘xf6+ ♕xf6 14 dxe6 fxe6 15 ♖he1 ♘c4 16 ♗xc4 bxc4 17 ♕e3 ♗d5 = Xu Yuhua-Zhukova, New Delhi FIDE wom 2000.

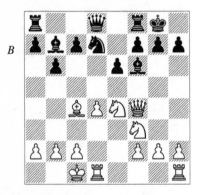

11...♕b8!?

Black reacts by moving the queen away from the d-file, and so prepares ...c5. This appears to give Black good chances of equality, but the alternatives are also worth noting:

a) 11...♗e7 12 d5! exd5 13 ♗xd5 ♗xd5 14 ♖xd5 ♕c8 15 ♘d4 ♘f6 16 ♖e5 ♘xe4 17 ♖xe7 ♘d6 18 ♖he1 ± Shirov-M.Gurevich, New Delhi FIDE 2000.

b) 11...♗d5 12 ♗d3 ♗e7!? (12...c5 13 c4 ♗b7!? also looks feasible) 13 c4 ♗b7 14 g4 ♘f6 15 ♘xf6+ ♗xf6 16 ♗e4 ♗xe4 17 ♕xe4 ♕e7 18 h4 ♕b4 with counterplay, Bologan-M.Gurevich, Belfort 1998.

12 ♖he1 (D)

12 ♘e5 c5 13 ♘xf6+ ♘xf6 14 dxc5 ♖c8!? is also fine for Black.

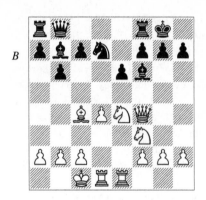

12...c5

Or:

a) 12...♗d5 13 ♗xd5 exd5 14 ♘xf6+ ♘xf6 15 ♖e7 looks better for White.

b) 12...♗e7 13 d5! exd5 14 ♗xd5 leaves White better after either 14...c6 15 ♕xb8 ♖axb8 16 ♗c4 ♘f6 17 ♘eg5 or 14...♘f6 15 ♗xb7 ♕xb7 16 ♘xf6+ ♗xf6 17 g4.

13 ♕g4?!

A much more critical line is 13 ♕xb8 ♖axb8 14 d5 exd5 (14...b5 15 dxe6 bxc4 16 exd7 ♗xe4 17 ♖xe4 ♗xb2+ 18 ♔d2 ±) 15 ♗xd5, and now Black must react accurately:

a) 15...♗xd5 16 ♖xd5 ♖fd8 17 ♖ed1 ♖e8 18 ♖xd7 ♖xe4 19 ♖xa7 ±.

b) 15...♗d8 16 ♗xb7 ♖xb7 17 ♘d6 and White is much better.

c) 15...♗e7! 16 ♘c3 ♗f6 17 ♘b5 a6 18 ♘c7 ♗d8 19 ♗xb7 ♖xb7 is equal.

13...cxd4 14 ♘xd4 ♗xe4 15 ♕xe4 ♘c5

∓ M.Freitag-Z.Schneider, Feldbach 1997.

6 Steinitz Variation: Introduction

1 e4 e6 2 d4 d5 3 ♘c3 ♘f6 4 e5 *(D)*

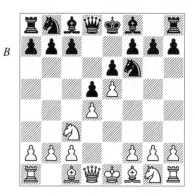

This pawn advance characterizes the Steinitz Variation. Steinitz's idea was to maintain a space advantage by fortifying the e5-pawn with f4. Today, this is a very popular method of play but Boleslavsky's 7 ♗e3 (after 4...♘fd7 5 f4 c5 6 ♘f3 ♘c6), which we look at in the next chapter, has completely superseded Steinitz's own 6 dxc5.

We now consider:

A: 4...♘e4   67
B: 4...♘fd7   68

The latter is standard; in this introductory chapter we only consider alternatives to the continuations 5 f4 c5 6 ♘f3 ♘c6 7 ♗e3 and 5 ♘ce2.

A few provocative types have tried 4...♘g8. Here White even has the option of transposing into the Advance Variation (*1 e4 e6 2 d4 d5 3 e5*) with the paradoxical 5 ♘b1(?!). This is just a joke of course; White is better after simple development with 5 f4, 5 ♘f3 or 5 ♗e3.

A)

4...♘e4

This is quite rare but is employed by some players as a surprise weapon.

5 ♘xe4

This could also arise from the Tarrasch Variation (*3 ♘d2 ♘f6 4 e5 ♘e4 5 ♘xe4*) from where it arrives more commonly. Here, White has an additional possibility in 5 ♘ce2!? f6 6 ♘f4 (6 f3 ♘g5 is not convincing as the knight can hop back to f7 where it usefully increases the pressure on e5) 6...♕e7 7 ♘f3 (or 7 ♗d3 ±) 7...♗d7 8 ♗d3 ♘c6 9 0-0 0-0-0 10 c4!, when White was much better in Arakhamia-Nolan, Aberdeen 1998.

5...dxe4 6 ♗e3

6 ♗c4 a6 (6...c5 7 d5 is good for White; for example, 7...exd5 8 ♕xd5 ♕xd5 9 ♗xd5 ♘c6 10 ♗xe4 ♘xe5 11

♗f4 ♘c6 12 ♘f3 ± Dvoirys) 7 a4 b6. Black intends first to increase his control over d5 and then either to play ...c5 or just to blockade the d5-square by ...♘c6-e7. White has tried various replies:

a) 8 d5?! is positionally desirable but White wastes time and now falls behind in development: 8...♗b7! 9 dxe6 ♕xd1+ 10 ♔xd1 fxe6 11 ♗xe6 ♘c6 12 ♗e3 (if 12 ♗f4, Black regains his pawn with 12...♗c5 13 ♘h3 ♗d4) 12...♘xe5 is slightly better for Black, Imanaliev-Malaniuk, Frunze 1987.

b) 8 ♘h3 ♗b7 9 ♘f4 ♘c6 10 ♗e3 (10 c3 ♘e7 11 ♕b3!? also looks good for White, Bryson-Nolan, Scottish Ch (Largs) 1998) 10...♘e7 11 0-0 g6 12 ♕e2 ♘f5 13 ♖fd1 ♗h6 14 a5! with a slight advantage for White, Aseev-Lputian, USSR Ch (Lvov) 1984.

6...c5

Black must react quickly; otherwise White just plays ♘e2-g3 and Black will have trouble defending his e4-pawn.

7 dxc5 ♘d7 8 ♕g4

This is critical and definitely better than 8 b4? b6!, when White's queenside is seriously weakened. Now White goes immediately for the e4-pawn.

8...♘xc5 9 ♗b5+

9 ♗xc5 ♗xc5 10 ♕xg7 is greedy but also risky. 10...♕a5+ 11 c3 ♖f8 12 ♘e2 ♗d7 13 ♕f6 ♗a4 14 ♘g3? (14 ♕f4 is necessary, although Black has compensation after 14...0-0-0) and now Pytel suggests 14...♗a3 (14...♗d4? 15 ♘xe4 ♗xe5 16 ♕h4 left Black in

trouble in Tringov-Bednarski, Varna 1972) 15 ♖b1, continuing 15...♖d8 (Pytel gives this an '!' but I think it really deserves a '?') but this looks very unconvincing in view of the reply 16 ♘xe4 ♗c2 17 bxa3!. Instead, Black has 15...♗xb2 16 ♖xb2 ♕xc3+ 17 ♖d2 ♕c1+ 18 ♔e2 ♗b5+ 19 ♔e3 ♕c3+ 20 ♗d3 ♗xd3 21 ♖hd1 ♕c5+ 22 ♔f4 ♕d4 with a large advantage for Black.

9...♘d7 10 ♘e2 ♕a5+ 11 ♘c3 a6 12 ♗xd7+ ♗xd7 13 ♗d4 ♗c6 14 0-0-0 0-0-0

This position has been reached a number of times, with reasonable results for Black after 15 ♔b1 ♖xd4! 16 ♖xd4 ♕xe5. Instead, 15 ♕f4!, as in Seul-Zach, Biel 1997, looks very good for White.

B)

4...♘fd7 (D)

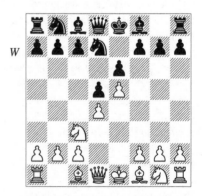

The coverage now divides into:

The Shirov/Anand Variation, 5 ♘ce2, which incidentally was one of Steinitz's ways of playing this position too, is covered independently in Chapter 8.

B1)

5 ♘f3

This is a sensible developing move, but now White cannot support his centre with c3 and/or f4 because the pawns are both blocked by knights. Therefore Black can break up the centre with ...c5 and ...f6. This leads to an interesting strategic struggle since the pawn-structure is defined by white pawns on the second rank (a-c and f-h) against the three black pawn islands a7+b7, d5+e6 and g7+h7. This means White will be attempting to gain control over the central dark squares, e5 in particular, while Black in turn will try to break this stronghold and seek counterplay on the semi-open c- and f-files.

5...c5

5...♗e7 is somewhat passive since Black loses a tempo if he later plays ...c5, White captures and Black recaptures with the bishop. 6 ♗d3 b6 7 h4!? h6 8 ♘e2 ♗a6 9 ♗xa6 ♘xa6 10 ♖h3 c5 11 ♖g3 ♗f8 12 c4!? ♘c7 13 ♘f4 cxd4 14 cxd5 ♘xd5 15 ♘xd5 exd5 16 ♖g4 ± Khasangatin-Sabaev, Pardubice 1988.

6 dxc5

With this, White seeks a fairly simple piece deployment. The light-squared bishop goes to d3, the other to f4, White castles and plays ♕e2 and/or

♖e1 and then sees how events unfold. Another line is 6 ♗b5 ♘c6 7 0-0 but Black has more than one satisfactory route to equality. One is 7...cxd4 8 ♘xd4 ♕c7 followed by ...a6. This is good and solid. Black can also maintain the central tension and simply develop with 7...♗e7 but also just 7...a6 looks good; e.g., 8 ♗xc6 bxc6 9 ♘e2 a5!? 10 ♘g3 ♕b6 11 ♖e1 cxd4 12 ♘xd4 ♗c5 13 c3 0-0 with a comfortable position for Black, as in Van de Oudeweertering-Vedder, Dutch Cht 1994.

6...♘c6 7 ♗f4 ♗xc5

Another option is 7...♘xc5 but 8 ♗d3 ♗e7 9 h4!? gives White some attacking chances. The idea of advancing the h-pawn in this type of French position is very common. Either White creates dark-squared weaknesses by advancing it all the way to h6, or White will gain a potential target on g7 if Black plays ...h6. Then a rook-lift to the third rank with ♖h3 becomes an option.

8 ♗d3 (D)

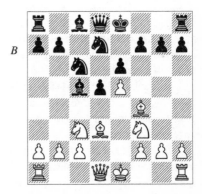

8...f6

This has to be played now. After 8...0-0?? White has the standard Greek Gift sacrifice, 9 ♗xh7+!, and 8...h6 only provides White with a target for a coming attack.

9 exf6 ♘xf6

9...♕xf6!? retains better control over e5 but also hinders the smooth development that Black obtains in the main line. However, this seems to be a very serious alternative. White has two options:

a) 10 ♗g5 ♕f7 11 ♕e2 0-0 12 0-0-0 h6 13 ♗h4 (Morozevich-Bareev, Sarajevo 1999; Bareev thinks 13 ♗d2 is better) 13...♗b4 14 ♗g3 (in Deseatnicov-Radjabov, Oropesa del Mar U-18 Wch 1999, White played the miserable 14 ♘b5? a6 15 ♘c7? only to discover that his knight was lost after 15...♕f4+) 14...♗xc3 15 bxc3, and now Bareev proposes 15...e5 16 ♘xe5 ♘dxe5 17 ♗xe5 ♖e8 18 f4 ♘xe5 19 fxe5 ♕f4+ 20 ♕d2 ♕xd2+, when Black should have no real problems in the endgame. The preparatory 15...♖e8 (or 15...♕e7) also looks worth a try, if Black is not satisfied with the endgame. It should be mentioned that White cannot really avoid the doubled pawns on the c-file.

b) 10 ♗g3 0-0 11 0-0 ♘d4 12 ♘xd4 ♗xd4 13 ♕h5 g6 14 ♕e2 a6 15 ♖ae1 ♘c5 (Rogers-Draško, Tallinn 1985) 16 ♗e5 is roughly equal.

10 0-0 0-0 11 ♘e5 ♗d7 12 ♕e2 ♕e7 13 ♖ae1 ♖ae8 14 ♔h1 a6 15 ♗g3 ♘xe5 16 ♗xe5 ♗c6

This series of moves has flowed very naturally. The type of position we have reached has occurred several times. This position is roughly equal, which to some extent was borne out by the fact that Rogers-Psakhis, Wijk aan Zee 1997 was agreed drawn after 17 a3. Black has no problems after 17...g6! followed by ...♘d7 but note that the immediate 17...♘d7 is wrong due to 18 ♕h5!.

B2)

5 f4 c5 *(D)*

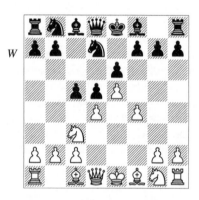

6 ♘f3

6 dxc5 ♗xc5 7 ♘f3 is an alternative, and the choice of Steinitz. Then:

a) The game Steinitz-Sellman, Baltimore 1885 illustrated White's concept. It went 7...a6 8 ♗d3 ♘c6 9 ♕e2 ♘b4?! (9...b5 worked well for Black in Safianovsky-Vaïsser, Cappelle la Grande 1993, which continued 10 ♗d2 ♘b6 followed by ...♘c4, but White should consider 10 ♘g5!?) 10 ♗d2 b5 11 ♘d1 ♘xd3+ 12 cxd3 ♕b6? (12...b4 is better) 13 b4! ♗e7 14 a3 and White is much better.

b) Nowadays, I think most French players would prefer, or at least consider, attacking White's centre immediately with 7...♘c6 8 ♗d3 f6 9 exf6 ♘xf6 10 ♕e2 0-0 11 ♗d2 a6 12 0-0-0 ♕c7, followed by ...b5, when Black had counterplay in Georgadze-Dvoretsky, USSR Cht (Moscow) 1967.

6...a6!?

Other moves:

a) After 6...♘c6, 7 ♗e3 is the next chapter, while 7 ♘e2 is a line of the Tarrasch Variation (*3 ♘d2 ♘f6 4 e5 ♘fd7 5 f4 c5 6 ♘df3 ♘c6 7 ♘e2*).

b) 6...♕b6 and now:

b1) 7 ♗e3 and here: 7...a6 – *6...a6 7 ♗e3 ♕b6*; 7...♘c6 – *6...♘c6 7 ♗e3 ♕b6* (Chapter 7, Line B).

b2) 7 ♘a4 ♕c6 8 ♘xc5 ♘xc5 9 dxc5 ♗xc5 10 ♗d3 ♕b6 11 c3 a5 12 ♕b3 ♘c6 13 ♕xb6 ♗xb6 14 ♔e2 ♗c5 15 ♗e3 b6 = Barkhagen-Gleizerov, Stockholm 1998.

7 ♗e3 *(D)*

A very notable idea here, pointed out by GM Peter Heine Nielsen, and actually played in a number of games, is 7 ♘e2!?. White gets the Shirov/Anand Variation (Chapter 8) in a good version since Black has wasted time on ...a6, and Anand doesn't seem bothered about the fact that Black can capture on d4 without White being able to recapture with a pawn. Obviously, since otherwise ...a6 is just a waste of time, Black should now play 7...cxd4 8 ♘exd4 ♘c6.

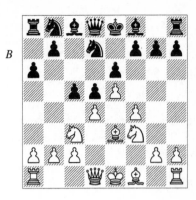

7...♕b6

This idea, which is a sort of accelerated version of the more common 6...♘c6 7 ♗e3 ♕b6 line, has been known for some time but only received serious attention after Morozevich used it to win against Lutz at the 1998 Elista Olympiad.

A less important sideline for Black is 7...b5 8 ♕d2 ♗b7 followed by ...b4 but I don't think this is significantly different from Line C of the next chapter, and to be honest I would rather have my knight on c6 than my bishop on b7.

8 a3

This is considered the most serious test. Of course, it is the usual trick: Black cannot take on b2 due to 9 ♘a4, trapping the queen. White now wishes to maintain the tension and at some point perhaps threaten ♘a4. Other continuations are:

a) 8 ♕d2?! ♕xb2 9 ♖b1 ♕a3 10 ♗e2 ♘c6 11 0-0 cxd4 12 ♘xd4 ♘xd4 13 ♗xd4 ♗c5 14 ♔h1 ♗xd4 15 ♕xd4 ♕c5 16 ♕d3 0-0 ∓ Barkhagen-Ulybin, Gothenburg 1999.

b) 8 ♖b1 ♘c6 9 ♕d2 ♕c7 10 ♗e2 ♗e7 11 0-0 0-0 12 ♘d1 cxd4 13 ♘xd4 ♘c5 14 ♘f2 ♗d7 15 c3 b5 = Timman-Bareev, Moscow 1993.

c) 8 ♘a4 and then:

c1) 8...♕c6 9 ♘xc5 ♘xc5 10 dxc5 ♗xc5 11 ♕d2 ♕b6 12 ♗xc5 ♕xc5 13 0-0-0 ♘c6 14 ♔b1 ± Ulybin-Alavkin, Krasnodar 1997.

c2) 8...♕a5+ 9 c3 cxd4 10 b4 ♕c7 (D).

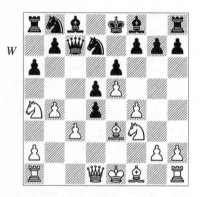

This is an important position. White has the choice between recapturing on d4 with the bishop or the queen:

c21) Not 11 ♘xd4?? in view of 11...b5.

c22) 11 ♗xd4 ♘c6 should be fine for Black. White would like to preserve his dark-squared bishop but this is not easy without allowing Black a strong attack:

c221) If White chooses 12 ♗e3, he could be in trouble after 12...b5 13 ♘b2 ♘cxe5! (13...f6 is also OK, but this looks even stronger) 14 fxe5 (14 ♘xe5 ♘xe5 15 fxe5 ♕xc3+ 16 ♕d2

♗xb4 ∓) 14...♕xc3+ 15 ♕d2 ♗xb4 16 ♔f2 ♕xd2+ 17 ♘xd2 ♘xe5 and with four sound pawns for a piece Black is definitely in very good shape, Sedlak-Radjabov, Aviles 2000.

c222) 12 ♖c1 is probably best, when Luther-Gleizerov, Cappelle la Grande 1998 was agreed drawn after 12...♘xd4. Indeed, after 13 ♘xd4 b5 14 ♘b2 ♘b6 Black has nothing to worry about.

c23) 11 ♕xd4 and now:

c231) 11...♘c6 12 ♕d2 b5 13 ♘b2 f6 14 a4 (after 14 exf6?! ♘xf6 15 ♗d3 ♗d6 16 0-0 0-0 17 a4 ♖b8 Black was doing well in Lutz-Morozevich, Elista OL 1998 because the knight is misplaced on b2 and Black has good chances of breaking open the centre with ...e5) 14...♖b8 (14...bxa4 15 exf6 ♘xf6 16 ♗d3 a5 17 ♖xa4 ♘e4 18 ♗xe4 dxe4 19 ♘g5 looked better for White in Wiersma-Barsov, Dieren 1999) 15 axb5 axb5 16 ♘d4! ♕xd4 17 ♗xd4 fxe5 18 fxe5 ♗e7 19 ♖a7 ♕c6 20 ♕f4! ± Skripchenko-Matveeva, Belgrade wom 1996.

c232) 11...a5 12 b5 b6 13 ♗e2 ♘c5 14 0-0 ♘bd7 15 ♘b2 ♗e7 16 c4 ♗b7 17 cxd5 ♗xd5 18 ♘c4 0-0 = Van der Weide-Radjabov, Wijk aan Zee 2001.

8...♘c6 (D)

9 ♗e2

If 9 dxc5 ♗xc5 10 ♘a4 ♕a5+ 11 b4 ♕xa4 12 bxc5, Black has two options:

a) 12...0-0 13 c4 ♕a5+ 14 ♕d2 ♕xd2+ 15 ♔xd2 actually looks a bit better for White. In Klimov-Kruppa, St Petersburg 2000 Black was worse

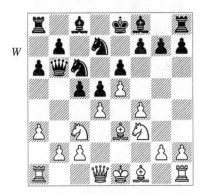

W

after 15...d4 16 ♘xd4 ♘a5 17 ♔c2 ♘xc5 18 ♘c6 ♘xc6 19 ♗xc5 ♖d8 20 ♗b6 and 15...♖d8 16 ♖d1 d4 17 ♘xd4 ♘xd4 18 ♗xd4 ♘xe5 19 fxe5 ♖xd4+ 20 ♗d3 doesn't solve all his problems either.

b) 12...f6! (this looks much better because White does not get enough time to consolidate) 13 c4 ♕a5+ 14 ♕d2 ♕xd2+ 15 ♔xd2 fxe5 16 cxd5 exd5 17 fxe5 0-0 and White is the one who is struggling to equalize, Berndt-Soln, Bled 2000.

9...♕a7

A recent and very solid move. Black steps out of any ♘a4 ideas and prepares to advance the b-pawn. The other option is 9...cxd4 10 ♘xd4 ♗c5 11 ♘a4 ♕a5+ 12 c3 ♗xd4 13 ♗xd4 ♘xd4

14 ♕xd4, which has been the centre of some discussion:

a) 14...b6 15 ♗d1 ♕b5 16 b4 a5 17 ♘b2 ♕c6 18 ♗f3 axb4 19 cxb4 b5 20 ♔f2 ♕b6 21 ♔e3 was very comfortable for White in Topalov-Korchnoi, Dos Hermanas 1999.

b) 14...♕c7 15 b4 b6 (I tried 15...0-0 16 0-0 b5 in Nunn-S.Pedersen, Oxford 1998, and felt that Black was worse after 17 ♘b2 ♗b7 18 ♗g4!? ♖ac8 19 ♖f3, so I am surprised that Black has successfully followed this idea, but first losing a tempo with the b-pawn!) 16 0-0 0-0 17 ♖ac1 (17 ♘b2! looks better; if 17...b5, 18 a4 is annoying and 17...♗b7 18 c4 f6 19 exf6 ♘xf6 20 ♖ac1 ♖ad8 21 c5 also appeared pleasant for White in E.Berg-Radjabov, Aviles 2000) 17...b5 18 ♘b2 ♗b7 19 a4 (in view of Nunn-Pedersen above, I suppose 19 ♗g4 should be considered) 19...bxa4 20 ♖a1 ♗c6 21 ♘xa4 ♗b5! and Black was doing fine in the game Guedon-M.Gurevich, Antwerp 1999.

10 ♕d2 cxd4 11 ♘xd4 ♗c5 12 ♖d1 0-0 13 0-0 b5 14 ♗f3 ♗b7 15 ♕f2 ♘xd4 16 ♗xd4 ♗xd4 17 ♖xd4 ♖fc8

The position is equal, Mitkov-Bagirov, Batumi Echt 1999.

7 Steinitz Variation: Main Line (7 ♗e3)

1 e4 e6 2 d4 d5 3 ♘c3 ♘f6 4 e5 ♘fd7 5 f4 c5 6 ♘f3 ♘c6 7 ♗e3 *(D)*

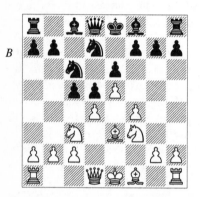

This is the main line of the Steinitz Variation. 7 ♗e3 was Boleslavsky's contribution. White reinforces his centre and perhaps prepares to castle queenside after 8 ♕d2. This may lead to sharp positions with opposite-side castling but frequently White aims at just keeping control of the d4-square, and thus in the long term plays against a bad light-squared bishop.

We shall look at:

A)

7...♗e7

This is an 'older' Morozevich idea. Black simply develops and also introduces the possibility of playing an ...f6 break.

8 dxc5!?

A plan like 8 ♕d2 0-0 9 0-0-0 is less impressive when the central tension hasn't been clarified. Black can play 9...c4!?, when ...b5 will soon be a real threat to White.

8...♘xc5

8...♗xc5!? isn't bad, even though Black has lost a tempo with his bishop. 9 ♕d2 0-0 10 0-0-0 ♕b6 11 ♗g1 ♗xg1 12 ♖xg1 ♘c5 was roughly equal in Ivanchuk-Korchnoi, Roquebrune Amber rpd 1992 but this needs further tests.

9 ♗e2 0-0 10 0-0 ♗d7

10...f6 11 exf6 ♖xf6 12 ♕d2 ±.

11 a3 ♗e8 12 ♕e1!? ♖c8

Psakhis suggests 12...f6!? 13 b4 ♘d7 14 ♘d4 ♘xd4 15 ♗xd4, with only a slight advantage to White.

13 ♖d1 ♕c7 14 b4! ♘d7 15 ♘b5 ♕b8 16 ♗d3

± Ivanchuk-Morozevich, Amsterdam Donner mem 1996.

B)
   7...♕b6 8 ♘a4
   8 a3 cxd4 9 ♘xd4 – 7...cxd4 8 ♘xd4
♕b6 9 a3 =.
   8...♕a5+ 9 c3 *(D)*

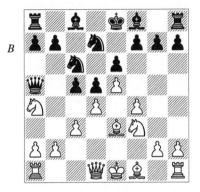

This line was first played in a simultaneous game (with Alekhine as White) but it only really caught on in tournament practice when Portisch introduced the variation 9...cxd4 10 b4 ♘xb4 11 cxb4 ♗xb4+ against Bronstein at the Amsterdam Interzonal in 1964. Nowadays, the view upon this idea is rather pessimistic though, and it is thought that Black should instead aim to keep the position closed with 9...c4, or try the slightly provocative 9...b6. The latter does, by the way, score excellently in practice and has the further incentive that it receives little mention in the majority of opening manuals.

Thus there are three main options for Black:

B1: 9...cxd4?!   75
B2: 9...c4   76
B3: 9...b6!?   78

B1)
   9...cxd4?!
   This is an exciting line but Black is not really going into it any more, for good reasons.
   10 b4 ♘xb4
   10...♕c7 11 ♘xd4 ♘xd4 12 ♗xd4 b6 is feasible but 13 ♗d3 gives White splendid chances on the kingside. This is hardly a line that makes the variation playable for Black.
   11 cxb4 ♗xb4+ 12 ♗d2 ♗xd2+ 13 ♘xd2 *(D)*

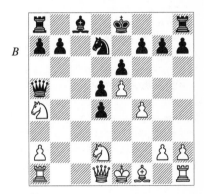

   13...g5!?
   This seems the best chance to mix things up. The other line is 13...b6, with the idea of exchanging a minor piece with ...♗a6 or ...♘c5. In that event White has several options, but I think the clearest route to an advantage is 14 ♗d3! ♗a6 (14...♘c5 15 ♘xc5 bxc5 16 0-0 is very good for White: 16...0-0? is unplayable according to Timman due to 17 ♗xh7+! ♔xh7 18 ♕h5+ ♔g8 19 ♘f3 f6 20 ♘g5 +–, and 16...c4 allows White to return the piece

for a strong attack by 17 ♗xc4 dxc4 18 ♘xc4 ±) 15 ♘b2 ♘c5 (15...♗xd3 16 ♘xd3 ♘c5 17 ♘f2! ♘a4 18 0-0 ♘c3 19 ♕g4 0-0 20 ♘f3 ± Timman-Korchnoi, Brussels 1987) 16 ♗xa6 ♕xa6 17 ♕e2 (Ghinda's 17 a4!, to keep the queen out of a3 and only then preparing ♕e2 and ♘f3, is perhaps a clearer route to an advantage) 17...♕a3 18 ♕b5+ ♔e7 19 0-0 ♕e3+ 20 ♖f2 ♖he8 21 ♘f1 ♕c3 22 ♖f3 d3 23 ♖d1 ♕d4+ 24 ♔h1 ± Nunn-Zysk, Bundesliga 1987/8.

14 ♖b1!

If White continues passively with, for instance, 14 g3, Black's ...b6 idea will gain in strength. The opening of the kingside is clearly in Black's favour, so White should play energetically to increase his lead in development and attempt to bring the a4-knight into play. If instead 14 ♘b2 gxf4 15 ♘d3, Black obtains adequate counterplay by continuing 15...b6! 16 ♔f2 (16 ♕g4 ♗a6 17 ♕xf4 ♖c8 is maybe even better for Black according to Anand) 16...♗a6 17 ♘f3 ♖c8, as in Anand-Dreev, Madras Ct (6) 1991.

14...a6

14...gxf4 is answered by 15 ♗b5. Then:

a) 15...a6 16 ♗xd7+ ♗xd7 17 ♘b6 ♖d8 18 a4! is White's idea. Because Black's pieces (particularly the queen) are out of play on the queenside, White prepares to castle, take the f4-pawn and launch an attack on the kingside. This might sound simplistic, but it looks very effective.

b) 15...♖b8 also led Black into difficulties in Short-Timman, Amsterdam 1994, after 16 ♘c5! ±.

c) The best option seems to be to unpin the d7-knight with 15...♔f8, but even this doesn't look satisfactory for Black. Kaminski suggests 16 ♕e2 d3, giving the continuation 17 ♕f2 ♘xe5 18 ♕xf4 ♘g6 19 ♕f6 with compensation for White, which I find quite attractive. I also have a feeling that Black is struggling after 17 ♕xd3 ♘xe5 18 ♕d4 ♘g6 19 0-0 a6 20 ♗e2.

15 ♘b2 ♘c5

Kaminski suggests 15...gxf4 as an improvement but I don't believe it is a very serious attempt to rehabilitate the line. White is clearly better after 16 ♘d3. A possible line is 16...b5 17 ♗e2 ♘b6 (Black cannot just sit and wait for White to castle and take on f4) 18 0-0 ♘c4, when White has the choice between returning the piece by 19 ♘xc4 dxc4 20 ♘xf4 d3 21 ♗xd3 cxd3 22 ♕xd3 with a promising attack, and the fairly simple 19 ♘b3 ♕b6 20 ♖xf4 ±.

16 ♗d3 ♗d7 17 0-0 ♕xa2 18 fxg5 ♕a3 19 ♘f3

± Kuczynski-Dolmatov, Polanica Zdroj 1993.

B2)

9...c4 10 b4 *(D)*

Black was threatening 10...b5 so apart from being logical this is also more or less forced.

10...♕c7

I am surprised that so little attention that has been paid to 10...♘xb4 11

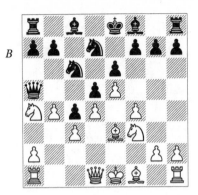

B

cxb4 ♗xb4+ 12 ♔f2 b5. Black gains two solid pawns for a piece and strong queenside pressure. There is room for plenty of new ideas here but I will only state that I would clearly prefer 13 ♘c5! to 13 ♘b2 ♗c3 14 ♕c2 b4 15 ♗e2 ♘b6, when Black obtains good compensation.

11 g3!?

Other moves:

a) 11 g4!? b5 12 ♘c5 a5 13 a3 axb4 14 axb4 ♖xa1 15 ♕xa1 h5 16 gxh5 ♖xh5 17 ♗e2 ♘xc5 18 dxc5 ♗e7 19 0-0 ♖h8 20 ♘d4 ♘xd4 21 ♗xd4 ♕b7 22 ♗g4 g6 and Black has reasonable chances of just blockading the position, Luther-Bareev, Tilburg 1994.

b) 11 ♗e2 ♗e7 and here:

b1) 12 0-0 and then:

b11) 12...b5!? 13 ♘c5 a5 14 a3 ♘xc5 15 dxc5 0-0 16 ♘d4 ♘xd4 17 ♗xd4 ± Anand-Dreev, Biel IZ 1993.

b12) 12...f5 13 g4 (this looks like a direct attempt to refute Black's opening but Anand's suggestion, 13 ♘b2!, intending a4, ♕c2 and ♘d1-f2 may be more sensible, and is probably slightly

better for White) 13...fxg4 14 ♘g5 ♘f8 15 ♗xg4 h6 16 ♘h3 (Kamsky-Bareev, Biel IZ 1993) and now Bareev suggests that 16...b6! is OK for Black.

b2) Short seems to like 12 a3!?. Then:

b21) If 12...b5 13 ♘c5 ♘xc5 14 dxc5 a5, White can consider keeping the rooks on the board with 15 ♖c1!?.

b22) 12...f5 13 ♖g1 ♘f8 14 g4 fxg4 15 ♖xg4 g6 16 ♗f2 and now, rather than 16...b6 17 ♘b2 ♗d7 18 a4 ± Short-Psakhis, Moscow OL 1994, 16...♘d8! (as proposed by Lutz) solves Black's problems. The idea is that White doesn't have time to regroup with 17 ♘b2, due to 17...a5! 18 b5 a4!. Hence, the whole plan with 13 ♖g1 may be wrong, and White should instead consider 13 ♘b2 or 13 h3.

b3) 12 g4!? b5 13 ♘c5 a5 14 a3 0-0 15 0-0 axb4 16 axb4 ♖xa1 17 ♕xa1 ♘xc5 18 dxc5 f6 19 exf6 ♗xf6 20 g5! and now:

b31) 20...♗d8 21 ♕c1 ♕b8 22 ♕d2 ♗c7 23 ♘d4 ♘xd4 24 ♕xd4 ♗b7 25 ♕d2! and White was better in Kamsky-Bareev, Madrid 1994.

b32) Bareev suggests that Black should play 20...d4!?, immediately getting rid of his d-pawn to open the position for his minor pieces; e.g., 21 cxd4 ♗d8 intending ...♗b7 and ...♘e7, with compensation.

11...♗e7 12 ♗h3 *(D)*

This is not only perhaps to support an f5 break himself but also to discourage ...f5 from Black. For example, after 12 ♗g2, Black can try 12...f5.

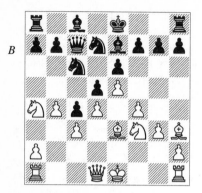

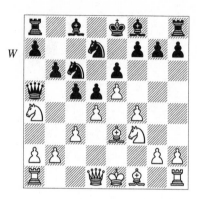

12...b5 13 ♘c5 a5 14 a3 axb4 15 axb4 ℤxa1 16 ♕xa1 ♘xc5 17 dxc5 0-0 18 ♘d4

This is a quite normal move but I wonder why White plays it so early. This seems like something White can always do. 18 0-0 appears more flexible. Then White can also consider putting his bishop on d4 and playing for an attack on the kingside. Svidler suggests that Black should seek counterplay with 18...f5 or 18...f6 (I suppose this is what 18 ♘d4 intends to prevent), but he also arrives at the conclusion that White is slightly better after the more or less forced 19 exf6 ♗xf6 20 ♘d4 ♘xd4 21 ♗xd4 e5 (21...♗xd4+ 22 cxd4 ±) 22 ♗xc8 ℤxc8 23 fxe5 ♗xe5 24 ♗xe5 ♕xe5 25 ℤe1 ♕f6 26 ♕d1.

18...♘xd4 19 ♗xd4 ♗b7 20 0-0 ℤa8 21 ♕b1 ♗c8 22 ♗g2 ℤa6

Black doesn't look worse, Svidler-Bareev, Russian Ch (Elista) 1997.

B3)

9...b6!? *(D)*

No hidden intentions here: Black wants to exchange his light-squared bishop. The only problem is that it looks like Black's queen could run into trouble because its retreat is cut off, but closer scrutiny reveals that Black has nothing to fear in that direction.

10 ♔f2

This type of king move is very common in positions with this type of pawn-structure. White needs to hide his king somewhere and plans to castle 'by hand'. Otherwise:

a) The problem is the knight on a4, which means that White couldn't simply play 10 ♗e2 ♗a6 11 0-0?, due to 11...♗xe2 12 ♕xe2 ♕xa4.

b) 10 a3?! (this is hardly the way White should play, but I am mentioning it for the record) 10...c4 and now:

b1) 11 ♗e2 ♗a6 12 ♕c2? is an attempt to avoid playing b4, but apart from 12...♗b5 13 ♗d1 ♗e7, which was certainly fine for Black in E.Berg-Kania, Copenhagen 1996, Black can play to win a pawn with 12...b5 13 ♘c5, and now 13...♘xd4 14 ♘xd4

♗xc5 or 13...♘xc5 14 dxc5 ♕c7 with the idea of ...♘a5.

b2) 11 b4 cxb3 12 ♕xb3 ♗a6 13 f5 ♗e7 14 g4 ♖c8 15 ♗d2 0-0 16 ♘b2 ♗xf1 17 ♖xf1 ♕a6 and Black is doing fine, Kovačević-O.Danielian, Leningrad 1991. He has excellent chances on the queenside, while White's attack is not going very far as long as his own king is exposed in the centre.

c) 10 ♗d2!? c4 11 b4 is White's main alternative. Now Black has the choice between keeping the position closed by retreating the queen, and an interesting piece sacrifice:

c1) 11...♕a6 used to have quite a good reputation, mainly based on ideas such as 12 ♘b2 b5 13 a4 bxa4 14 ♘xa4 ♕b5 15 ♘c5 a5, when the queenside opens in Black's favour. However, White should not pursue such a fast opening of the queenside. Instead, White looks slightly better if he keeps his knight on a4 for a while, and continues 12 ♗e2 ♗e7 13 0-0, with the idea of pressing on the kingside. In Gofshtein-Zifroni, Tel-Aviv 1995, Black reacted with 13...f5 but ran into considerable trouble after 14 g4! fxg4 15 ♘g5 ♘f8 16 ♗xg4 g6 17 ♘b2 ♗d7 18 a4 ♘d8 19 ♕f3 ♕c8 20 ♕h3.

c2) 11...♘xb4!? 12 cxb4 ♗xb4 13 ♕c2 ♗xd2+ 14 ♘xd2 b5 15 ♘c3 b4 and here:

c21) 16 ♕a4?! ♕b6!? 17 ♘b5 0-0 18 ♘f3 f6 (18...♘b8!?) 19 ♘d6 fxe5! 20 ♘xc8 ♖axc8 21 ♕xd7 ♖c7 22 ♕a4 e4 ∓ Stripunsky-Hmadi, Pardubice 1995.

c22) 16 ♘d1 0-0 17 ♗e2 f6 18 ♘f3 ♕b6 19 ♕d2 a5!? 20 ♘f2 ♗a6 21 ♕e3 c3 22 ♘d3 ♖ac8 23 0-0 f5 with good compensation for Black, Neumeier-Weinzettl, Vienna 1998.

10...♗a6 (D)

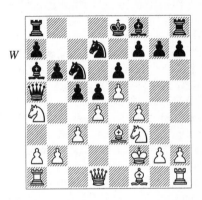

11 ♗xa6

With this White decides to clarify the situation straight away. He could also wait, but Black will not exchange on f1 voluntarily, so there seems no real point in that. Otherwise:

a) 11 h4 has been played a few times but it is not really clear what the purpose is. Ochoa-Sarmiento, Las Palmas 1994 continued 11...♗e7 12 ♗xa6 ♕xa6 13 b3 ♖c8 14 ♕e2 ♕xe2+ 15 ♔xe2 h5 16 ♖ac1 0-0, when Black was doing fine, and White wished he had never played h4 in the first place.

I tried to make a few more direct continuations work, and particularly line 'c' might be worth noting:

b) 11 b4 (note that this would work if Black had played not 10...♗a6, but, for example, 10...♗e7?) 11...cxb4 12 cxb4 ♘xb4 (12...♗xb4? drops a piece to 13 a3) 13 a3 ♘d3+ 14 ♗xd3 ♗xd3 15 ♘xb6 (15 ♕xd3 ♕xa4 16 ♖hc1 ♗e7 appears insufficient for White) 15...axb6 16 ♕xd3 and at this point both 16...♗e7 and 16...♕a4 17 f5 ♗e7 18 ♖hc1 0-0 19 ♔g1 ♖fc8 should be fine for Black.

c) 11 c4!? ♗xc4 12 ♗xc4 dxc4 13 d5 exd5 (13...♘b4!? 14 dxe6 fxe6 might be Black's best but is far from clear after 15 ♘g5!) 14 ♕xd5 (14 ♘g5 ♘b4! –+) 14...♕xa4 15 b3 cxb3 16 axb3 ♕b5 17 ♘d4! (this is the real point; 17 ♘g5 0-0-0 18 ♘xf7 ♗e7 19 ♘xh8 ♖xh8 20 ♖hd1 ♖d8 is good for Black) 17...♘xd4 18 ♕xa8+ ♔e7 19 ♗xd4 cxd4 20 ♖xa7. Starting from Black's 13th move, this has all been forced, and although it looks as if Black should be able to parry White's attack, I am still searching for a convincing idea to refute it. Here are a few lines to persuade you that matters are far from easy:

c1) 20...g6, intending simply to develop, is risky since 21 ♖d1 ♗g7 22 ♕e4 picks up the d-pawn with Black ending up in an annoying pin.

c2) 20...♕c5 21 ♖ha1! and now:

c21) 21...d3+ 22 ♔f3 is actually real trouble for Black since 23 ♖xd7+ is threatened.

c22) Going for an 'improved' version of line 'c1' with 21...g6 could be tried, since then 22 ♖xd7+? backfires after 22...♔xd7 23 ♖a7+ ♔e6 24 ♕e8+ ♔f5 25 ♕xf7+ ♔e4 26 ♖c7 ♕d5 27 ♕f6 ♗c5!, with a strong attack for

Black. However, 22 b4! wins more or less by force: 22...♕xb4? 23 ♖xd7+ mates, while 22...♕b5 23 ♖xd7+ ♔xd7 24 ♖c1! is decisive.

c3) 20...♕xb3 21 ♖ha1!? (21 ♖e1!? might be safer) 21...♕e3+ 22 ♔f1 ♕xf4+ 23 ♔g1 ♕xe5 24 ♕c6 ♕e6 25 ♕a4 is not very clear since Black is struggling with his king's position.

11...♕xa6 12 ♖f1 ♗e7 13 g3 ♖c8 14 ♔g2 0-0

Hernandez Padron-Rojo Huerta, Alcobendas 1994. Chances are roughly equal. White should aim for a kingside attack, while Black has sufficient counterchances on the queenside by doubling rooks on the c-file and exchanging on d4.

C)

7...a6 (D)

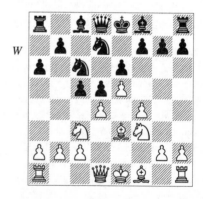

Rather than immediately intensifying the pressure against d4 or just finishing his kingside development, which we saw in the last two main lines, Black here prepares to gain space on the queenside. Moreover, there is a certain flexibility with this move, because Black may also exchange on d4, when ...a6 usually suits his needs anyway, and thus isn't just going to be a waste of time.

8 ♕d2 b5 9 dxc5

White immediately releases the central tension. White now wants to play for domination of the d4-square. We should note that it is generally premature for White to castle queenside before exchanging on c5.

There are a few alternatives, but Black equalizes comfortably against all of them:

a) 9 h4 ♗b7 10 h5 b4 11 ♘a4?! (11 ♘d1 is better), Anand-Dreev, Madras Ct (4) 1991, and now Anand gives 11...♘xd4! 12 ♘xd4 cxd4 13 ♗xd4 ♗c6 ∓.

b) 9 ♘e2 ♗b7 10 g3 ♖c8 11 ♗h3 g6 12 0-0 cxd4 13 ♘exd4 ♘c5 14 ♕e2 ♘xd4 15 ♘xd4 h5 = Timman-Bareev, Linares 1992.

c) 9 ♗e2 and now:

c1) 9...♕b6! 10 ♘d1 (10 0-0 cxd4 11 ♘xd4 ♗c5 12 ♖ad1 ♗b7 has been played a few times but is comfortable for Black) 10...b4 11 0-0 cxd4 12 ♘xd4 ♘xd4 13 ♗xd4 and now 13...♗c5 14 c3 ♘b8 was solid for Black in the game Salmensuu-Dolmatov, Ubeda 2000. 13...♕xd4+ 14 ♕xd4 ♗c5 is also possible. The problem for Black in this type of position is that it is generally very difficult for Black to win.

c2) Thus, GM Mikhail Gurevich often simply plays 9...♗e7!? 10 0-0

0-0 and only later exchanges on d4. This gives White some play on the kingside but usually Black's position is solid enough.

9...♗xc5 (D)

Black has no reason to be dissatisfied with the main line, but there are a few alternatives:

a) 9...♘xc5 10 ♕f2 is probably a little better for White; e.g., 10...♘e4 11 ♘xe4 dxe4 12 ♘d2 ♗b7 13 a3!, cutting out ...♘b4 ideas.

b) 9...b4 is interesting though, and can lead to more exciting positions; for example, 10 ♘a4 (Ziatdinov's suggestion 10 ♘xd5 exd5 11 ♕xd5 ♘db8 12 ♕xd8+ ♔xd8 13 ♘d2 still needs to be tested) 10...♕a5 11 ♘b6 ♘xb6 12 cxb6 ♗c5 13 ♗xc5 ♕xc5 14 0-0-0 (14 ♕f2 ♕xf2+ 15 ♔xf2 ♖b8 is just equal) 14...♕xb6 15 h4 h5 16 ♖h3 a5 17 ♔b1 with an edge for White, Magem-Vaïsser, Escaldes Z 1998.

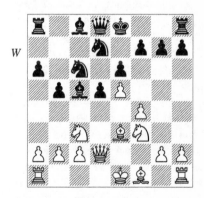

10 ♗xc5 ♘xc5 11 ♕f2

White usually wants to castle kingside, and covering the g1-a7 diagonal makes this possible. White also has in mind to continue with ♗d3 and ♘e2, increasing his control over d4.

11...♕b6 12 ♗d3 *(D)*

This move is White's most logical continuation. He carries on with development and keeps e2 as a useful retreat-square for the c3-knight. Nevertheless, there is very interesting alternative in 12 b4, which is a direct way of playing for an attack against Black's queenside. Black has two replies:

a) 12...♘xb4 13 ♖b1 and now:

a1) 13...♘c6 14 ♗xb5 ♗d7 15 0-0 ♕a7 (this might be a waste of time since White is not threatening any discovered bishop moves; 15...0-0 should be considered) 16 ♗xc6 ♗xc6 17 ♘d4 ♖c8 18 f5 exf5 19 ♘xf5 0-0 20 ♖b4! with a strong attack for White in Feletar-Kovačević, Pula 2000.

a2) 13...d4!? (after this I don't see how White obtains an advantage) 14 ♘xb5 (14 ♘xd4 ♕a5! 15 ♘dxb5? ♘e4! 16 ♕f3 ♘d5! 17 ♕xe4 axb5 18 ♖b3 ♗d7 =) 14...♘e4 15 ♕e2 ♘c3 16 ♘xc3 dxc3 17 ♖b3 ♕a5 with counterplay.

b) 12...♘d7! 13 a4 (better than 13 ♕xb6?! ♘xb6 14 a4 ♘xb4 15 ♘d4 bxa4 16 ♘xa4 ♘xa4 17 ♖xa4 a5 ∓ Kreuzholz-Newton, Germany 1998/9) 13...♘xb4 (13...♕xf2+ 14 ♔xf2 bxa4 15 b5 axb5 16 ♗xb5 ♗b7 17 ♘xa4 ♔e7 = Langheinrich-Holzke, Bundesliga 2000/1) 14 axb5 ♕c7! ∓ Tissir-Vysochin, Cappelle la Grande 2001.

12...♖b8

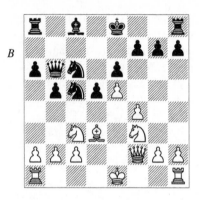

This is a very solid move. Black intends to go for an ending with ...♘a4, which gives him very few chances of winning but on the other hand he shouldn't have trouble drawing. As an alternative, there is 12...b4 13 ♘e2 a5 14 0-0 ♗a6, when White usually continues 15 ♔h1, which makes it possible for him to use his queen more actively. Now 15...♘e7 16 ♖fd1 h6 17 ♘g3!? g6 18 ♘e2 h5 19 ♘ed4 gave White a small edge in Rowson-Barsov, York 1999.

13 0-0 ♘b4

Black can also play 13...♘a4 immediately: 14 ♘xa4 bxa4 15 ♕xb6 ♖xb6 16 b3 with approximately equal play, Mokry-Schmidt, Moscow OL 1994.

14 ♖fd1 ♘a4 15 ♘xa4 ♕xf2+ 16 ♔xf2 bxa4 17 b3 ♔e7 18 ♘d4 ♗d7

GM Piotr Kiriakov is a great expert in this endgame. He usually draws it with no real trouble, but it is important not to exchange on b3 too early. For example, after 19 c3 ♘xd3+ 20 ♖xd3 h6!? followed by ...♖hc8 and ...a5,

Black has ideas of exchanging on b3 followed by ...a4.

D)

7...cxd4 8 ②xd4 *(D)*

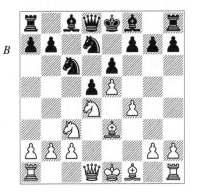

Now:
D1: 8...②xd4   83
D2: 8...♕b6   84
D3: 8...&c5   87

D1)

8...②xd4 9 &xd4 ②b8

An almost comic situation has come about. Black has spent two moves with his queen's knight, only to exchange it on d4, and has then taken three moves with his king's knight to bring it to b8! Obviously, Black cannot count on equal play with this kind of strategy. An alternative is 9...&c5, but White obtains a pleasant game with 10 &xc5 ②xc5 11 ♕d4 ♕b6 12 0-0-0 a6 13 h4 &d7 14 ♖h3 &c6 15 ♖g3 g6 16 h5 ± Cherevatenko-Brabec, Ceske Budejovice 1995.

10 &d3

With this move, White seeks to use his space advantage on the kingside to launch an attack. Another idea is simply to play for control over d4 with 10 ♕d2 ②c6 11 0-0-0. White is just going to sit on d4, and whether it is with a bishop, knight, queen or rook doesn't really matter. Sometimes it is even possible to break with f5.

10...②c6 11 &f2 g6

Perhaps this is not strictly necessary, but otherwise ♕h5 can be annoying. A short summary of other moves:

a) 11...&e7 12 ♕h5 ♕a5 13 0-0 g6 14 ♕h6 &f8 15 ♕h3 ± Nunn-Sutton, Peterborough 1984.

b) 11...g5 is a creative attempt to unbalance the position right from the start. After 12 g3 h5 13 ♕e2 &d7 14 a3 a6, Black might even have had an acceptable game in Diesen-Bednarski, Polanica Zdroj 1978. However, I don't trust the idea. For example, 12 ♕h5 gxf4 13 0-0 should be good for White.

12 a3

This is one of those little rook's pawn moves that aren't really essential, but are quite useful nevertheless. It is not clear that Black really wants to go ...②b4 or ...&b4 but White is ahead in development and can therefore afford the time to prevent it in any case.

12...&d7 13 0-0 h5

13...a6!? to prevent ②b5 might be superior, but White is better at any rate.

14 ②b5 a6 15 ②d6+ &xd6 16 exd6

It should be quite clear that White has few chances of preserving this pawn but Black has created so many weaknesses on the dark squares that it is worth a pawn to get rid of Black's dark-squared bishop.

16...♕b8

So far we have followed Nunn-Schulz, Bundesliga 1984/5. Nunn chose to go straight for Black's centre with 17 c4 but later considered it better for White to play on the dark squares with 17 ♗h4! ♕xd6 18 ♗f6 ♖g8 19 ♕e2, when Black's king is caught in the centre and White has plenty of time to open the position with c4 or f5.

D2)
8...♕b6 (D)

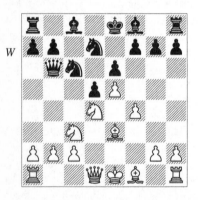

A provocative line. As in the Najdorf Poisoned Pawn, Black goes for the b-pawn. If White spends time protecting the pawn, Black will put further pressure on the d4-knight with ...♗c5.

9 ♕d2

The only critical line. White sacrifices a pawn but obtains a large lead

in development in return. Moreover, 9...♗c5 is now pointless since White has 10 ♘a4. Other 9th moves look harmless:

a) 9 a3 ♗c5 10 ♘a4 ♕a5+ 11 c3 ♗xd4 12 ♗xd4 ♘xd4 13 ♕xd4 b6! 14 ♕b4 ♕xb4 15 axb4 ♔e7 16 ♗b5 ♗b7 = Nunn-Ehlvest, Reykjavik 1988.

b) 9 ♗e2 ♗c5 (9...♕xb2?! 10 ♘db5 ±) 10 ♘a4 ♕a5+ 11 c3 ♘xd4 12 ♗xd4 ♗xd4 13 ♕xd4 b6 14 ♗d1 (White intends to free his knight with b4 and ♘b2) 14...♕b5 15 b4 ♗a6 16 ♘b2 ♕c6 17 ♔f2 ♖c8 18 ♖c1 0-0 = Aseev-Dreev, Frunze 1988.

c) 9 ♘cb5 a6! 10 ♘f5 ♗c5 and now:

c1) 11 ♗xc5?! ♘xc5 12 ♘bd6+ ♔f8 13 ♕h5 ♘d8 14 ♘xg7 ♕b4+! 15 c3 ♕xb2 16 ♖d1 ♕xc3+ 17 ♖d2 h6! 18 ♘ge8 ♘e4! 0-1 Hübner-Korchnoi, San Francisco 1995.

c2) 11 ♘bd6+ ♔f8 12 ♕h5 ♘d8 (Byrne and Mednis give 12...♘cxe5(?) 13 fxe5 ♘xe5, continuing 14 ♘xc8(?) ♖xc8 15 ♗xc5+ ♕xc5 16 ♘g3 ♕b4+ '∓'; indeed, this position is probably just won for Black, but 14 ♕g5! +− {Nunn} decides matters in White's favour) 13 ♘xg7 ♗xe3 14 ♘xe6+! fxe6 15 ♕h6+ ♔g8 16 ♕g5+ ♔f8 17 ♕h6+ ♔g8 18 ♕g5+ ½-½ Lengyel-Züger, Budapest 1994.

9...♕xb2 10 ♖b1 ♕a3 11 ♗b5 (D)
11...♘db8

This move has a very reasonable score for Black in practice, but I find it very hard to believe that Black can afford such a luxury. Black should

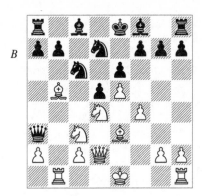

already be considering how to counter White's f5, but the price of maintaining the tension is a further delay in development. 11...♘xd4 12 ♗xd4 ♗b4 13 0-0 is somewhat more logical but it also gives White a menacing attack, which is enhanced considerably by the dark-squared bishop's appearance on d4. Black has two options:

a) 13...a6 14 ♖b3 (14 ♗d3 permits 14...♗c5, when Black has little to fear) 14...♕a5 15 ♖fb1! and now:

a1) Black normally plays 15...♗e7, when the key line continues 16 ♗xd7+ ♗xd7 17 ♖xb7 ♖c8 (17...♗c5 18 ♖b8+ ♔e7 19 ♖1b5 ♗xd4+ 20 ♕xd4 ♕a3 21 ♖xh8 axb5 22 ♖xa8 ♕xa8 23 ♕c5+ ♔d8 24 ♔f2 ±) 18 ♕e3! and White is better; e.g., 18...♖c4 19 f5! exf5 20 ♖xd7! ♔xd7 21 ♖b7+ ♔e8 22 e6, with a winning attack, Soffer-Blauert, Budapest 1998.

a2) 15...♕xb5 (the only move according to Ki.Georgiev) 16 ♖xb4 ♕c6 17 f5 h6 18 f6 gxf6 19 exf6 ♕d6 20 a4 and White is better, Ki.Georgiev-Dolmatov, Moscow 1990.

b) 13...0-0 14 ♖b3 (14 f5 and 14 ♖f3!? can also be considered) 14...♕a5 (D).

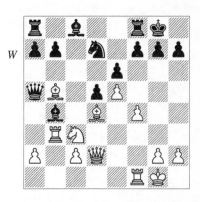

There are now several ways for White to continue. Even a move like 15 ♖fb1 is possible, but I think it is more logical to play for an attack on the kingside. With that aim in mind, there are two logical continuations:

b1) 15 f5, as we shall see, is not an outright blunder! Now:

b11) 15...♕xb5? (Black decides to verify whether White really wanted to put a piece *en prise*, but after this he is virtually lost) 16 f6! h6 17 fxg7 ♔xg7 18 ♕f4 (18 ♖f4 is also good) 18...♕c4 19 ♘b5! and White had a decisive attack in the game Solodovnichenko-I.Timoshenko, Alushta 1999.

b12) 15...exf5! is much more critical. I am not sure what White actually gains from the early f5 since a further pawn sacrifice with e6 does not impress. White can try something like 16 ♕f2 ♘b6 17 ♕h4!? (17 ♖fb1 ♗e7 18 a4!? ♗e6 19 ♗d3 ♘c4 20 ♖xb7 ♗g5 is not clear either) 17...a6 18 ♖fb1, but 18...axb5 19 ♖xb4 ♘c4 20 ♖xb5 ♕d8 21 ♕g3 ♗e6 seems to maintain the balance.

b2) 15 ♕f2. It is debatable whether the queen is better here or on e3; I prefer it here. Then:

b21) 15...♘b6?! 16 a3 (16 g4 is also good for White according to Ernst, who gives 16...♘c4 17 f5 a6 18 f6 ±) 16...♗e7 17 ♘e4! ♘c4?! (17...dxe4 18 ♗c3 ♕xa3 might be the only defence) 18 ♘f6+ ♗xf6 19 exf6 +− Ziatdinov-Züger, Berne 1994.

b22) 15...f5 16 ♖fb1 ♗e7 (alternatively, 16...♗xc3 17 ♗xc3 ♕c7 18 ♗b4 ±) 17 ♗xd7 ♗xd7 18 ♖xb7 ♖fd8 19 ♖1b3!?, intending ♗xa7, gave White slightly the better game in Bangiev-Buchenau, Emden 1995.

We now return to the position after 11...♘db8 (D):

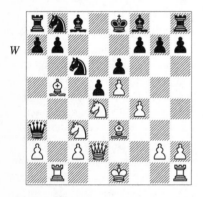

12 ♗xc6+

This is how Fedorov plays. The idea of this voluntary exchange is not to allow Black to recapture with the knight.

However, it is not clear if this move is best. Otherwise:

a) If White plays 12 0-0 a6 13 ♗xc6+, then 13...♘xc6 (13...bxc6? − *12 ♗xc6+ bxc6 13 0-0 a6* ±) looks like a reasonable reply.

b) 12 f5!? ♗b4 13 ♖b3 ♕a5 14 0-0 exf5!? (14...a6!?) 15 ♖fb1 f4! 16 ♖xb4 fxe3 17 ♕xe3 0-0 18 ♗xc6 ♘xc6 19 ♖b5 ♕a6 20 ♖xd5 ½-½ Dolmatov-Volkov, Kstovo 1997.

c) 12 0-0!? a6 13 f5!? axb5 (the line 13...♗b4!? 14 ♖b3 ♕a5 15 ♗xc6+ ♘xc6 16 ♘xc6 bxc6 17 f6 is not clear but probably favourable for White) 14 fxe6 ♗xe6 15 ♘xe6 fxe6 16 ♘xb5 ♕a5 17 ♕f2 ♘xe5 18 ♗b6 ♕a4 19 ♗c5 ♘f3+?! (Black should try 19...♗xc5 20 ♕xc5 and now not 20...♘bc6? 21 ♕d6! +−, but 20...♘bd7! might survive) 20 gxf3 ♘a6 (or 20...♕c4 21 ♗xf8 ♔xf8 22 ♕b6 ♘c6 23 ♘c7 ±) 21 ♗xf8 ♔xf8 22 ♖fe1 ♖e8 23 ♘d6 ±.

12...bxc6

12...♘xc6 13 ♘cb5 ♕xa2 14 0-0 gives White more than enough compensation for the pawns.

13 0-0 ♗c5!?

It is interesting that in a later game Volkov preferred 13...a6?:

a) Fedorov-Volkov, Russian Cup 1997 continued 14 ♖b3 ♕a5 15 ♖xb8 ♖xb8 16 ♘xc6 ♕c7 17 ♘xb8 ♕xb8 18 f5, which looks dangerous for Black.

b) 14 f5! (D) looks even stronger.

In *NCO*, Nunn provides excellent analysis of this move. Now:

b1) 14...exf5 15 ♘xc6! ♘xc6 16 ♘xd5 ♖b8 17 ♘c7+ ♔e7 18 ♖xb8

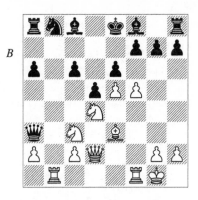

B

♘xb8 19 ♖f3 f6 20 ♕d5 and White wins (Nunn).

b2) 14...♗b4 15 fxe6 ♗xe6 (alternatively, 15...fxe6 16 ♖xb4 ♕xb4 17 ♘e4! ♕xd2 18 ♘d6+ ♔d8 19 ♗xd2 a5 20 ♖f7 h6 21 ♖xg7 +−) 16 ♖b3 ♕a5 17 ♘xe6 fxe6 18 ♕d4 ♗e7 (18...♗xc3 19 ♕g4 ♕c7 20 ♕xe6+ ♕e7 21 ♕c8+ ♕d8 22 ♕b7 +−) 19 ♕g4 ♘d7 20 ♕xe6 gives White a decisive attack.

b3) 14...c5 15 fxe6 fxe6 16 ♕f2 cxd4 17 ♕f7+ ♔d8 18 ♗g5+ ♗e7 19 ♖b3 ♕c5 20 ♘a4 (+− Nunn) 20...♕c7 21 ♕xg7 ♖e8 22 ♗xe7+ ♕xe7 23 ♖f7 +−.

14 ♖b3

14 ♔h1 0-0 15 g4 could be worth a try.

14...♕a5 15 ♖fb1 ♗b6 16 ♕c1!? ♗xd4 17 ♗xd4 ♘d7 18 f5!?

Fedorov also mentions 18 ♖a3!? ♕c7 19 ♘a4 with compensation.

18...exf5 19 e6

The straightforward 19 ♕g5 should perhaps be considered.

19...fxe6 20 ♕g5 ♕d8! 21 ♕xg7 ♖f8

Fedorov-Volkov, Omsk 1996. Now Fedorov mentions 22 ♘a4 with compensation for White.

D3)

8...♗c5 9 ♕d2 *(D)*

9 ♗e2 ♕b6 − 8...♕b6 9 ♗e2 ♗c5 =.

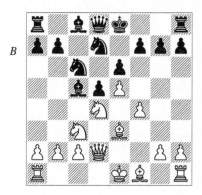

B

Now Black has two main options:
D31: 9...♘xd4   87
D32: 9...0-0   90

D31)

9...♘xd4 10 ♗xd4 ♗xd4 11 ♕xd4 ♕b6 *(D)*

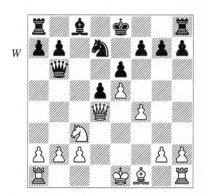

W

This is a solid line for Black. There is a chance that the better player will simply outplay the other never mind the colour. The reason is that the endgame is going to be roughly balanced, perhaps with a slight edge for White, but the player who understands the position better is liable to gain the upper hand. In the first place it is a fight for the d4-square but other important factors are that Black has play on the semi-open c-file, while White may seek a way through on the kingside.

12 ♕xb6

This is considered best. The queens are going to be exchanged anyway, and practice has shown that Black has an easier game if in the following play he has the option of challenging White on the d4-square by the manoeuvre ...♘b8-c6. Hence, White forces the black knight to go to b6. The alternatives are:

a) 12 0-0-0 ♕xd4 13 ♖xd4 ♚e7 (since we can already speak of an endgame, or perhaps more precisely a queenless middlegame, the king is better off in the centre) 14 h4 (a typical French idea: if White is allowed to advance his pawn further, Black may experience problems with his kingside pawns) 14...h5 15 ♗e2 ♘b8 16 ♖d2 ♗d7 17 ♖hd1 g6 18 b3 ♗c6 (18...♘c6? 19 ♘e4! ±) 19 ♗f3 ♘d7 20 ♘e2 ♖hc8 21 ♘d4, Leko-Ružele, Debrecen Echt 1992. White has a slight but fairly clear advantage due to the knight established on d4 and his spatial plus, which makes it possible for him to switch between

playing on the kingside or the queenside.

b) 12 ♘b5 ♕xd4 13 ♘xd4 ♚e7 (D) (13...♘c5 14 ♗d3 ♗d7 is another idea, but White has an edge because Black is again far away from challenging the d4-knight) and now:

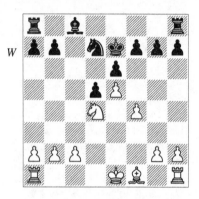

b1) 14 h4 and then:

b11) 14...h5 15 ♖h3! worked well for White in Gofshtein-Chernin, Brno 1993. After 15...a6 (15...♘b8 16 ♖c3!) 16 ♖c3! White was ready to answer 16...♘b8 with 17 ♖c7+!, and hence Black was forced into a very passive set-up where it was almost impossible to get the c8-bishop out.

b12) 14...f6! is a much better idea. Now both 15 exf6+ gxf6 16 ♗d3 ♘c5 and 15 ♘f3 fxe5 16 fxe5 ♘c5 look alright for Black.

b2) 14 g3 ♘b8! (14...f6 might again be considered) 15 ♚d2 ♗d7 16 ♗d3 ♘c6 17 ♘f3 h6 and Black was close to equality in Short-Chernin, Montpellier Ct 1985.

12...♘xb6 13 ♘b5

This is the most common. White immediately heads for the d4-square. In this type of position White should in most cases deny Black the chance to exchange his light-squared bishop. Hence, for example after a ♘b5 sortie, if Black replies ...♗d7 at some point, White should immediately move the knight to d4.

Another important option for White is 13 a4, which requires accurate play from Black. He must now consider whether he wants to allow a5:

a) 13...a5 (it looks like a definite achievement for White that the b5-square is now weakened but this advantage is far from easy to exploit) 14 ♔d2 (14 ♘b5 ♔e7 15 b3 ♗d7! and now 16 ♘d4 f6 is fine for Black, while Black has no problems after 16 ♔d2 ♗xb5! 17 ♗xb5 ♖ac8 either) 14...♗d7 15 b3 ♔e7 16 ♖e1 ♖ag8!? 17 h4 h6 18 ♗d3 g5 19 hxg5 (19 fxg5 hxg5 20 h5 g4! is very risky for White; the h-pawn can turn out to be weak, while White can also experience difficulties protecting his e-pawn after moves like ...♖g5, ...♗e8/c6 and ...♘d7) 19...hxg5 20 g3 ♗c6 21 ♖xh8 ♖xh8 22 ♘e2 ♘d7 23 ♘d4 ♖h3! = Short-Korchnoi, Groningen FIDE 1997.

b) 13...♔e7 14 a5 ♘d7 15 ♔d2 g5! 16 g3 gxf4 17 gxf4 f6 18 ♖g1 (18 exf6+ ♘xf6 19 ♗d3 ♗d7 gives Black no reason to worry, Short-Timman, Novgorod 1995) 18...fxe5 19 ♗h3 exf4 20 ♖ae1 ♘f8 (20...♘f6 21 ♖g7+ ♔f8 22 ♖c7 ♘e8 23 ♖c5 with compensation for White) 21 ♘xd5+ ♔d6

22 ♘xf4 e5 23 ♖g3! ♗xh3 24 ♖d3+ ♔c6 25 ♖c3+ ♔d6 26 ♘xh3 ± Kasparov-Bareev, Novgorod 1997.

13...♔e7 14 ♗d3 *(D)*
14 ♘d4 ♘a4 15 0-0-0 ♗d7 16 ♗d3 comes to the same thing.

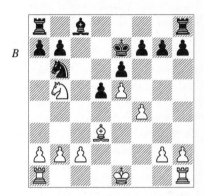

14...♗d7 15 ♘d4 ♘a4 16 0-0-0 g6!?
Mikhail Gurevich has an excellent understanding of most French positions. Here he wants to keep his knight on a4 for as long as possible in order to avoid a white set-up with b3. The main line used to be 16...♘c5, when after 17 ♔d2 g5! Black equalized in a number of games. A more accurate plan for White is 17 ♖hf1, when 17...g5 can be met by 18 f5!. Black can instead adopt a set-up with ...g6 and ...h5, when White is only microscopically better. A first-class example of how White's advantage can grow if Black plays too passively is the game Nunn-Daly, Kilkenny 1996, which, for its instructional value, I give in full: 17...h5 18 ♔d2 g6 19 g3 ♖ac8 20 ♖de1 ♖c7 21 h3 a6 22 b3 ♖cc8 23 ♖e3 ♖h6 (a rather peculiar

move, but Black has decided just to sit and wait, and perhaps he intends to double on the h-file if White decides to play for g4) 24 a4 ♖hh8? (Black should prevent White's next move by playing 24...a5) 25 a5 ♖c7 26 ♖b1 ♖hc8 27 ♖ee1 ♖h8 28 ♖a1 ♗e8 29 ♖a3! ♗d7 30 b4 ♘xd3 31 cxd3 ♖hc8 32 ♖a2 ♗b5 33 ♖c2 ♖xc2+ 34 ♘xc2 ♗d7 35 ♘d4 ♖h8 36 ♖c1 ♖c8 37 ♖xc8 ♗xc8 38 b5 (White has got what seems to be the maximal achievement in this line: a knight vs bad bishop endgame, which Nunn converts smoothly into victory) 38...♗d7 39 bxa6 bxa6 40 ♔c3 ♔d8 41 ♔b4 ♔c7 42 ♔c5 ♗a4 43 ♘f3 ♔d7 44 d4 ♗d1 45 ♘g5 ♔e7 46 ♘h7 ♗e2 47 ♔b6 ♗c4 48 ♘g5 ♗e2 49 ♔b7 ♗f1 50 ♘f3 ♔d7 51 h4 ♗e2 52 ♘e1 ♗b5 53 ♘c2 ♗c6+ 54 ♔b6 ♗b5 55 ♘b4 ♗c4 56 ♘xa6 ♗xa6 57 ♔xa6 ♔c6 58 ♔a7 ♔c7 59 a6 ♔c8 60 ♔b6 1-0. Perhaps Black can defend better in the endgame, but there is no question that the task is very awkward.

17 ♖df1 h5 18 g3 a6 19 ♖f3 ♖ac8 20 h3 ♖c7 21 ♖hf1 ♘b6!? 22 ♔d2

22 b3 is a better chance of maintaining an advantage but Black has good equalizing chances after 22...♘c8, with the idea of ...♘a7-c6.

22...♘c4+ 23 ♗xc4 dxc4!? 24 ♔e3 ♖c5 25 c3 ♖a5 26 a3 ♖d5

= Fedorov-M.Gurevich, Comtois 1999.

D32)
9...0-0 (D)

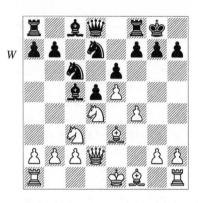

10 0-0-0
Recently, Kasparov experimented with 10 g3, which introduces the idea of White castling kingside instead. After this White is very flexible, and Black's set-up is therefore less straightforward than in the main line, because White has ideas of playing ♗g2 and 0-0, and primarily concentrating on controlling the d4-square. Such a set-up would also have the advantage of taking the sting out of ...f6 breaks. Black has tried:

a) 10...♕e7?! 11 0-0-0! ♘b6 (playing 11...a6 seems a more normal set-up but Shirov was, maybe rightly, worried that the queen wouldn't be very suitably placed on e7) 12 ♘b3! ♗xe3 13 ♕xe3 ♗d7 14 ♔b1 ♖fc8 15 g4 with the better game for White, Kasparov-Shirov, Astana 2001.

b) 10...♘xd4 11 ♗xd4 ♗xd4 12 ♕xd4 ♘b8!? 13 0-0-0 ♘c6 14 ♕f2 ♗d7 15 ♔b1 ♕a5 16 ♗d3 ♖fc8 17 ♕e1 ♘b4 18 a3 ♘xd3 19 ♖xd3 ♖c4 20 ♕d2 ♖ac8 21 ♘e2 ♕xd2 22 ♖xd2 ♖e4 23 ♘c3 ♖ec4 24 ♖e1 with a slight advantage for White, Anand-Shirov, Leon adv 2001.

c) 10...a6 11 ♗g2 ♘xd4 12 ♗xd4 b5 13 ♘e2 ♕c7 14 ♗xc5 ♘xc5 15 ♘d4 ♗b7 16 0-0 ♘e4 17 ♕e3 b4 and Black had good counterplay in Kuczynski-Gunnarsson, Ohrid Ech 2001.

10...a6 *(D)*

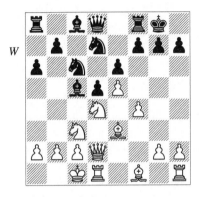

11 h4

With this White aims for a kingside attack, either by throwing the h-pawn further forward or by lifting the rook up to the third rank. White has tried a great number of other ideas, of which 'd' and 'e' clearly could be real alternatives to the main line:

a) 11 g4?! (throwing the g-pawn forward is rarely very dangerous for Black; there are other ways of preparing f5 and the g-pawn in itself is just in the way of a possible attack on the g-file) 11...♘xd4 12 ♗xd4 b5 13 g5?! b4 14 ♘a4 a5 15 ♗e3 ♕c7 16 ♖g1 ♘e7 17 ♗b5 ♖b8 18 ♕e2 ♗b7 with a slight advantage for Black, Hodgson-Bareev, Sochi 1987.

b) 11 ♕f2 ♗xd4 12 ♗xd4 b5 13 ♗d3 b4 14 ♘e2 a5 15 ♔b1 ♗a6 = Mainka-Lautier, Dortmund 1989.

c) 11 ♘ce2 ♘a5! (11...♕e7!? 12 ♔b1?! f6! 13 exf6 ♘xf6 14 g3 ♘e4 15 ♕c1 e5 16 fxe5 ♗g4! was good for Black in R.Moor-S.Pedersen, Zug 1999 but I am sure White can find more useful things to do on move 12) 12 ♘g3 (12 ♘g1!?) 12...b5 13 b3 ♗b7 14 ♔b1 ♖c8 looked fine for Black in Anand-Shirov, Monaco Amber rpd 1999.

d) 11 ♔b1!? ♘xd4 12 ♗xd4 b5 13 ♕e3 ♕c7 (13...♕e7 could also be considered) 14 ♗d3 (rather than going for an attack, White has aimed to develop his light-squared bishop and primarily concentrate on central control) 14...♗xd4 15 ♕xd4 ♗b7 16 ♖he1 ♘c5 17 ♘e2 ♖ac8 (17...♖fc8!?) 18 ♕e3 ♘e4!? 19 ♘d4 ♕e7 20 ♘f3 with perhaps a slight edge for White, J.Polgar-Luther, Ohrid Ech 2001.

e) 11 ♘b3!? (not a new move but an idea that has been polished recently) 11...♗b4 12 ♗d3 (after 12 a3 ♗e7, Black can expect counterplay thanks to the exposed a3-pawn) 12...b5 13 g4!? (the other idea is 13 ♖hf1 ♗b7 14 ♖f3 ♖c8 15 ♖h3 but 15...f5 16 exf6 ♘xf6 17 ♗c5 ♖f7 secured Black approximately equal play in Gallagher-Brynell, Gausdal 2001; with the text-move, White wants to make an ...f6/f5 push less attractive for Black) 13...♗b7 14 ♖hg1 ♖c8 (14...♘b6 or 14...f6 might be better) 15 ♖g3 ♘a5 16 ♖h3 g6 17 ♗d4 ± Nijboer-Sielecki, Dutch Cht (Breda) 2001.

11...♘xd4

11...♕c7 has been played by Bareev but since Black's plan is essentially the same as in the main line, namely to exchange on d4 followed by advancing his queenside pawns, the queen move seems unnecessarily committal and much less flexible than the main line.

Alternatively, Black can take on d4 with the bishop. This often leads to the same thing as taking with the knight, but there are a few differences which I will try to point out. After 11...♗xd4 12 ♗xd4 b5 White can try to preserve his bishop. Best seems 13 ♗g1! (in view of a coming ...♘c5-e4, this is better than 13 ♗f2; 13 ♖h3 b4 14 ♘a4 ♘xd4 15 ♕xd4 – *11...♘xd4 12 ♗xd4 b5 13 ♖h3! b4 14 ♘a4 ♗xd4 15 ♕xd4*) 13...♕a5 (13...b4 14 ♘a4 ♕c7 15 ♔b1 a5 16 h5 ♘a7 17 h6 g6 18 ♖c1 ± Vasiukov-Dizdar, Voskresensk 1990; I expect that Black can improve on this but nevertheless I like White's concept) 14 ♔b1 b4 15 ♘e2 ♘c5 (15...f6!?) 16 ♖h3! ♘e4 17 ♕e1 ♖b8 18 ♘c1 with slightly the better chances for White, Nunn-S.Lalić, Hastings 1994/5. In fact this came from a slightly different move-order, as White played 13 ♖h3 ♕a5 14 ♔b1 b4 15 ♘e2 ♘c5 and only then 16 ♗g1.

12 ♗xd4 b5 *(D)*

13 ♖h3!

This excellent rook move is one idea behind White's 11th move. It has several points, of which the main ones are the possibility of attacking with ♖g3

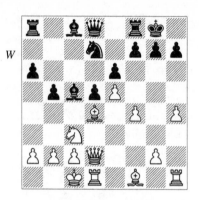

and the supervising of the queenside. Some alternatives:

a) 13 ♗xc5 ♘xc5 14 ♕d4 is a dubious attempt to stop Black's queenside expansion. White has little hope of halting ...b4 forever, and the game Apicella-M.Gurevich, Clichy 2001 produced a good and simple example of how Black soon takes over the initiative: 14...♕c7 15 a3 (the immediate 15 f5 is also feasible but Black plays 15...♖b8, threatening ...b4) 15...♗d7 16 f5 ♖fc8 17 f6 gxf6! (this is safe; 17...♘e4 18 ♗d3 ♘xc3 19 ♕g4 g6 20 ♕g5 is tricky) 18 exf6 ♔h8. Black is already better. His kingside is fairly safe and he is only two or three moves away from a winning queenside attack with ...♖ab8, ...a5 and ...b4.

b) 13 h5 b4 and then:

b1) 14 ♘e2 a5 15 ♕e3 ♕c7 16 ♔b1 ♗a6 17 ♗xc5 ♘xc5 18 ♘g3 (White wants to cover the e4-square but the knight is out of play, and White now has no real hopes of a successful kingside attack) 18...♖fc8 19 ♖c1 a4 20 ♗xa6 ♖xa6 21 ♖hd1 a3 22 b3 ♖c6 23

♕d4 ♘a6 24 ♖d2 ♕e7 and Black was better in Topalov-Morozevich, Sarajevo 1999.

b2) 14 ♘a4 ♗xd4 15 ♕xd4 ♕a5 (15...a5 16 ♗b5 ♖b8 17 ♗d3 ♕c7, with similar ideas as in the main line, is also viable but it makes sense to exert more concrete pressure on White's queenside, when there isn't the option of breaking with c3) 16 b3 ♗b7 (with the rook on h3 instead of the pawn on h5, White would have the very sensible option of playing 17 c3; obviously this would now be way too risky). Now:

b21) 17 f5?! ♗c6 18 f6 (18 ♘b2 is possible but unconvincing; 18...♕xa2 19 ♖h3 could be an idea but I don't really believe it for White, while the alternative 18...♕c7!? should also be fine for Black) 18...gxf6 19 exf6 ♔h8 20 ♗d3 ♗xa4 21 ♕f4 ♖g8! 22 bxa4 ♕xa4 23 ♔b1 ♘c5 24 g3 ♖ac8 –+ Gallagher-Barsov, Berne 1994. This is a good example of the fact that Black's position is solid enough to withstand a direct knock-out attempt, despite having very few pieces to defend the king.

b22) 17 ♔b1 ♗c6 18 ♘b2 ♕c5 19 ♕d2 a5 and Black was doing well in Belotti-Luther, Saint Vincent 1998.

We now return to 13 ♖h3 (D):

13...b4

Nowadays this is the most common, but French experts such as Knaak (when he was active) and M.Gurevich also like 13...♗b7. The idea is that only after White has played his next move, say 14 h5 or 14 ♔b1, does Black

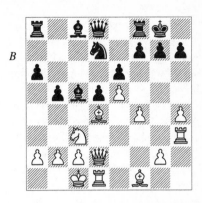

B

continue with 14...b4 15 ♘a4 ♗xd4 16 ♕xd4 ♕a5 17 b3 ♗c6. This cuts across White's idea of meeting this type of plan with c3, as in note 'b2' to Black's 15th move.

We shall look at White's most critical replies:

a) 14 h5 b4 15 ♘a4 ♗xd4 16 ♕xd4 ♕a5 17 b3 ♗c6 18 ♘b2 ♖fc8!? (it is often too dangerous for Black to take the pawn in these positions) 19 ♘d3 ♗b5 20 ♔b1 ♕c7 21 ♖c1 a5 and Black was doing well in Zelčić-Dizdar, Pula 1999.

b) 14 ♖g3!? b4 15 ♘a4 ♗xd4 16 ♕xd4 ♕a5 17 b3 ♗c6 and now:

b1) 18 ♘b2 ♘c5 19 ♗d3 ♖fd8 20 f5 exf5 21 ♗xf5 ♘e4 22 ♗xe4 dxe4 23 ♘c4 ♖xd4 24 ♘xa5 ♖xd1+ 25 ♔xd1 ♖d8+ 26 ♔e1 ♗d5 gave Black enough counterplay in Dutreeuw-M.Gurevich, Brussels 1995.

b2) 18 f5!? ♗xa4 19 f6 g6 20 ♕f4 ♔h8 21 h5 ♖g8 22 hxg6 fxg6 23 ♖h3 ♘f8 24 bxa4 (24 ♗d3? fails against 24...♗e8! –+, but Black must avoid 24...♗c6? 25 ♖dh1, with the point

25...♕c7 26 f7 ♖g7 27 ♖xh7+ ♘xh7 28 ♖xh7+ ♖xh7 29 f8♕+ ♖xf8 30 ♕xf8#) 24...♕xa4 25 ♔b1 a5 26 ♗d3 and White has some compensation for the pawn.

c) 14 g4!? b4 15 ♘e2 a5 16 g5 ♗a6 17 h5 ♖c8 18 ♔b1 ♕b6 19 g6 fxg6 (19...h6 20 ♖e3! ♗xe2 21 ♖xe2 a4 22 ♗h3 b3 23 cxb3 axb3 24 a3 was better for White in Grünfeld-M.Gurevich, Haifa 1995) 20 hxg6 hxg6 21 ♖g3 ♗xd4 22 ♘xd4 ♗xf1 23 ♖xg6! (an amazing discovery; when analysing this position before, in the notes to the above-mentioned Grünfeld-M.Gure-vich game, M.Gurevich only gave 23 ♖xf1 ♘xe5 24 ♖fg1 ♖c3! with coun-terplay) 23...♖ce8 (23...♗h3 24 ♖h1 and now 24...♔f7? loses to 25 f5! ♗xf5 26 ♘xf5 ♔xg6 27 ♕g2+, mat-ing, while 24...♖c3 25 ♔a1 ♖c4 26 ♕e3! is good for White) 24 ♕e3! ♗f7 (24...♗a6 25 ♖dg1 ♖e7 26 ♕g3 +– Coco) 25 ♖xf1 ♘f8 26 ♖g2 g6 27 ♕d3 and White went on to win in Coco-Daconto, corr. 1995-6.

14 ♘a4

White can also play 14 ♘e2 but it is important to try to slow down Black's queenside expansion. After 14...a5 15 ♕e3 ♕c7 16 ♗xc5 ♘xc5 17 ♘d4 a4 18 ♔b1 a3! 19 b3 ♗a6 20 ♗xa6 ♖xa6, Black had a very good position in J.Polgar-Shirov, Prague (2) 1999. Black will follow up with ...♘e4, threatening ...♘c3+, and will possibly open the position further by means of ...f6.

14...♗xd4 15 ♕xd4 (D)
15...a5

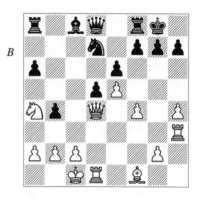

B

This is the positional approach. Black is simply intending to exchange his bad bishop. At the same time, lots of White's attacking potential will be removed. It looks slow at first sight, so a question of the utmost importance is whether White's attack (based on ♖g3 and f5) is going to win through.

Black has two alternative plans, which are both based on more con-crete counterplay:

a) 15...♕a5 16 b3 ♗b7 and now:

a1) 17 ♖g3 ♗c6 18 ♘b2 ♘c5 19 ♗d3 ♖fd8 20 f5 exf5 21 ♗xf5 ♘e4! favoured Black in Dutreeuw-M.Gure-vich, Brussels 1995.

a2) 17 c3!? ♖fc8 (17...f6 18 cxb4 fxe5 19 bxa5 exd4 20 ♖f3 e5 21 fxe5 ♘xe5 22 ♖xf8+ ♖xf8 23 b4!? ±) 18 ♔b2 bxc3+ 19 ♖xc3 ♖xc3 20 ♕xc3 ♕xc3+ 21 ♘xc3 and White was better in Nijboer-Luther, Leeuwarden 1992.

b) 15...f6 (this was devalued by Kasparov but might not be that clear) 16 ♕xb4!? (16 exf6 ♕xf6 17 g3 is un-tested but I believe Black should have enough counterplay to compensate for his many weaknesses) 16...fxe5 and now:

b1) 17 fxe5 ♘xe5 18 ♖e3 went very well for White in Thorhallsson-Limp, Istanbul OL 2000: 18...♘f7?! (Black could consider 18...a5!?) 19 g3 ♘d6 20 ♗h3 ♘f5 21 ♖f3 ♘d6?! 22 ♖xf8+ ♕xf8 23 ♘b6 ♖b8 24 ♕c5 ±. This idea requires further tests.

b2) 17 ♕d6!? ♕f6 18 f5 (D) (!! – Kasparov) 18...♕h6+ 19 ♔b1 was a highly praised idea by Kasparov. Now, there are two options for Black:

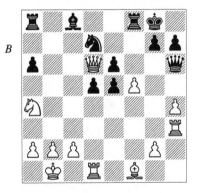

B

b21) 19...♖xf5 20 ♖f3! ♖xf3 (or 20...♕f6 21 ♖xf5 ♕xf5 22 ♗e2 ±) 21 gxf3 ♕f6 22 ♗h3 ♔f7 23 c4! opens up lines against the enemy king. Now 23...dxc4 24 ♘c3! gave Black irremediable problems in Kasparov-Short, Amsterdam 1994. Instead, 23...d4 is a better chance. Then 24 f4! exf4 25 ♖e1 looks dangerous; e.g., 25...♕g6+ 26 ♔a1 ♘f6 27 ♕c7+ ♔g8 28 ♘b6 ♕g3 29 ♖h1 ♕f3 30 ♖g1 +− (Nunn)

b22) 19...♘f6!? 20 ♕xe5 (20 ♘b6?! ♘e4 21 ♕c7 ♖f7 22 ♕d8+ {22 ♕c6!?

♗b7 23 ♕xe6 is messy} 22...♖f8 23 ♕c7 ♖f7 24 ♕xe5 ♖xf5 25 ♕d4 ♖b8 gave Black good counterplay in Wedberg-Brynell, Swedish Ch (Linköping) 2001) 20...♘e4 and now 21 g4?! ♘f2 22 ♘b6 ♘xd1 23 ♘xa8 ♘f2 24 g5 ♕h5 25 ♗e2 ♖xf5 again gives Black counterplay, but 21 ♕d4 ♖xf5 22 ♖f3 (Nunn) could well be favourable for White.

16 ♗b5

This move cleverly prevents the exchange of bishops because 16...♗a6? would now fail to 17 ♗xd7 ♕xd7 18 ♘b6.

An interesting pawn sacrifice was tried in Nijboer-Korchnoi, Arnhem 1999: 16 c4!? bxc3 17 ♖xc3 ♕xh4 18 g3 ♕d8 19 ♔b1 ♗a6 20 ♗xa6 ♖xa6 21 ♖h1, when White had clear compensation (but probably no more than that) due to the semi-open h-file and control of the c-file.

16...♖b8 (D)

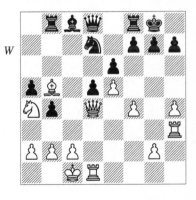

W

17 ♗d3

Other moves:

a) 17 c4?! bxc3 18 ♘xc3 ♕b6 19 ♕xb6 ♖xb6 20 b3 f6! ∓ left White's pieces somewhat uncoordinated in Yurtaev-Goloshchapov, Calcutta 2000.

b) 17 ♗xd7?! ♗xd7 18 ♘c5 ♖c8 19 ♖d2 ♕c7 20 ♘xd7 ♕xd7 was very good for Black in Wells-Glek, Vienna 1998, because his attack is slightly faster.

c) 17 ♗e2 ♗b7 18 ♔b1 ♗c6 19 ♘c5 ♗b5 20 ♗d3 ♘xc5 21 ♕xc5 ♕d7 22 ♕f2 ♗xd3 23 ♖hxd3 ♖b5 24 h5 ♖c8 25 h6 ♖bc5 and again Black's attack is the more dangerous, de la Riva-Glek, Saint Vincent 1999.

17...f6!? *(D)*

In my opinion this thematic break is the simplest way to equalize. Some alternatives:

a) 17...♕c7 18 ♖e1 (18 h5 ♕c6 19 b3 ♗a6 20 f5 ♖bc8 21 ♖d2 ♗xd3 22 ♖hxd3 ♕c7 23 ♖e2, Berndt-Furlan, Bled 2000, 23...exf5 24 ♕xd5 ♘c5 25 ♘xc5 ♕xc5 =) 18...♕c6 19 b3 ♗a6 20 ♗xa6 ♕xa6 has been seen in a couple of games and is fine for Black. On 21 ♖g3, as played in Arakhamia-Matveeva, Kishnev wom IZ 1995, Black's best is probably 21...♔h8 intending to meet 22 f5 with 22...exf5.

b) 17...♗b7 18 f5 and then:

b1) 18...♕c7 19 ♖e1 exf5 20 ♗xf5 ♗c6 21 ♘c5 ♘xc5 22 ♕xc5 ♖fe8 23 ♖he3 leads to a slight advantage for White, Fedorov-Korchnoi, Batumi Echt 1999.

b2) 18...♗c6 19 ♘c5 (19 ♖g3!? exf5! 20 ♗xf5 ♗xa4 21 ♖xg7+ ♔xg7 22 ♕g4+ ♔h6 23 ♕f4+ ♔g7 24 ♕g4+ =) 19...♘xc5 (19...♕b6 20 f6! is too dangerous for Black; one pretty line is 20...♘xc5 21 ♕g4 g6 22 ♕g5 ♘xd3+ 23 ♖dxd3 ♔h8 24 h5 ♖b7 25 ♕h6 ♖g8 26 hxg6 fxg6 27 ♕xh7+ ♖xh7 28 ♖xh7+ ♔xh7 29 ♖h3# – Antić) 20 ♕xc5 ♕b6 21 ♕xb6 ♖xb6 with approximately equal chances, Marjanović-Antić, Yugoslav Ch 2000.

c) 17...♘b6!? is given by Glek. The idea is 18 ♘c5 ♘d7, when White cannot really avoid an exchange of knights. After 19 h5 ♘xc5 20 ♕xc5 a4 21 h6 g6 Black has counterplay.

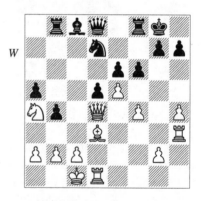

18 exf6

18 ♖g3 fxe5 19 fxe5 ♕c7 20 ♖e1 ♕c6 21 b3 ♗a6 is fine for Black.

18...♕xf6 19 ♕xf6 ♘xf6 20 ♖f3 ♘e4

The position is equal.

8 Shirov/Anand Variation (5 ♘ce2)

1 e4 e6 2 d4 d5 3 ♘c3 ♘f6 4 e5 ♘fd7 5 ♘ce2 *(D)*

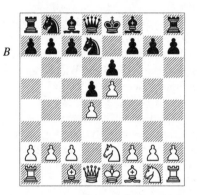

I have dubbed this the Shirov/Anand variation. Shirov did a lot to promote this line for White in the early and mid-1990s while nowadays he is fighting the black side against Anand. It is a logical line where White attempts to maintain a space advantage by defending his centre with c3 and f4, against Black's pawn breaks ...c5 and ...f6. The drawback is of course that White's development is temporarily halted.

5...c5 6 c3

We have already reached an interesting moment. Recently, against Shirov, Anand chose 6 f4, which is an unusual

but probably clever move-order. It has the advantage of avoiding Line B (6 c3 cxd4 7 cxd4 f6), and Anand argues that 6...cxd4 7 ♘xd4 isn't necessarily a bad bargain for White since in many lines where Black takes on d4, White recaptures with a knight anyway. Obviously, this needs some practical tests and current examples are practically non-existent. One interesting thing, though, is that *5 f4 c5 6 ♘f3 a6* is a popular line for Black but then *7 ♘e2!?* is an improved version of Anand's idea since ...a6 is pointless.

We now look at:

A: 6...♘c6   97
B: 6...cxd4   104

A)

6...♘c6 7 f4 *(D)*

White's most logical move. He reinforces e5 and seizes more space.

After 7 ♘f3 Black has several sensible replies but the simplest might be 7...cxd4 8 cxd4 f6 9 ♘f4 ♗b4+ 10 ♗d2 ♕e7 11 ♗xb4 ♕xb4+ 12 ♕d2 ♔e7! 13 exf6+ gxf6 14 ♕xb4+ ♘xb4 15 ♔d2 ♘b6 16 a3 ♘c6, which is very similar to the endgame arising after Black's 15th move in Line B. After 17

♗b5 it would make sense to consider 17...♘a5 or 17...♘d8, since as we see in Line B, Anand was successful in a similar position with an exchange of his bishop for the knight.

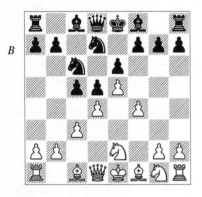

B

Now:

A1: 7...b5   98
A2: 7...♕b6   99

A1)

7...b5 8 a3

It makes sense for White to attempt to prevent Black from playing ...b4. For example, 8 ♘f3 b4 gives Black a promising position:

a) 9 f5 bxc3 10 fxe6 fxe6 11 bxc3 cxd4 12 cxd4 ♗b4+ 13 ♗d2 0-0 was fine for Black in Sax-Korchnoi, Wijk aan Zee 1991.

b) 9 h4 a5 10 ♖h3 ♗a6 11 ♗e3 ♖c8 (the queenside pressure is getting annoying) 12 f5 bxc3 13 bxc3 cxd4 14 ♗xd4 exf5 ∓ Ledger-Summerscale, British League (4NCL) 2000/1.

8...cxd4

Otherwise:

a) In such situations Black would usually consider 8...c4 but here White obtains too much play on the kingside. 9 ♘f3 ♘b6 10 g4 was very good for White in Anand-Morozevich, Frankfurt rpd 2000.

b) On 8...b4, Shirov gives 9 axb4 cxb4 10 ♘f3 as better for White, which seems right because White has good chances on the kingside. Incidentally, 9 dxc5!? might also be an idea, intending to meet 9...bxa3 with 10 b4!.

c) Instead, 8...a5 is logical. Then 9 ♘f3 ♗a6 10 h4 b4 11 h5 ♗e7 12 f5 exf5 13 ♘g3 ♗xf1 14 ♔xf1 looked promising for White in Waitzkin-Thorhallsson, Bermuda 1999.

9 ♘xd4 ♘xd4 10 cxd4

Shirov once tried 10 ♕xd4 but after 10...♗c5 11 ♕d3 0-0 12 ♘f3 f6 the position looked promising for Black in Shirov-Bareev, Hastings 1991/2.

10...b4 11 a4

White wishes to keep the queenside relatively closed, and then later try to exploit his space advantage on the kingside. However, 11 ♘f3!? is worth noting. Then:

a) 11...♘b6 12 a4 – *11 a4 ♘b6 12 ♘f3*.

b) 11...♕b6 has been suggested but 12 a4 looks like a good version of the main line.

c) 11...bxa3 12 bxa3 and then:

c1) 12...♗a6 13 ♗xa6 ♕a5+ 14 ♗d2 ♕xa6 15 ♕e2 ♕xe2+ 16 ♔xe2 gave White a pleasant endgame advantage in Barsky-Castañeda, Russia 1993.

c2) Another idea is 12...♘b6, intending ...♗d7, ...♖c8 and ...♘c4.

11...♕a5!?

11...♘b6 12 ♘f3 ♗e7 13 b3 a5 14 ♗b5+ ♘d7 15 0-0 was very good for White in Shirov-Korchnoi, Lucerne Wcht 1993.

12 ♗d2

Back in 1993, Shirov gave 12 ♕d3 as '±'. This suggestion should be seriously considered. Black should probably still try to get in ...♗a6, for example with 12...♖b8 13 ♗d2 ♗e7 14 ♘f3 ♖b6 ±/=.

12...♗e7 13 ♘f3

Anand-Shirov, Leon adv 2000. Now 13...♗a6 leaves Black close to equality.

A2)

7...♕b6 8 ♘f3 f6 (D)

Black can also play 8...♗e7 but there is a clear danger of him just being worse if he doesn't create some counterplay soon. In Lalić-Speelman, Hastings 2000 White had a pleasant space advantage after 9 g3 a5 10 h4 a4 11 ♗h3 ♘db8 12 h5. 9 a3 is equally sensible.

Now:

A21)

9 g3

Although in line with White's general ambitions, this move has gone out of favour. The reason is that a timely ...♗b4+ is supposed to solve Black's

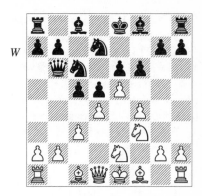

problems. However, this seems to be based on not very well checked analysis, and I wouldn't be surprised if this line becomes fashionable again. Recently, White has been postponing development further in order to take away the option of a bishop check on b4 (see Line A22).

9...cxd4 10 ♘exd4!

An exchange of knights greatly helps White, while now Black must also take into account the fact that e6 is suddenly attacked.

White has also played the more natural 10 cxd4 *(D)*:

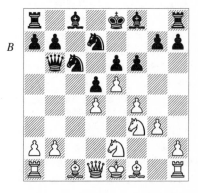

a) 10...fxe5 11 fxe5 ♗b4+ and then:

a1) 12 ♗d2? 0-0 13 ♗g2 ♘dxe5! (13...♖xf3!? 14 ♗xf3 ♘xd4 15 ♘xd4 ♕xd4 16 ♗xb4 ♕xb4+ 17 ♕d2 ♕xd2+ 18 ♔xd2 ♘xe5, as in Sherzer-Sisniega, Philadelphia 1987, also offers Black a promising endgame but the text is clearer) 14 dxe5 ♘xe5 and now White has tried a variety of things but is suffering in all lines:

a11) 15 ♘ed4?! ♘d3+ 16 ♔e2 ♘xb2 gave Black a decisive attack in Hamann-Uhlmann, Halle 1963.

a12) 15 ♘f4 ♕e3+ 16 ♔f1 ♗xd2 17 ♕xd2 ♕xd2 18 ♘xd2 g5 –+ Boulkrouche-Schäfer, Sofia 1994.

a13) 15 ♗xb4 ♕xb4+ 16 ♔f2 ♕e4 (16...♗d7!?, with the point 17 ♕d4 ♕d6!, also looks good) 17 ♘c3 ♘d3+! (after 17...♘g4+ 18 ♔f1 ♘e3+ 19 ♔e2 ♘xd1+ 20 ♘xe4 dxe4 21 ♖hxd1 exf3+ 22 ♗xf3 e5 Black has an extra pawn but it is difficult to exploit due to White's active pieces) 18 ♔f1 ♕c4 19 ♕e2 e5 20 h3 e4 21 ♔g1 exf3 22 ♗xf3 (Hartwig-Seifert, Germany 1998/9) 22...♘h8! is very good for Black.

a2) 12 ♘c3 0-0 13 ♗f4 ♗e7 *(D)* is a critical position. White has some extra space but his king is not safe and Black may contemplate various types of sacrifices to destroy White's centre. Now:

a21) 14 ♗h3 ♕xb2! 15 ♕c1!? (15 ♗xe6+ ♔h8 16 ♘xd5 ♘dxe5! causes trouble for White) 15...♕xc1+ 16 ♖xc1 was played in Anand-Sisniega, Philadelphia 1987. Now Sisniega thinks 16...♘db8, intending to meet 17 ♘b5

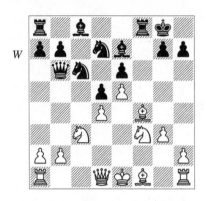

with 17...♘a6, is the simplest, keeping a reasonably clear advantage for Black.

a22) 14 ♘a4 ♕a5+ 15 ♘c3 ♕b6 is just a repetition. Black may avoid this with 16 ♘a4 ♕d8, as in Jaracz-Gleizerov, Katowice 1991 but then 17 ♗d3 or 17 h4!? is ±.

a23) 14 ♕d2?! allows the thematic 14...g5!, which was given by Sisniega in *Informator 44* and had apparently been played in Alapin-Maroczy, Vienna 1908(!), but Dolmatov was obviously unaware of this: 15 ♘xg5 ♗xg5 16 ♗xg5 ♘xd4 17 ♗g2 ♘xe5 18 0-0-0 ♖f2! –+ Dolmatov-Bareev, Russian Ch (Elista) 1997.

a24) 14 a3! ♖f7 15 ♘a4 ♕d8 16 h4!? ♘f8 17 ♖c1 ♗d7 18 b4 was better for White in Ghinda-Prandstetter, Bucharest 1980.

b) All the above lines indicate that White's options are largely increased by the exchange of f-pawns. Hence, 10...♗b4+!? 11 ♘c3 0-0 is supposed to be the most accurate move-order. Then after 12 a3 ♗e7 (compared to line 'a2', White doesn't have ♗f4 available to block the f-file and hence Black can decide at which moment to open the file, assuming that White intends to maintain the centre as it is) 13 ♗h3 (13 exf6!? might be worth considering; for example, 13...♗xf6 14 ♘a4 ♕d8 15 ♗h3 or 13...♘xf6 14 ♗d3) 13...fxe5! 14 ♗xe6+ ♔h8 15 ♘xd5 ♕d8 we have:

b1) 16 ♘xe7 ♕xe7 17 d5 e4 18 ♘g5 ♘c5! and now:

b11) 19 ♗xc8?! ♘d3+ 20 ♔f1 ♖axc8 21 dxc6 ♕xg5 22 cxb7 ♖b8 23 ♔g2 ♕f6 24 ♕e2 ♖xb7 and Black is slightly better, Lukin-Se.Ivanov, USSR 1984.

b12) 19 ♘xh7?! is complicated but more dangerous for White, a sample line being 19...♘d3+ 20 ♔d2 ♗xe6 21 ♘xf8 ♖xf8 22 ♕h5+ ♔g8 23 dxc6 ♘f2 24 ♖f1 ♖d8+ 25 ♔c2 ♕d6 26 ♕e2 ♕xc6+ 27 ♔b1 e3 with a winning attack for Black.

b13) More resilient is 19 0-0! ♗xe6 20 dxe6 ♘xe6 21 ♘xe4 ♘xf4 = (Yudasin and Se.Ivanov).

b2) 16 ♗xd7 ♗xd7 17 dxe5 ♗g4 18 0-0 ♗c5+! 19 ♗e3 ♗xe3+ 20 ♘xe3 ♕b6! 21 ♕d2 ♗xf3 22 ♖xf3 ♘d4! (22...♘xe5? 23 ♖f2 ±) and now:

b21) 23 ♖ff1?! ♘b3 24 ♕f2 ♘xa1 25 ♖xa1 ♖ae8! (this is the problem: White is not as organized as he is in line 'b22') 26 ♖c1 g5 (26...♖xe5?? 27 fxe5 ♖xf2 28 ♖c8+) 27 ♘g4 ♕xf2+ 28 ♔xf2 gxf4 29 ♖c7 fxg3+ 30 ♔xg3 ♖g8 ∓ Smagin-Dimitrov, Prilep 1992.

b22) 23 ♖af1! ♘xf3+ 24 ♖xf3 is unclear – Smagin.

10...fxe5

Or 10...♘xd4 11 cxd4 ♗b4+ 12 ♔f2 fxe5 13 fxe5 0-0 14 ♔g2 ♗e7 15 ♗d3. White has managed to catch up in development, bring his king into safety and maintains a space advantage. This should add up to an advantage but Black is solid and may have some prospects on the queenside. Psakhis-Dizdar, Zagreb 1993 continued 15...♖f7! (alertly making room for ...♘f8 to defend h7) 16 h4 ♘f8 17 ♘g5 (straightforward; 17 ♖b1 intending ♗e3 would also give White an edge) 17...♗xg5 18 hxg5 g6 19 ♖h4 ♗d7 20 a4!?. White has a slight, but not very significant, advantage.

11 fxe5! *(D)*

Keeping it simple. Instead, 11 ♘xe6 e4! 12 ♘fd4 ♘f6 doesn't look like a great problem for Black.

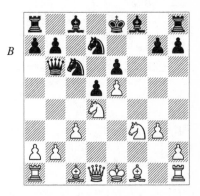

11...♗c5?!

'!' – Knaak, but it doesn't look very good. Otherwise:

a) 11...♘dxe5?! 12 ♘xe5 ♘xe5 13 ♕h5+ ♘g6 (13...♘f7 14 ♗b5+ ♔e7 15

0-0 +−) 14 ♗d3 e5 15 ♗xg6+ ♕xg6 16 ♕xe5+ and White has a clear advantage.

b) 11...♗e7?! (this attempt to improve on Knaak's idea doesn't work) 12 ♘xe6 (12 ♗h3? ♘dxe5) 12...♘dxe5 13 ♘xg7+ ♔f8 14 ♘xe5 ♘xe5 15 ♕h5 ♔xg7 16 ♕xe5+ ♗f6 17 ♕h5 and Black doesn't have enough compensation.

c) Black's best might be 11...♘xd4 12 cxd4 ♗b4+ 13 ♔f2 – *10...♘xd4 11 cxd4 ♗b4+ 12 ♔f2 fxe5 13 fxe5 ±/=*.

12 ♘xe6!

This move is underestimated by Knaak, who gives 12 ♗d3 g6 13 ♘xc6 (13 ♘xe6?! ♗f2+ 14 ♔e2 ♘dxe5 ∓) 13...bxc6 14 ♕e2 (14 b4?! ♗f2+ 15 ♔e2 0-0 intending ...♖xf3 is dangerous for White) 14...a5 with an unclear position.

12...♘dxe5

12...♗f2+ 13 ♔e2 ♘dxe5 14 ♕xd5 is also bad for Black.

13 ♘xc5!

Overlooked by Knaak, whose main point was 13 ♘xg7+? ♔f8 ∓, when on 14 ♘xe5, Black throws in 14...♗f2+.

13...♕xc5

The alternative 13...♘xf3+ 14 ♕xf3 ♕xc5 15 ♕e2+! ± is similar.

14 ♘xe5 ♘xe5 15 ♕h5+ ♘g6 16 ♕e2+!

The main point. White follows with ♗e3 and ♗g2, with a clear, perhaps winning, advantage.

A22)

9 a3 *(D)*

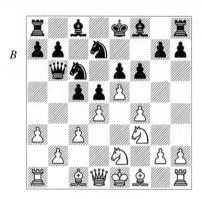

This is a move with various purposes. First of all, White denies Black the possibility of ...♗b4+ but secondly White may also use it to gain space on the queenside with b4.

9...♗e7

Or:

a) 9...cxd4 10 ♘exd4 fxe5 11 fxe5 ♘xd4 12 cxd4 a5 13 ♗d3 is much better for White, Vuković-Drei, Saint Vincent Ech 2000.

b) 9...a5 10 g3 cxd4 11 cxd4 (11 ♘exd4! is stronger – compare with Line A21) 11...♗e7 12 ♗h3 fxe5 13 fxe5 0-0! 14 ♗xe6+ ♔h8 15 ♗xd5 ♘dxe5! 16 dxe5 ♗g4 17 ♗xc6 ♕xc6 18 ♘ed4 ♕e4+ 19 ♕e2 ♗xf3 20 ♘xf3 ♕xf3 21 ♕xf3 ♖xf3 with counterplay, Kalinin-Boog, Hamburg 1994.

10 h4

This is not a random attacking move (though it may at some stage be helpful in an attack) but just as much a prophylactic measure against Black's counterplay. With it, White rules out counterplay based on ...g5 and also prepares to defend against possible

exchange sacrifices on f3 by playing
♖h3. Other moves:

a) 10 f5?! cxd4! 11 fxe6 (11 cxd4
fxe5 12 fxe6 ♘f6! 13 dxe5 ♘g4! 14
♘ed4 0-0 ∓) and now:

a1) 11...♘dxe5 12 ♘fxd4 ♗c5! 13
♘f4 ♘xd4!? 14 cxd4 ♗xd4 15 ♕a4+
♘c6 16 ♗d3 (16 ♘xd5 ♕d8 17 ♘f4
g5 ∓) 16...g5! and the complications
favour Black, Morozevich-Gleizerov,
Alushta 1993. This is all very sharp.

a2) Gleizerov's idea 11...♘c5! may
be simpler.

b) 10 ♘g3 0-0 11 ♗d3 cxd4 12
cxd4 (12 ♘g5? fxg5 13 ♕h5 h6 14
♕g6 ♘dxe5 15 fxe5 ♘xe5 16 ♕h7+
♔f7 −+) 12...fxe5 13 fxe5 ♘dxe5 (this
leads to very sharp play; Euwe recommended 13...a5, while 13...♖xf3!? may
also be worth a shot) 14 dxe5 ♘xe5 15
♗e2 ♗d7! gives Black good compensation for the piece; for example, 16
♖f1 (16 ♘xe5? ♕f2+ 17 ♔d2 ♖ac8!!
18 ♕b3 ♗g5+ 19 ♔d3 ♖f4!! 20 ♘f3
♗e8 0-1 Kengis-Djurhuus, Gausdal
1991 – a fantastic miniature) 16...♘g4
(16...♗f6!?) 17 ♕d4 ♕xd4 18 ♘xd4
♘xh2 19 ♖xf8+ ♖xf8 20 ♘f3 ♗d6 21
♘h1 ♘g4 with compensation – Djurhuus.

c) 10 b4 cxd4 and now:

c1) 11 ♘exd4?! (often this type of
move is a good idea but this is one case
where it is not) 11...fxe5! 12 fxe5 (12
♘xe6 is met by 12...♘f6!, with the
point 13 ♘xg7+ ♔f8 14 b5 ♘e4!? 15
♕c2 ♘d8 16 ♘h5 ♕g6 ∓) 12...♘dxe5
13 ♘xe5 ♘xe5 14 ♕h5+ ♘g6 15 ♗d3
(15 ♗b5+ ♗d7 ∓) 15...0-0 16 ♗xg6

hxg6 17 ♕xg6 ♗f6 18 ♗e3? e5 19
♘c2? ♗h4+ 0-1 F.Meyer-S.Pedersen,
Germany 1999.

c2) 11 cxd4 0-0 (11...a5 12 b5!
♕xb5 13 ♘c3 ♕b6 14 ♖b1 ♕d8 15
♗d3 gave White excellent compensation for the pawn in Lanka-Glek, Zil-
lertal 1993) 12 ♖b1 a5 13 b5 a4 14
exf6 ♘xf6 15 ♘c3 ♘d8 16 ♗d3 ♘f7
is unclear – Shirov.

10...0-0 11 ♖h3 a5

11...♘a5?! 12 b4 cxb4 13 axb4 ♘c4
14 ♘g3 was very good for White in
Anand-Shirov, Frankfurt rpd 2000 as
White is already developing a promising attack.

12 b3 *(D)*

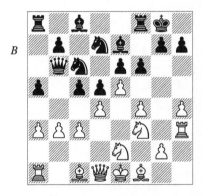

12...♕c7!

This might be an improvement over
the previously played 12...♕d8:

a) 13 ♘g3 ♘b6 14 ♗d3 f5 15 ♗c2
♗d7 16 ♗e3 cxd4 17 cxd4 a4 18 b4
♘a7 was fine for Black in Smirin-
Psakhis, Las Vegas FIDE 1999.

b) White should consider Anand's
idea, 13 ♘eg1, when there is now a

significant difference in at least one of the key lines: 13...cxd4 14 cxd4 b6 15 ♗d3 fxe5 16 fxe5 is now very good for White since here there are no sacrifices on e5.

13 ♘eg1 b6

Anand-Shirov, Teheran FIDE Wch (4) 2000 went 13...a4?! 14 b4 fxe5 15 fxe5 ♘dxe5 16 dxe5 ♘xe5 17 ♘xe5 ♕xe5+ 18 ♕e2 and Black's sacrifices were repelled.

14 ♗e3

This might be slightly unambitious but Anand does not believe in 14 ♗d3 cxd4, when he gives:

a) 15 ♗xh7+? ♔xh7 16 ♘g5+ fxg5 17 ♕h5+ ♔g8 18 hxg5 ♘dxe5 19 fxe5 ♕xe5+ 20 ♘e2 ♗a6 −+.

b) 15 cxd4 fxe5 16 fxe5 ♘cxe5 with no assessment but presumably this means that Black is clearly better or winning.

14...♗a6 15 ♗xa6 ♖xa6

The position is equal – Anand.

B)

6...cxd4 7 cxd4 f6 *(D)*

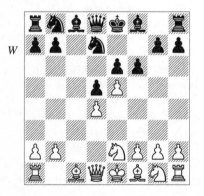

This is a trendy line, but in view of Anand's move-order (6 f4) we might not see much more of it.

8 ♘f4

White has other options worth noting:

a) 8 exf6 ♘xf6 9 ♘f3 ♘c6 10 ♘c3 ♗d6 11 ♗d3 0-0 = Nijboer-Glek, Wijk aan Zee 1999.

b) 8 f4 is a sharp continuation but Black ought to be OK. 8...fxe5 and now:

b1) 9 dxe5 ♕b6 10 ♘c3 ♘c6 11 ♘f3 ♗b4 12 ♗d2 ♘c5 13 a3 ♗xc3 14 ♗xc3 0-0 15 g3 ♗d7 was fine for Black in Bologan-Short, Beijing 2000.

b2) 9 fxe5 ♗b4+ 10 ♔f2 0-0+ 11 ♘f3 ♘c6 12 a3 ♘dxe5! (12...♗a5 is safer, but I think the sacrifice is justified) 13 axb4 ♕h4+ 14 ♔g1?! (14 ♘g3 ♘xd4 15 ♗e2 ♗d7 also gives Black good compensation) 14...♘xf3+ 15 gxf3 ♖xf3 16 ♘g3 and now 16...♕g4! is strong, although 16...♘xd4, as in J.Polgar-Gi.Hernandez, Merida 2000, also looks sufficient.

8...♗b4+ 9 ♗d2 ♕b6

Stronger than 9...♕e7 since Black attacks d4.

10 ♗xb4

Or:

a) On 10 exf6, 10...♘xf6 11 ♕a4+ ♘c6 12 ♗xb4 ♕xb4+ 13 ♕xb4 ♘xb4 was fine for Black in Vuković-Piskov, Yugoslav Cht 1994 but Black could also consider 10...0-0!?.

10 ♕h5+ g6 11 ♘xg6 ♗xd2+ 12 ♔xd2 ♕xb2+ 13 ♔e3 ♕xa1 14 ♘xh8+ ♔d8 is a line given by Sakaev. The

position is a mess but Black's chances look preferable.

10...♕xb4+ 11 ♕d2 ♕xd2+ 12 ♔xd2 ♘e7 *(D)*

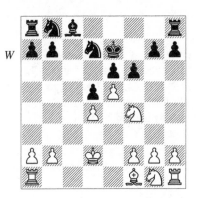

This has all been more or less forced. The position should be approximately equal but if I had to take a side, I would actually prefer Black. White is going to end up with a weak pawn on e5 if he doesn't take on f6, while that exchange would give Black a strong centre. Nonetheless, Anand has won a good game from this position as White.

13 exf6+

It is very natural for White to avoid a black exchange on e5, but 13 ♘f3 should also be considered:

a) 13...fxe5 14 ♘xe5 ♘xe5 15 dxe5 ♘c6 16 ♘d3, with approximately equal chances.

b) Against 13...♘c6, White can try 14 exf6+ gxf6 15 ♗b5, when he will be able to achieve the strategically desirable exchange of his bishop for one of Black's knights.

13...gxf6 14 ♖e1 ♘b6 15 ♘f3 ♘c6

Black could also consider 15...♔d6, as this is a logical square for the king. Then, for example, 16 ♗d3 ♘c6 – *15...♘c6 16 ♗d3 ♔d6*.

16 ♗b5

16 ♗d3 ♔d6 (intending ...e5) 17 ♘h5 ♖f8! 18 ♗xh7 e5 19 ♘g3 e4 20 ♘h4 ♘xd4 is very pleasant for Black, Bezgodov-Sakaev, Moscow 1999. The sacrifice of the h-pawn is clever and demonstrates how quickly Black's central advance can become dangerous for White.

16...♗d7

It is difficult to criticize such a natural move but the fact is that White is happy to exchange his bishop for Black's knight, as this gives him increased control over the e5-square. Hence, Anand suggests 16...♘a5 or 16...♘d8 followed by ...a6, driving the white bishop back.

17 ♗xc6 bxc6 18 ♖e2! ♖ae8 19 ♖he1

From this point Anand-Bareev, Shenyang FIDE WCup 2000 continued 19...♔f7 20 ♔c1!?, when White's position was somewhat more pleasant to play due to his superior control of the c5- and e5-squares. Instead, Anand suggests 19...♔d6! as a better try for Black.

9 Classical Variation

1 e4 e6 2 d4 d5 3 ♘c3 ♘f6 4 ♗g5 ♗e7 *(D)*

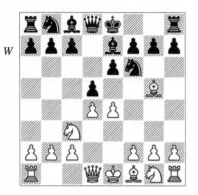

The Classical Variation has lost some of its popularity during the last few years, with the Burn and Rubinstein Variations taking all the limelight.

Fashion plays a large role in this, and the Classical Variation remains a solid defence that certainly shouldn't be neglected. It quickly leads to a typical French position with a basic structure characterized by a closed centre, in which Black plays for the ...c5 and ...f6 breaks. The Classical Variation attracts strong defensive and strategic players.

5 e5

5 ♗xf6 ♗xf6 6 e5 ♗e7 is seen occasionally. The aggressive 7 ♕g4 is White's best but nothing that Black should be afraid of. He can play 7...g6, but 7...0-0 8 ♗d3 c5 9 ♕h3 g6 10 dxc5 ♘d7 (10...♘c6 is also good, with the idea of meeting 11 f4 with 11...♕a5) 11 f4 ♘xc5 12 0-0-0 b5!? 13 ♘ce2 ♕a5 14 ♔b1 ♘a4 was very good for Black in Maier-Moskalenko, Groningen 1989.

5...♘fd7

There are two minor alternatives:

a) 5...♘e4?! 6 ♗xe7 gives Black two unsatisfactory options:

a1) 6...♘xc3 7 ♕g4! ♕xe7 8 ♕xg7 ♕b4 9 ♕xh8+ ♔d7 10 ♘f3! ♕xb2 11 ♔d2! ♘b1+?! (or 11...♘e4+ 12 ♔e3 ♕xc2 13 ♗b5+ c6 14 ♗e2 ± L.Dominguez) 12 ♖xb1 ♕xb1 13 ♕xh7 +− L.Dominguez-Heidenfeld, Istanbul OL 2000.

a2) 6...♕xe7 7 ♘xe4 dxe4 8 ♕e2 b6 9 0-0-0 (9 ♕xe4? ♕b4+) 9...♗b7 10 g3 c5 11 ♗g2 ♘c6 12 dxc5 0-0 13 ♗xe4 ♘xe5 14 f4 ♗xe4 15 ♕xe4 ♘g4 16 ♕f3 ± Tseshkovsky-Lputian, Kropotkin 1995.

b) 5...♘g8 is feasible but a little passive. White's standard 6th moves in the main line (6 ♗xe7 and 6 h4) are no longer effective, but if White retreats his bishop, he can expect some advantage:

b1) 6 ♗xe7 makes little sense as Black has the natural reply 6...♘xe7.

b2) 6 h4?! ♗xg5 7 hxg5 ♕xg5 8 ♘h3 ♕e7 9 ♘f4 (9 ♕g4 f5 is also good for Black, as shown in some old games by Heidenfeld) 9...g6 denies White sufficient compensation for the pawn. The black knight is well placed to hold the kingside together.

b3) Even 6 ♗c1 suffices for an edge – *3...♗e7 4 e5* ±.

b4) 6 ♗e3 b6 7 h4! (threatening h5) 7...h5 8 ♗e2 (8 g4!?) 8...g6 9 ♘f3 ♗a6 10 ♕d2 ♕d7 11 ♗g5 ♗xe2 12 ♘xe2 ♘c6 13 ♘f4 0-0-0 14 c3 ± Vera-Bischoff, Pau 1988.

6 ♗xe7

6 h4 is analysed in the next chapter.

6...♕xe7 *(D)*

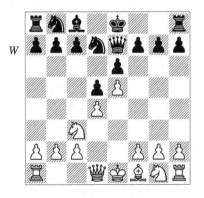

7 f4

This has become White's most popular choice, but there are a few notable alternatives:

a) 7 ♘b5 is called the Alapin Variation. It is interesting, though, that Alapin was more frequently on the

black side against this. The verdict nowadays is that it is not very dangerous. 7...♘b6, and then:

a1) 8 c3 a6 9 ♘a3 c5 10 ♘c2 ♘c6 11 f4 ♘a4!? 12 ♖b1 b5 13 ♘f3 ♗d7 was roughly equal in, for example, Em.Lasker-Lilienthal, Moscow 1934.

a2) 8 a4!? a6 9 a5 axb5 10 axb6 ♖xa1 11 ♕xa1 c6!? 12 ♕a8 ♕b4+ 13 c3 and now:

a21) The simplest is 13...♕a4!? 14 ♕xb8 ♕a1+ 15 ♔e2 ♕xb2+, with perpetual check.

a22) In Ljubojević-Korchnoi, Belgrade 1987 Black also managed to equalize but with slightly more difficulty: 13...♕xb2 14 ♘e2 b4 15 ♕xb8 0-0 16 cxb4 ♕xb4+ 17 ♔d1 c5! 18 ♕c7 ♕a4+ 19 ♔d2 ♗d7! 20 ♔e3 ♖c8 21 ♕xb7 cxd4+ 22 ♘xd4 ♖c3+ 23 ♗d3, and now 23...♖xd3+ 24 ♔xd3 ♕c4+ 25 ♔e3 ♕c3+ 26 ♔e2 ♕c4+ 27 ♔f3 ♕d3+ 28 ♔g4 ♕g6+ would be a perpetual check, while Korchnoi decided to play for more with 23...g5!?.

b) 7 ♕d2 is an interesting move-order, which Black should be aware of. If 7...0-0, White can transpose to the main lines with 8 f4 c5 9 ♘f3; this is bad news for Black if he wants to meet *7 f4* with *7...a6* (Line B). Thus we shall look at two lines for Black:

b1) 7...a6 8 ♘d1!? (8 f4 c5 9 ♘f3 ♘c6 10 dxc5 – *7 f4 a6 8 ♘f3 c5 9 dxc5 ♘c6 10 ♕d2*) 8...c5 9 c3 ♘c6 10 f4 and now:

b11) 10...b5 11 ♘f3 f5! 12 ♘e3 ♘b6 gave Black counterplay in Winawer-Blackburne, Paris 1878.

b12) A more recent example is the game Sakaev-Volkov, New Delhi FIDE 2000, where Black launched a more aggressive idea with 10...cxd4 11 cxd4 g5!?, but 12 fxg5 h6 13 ♘f3 hxg5 14 ♘f2 ♖g8 15 h3!, intending to castle queenside, favoured White.

b2) 7...0-0 8 f4 (here the 8 ♘d1 idea is less attractive, owing to 8...c5 9 c3 ♘c6 10 f4 f6 11 ♘f3 cxd4 12 cxd4 fxe5, when 13 fxe5 runs into 13...♖xf3 14 gxf3 ♕h4+, and 13 dxe5 ♕b4! was very good for Black in Thomas-Lilienthal, Ujpest 1934) 8...c5 9 ♘b5 (9 ♘f3 ♘c6 10 dxc5 – 7 f4 0-0 8 ♘f3 c5 9 dxc5 ♘c6 10 ♕d2) 9...a6! 10 ♘d6 cxd4 11 ♘f3 ♘c6 12 ♗d3 f6 ∓ Asztalos-Spielmann, Bled 1931.

We now return to 7 f4 (D):

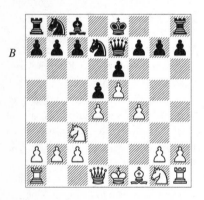

Now:

A: 7...0-0   108
B: 7...a6   117

A)

7...0-0 8 ♘f3 c5
Here we consider:

A1:	9 ♗d3	108
A2:	9 ♕d2	109
A3:	9 dxc5	110

A1)

9 ♗d3 (D)

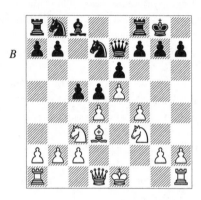

9...f6!

In the Classical Variation, Black nearly always answers ♗d3 with ...f6. Here, the threat of ♗xh7+ almost compels the reply. 9...f5 should transpose to the main line, although White also has the option of keeping the position closed, and 9...cxd4? is very bad, owing to 10 ♗xh7+! ♔xh7 11 ♘g5+ ♕xg5 (11...♔g6 12 ♕d3+ f5 13 exf6+ ♔xf6 14 ♕xd4+ ♔g6 15 ♕d3+ ♔f6 16 0-0-0 ♘c5 17 ♕h3 +−) 12 fxg5 dxc3 13 ♕h5+! ♔g8 14 0-0 ♘xe5 15 ♖ae1 ♘g6 16 ♖e3 e5 17 g4, when White has a decisive attack, Szilagyi-Harding, corr. 1988 (and others).

10 exf6 ♕xf6

This seems best. Black gains a tempo due to the attack on f4 and keeps the knight on d7 to recapture on c5. After

10...♘xf6 11 dxc5 ♕xc5 12 ♕d2 ♘c6 13 0-0-0 White has a slight advantage due to his good piece configuration, control of e5 and possible play against the backward e6-pawn.

11 ♘g5

11 g3 ♘c6 (11...cxd4?! 12 ♘b5! ♘c6 13 ♘g5 ±) 12 dxc5 – *9 dxc5 ♘c6 10 ♗d3 f6 11 exf6 ♕xf6 12 g3 ±/=.*

11...♕xf4

Stronger than 11...g6 12 ♕g4, when White gets an attack.

12 ♗xh7+ ♚h8 13 ♕h5

On 13 ♕d2, the simplest reply is 13...♕xd2+ 14 ♚xd2 ♖f2+ 15 ♘e2 ♘f8!, when White is in big trouble, Kostakiev-Strelkov, corr. 1988.

13...♘f6!?

13...♕f2+ 14 ♚d1 ♘f6 is also feasible but White can be happy that the g5-knight is not attacked any more. Hence 15 ♕h3 is an option, but it is no more than a draw though: 15...♕xd4+ 16 ♗d3+ ♚g8 17 ♘xe6 ♕e5! (17...♖e8 18 ♘xd4! ♗xh3 19 gxh3 cxd4 20 ♘b5 gives White an edge) 18 ♗f5 (18 ♖e1 ♗xe6 19 ♕xe6+ ♕xe6 20 ♖xe6 ♘c6 = Paoli) 18...g6 19 ♕h6 ♗xe6 20 ♕xg6+ = Stetsko.

14 ♘f7+

This is White's only chance. After 14 ♕g6 the white pieces are only stepping on each other's toes.

14...♖xf7 15 ♕xf7 ♚xh7 16 ♖f1

White hopes that he will get a rook to the third rank to mix things up. Black must be careful but as the following analysis shows, White's compensation is insufficient: 16...♕xd4 17

♖d1 ♕h4+! 18 g3 ♕g5 (18...♕h5 19 ♖xf6 ♕e5+ 20 ♘e4 ♕xe4+ 21 ♚f2 and Black has no more than a draw) 19 ♖f4 ♘g4 20 ♘e4 dxe4 21 h4 ♘e5 22 hxg5 ♘xf7 23 ♖xf7 ♚g6 24 ♖f8 ♘c6 –+.

A2)

9 ♕d2 ♘c6 10 dxc5 *(D)*

White does best to release the tension. If 10 0-0-0?!, Black can advantageously close the queenside with 10...c4 and threaten to build up an attack with ...b5-b4. White has to take some untraditional measures against this, which are unlikely to work well. For example, Bologan-Gleizerov, Calcutta 1999 continued 11 ♘b5 ♘b6 12 h4 ♗d7 13 ♘d6 ♖ab8 14 f5 f6! 15 ♕f4 exf5 16 g3 ♘c8 and Black was much better.

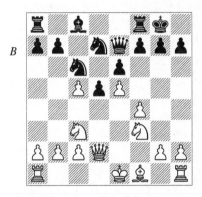

10...♘xc5

An alternative way to reach the main line is 10...f6 11 exf6 ♕xf6 12 g3 ♘xc5, while 10...♕xc5 transposes to Line A32.

11 0-0-0 f6

11...♗d7 is also sensible, waiting to decide whether to break with ...f6. However, if Black waits too long, there is a large risk that he will become too passive. An example of this is Dolmatov-Aris, Jakarta 1997: 12 ♕e3 b6 13 g3 ♖ac8 (it is about time for Black to play ...f6, either here or on the next move) 14 ♔b1 ♖fd8? (this looks like a step in the wrong direction) 15 ♗e2 ♗e8 16 ♖he1 a6 17 f5 ±.

12 exf6 ♕xf6 13 g3 ♖d8

This is essential preparation because 13...♗d7? can be met by 14 ♘xd5! exd5 15 ♕xd5+, winning material.

14 ♕f2!

It looks like a sensible idea to move the queen away from the d-file, although this is far from imperative. 14 ♗d3 also makes sense but has so far not given White anything tangible in the opening; for example: 14...♗d7 15 ♖he1 ♖ac8 16 ♔b1 ♗e8 17 ♘e5 ♘xe5 18 ♖xe5 ♘d7 19 ♖ee1 ♗h5 20 ♗e2 ♗g6 21 ♗g4 ♖c6 22 ♕d4 ♕xd4 23 ♖xd4 ♔f7 with approximately equal play, Mukhaev-Gleizerov, Russia Cup (Tomsk) 1998.

14...b6

14...d4? 15 ♘b5 e5 16 ♘g5! led to a disastrous position for Black in Sadvakasov-R.Bagirov, Istanbul OL 2000.

15 ♗g2 ♗d7 16 ♖he1 ♖ac8 17 ♘e5 ♘xe5 18 ♖xe5

± Goloshchapov-Vysochin, Ordzhonikidze Z 2000.

A3)

9 dxc5 *(D)*

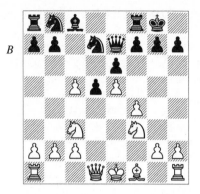

This is White's most common continuation, although it is also often implemented after *9 ♕d2 ♘c6* and only then *10 dxc5*. After *10...♕xc5* we then arrive at Line C2, while Black in this line has the additional possibility of capturing with the knight on c5 – see Line B.

We now look at:

A31: 9...♘c6   111
A32: 9...♕xc5   113

The former is the most flexible, as Black keeps the option open whether to capture with the knight or the queen on c5. Usually, in this line Black takes with the knight on c5 but it is a good idea to wait a few moves. After the immediate 9...♘xc5 10 ♗d3, Black has some problems:

a) 10...♘c6 – *9...♘c6 10 ♗d3 ♘xc5* ±.

b) 10...♘xd3+ 11 cxd3 is better for White.

c) That leaves 10...f6, but in this case White doesn't need to take on f6 since Black has lessened the pressure

against e5, and can continue simply
with 11 0-0 ±.

A31)

9...♘c6 10 ♗d3 f6

On 10...♘xc5 White should simply
reply 11 0-0, with the better game; he
then threatens ♗xh7+. However, the
immediate 11 ♗xh7+ ♔xh7 12 ♘g5+
♔g6 13 ♕g4 only looks like a draw:
13...f6 (13...f5? 14 ♕g3 ±; 13...♘xe5
14 ♕g3 f6 15 ♘f3+ ♔f7 16 fxe5 ±) 14
♘ge4+ ♔f7 15 exf6 gxf6 16 ♕h5+
♔g7 17 ♕g4+ =.

11 exf6

If 11 0-0, 11...fxe5 12 fxe5 ♘dxe5
looks safe enough, for on 13 ♘xe5?!
Black has the clever 13...♕xc5+ 14
♔h1 ♖xf1+ and the knight is won back
without running into a ♗xh7+ trick.

11...♕xf6

This is best as Black gains a tempo
by attacking f4 and also forces White
to weaken his kingside with g3. Other
moves allow White a pleasant advantage:

a) 11...♖xf6 12 ♕d2 ♘xc5 13 0-0
♘xd3 14 cxd3 ♗d7 15 ♖ae1 ♕b4 16
g3 ♗e8 17 a3 ♕b6+ 18 ♔g2 ± Gli-
gorić-Yanofsky, Dallas 1957.

b) 11...♘xf6 12 0-0 ♕xc5+ 13 ♔h1
♕d6 14 ♕d2 ♗d7 15 ♖ae1 and again
White is better as he has established
good control over the e5-square, Jo-
hansson-Ståhlberg, Stockholm 1967.

12 g3 ♘xc5 *(D)*

13 0-0

Other moves don't promise White
anything:

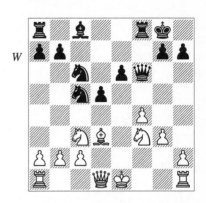

a) 13 ♕d2 ♘xd3+ 14 ♕xd3 (14
cxd3 e5! is comfortable for Black; e.g.,
15 0-0 ♗h3 16 ♖fe1 ♖ae8) 14...♗d7
15 0-0-0 ♗e8 16 ♖he1 ♗g6 17 ♕e3
♗h5 18 ♖d2 ♗xf3! (a well-timed exchange before White gets the chance
to play ♘e5) 19 ♕xf3 ♖ac8, Borkow-
ski-Lada, Polanica Zdroj 1992. The
position is dynamically balanced. White
has some pressure on the semi-open
e-file but this is outweighed by Black's
counterplay on the queenside.

b) 13 ♘g5 ♘xd3+ 14 ♕xd3 ♕f5
15 ♕xf5 ♖xf5 16 0-0-0 h6 17 ♘f3 g5
18 ♘e2 ½-½ Vallejo Pons-Comas
Fabrego, Pamplona 1998/9.

13...♗d7 14 ♕d2

Simple chess. In an ideal world
White would follow up with ♖ae1,
hope that Black exchanges on d3, and
then occupy e5 at some point, thus obtaining a knight vs bishop scenario
with a backward pawn on e6. This
type of position is usually very difficult for Black. Other moves are:

a) 14 ♕e2 ♘d4! 15 ♘xd4 ♕xd4+
16 ♕f2 ♕b4 17 a3 ♕b6 18 ♕d4 ♖ac8

19 ♖ab1 ♗e8 20 ♖f2 ♗h5 = Lanc-Züger, Prague 1989.

b) 14 ♗b5!? (a positionally subtle move as White is about to exchange on c6, thus obtaining a knight against Black's light-squared bishop) 14...d4 (14...♘b4 15 ♕d4! ♕xd4+ 16 ♘xd4 ♗xb5 17 ♘cxb5 a6 18 c3 ♘bd3 19 ♘c7 ♖ac8 20 ♘cxe6 ♘xe6 21 ♘xe6 ♖f6 22 f5 ♘xb2! 23 ♖ab1 ♘a4 24 ♖xb7 ± Fernandez Garcia-Vera, Las Palmas 1988) 15 ♗xc6 (15 ♘e2 ♖ad8!? with counterplay) 15...dxc3 16 ♗xd7 cxb2 17 ♖b1 ♖ad8 = Jenni-Bagirov, Biel 2000.

14...♘xd3

This is the correct moment for the exchange, before White reinforces his control of e5 with ♖ae1. If Black delays by 14...♗e8 15 ♖ae1, he can expect problems:

a) 15...♘xd3 is met by 16 cxd3 ♗g6 17 ♘e5, with an edge for White.

b) Instead in Leko-Volkov, New Delhi FIDE 2000, Black further postponed the exchange on d3 but was worse anyway: 15...♖d8 16 a3 (an interesting waiting move; if 16 ♘e5 ♘xe5 17 ♖xe5 Black puts his bishop on c6, where it is much better than it is on h5) 16...♗h5 17 ♘e5 ♘xe5 18 ♖xe5 ±.

15 cxd3 *(D)*

15 ♕xd3 ♗e8 16 ♖ae1 ♗g6 17 ♕d2 ♖ac8 is fine for Black because he has counterplay on the queenside. This is removed by capturing with the pawn on d3, but then another option becomes available for Black...

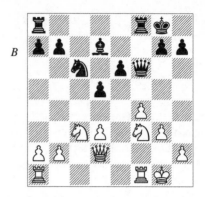

B

15...e5!

Black sacrifices a pawn to avoid the prospect of a passive position if White is allowed time to play a rook to the e-file. However, perhaps 15...d4 16 ♘e4 ♕f5 is a viable and less complicated alternative, as in Galliamova-Zhukova, Istanbul wom OL 2000. Black intends to put her queen on d5 and prepares ...e5 without sacrificing a pawn.

16 ♖ae1

16 ♘xe5 ♘xe5 17 fxe5 ♕xe5 18 d4 ♕h5 has been played in several games but is not a problem for Black. Not even if both rooks disappear can White hope for an advantage as the position is too open for him to make real progress in a queen + knight vs queen + bishop position.

16...exf4

16...♗h3 17 ♖f2 d4 18 ♘e4 ♕f5 is an interesting alternative. The position is complex, but I think White has better chances of obtaining an advantage than in the main line:

a) 19 ♘xe5 ♘xe5 20 fxe5 ♕xe5 21 ♖xf8+ (21 ♘f6+ ♕xf6 22 ♖xf6 ♖xf6 is fine for Black as ...♖af8 comes next, and White cannot make progress due to the threat of ...♖f1+) 21...♖xf8 22 ♘f2 ♛h5! 23 ♛b4 ♗g2! 24 ♛xd4 ♗c6 25 ♖e7 ♛g5 = de Firmian-Chernin, New York 1988.

b) 19 ♘h4 ♛d7 20 f5! ♗xf5 21 ♘c5 ♛c8 (21...♛d5? 22 ♘xf5 ♛xc5 23 ♛g5 g6 24 ♖c1! ♛b4 25 ♖cf1 gave White too strong an attack in Sax-Jurković, Tucepi 1996) 22 ♖xf5 ♖xf5 23 ♘xf5 ♛xf5 24 ♖f1 ♛g6 25 ♘xb7 e4 26 dxe4 ♛xe4 27 ♘d6 ♛e5 with a roughly equal position.

c) 19 ♘fg5!? ♗g4 (19...exf4 20 ♖xf4 ♛d7 21 ♘xh3 ♛xh3 22 ♖ef1 ± A.Sokolov) 20 h3! ♗xh3 21 ♖h2 exf4 22 ♖xh3! (stronger than 22 ♘xh3 ♘e5!, when Black has counterplay) 22...h6 23 gxf4 hxg5 24 ♛h2 ♛g4+ 25 ♔h1 ♛xf4 26 ♖h8+ ♔f7 27 ♘d6+ ♛xd6 (27...♔f6 28 ♖h6+ g6 29 ♘e4+ ♔g7 30 ♖h7+ ♔g8 31 ♖h8+ ♔f7 32 ♛h7+ ♔e6 33 ♘xg5+ ♔d5 34 ♛d7+ ♛d6 35 ♖h7 ♛xd7 36 ♖xd7+ ♔c5 37 ♘e6+ ♔b6 38 ♘xf8 ♖xf8 39 ♔g2 and White should win) 28 ♛xd6 ♖xh8+ 29 ♔g2 ± Am.Rodriguez-Stojanović, Linares open 1997.

17 ♘xd5 ♛d6 18 ♘xf4 ♗g4! 19 ♛e3 ♖ad8 20 ♖f2 h6!? 21 h4 ♖f7 22 ♘d2 ♛b4!

Black has good compensation for the sacrificed pawn, Arnason-Bareev, Sochi 1988.

A32)

9...♛xc5 *(D)*
10 ♛d2

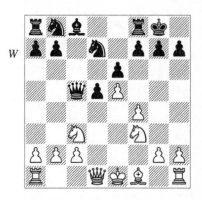

Another interesting option is 10 ♗d3!? ♛e3+ (10...♘c6?? 11 ♗xh7+ ♔xh7 12 ♘g5+ +−) 11 ♘e2 ♘c6 12 ♛d2 ♛xd2+ 13 ♔xd2. This type of position is usually somewhere between equal and slightly better for White. Pluses for White are his control over the d4-square and the better minor pieces.

It is interesting that Gufeld and Stetsko regard Black's 9th move as dubious in view of 10 ♛d4 (they give it a '!'). Naturally, 10 ♛d4 remains a viable option but I don't share their view that it promises White an advantage. While I trust that Black should be able to equalize after 10...♘c6 11 ♛xc5 ♘xc5, I think that Gleizerov's move 10...b6!? could be even simpler. Then Suetin-Gleizerov, Berlin 1994 was drawn after 11 0-0-0 ♘c6 (11...♗a6!? deserves attention) 12 ♛d2 a6 13 ♗d3 f5. Actually, this ought to receive more attention. Black has the extra move ...b6 compared to the main line but this is perhaps not an advantage as it obstructs ...♘b6.

10...♘c6 11 0-0-0

11 a3!? is a slightly unorthodox idea. The intention is not to prevent ...♘b4 but rather to advance the b-pawn. A few examples:

a) 11...♘b6 12 b4! ♕e7 13 ♗d3 ♗d7 14 0-0 ♖ac8 15 ♘b5 f6 16 ♕e3! ± Smyslov-Nikolenko, Cappelle la Grande 1995.

b) 11...f6!? 12 exf6 ♖xf6 13 0-0-0 ♘b6 14 g3 ♗d7 15 h4 ♖c8 16 ♔b1 ♘a5 17 ♘e5 ♘ac4 18 ♗xc4 ♘xc4 19 ♘xc4 ♕xc4 20 h5 ± Bruzon-Hernando Rodrigo, Santa Clara 1999.

c) 11...a6!? (maybe best; now it would be dangerous to castle queenside, so White has to proceed with the b4 idea) 12 b4 ♕b6 (12...♕a7!?) 13 ♗d3 f6 14 exf6 ♘xf6 15 ♘a4 ♕a7 16 ♕f2 ♕xf2+ 17 ♔xf2 = Kovalevskaya-Matveeva, Belgrade wom 2000.

11...♘b6 (D)

11...f6 12 exf6 ♘xf6 is typically French but White retains slightly the better chances in view of the d4- and e5-squares; e.g., 13 ♗d3 ♗d7 14 ♖he1 ♖ac8 15 ♔b1 a6 16 ♘e5 ♘xe5 17 ♖xe5 b5 18 h3 ♕b6 19 ♘e2 ♗e8 20 ♘d4 ± V.Ivanov-Nikolenko, Moscow 1995.

12 ♔b1

With this move White introduces the idea of playing ♘b5. White has a range of other possibilities:

a) After the immediate 12 ♘b5?!, 12...♘c4 13 ♗xc4 ♕xc4 solves Black's problems since White does not have time to play ♘d6 due to the threat of ...♕xa2.

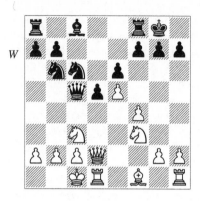

b) 12 ♗d3 and then:

b1) 12...♘c4 (the type of position arising after this is usually in White's favour) 13 ♗xc4 ♕xc4 14 ♔b1 f6 15 exf6 ♖xf6 16 g3 ♗d7 17 ♖he1 ♗e8 18 ♘e5 ♘xe5 19 ♖xe5 ± Toth-Hoang Than Trang, Budapest 1995.

b2) 12...♗d7 and now:

b21) 13 ♔b1 – 12 ♔b1 ♗d7 13 ♗d3.

b22) White has also tried the direct 13 ♗xh7+!? ♔xh7 14 ♘g5+ ♔g8 15 ♕d3. We shall soon become familiar with this attacking idea. Black has to move the rook:

b221) 15...♖fc8!? 16 ♕h7+ ♔f8 17 ♕h5 (17 ♖he1 ♘b4 ∓) 17...♗e8 18 ♕h8+ ♔e7 19 ♕xg7 ♘b4 ∓.

b222) 15...♖fe8 16 ♕h7+ ♔f8 17 ♖he1!? ♘c4!? (17...♕b4 18 ♕h8+ ♔e7 19 ♕h4 ♔d8!? 20 ♘xe6++ ♔c8 21 a3 ♕e7 22 ♘g5! and White keeps his attack going, Van der Wiel-Korchnoi, Amsterdam 1991) 18 ♕h8+ ♔e7 19 ♕h4 ♖h8 20 ♘h7+ f6 (20...♔e8 21 ♘f6+ gxf6 22 ♕xh8+ ♕f8 23 ♕xf8+ ♔xf8 24 exf6 ± Zso.Polgar-Somlai,

Budapest 1991) 21 exf6+ ♔d8 22 fxg7+ ♔c7 23 gxh8♕ ½-½ P.H.Nielsen-Ulybin, Mamaia jr Wch 1991. The position looks very unclear after 23...♖xh8 24 a3 d4 25 ♘e4 ♕b5 26 b3 ♘xa3.

c) 12 h4!? (White wants to play h5-h6 to create weaknesses on the black kingside; this is a sensible idea in itself but it is time-consuming and gives Black a couple of moves to step up his attack on the queenside) 12...♗d7 (12...f6 13 exf6 ♖xf6 14 ♗d3 ♗d7 15 ♖he1 ♘c4 16 ♗xc4 ♕xc4 17 g3 ♗e8 18 ♘e5 ♘xe5 19 ♖xe5 ♗g6 20 b3 ♕b4 21 ♔b2 ♖c8 22 a3 ♕c5 23 ♖c1!, intending ♘e2-d4 ±, Kruppa-Ulybin, Minsk 1997) 13 h5 ♖fc8. Black could also put the other rook on c8 but I think most players would prefer this move, as it keeps the rook participating in the attack and vacates f8 as a possible escape-route for the king. After 14 h6 g6 a critical position arises:

c1) 15 ♘h2?! (White's knight is heading for f6 but this is premature) 15...♘b4! (threatening ...d4 or ...♘a4) 16 a3 a5! 17 ♘g4 ♗a4! 18 ♗d3 ♘c4 19 ♗xc4 ♕xc4 20 ♘f6+ ♔h8 21 axb4 axb4 with a probably decisive attack for Black, Vogt-Züger, Lucerne 1994.

c2) 15 ♔b1 ♘a5 16 ♕d4 ♕e7 (White has a slight advantage if the queens are exchanged) 17 ♖h3 ♘bc4 18 ♘d2 b5 19 ♗xc4 ♘xc4 20 ♘xc4 bxc4 21 ♔c1 ♖c7 22 ♖dh1 ♖b8 23 ♘d1 is slightly better for White, Rausis-Züger, Cattolica 1994.

d) 12 ♘d4!? ♗d7 and now:

d1) 13 ♔b1 ♖ac8 14 ♗e2 ♘xd4 (14...♘a5 15 ♘b3 ♘xb3 16 cxb3 ± Wedberg) 15 ♕xd4 ♕a5 (15...♕xd4 is equal according to Korchnoi) 16 ♖hf1 ♘c4 17 ♖f3 b5 18 ♗xc4 ♖xc4 19 ♕d2 b4 20 ♘e2 ♖fc8 21 ♘d4 ± Wedberg-Korchnoi, Haninge 1988.

d2) 13 h4 ♖fc8 14 ♖h3 ♘a5!? (or 14...♘xd4 15 ♕xd4 ♕xd4 16 ♖xd4 ♖c5 17 ♗e2 ♖ac8, with roughly equal chances) 15 ♘b3 ♘xb3+ 16 axb3 a5 is equal, Rowson-Hanley, British League (4NCL) 2000/1.

12...♗d7 *(D)*

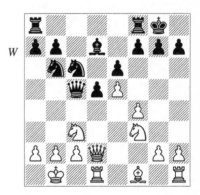

13 ♗d3

13 ♘b5 is an important alternative that is now regarded as harmless due to 13...♘a4! (13...♖ac8?! 14 ♘d6 ♖c7 15 ♗b5!? f6 16 ♗xc6! ♕xc6 17 ♘d4 ♕a4 18 ♖he1 ± Groszpeter-I.Almasi, Hungarian Cht 1995), and now:

a) 14 ♘d6?! f6 15 ♗e2 fxe5 16 fxe5 ♘xe5 17 ♘xe5 ♕xd6 18 ♘xd7 ♕xd7 19 ♖he1 (Hjartarson-Brynell, Stockholm 1996) 19...♘c5 is favourable for Black.

b) 14 ♘bd4 ♕b6 15 ♘b3 a5 16 c3 (Borik-Blauert, 2nd Bundesliga 1997/8) 16...♖fc8 17 ♗d3 ♘e7 18 ♔a1 ♗b5 is fine for Black.

13...♖ac8

In the following play Black must be alert to possibilities of ♗xh7+. It is tempting but White is probably not yet threatening it. The question again is which rook Black should put on the c-file. In this case the queen's rook is right, because on 13...♖fc8, 14 ♘b5! is much stronger as Black cannot counter in the centre. Then, for example, 14...h6 15 ♘d6 ♖c7 16 c3! is good for White. Alternatives for Black on move 13 are:

a) 13...f6 14 exf6 ♖xf6 15 ♖he1 ♘c4 16 ♗xc4 ♕xc4 17 g3 – *12 ♗d3 ♘c4 13 ♗xc4 ♕xc4 14 ♔b1 f6 15 exf6 ♖xf6 16 g3 ♗d7 17 ♖he1* ±.

b) 13...♘b4 14 a3 a5 15 ♖hf1 ♖fc8 16 ♕f2 ♘xd3 17 cxd3 ♘a4 18 ♘xa4 ♗xa4 19 ♕xc5 ♖xc5 20 ♖c1 b6 21 ♘d4 ♖ac8 22 b3 ♗d7 23 ♔b2 gives White a slight advantage, Z.Almasi-Züger, Horgen 1995.

c) 13...♘a5 14 ♗xh7+!? ♔xh7 15 ♘g5+ ♔g8 16 ♕d3 ♖fe8 (16...♖fc8 17 ♕h7+ ♔f8 18 f5! exf5 19 ♕h8+ ♔e7 20 ♕xg7 ±) 17 ♕h7+ ♔f8 18 ♕h8+ (after 18 ♘ce4 dxe4 19 ♘xe4 ♕c6! 20 ♖d6 ♕b5 21 ♕h8+ ♔e7 22 ♕h4+ ♔f8 White had to content himself with a repetition by 23 ♕h8+ ♔e7 24 ♕h4+ ♔f8 in Glek-Morozevich, St Petersburg 1998) 18...♔e7 19 ♕xg7 (19 ♕h4!? ♖h8! 20 ♘h7+ ♔e8 21 ♘f6+ gxf6 22 ♕xh8+ ♕f8 23 ♕xf6

♘ac4 24 ♖d3 ♕b4 25 b3 ± Grabics-Matveeva, Istanbul wom OL 2000) 19...♔d8 20 ♘xf7+ ♔c7 21 ♘d6 ♘ac4 22 ♘cb5+! ♔b8 23 ♘xc4 ♕xc4 24 ♘d6 and White is better according to Finkel.

14 ♘b5 (D)

Again 14 ♗xh7+ ♔xh7 15 ♘g5+ ♔g8 16 ♕d3 ♖fe8 17 ♕h7+ ♔f8 must be carefully checked:

a) 18 ♘ge4 dxe4 19 ♘xe4 ♕b4 20 ♕h8+ ♔e7 21 ♕h4+ is just a draw.

b) 18 ♕h8+ ♔e7 19 ♕h4 (19 ♕xg7 ♔d8 20 ♘xf7+ ♔c7 21 ♘d6 ♖g8 makes a significant difference compared to *13...♘a5*, since Black's king can now escape via b8) 19...♖h8 20 ♘h7+ ♔e8 21 ♘f6+ gxf6 22 ♕xh8+ ♕f8 23 ♕xf6 ♘c4 24 a3 with an unclear position.

c) 18 ♕h5 ♔e7 19 ♘xf7 ♘a5! 20 ♘d6 ½-½ Sax-Timman, Rotterdam 1989. Now Timman gives 20...♔d8 21 f5! exf5 22 ♘xe8 ♗xe8 23 ♕xf5 with an unclear position.

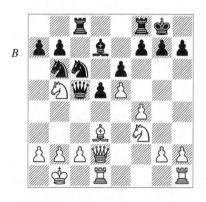

14...f6!

This is the reason why Black should put his queen's rook on c8.

15 exf6 ♖xf6 16 ♘bd4 ♘xd4 17 ♘xd4 ♘a4 18 ♘b3 ♕c7!

An improvement over Z.Almasi-Sermek, Mitropa Cup (Bükfürdo) 1995, in which White obtained an advantage after 18...♕b6 19 ♖he1 ♗b5 20 ♗xb5 ♕xb5 21 ♖e5.

19 g3 e5 20 fxe5 ♕xe5 21 ♕c1 ♖f2

Naiditsch-Blauert, Budapest 1998. Black has active piece-play to compensate for his structural inferiority.

B)

7...a6 *(D)*

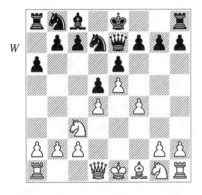

This has become a more popular way of playing the Classical Variation. Black postpones castling in return for an immediate advance on the queenside. This cuts out White's perhaps most dangerous set-up with an early ♗d3.

8 ♘f3

This is the most natural but Black should be aware of a couple of alternatives:

a) 8 ♕h5!? c5 9 ♘f3 ♘c6 10 0-0-0 cxd4 11 ♘xd4 ♘xd4 12 ♖xd4 ♘b6 (12...b5 13 f5!? gives White an attack) 13 ♗d3 g6 14 ♕g5 ♕xg5 15 fxg5 ♘d7 16 ♖e1 b6 17 ♘d1 h5 = Sariego-Moskalenko, Cienfuegos 1989.

b) 8 ♕g4 g6 (safest; 8...0-0 9 ♗d3 f5 10 exf6 ♕xf6 11 ♘f3 c5 12 ♘g5 is unclear according to Hjartarson but Black appears to be in some danger) 9 ♘f3 c5 10 dxc5 ♘c6 11 0-0-0 ♘xc5 12 h4 h5 13 ♕g5 b5 14 ♗d3 b4 15 ♘e2 ♗d7 with roughly equal chances, Batričević-Kalezić, Tivat 2000.

8...c5

8...b6 is a set-up Ulybin has experimented with. It looks slightly passive but Black doesn't want to give White access to the d4-square. Now the critical line is 9 ♕d2 c5 10 ♘d1!? ♘c6 11 c3 f5!?, as in Khalifman-Ulybin, Russian Ch (Elista) 1995. Black's position is very solid but White ought to be a bit better. The game continued 12 ♘e3 ♗b7 13 ♗d3 g6 14 h3 h5, and now Curt Hansen suggests 15 g3!?, intending ♔f2, maybe followed by a3 and slowly preparing g4.

9 dxc5

White has also tried to delay this with 9 ♕d2 ♘c6 10 0-0-0 but this doesn't seem advisable, in view of 10...c4! 11 f5 ♘b6! 12 fxe6 ♖xe6!? 13 ♗e2 (Pelletier thinks White should play 13 ♘g5 but Black seems fine anyway) 13...h6 14 ♖df1, Pelletier-Züger, Swiss Ch (Pontresina) 2000, and now Pelletier suggests 14...♘d7! followed by ...b5 with a strong attack for Black.

9...♘c6 10 ♕d2 *(D)*

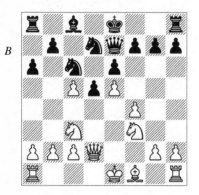

Here Black has two options:
B1: 10...♘xc5   118
B2: 10...♕xc5   119

B1)
10...♘xc5

This is considered slightly inferior to the queen capture since it becomes easier for White to gain control of d4. It has its pluses too, though, since often the knight goes to e4 and in combination with ...f6 creates counterplay.

11 0-0-0

The alternative is 11 ♗d3:

a) 11...0-0 is feasible since with the knight on c5 Black need not fear a ♗xh7+ sacrifice, but after 12 0-0 f6 13 exf6 ♕xf6 14 g3 White is practically a tempo up on Line A31 since Black has wasted time on ...a6. After 14...♗d7 15 ♖ae1 ♗e8 16 ♘e5 ♖c8 17 ♖f2 White was slightly better in Stefansson-Hjartarson, Reykjavik 1995.

b) 11...b5 12 0-0 ♗b7 13 ♖ae1 b4 14 ♘e2 0-0 15 ♘ed4 ♘xd4 16 ♘xd4

♘e4 17 ♕e3 f6! with counterplay in the game Messing-Kovačević, Croatian Cht (Tučepi) 1996.

c) 11...♗d7 12 0-0-0 b5 13 ♕e3 b4 14 ♘e2 a5 15 ♔b1 a4 16 ♘ed4 ♘xd4 17 ♘xd4 0-0 18 ♖he1 ♖fb8 gave both sides chances in Vujosević-Miljanić, Tivat 1997. White usually prepares f5, and Black has anticipated this by developing his bishop to d7 as opposed to a6. When White plays f5, Black would now capture on d3. Normally, White would like to recapture with the pawn but if White has already played f5, this won't be possible, and he would have to take back with the queen

11...b5 *(D)*

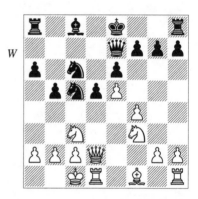

12 ♕e3!? b4 13 ♘e2 0-0 14 ♔b1

The alternative 14 g4 ♗b7 15 ♖g1 ♘e4 16 ♘g3 f6! led to a complicated position in the game Rogers-Soffer, Biel 1990.

14...♖b8

This move looks rather pointless. I would prefer to play the immediate 14...a5.

15 ♘ed4 ♘xd4 16 ♘xd4 ♗d7 17 ♗d3 a5 18 ♖hf1

Lutz-J.Pedersen, St Vincent Ech 2000. A position typical of the Classical French has arisen, which is probably somewhere between equal and slightly better for White. Black now committed the error of capturing prematurely on d3, which allowed White to recapture with the pawn, with a promising knight vs bad bishop scenario.

B2)
10...♕xc5 *(D)*

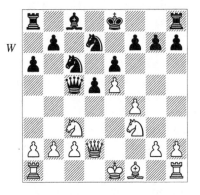

This is Short's preference. The queen is deployed actively and the d7-knight may come via b6 to c4 or a4, or support an ...f6 break. White has two plans. He can aim for a direct kingside attack, often initiated with h4-h5 and ♖h3 but prefaced by 0-0-0. Alternatively, White might attempt to gain control of the d4-square with a ♘e2-d4 manoeuvre.

11 ♗d3
11 0-0-0 is another option:

a) 11...b5 12 ♘e2!? 0-0 13 ♘ed4 ♗b7 14 h4 ♘xd4 15 ♘xd4 b4 16 ♖h3 ♖ae8!? 17 ♖e3 ♕b6 18 ♔b1 f6 with counterplay for Black, King-Short, British League (4NCL) 2000/1.

b) 11...♘b6!? 12 h4 ♗d7 13 ♖h3 h6 14 ♖g3 ♖g8 15 h5 0-0-0 16 ♔b1 f6! with approximately equal chances, Gi.Hernandez-Short, Merida 2001.

11...b5 *(D)*

In this case, 11...♘b6 is probably not the best idea: 12 a3 ♗d7 13 b4! ♕e7 14 ♕f2 ♕d8 15 0-0 ♘e7 16 ♘e2 ♕c7 17 ♘ed4 with a significant advantage for White, Palac-Kovačević, Belišče 1999. Black must often be wary of the 'anti-positional' b4 idea, which gains space for White on the queenside, and usually makes it easier to clamp down on the d4-square.

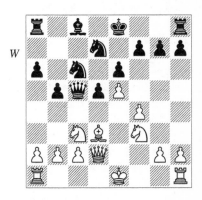

12 0-0-0

This is a normal continuation but it is far from certain that it is best. Maybe White is committing his king prematurely. There are three alternatives, all aiming for control of d4:

a) 12 ♕f2 is a common 'blunder' but incidentally White obtains quite reasonable compensation:

a1) After 12...♕b4 Black wins a pawn, but 13 0-0 ♕xf4 14 ♘e2 ♕h6 15 ♘ed4!? ♘xd4 16 ♘xd4 0-0 17 ♖ae1 ♗b7 18 ♖e3 g6 19 ♕g3 gave White good compensation in Antoniewski-M.Babula, Trinec 1998.

a2) Black can simply play 12...♗b7 13 ♕xc5 (13 a3 – *12 a3 ♗b7 13 ♕f2*) 13...♘xc5 14 ♘e2 d4!? 15 ♘exd4 ♘xd4 16 ♘xd4 0-0-0 ∓ Ståhlberg-Alekhine, Warsaw OL 1935.

b) 12 a3 ♗b7 13 ♕f2 h6!? 14 h4 0-0 15 ♕xc5 ♘xc5 16 b4 ♘d7 17 ♔d2 ♘b6 with roughly equal chances, Bologan-Short, Buenos Aires 2000.

c) 12 ♘e2!? ♘b6 13 b3! ♗d7 14 a3!? f6 15 ♘ed4 ♘xd4 16 ♘xd4 fxe5 17 fxe5 0-0 18 ♕b4! ± Tal-Lahav, Tel-Aviv 1990.

12...♘b6

Or:

a) It is worth noting that 12...0-0? is a disastrous mistake, as in Chandler-Agnos, London Lloyds Bank 1989: 13 ♗xh7+! ♔xh7 14 ♘g5+ ♔g8 15 ♕d3 ♖e8 16 ♕h7+ ♔f8 17 ♕h5! ♘d8 (or 17...g6 18 ♕h8+ ♔e7 19 ♕h4 +−) 18 ♘h7+ ♔g8 19 ♖d3 ♕e7 20 ♖h3 f6 21 ♘xf6+ ♘xf6 22 exf6 1-0.

b) A popular alternative plan is 12...b4 13 ♘e2 a5, intending ...♗a6.

13 h4 b4 14 ♘e2 ♗d7 *(D)*

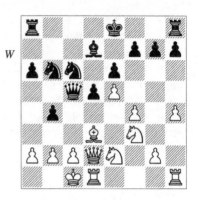

I like Black's attacking concept. It is straightforward and simple as long as you know what to do: don't castle; just keep going on the queenside.

15 ♔b1 h6 16 ♘g3

This looks sensible. White supports an f5 break and has ideas of jumping further to h5. However, it also removes a defender of the queenside. 16 ♘c1 might be better.

16...♘a4 17 ♔a1

17 f5 ♘c3+ 18 bxc3 bxc3 19 ♕c1 ♖b8+ 20 ♔a1 ♕a5 is too dangerous for White.

17...♘c3

Black has a strong attack and after 18 ♖de1 ♕a5 19 a3 ♖b8!? 20 f5 ♘b5 21 ♗xb5 ♖xb5, Black was much better in Savanović-Raičević, Yugoslav Cht (Nikšić) 1996.

10 Chatard-Alekhine Attack

**1 e4 e6 2 d4 d5 3 ♘c3 ♘f6 4 ♗g5 ♗e7
5 e5 ♘fd7 6 h4** *(D)*

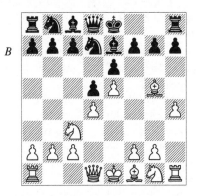

The move 6 h4 was first suggested and analysed by the French player Chatard, but only became well-known after the famous game Alekhine-Fahrni, Mannheim 1914. Hence the name of the line.

These days, 6 h4 remains a serious weapon but most experts consider that if Black has prepared accurately, he should have few problems reaching equality.

We look at four main lines for Black:

A:	**6...0-0**	122
B:	**6...a6**	124
C:	**6...c5**	127
D:	**6...♗xg5**	130

Some minor options are:

a) 6...h6 7 ♗e3 (7 ♕h5!?) 7...c5 8 ♕g4 g6 9 ♘f3 ♘c6 10 dxc5 ♘xc5 11 0-0-0 a6 12 ♗xc5!? ♗xc5 13 ♘e4 ♗e7 14 ♕f4 ± Hellers-Bareev, Gausdal 1986.

b) 6...f6 7 ♕h5+ ♔f8 8 exf6 ♘xf6 9 ♕e2 c5 10 dxc5 b6!? (10...♘a6 11 ♘f3 ♘xc5 12 0-0-0 b5 13 ♕e3! b4 14 ♘b5 ♗d7 15 ♘e5 ♗e8 16 ♘d4 ♕b6 17 ♗d3 ♖c8 18 ♖he1 a5 19 ♘g4! ± Vitomskis-Carleton, corr. 1996) 11 c6 ♘xc6 12 ♘f3 ♔f7 13 ♗f4 ± Stefansson-Bricard, Reykjavik 1993.

c) 6...♘c6!? and now:

c1) 7 ♗xe7 ♕xe7 8 a3 ♘b6 9 f4 ♗d7 10 ♕d2 0-0-0 11 ♘f3 ♔b8 12 h5 h6 13 ♘d1 f6 14 ♘f2 fxe5 15 fxe5 ♖hf8 was fine for Black in Nataf-Morozevich, Istanbul OL 2000. Black's idea needs more tests. Personally, I don't like the voluntary exchange on e7, even though White can rightfully claim that the c6-knight obstructs the c-pawn. However, it is not clear what is a useful move for White...

c2) On 7 ♘f3 Black has a better version of the *6...f6* line with 7...f6.

c3) If 7 ♗b5, then 7...♗xg5 8 hxg5 ♕xg5 is better for Black than the immediate *6...♗xg5*.

c4) Maybe 7 ♘h3 is an idea.

A)

6...0-0 *(D)*

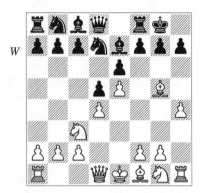

This should perhaps be taken more seriously than it used to be, if only because the renowned French expert and world-class player Mikhail Gurevich has played it in a couple of games. Black daringly castles into a dangerous attack but also prepares to counter with ...c5 without having to worry about ♘b5.

7 ♗d3

A safe line for White is 7 ♕g4 f5 (7...c5?! 8 ♗h6 g6 9 h5!? is too dangerous for Black; e.g., 9...cxd4 10 hxg6 fxg6 11 ♕xe6+ ♖f7 12 ♘xd5 – M.Gurevich) 8 ♗xe7 ♕xe7 9 ♕g5!. Then:

a) 9...♕b4 10 0-0-0 c5 11 ♕e7 and now:

a1) M.Gurevich suggests 11...♘b6!?, but I think White retains an advantage: 12 a3 ♕a5 13 ♕xc5 ♕xc5 14 dxc5 ♘6d7 15 ♘b5!?. Now both 15...♘c6 16 ♘c7 ♖b8 17 ♘xe6 ♖e8 18 ♘c7 ♖xe5 19 ♘f3 ± and 15...♘a6 16 ♘f3

♘axc5 17 ♘c7 ♖b8 18 b4 ♘e4 19 ♘xe6 ♘xf2 20 ♘xf8 ♘xf8 21 ♗d3 ± look good for White.

a2) 11...♕b6 12 ♘a4 ♕c6 13 ♘xc5 ♘xc5 14 ♕xc5 ♕xc5 15 dxc5 ♘d7 16 ♘f3 (M.Gurevich also considers 16 c4 ♘xc5 17 cxd5 exd5 18 ♖xd5 ♘e4, when Black has counterplay) 16...♘xc5 17 ♗d3 ♘e4 18 ♖hf1 ♗d7 19 ♘d4 ♖ac8 20 f3 ♘c5 21 b3 ± Hebden-M.Gurevich, British League (4NCL) 1997/8.

b) 9...♕xg5 10 hxg5 looks like a better choice for Black, although rather uninspiring:

b1) 10...c5 11 ♘b5 ♘c6 12 0-0-0 (this is given by M.Gurevich, but I would prefer 12 c3!, with a solid edge for White) 12...cxd4 13 f4 (13 ♘xd4 ♘dxe5) 13...♘c5 14 ♘f3 ♘e4 looks fine for Black.

b2) 10...a6! 11 ♘ce2 g6 (not really necessary; 11...c5 looks fine) 12 ♘f4 ♖e8 13 ♘f3 c5 14 c3 ♘c6, Brod-Beck, Austrian Cht 1995. Black seems to have reasonable chances of holding the position as the kingside can always be reinforced by ...♘f8.

7...c5

A new attempt by Black. 7...f5 has been more common but does not enjoy a good reputation. White has usually just left it as it is and aimed for a g4 thrust, with or without preparation:

a) 8 g4 c5 9 gxf5 cxd4 10 f6 ♗xf6! (10...♘xf6? 11 exf6 ♗xf6 12 ♕h5 g6 13 ♗xg6 ♕e7 14 ♘b5! ♘c6 15 ♗d3 e5 16 ♘e2 ♔h8 17 ♘c7 ♕xc7 18 ♗xf6+ 1-0 Sax-Donner, Amsterdam

1976) 11 exf6 ♘xf6 is unclear according to Sax.

b) 8 ♘h3! is better, heading for f4. 8...♘c6 9 ♘e2 (9 ♗b5!?) 9...♘b4 10 ♘ef4 ♘xd3+ 11 ♕xd3 ♘b6 12 0-0-0 ♗d7 (12...c5 13 dxc5 ♘c4 14 ♔b1! ♘xe5 15 ♕e2 ♗f6 16 ♘h5 ♗xg5 17 hxg5 ♘c4 18 ♘3f4 ± Zeziulkin) 13 ♖hg1!? ♘c4 14 g4 (14 ♔b1!?, with the point 14...c5 15 dxc5! ♘xe5 16 ♕e2 {Zeziulkin}, also looks good) 14...c5 15 dxc5!? ♕a5! 16 ♔b1 ± Zeziulkin-Lempert, Czestochowa 1991.

We now return to 7...c5 (D):

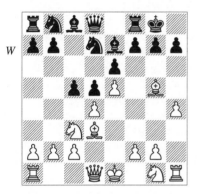

8 ♕h5!?

This is an extremely dangerous idea. Instead, 8 ♘h3 g6! (and not 8...cxd4? 9 ♗xe7 ♕xe7 10 ♗xh7+! ♔xh7 11 ♕h5+ ♔g8 12 ♘g5 +−) 9 f4 cxd4 10 ♘e2!? ♕a5+ 11 ♕d2 ♕xd2+ 12 ♔xd2 ♗b4+ 13 ♔d1 f6 gives Black excellent counterplay, Relange-M.Gurevich, Belfort 1997.

8...g6 9 ♕h6 cxd4

9...♘c6 10 ♗xe7 ♕xe7 11 h5 ♘b4 12 ♘f3 looks good for White.

10 ♘f3!

10 f4 is certainly inventive. Only with careful play can Black survive:

a) 10...dxc3 11 ♘f3 (11 h5? ♗xg5 12 fxg5 cxb2 13 ♖b1 ♕e7 −+) 11...cxb2 12 ♖b1 and now:

a1) 12...♖e8? 13 h5 ♕a5+ (13...♘f8 14 hxg6 fxg6 15 ♗xg6 +−) 14 ♔e2 ♗f8 15 ♕xh7+!! ♔xh7 16 hxg6++ ♔g8 17 ♖h8+!! ♔xh8 18 gxf7 +−. This line may not be that relevant but it was a pleasure to work out!

a2) 12...f6!? 13 h5 and at this point 13...fxg5? 14 hxg6 ♗b4+ 15 ♔e2 ♕e7 16 g7! ♕xg7 17 ♕xe6+ ♔h8 18 ♗xh7 gives White an irresistible attack, but 13...♖f7! appears to defend.

a3) Black's safest course is to play 12...♘xe5! 13 fxe5 – 10...♘xe5! 11 fxe5 dxc3 12 ♘f3 cxb2 13 ♖b1 =.

b) 10...♘xe5! 11 fxe5 dxc3 12 ♘f3 cxb2 13 ♖b1 f5! (13...♕c7 14 ♗xe7 ♕xe7 15 h5 ♘c6 16 hxg6 fxg6 17 ♗xg6 hxg6 18 ♕h8+ ♔f7 19 ♖h7+ ♔e8 20 ♖xe7+ ♘xe7 may be defensible for Black) 14 h5 (14 exf6 ♗xf6 15 ♗xf6 ♕xf6 16 h5 ♕g7 and Black defends) 14...♗xg5 (14...♗b4+ 15 ♔d1 ♕e8 16 ♗f6 ♖xf6 17 exf6 ♗f8 18 hxg6 ♕xg6 19 ♕xg6+ hxg6 20 ♘g5 ♘d7 21 f7+ ♔g7 22 ♘xe6+ ♔xf7 23 ♘xf8 ±) 15 ♘xg5 ♕e7! 16 hxg6 ♕b4+ 17 ♔f2 ♕f4+ 18 ♔g1 ♕e3+ 19 ♔f1 ♕f4+ with a perpetual check.

10...♘xe5!?

Not 10...dxc3? 11 h5! cxb2 12 ♖b1 ♗b4+ 13 ♔d1 f6 14 hxg6 +− Knaak.

11 ♘xe5 dxc3

Now White can try:

a) 12 ♘xg6 fxg6 13 ♗xg6 hxg6 14 ♕xg6+ ♔h8 and Knaak thinks White should be content with a perpetual. Perhaps it is possible to play for more; e.g., 15 ♖h3!? cxb2 16 ♖b1 ♗b4+ 17 c3 ♕c7 18 ♗f6+ ♖xf6 19 ♕xf6+ ♕g7 (19...♔h7!?) 20 ♕xg7+ ♔xg7 21 cxb4 and the endgame shouldn't be worse for White.

b) 12 ♖h3!? looks much more dangerous; e.g., 12...cxb2 13 ♖b1 ♕c7 14 ♗xe7 ♕xe5+ (14...♕xe7 15 h5 f6 16 hxg6 fxe5 17 g7! ♕b4+ 18 ♔d1 ♕g4+ 19 f3 ♕xg7 20 ♖g3 ♖f7 21 ♕xh7+ ♔f8 22 ♖xg7 ♖xg7 23 ♕h8+ ♖g8 24 ♕f6+ wins for White) 15 ♖e3 ♕c3+ 16 ♔f1 ♕g7 17 ♗xf8 ♔xf8 18 ♕f4 and I would prefer White's attacking chances.

B)

6...a6 (D)

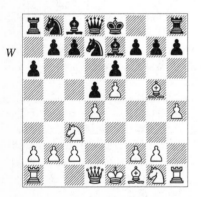

With this Black prepares ...c5 by first preventing a ♘b5 sortie. However, with White already showing his attacking tendencies on the kingside,

this is, in my opinion, a luxury Black can hardly afford.

7 ♕g4! ♗xg5

This is regarded as Black's best. The g-file is now blocked but instead the h-file is opened, and h7 becomes a serious weakness. Other moves are:

a) 7...h5 8 ♕g3 ♗xg5 9 hxg5 g6 10 0-0-0 b5 11 ♕e3 ♖g8 12 f4 ± Rõt-šagov-Bykhovsky, Cappelle la Grande 1993.

b) 7...f5 8 ♕h5+! g6 9 ♕h6 ♗xg5 10 hxg5 ♔f7 11 ♘ge2 ♘f8 12 0-0-0 ♖g8 13 g4 ± Yanofsky-Gudmundsson, Reykjavik 1947.

c) 7...♔f8 8 ♘f3 c5 9 dxc5 ♘c6 10 ♕f4 ♘xc5 11 0-0-0 b5 12 ♖h3 ♗d7 13 ♔b1 b4 14 ♘e2 ♘e4 15 ♗xe7+ ♕xe7 16 ♘g5 ♘c5 17 h5 h6 18 ♘f3 ♘e4 19 ♕e3 a5 20 ♘g3 ♘c5 21 ♘d4 ± Djurhuus-Minero Pineda, Santiago jr Wch 1990.

8 hxg5 c5

Other moves are simply too slow. Black must seek counterplay before White completes his development, after which White's h-file play and spatial plus will prevail.

9 ♘f3!

Otherwise:

a) 9 dxc5!? ♘xe5 10 ♕g3 ♘bc6 11 0-0-0 is dangerous for Black. Black must reckon with f4-f5 and various sacrifices on d5 which could favourably open the e-file for White:

a1) 11...♕a5 12 f4 ♘g6 13 f5 is good for White.

a2) Black should prophylactically retreat the knight first: 11...♘g6. Now:

a21) In the event of 12 f4, Black has 12...♕c7 13 ♘ge2 ♘ce7 with a solid position.

a22) 12 ♘f3 is hardly dangerous either. Black can then safely continue 12...♕a5 as there is now no real danger in the centre.

a23) That leaves 12 ♘e4, but I think 12...♕a5 13 ♘d6+ ♔e7 is actually more dangerous for White than it is for Black.

b) 9 g6 is a common lever but the timing is premature. With 9...f5! *(D)* Black obtains a good game:

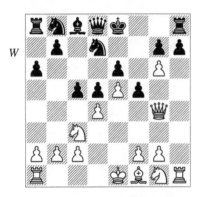

b1) 10 exf6 ♘xf6 11 ♖xh7 and now 11...♘xh7? 12 gxh7 ♔f8 13 ♗d3! is probably winning for White, Murei-Gruzmann, Moscow 1965. The h7-pawn shuts in the h8-rook and White is already threatening the decisive ♘f3-h4/e5-g6+. However, 11...♖f8! turns the evaluation in Black's favour. The queen must step aside, which allows ...cxd4 or ...♘xh7.

b2) 10 ♕f4 cxd4! (this move is far stronger than 10...h6 11 dxc5 0-0 12 0-0-0!, when White contemplates various sacrifices on d5 and h6) 11 ♖xh7 ♖g8 12 ♘ce2 ♕a5+ 13 ♔d1 ♘f8! 14 ♘xd4 (14 ♖h3 ♘c6 15 ♕g3 ♕b4! ∓) 14...♘xh7 15 gxh7 ♖h8 16 ♕g5 ♕c7 ∓.

b3) 10 ♕g3 and now:

b31) 10...h6 is the most common, but allows White an advantage; e.g., 11 ♘f3 0-0 12 0-0-0 ♘c6 13 ♘e2 cxd4 14 ♘exd4 ± Khalifman-M.Gurevich, Moscow 1987.

b32) 10...cxd4!? is stronger:

b321) 11 ♖xh7 ♖g8 12 ♘ce2 ♕a5+ 13 ♔d1 ♘c6 14 f4 (14 ♘f3 looks better; although the text-move is a better reinforcement of the e5-pawn, I think White should instead rely on rapid piece activity) 14...♕b4 (14...♘c5!?) 15 b3 ♘f8 (Kraft-Schmittdiel, Geneva 1997) 16 ♖h3 ♗d7 17 ♘f3 ♕a3 gives Black good counterplay.

b322) 11 gxh7 is perhaps more critical, and demands very accurate play from Black:

b3221) 11...dxc3? 12 ♕xg7 cxb2 13 ♕xh8+ ♔f7 14 ♕xd8 bxa1♕+ 15 ♔d2 ♕d4+ 16 ♗d3 +−.

b3222) 11...♕e7 12 ♘ce2 g5!? (12...♘c6 13 ♘f3 ♕b4+ 14 ♔d1 ±) 13 ♘f3 ♕b4+ (13...g4 14 ♘fxd4 ♘c6!? could also be possible) 14 ♔d1 g4 15 ♘fxd4 ♕xb2 16 ♖c1 ♘f8 17 f3 ♘c6 18 ♘xc6 bxc6 and Black seems fine. His king is relatively safe, while the h7-pawn will soon fall.

We now return to the position after 9 ♘f3 *(D)*:

9...♘c6

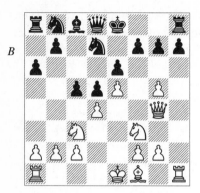

An important alternative is 9...cxd4 10 ♕xd4 ♘c6 11 ♕f4 (11 ♕a4!?). Now if White were allowed to finish his development in peace he would be much better, so the critical line runs 11...♕b6!? (11...♕c7 12 0-0-0 ♘dxe5 13 ♘xe5 ♕xe5 14 ♕xe5 ♘xe5 15 ♖e1) 12 0-0-0! (Gagarin mentions 12 ♖b1?! d4 13 ♘e4 ♘dxe5! 14 ♘d6+ ♔e7 15 ♘xe5 ♕a5+ 16 ♔d1 ♕xe5, when Black is much better) 12...♕xf2 13 ♖d2 (13 ♖xd5 exd5 14 ♘xd5 ♘dxe5) 13...♕c5 14 g6!? fxg6 15 ♗d3 but here White seems to have excellent compensation. For example:

a) Gagarin mentions 15...♘f8 16 ♘g5 ♕e7 17 ♖f2 h6 18 ♘f7 g5 19 ♘d6+ with compensation for White. This looks like quite an understatement, as White's attack appears decisive; e.g., 19...♔d8 20 ♕g3 ♘xe5 21 ♕xe5 ♘d7 22 ♕g3 ♖f8 23 ♖xf8+ ♕xf8 24 ♖f1 ♘f6 25 ♘a4 +–.

b) 15...♖f8 and then:

b1) 16 ♕g3 and now:

b11) 16...♕e3?! 17 ♖xh7 ♘dxe5?! 18 ♗xg6+ ♔d8 19 ♗e4! left White

with a probably decisive attack in Mirumian-Supatashvili, Ankara 1995.

b12) Instead 16...d4, with the point 17 ♘e4 ♕a5!, looks far from clear.

b2) I would prefer 16 ♕g5!. The idea is that after 16...♕e7 17 ♕g3 Black's queen is passive and h7 is still a problem for Black. Then 17...h6 18 ♗xg6+ ♔d8 19 ♖hd1 is good for White since Black's king is caught in the centre, and he has severe difficulties with the development of his bishop and a sacrifice on d5 is in the air.

We now return to the position after 9...♘c6 (D):

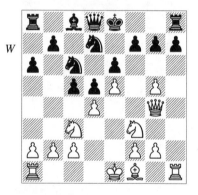

10 dxc5

10 g6!? f5 11 ♕g3 also looks good. The insertion of ♘f3 and ...♘c6 seems to White's advantage. Then:

a) 11...cxd4 12 gxh7! is good for White now that Black doesn't have the possibility of gaining space with ...g5.

b) 11...h6 12 ♘g5! and then:

b1) 12...♕e7 13 ♘f7 ♖f8 14 ♘e2! cxd4 15 0-0-0 ± Landa-Gleizerov, Bled 1990.

b2) 12...♘xd4 13 ♘f7 ♕a5 14 0-0-0!
(14 ♘xh8 ♘xc2+ 15 ♔d1 ♘xa1 16
♘f7 d4 17 ♘d6+ ♔d8 18 ♘c4 ♕b4 ∓)
14...♖g8 15 ♔b1 and White has excellent compensation. In Passos-Dutra
Neto, corr. 1993 White now obtained a
decisive attack, but in fact it is very
difficult for Black to improve: 15...b5
(this looks logical; if Black removes
the knight from d4, a sacrifice on d5 is
surely going to be lethal) 16 ♕h4 b4
17 ♖xd4!? cxd4? (this is definitely a
mistake; 17...bxc3 is better, when 18
♖a4 ♕c7 19 f4, intending to answer
19...♖b8 with 20 ♗xa6!, looks messy)
18 ♘xd5! (the point of the sacrifice;
the following play looks more or less
forced) 18...exd5 19 ♘d6+ ♔f8 20
♘xf5 ♘f6 21 exf6 ♗xf5 22 ♕f4
♗xc2+ 23 ♔xc2 ♖c8+ (23...b3+ 24
♔d1 +−) 24 ♔b1 ♕c7 25 fxg7+ ♔e8?
(this loses immediately, but 25...♔xg7
26 ♕xd4+! ♔xg6 27 ♗d3+ ♔f7 28
♕xd5+ ♔g7 29 ♕e6 should also be
pretty decisive) 26 ♗b5+! axb5 27
♖e1+ 1-0.

   **10...♘dxe5 11 ♘xe5 ♘xe5 12 ♕g3
♘g6 13 0-0-0 ♗d7**

13...♕e7!? might be better. Finkel
then gives 14 ♗d3!? (14 ♕e3 should
also be considered) 14...♕xc5 15 ♗xg6
fxg6 16 ♕e5 0-0 17 ♖d2!, when White
(who threatens ♕h2) has excellent
compensation.

   14 ♗d3 ♕b8 15 ♕e3 ♘e7

15...♕e5 16 ♘xd5! exd5 17 ♕xe5+
♘xe5 18 ♖de1 f6 19 gxf6 gxf6 20 f4
was more or less winning for White in
Hector-J.Hansen, Gausdal Z 1987.

   **16 ♗xh7 g6 17 ♗xg6! ♖xh1 18
♖xh1 ♘xg6 19 ♘xd5 ♗c6 20 ♘b6**

   ± Degraeve-M.Gurevich, Belfort
1997.

C)

6...c5!? *(D)*

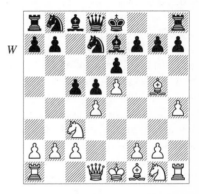

The most combative and the usual
choice of strong dynamic players like
GMs Ulybin and Gleizerov, both with
a life-long experience in the French.

7 ♗xe7

This simple exchange poses Black a
serious question: 'How to recapture?'.
If he takes back with the queen, White
can try ♘b5, and taking back with the
king isn't what Black really wants to
do.

We shall take a brief look at alternatives for White:

a) 7 ♕g4?! ♗xg5! 8 hxg5 (8 ♕xg5
♕xg5 9 hxg5 ♘c6 is at least fine for
Black) 8...cxd4 9 ♘b5?! (9 ♕xd4 ♘c6
10 ♕d2 ♘dxe5 11 f4 ♘g6 12 ♗d3
♘ce7 ∓) 9...♘xe5 10 ♕xd4 ♘bc6 ∓
Binder-Ripperger, St Ingbert 1994.

b) 7 ♘b5 is more testing but reacting actively with 7...f6! is good for Black. A few examples:

b1) 8 exf6 ♘xf6 9 ♘f3 ♘c6 10 ♗f4 0-0 11 ♗c7 ♕d7 12 ♘e5 ♘xe5 13 ♗xe5 a6 14 ♘c3 b5 15 a3 ♗d6 ∓ Ivanović-Miljanić, Nikšić 1991.

b2) 8 ♗d3 a6! (8...fxg5? 9 ♕h5+ ♔f8 10 hxg5 cxd4 11 g6 ♘c5 12 ♕f3+ ♔e8 13 ♘d6+ ♔d7 14 ♘f7 ♕a5+ 15 ♔f1 +−) 9 ♕h5+ ♔f8 10 ♖h3 (10 ♘h3? cxd4 11 ♘f4 ♘xe5 12 ♘xd4 ♕b6 −+ Ragozin-Yanofsky, Saltsjöbaden IZ 1948) 10...cxd4! leaves White with too many pieces hanging. Kapnisis-Ulybin, Ano Liosia 1997 finished shortly: 11 ♘f3?! (I suppose that 11 ♘xd4 is better but White is just a clear pawn down after 11...♘xe5) 11...axb5 12 ♗h6 ♕a5+ 13 ♗d2 (13 ♔f1 gxh6 14 ♕xh6+ ♔e8 15 ♗xh7 ♖f8 −+) 13...♗b4 0-1.

We now return to 7 ♗xe7 (D):

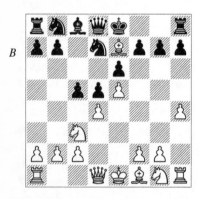

7...♔xe7

7...♕xe7 is obviously more natural but 8 ♘b5 is slightly annoying and almost forces Black to sacrifice the exchange. After 8...0-0 (8...♔d8?! 9 c3 ♘c6 10 ♘d6 a6 11 f4 f6 12 ♘f3 ± Dubois-Ruck Petit, France 1991) 9 ♘c7, we have:

a) 9...♘xe5 10 ♘xa8 cxd4 11 ♕xd4 ♘bc6 12 ♕d2 ♕d6 13 ♗e2 ♗d7 14 h5 f6 15 0-0-0 ♘f7 16 f4 ♖xa8 17 ♘f3 ± Khalifman-Levin, Riga 1988.

b) 9...♘c6 10 ♘xa8 cxd4 and now:

b1) 11 ♘c7 f6! can lead to entertaining play; e.g., 12 ♕d2 fxe5 13 ♘b5 a6 14 ♘a3 ♘f6 15 f3 e4 16 0-0-0 b5 and Black has counterplay, From-Hvenekilde, Copenhagen 1981.

b2) 11 ♘e2! is safer. Then 11...f6 12 ♘xd4 fxe5 (12...♘dxe5 13 ♗e2 ♘xd4 14 ♕xd4 ♘c6 15 ♕d2 ♕d6 16 0-0 ♗d7 17 c4 d4 18 b4! ♖xa8 19 c5 ± Zeziulkin-Maiorov, Krasnodar 1998) 13 ♘xe6! ♕b4+ 14 c3 ♕xb2 15 ♗e2 ♕xc3+ 16 ♔f1 ♖f6 17 ♘ac7 was winning for White in Moe-Hvenekilde, Aalborg 1965.

c) 9...cxd4 10 ♘xa8 and now:

c1) 10...♕b4+ 11 ♕d2 ♕xb2 12 ♖d1 ♘c6 13 ♘f3 ♘c5 14 ♗d3! ♗d7 (14...f6 15 exf6 ♖xf6 16 ♘c7 is also good for White) 15 ♘c7 ♖c8 (Christoffel-Guimard, Groningen 1946) 16 ♘xd5! exd5 17 0-0 is good for White; e.g., 17...♗g4 18 ♕g5!, with the point that 18...♗xf3 19 ♕f5! ♖e8?! (19...♗g4 20 ♕xg4 ♖e8 21 f4 ±) 20 ♕xh7+ ♔f8 21 ♖b1 ♕xa2 22 ♕h8+ ♔e7 23 ♕xg7 gives White a winning attack.

c2) 10...f6! 11 ♕xd4 ♘c6 12 ♕d2 fxe5 13 0-0-0 ♘f6 14 f3 ♕d6 15 h5 ♗d7 16 h6 g6 17 ♕g5 ♔f7 18 ♘e2

Ξxa8 19 ②c3 Ξc8 20 ♕xf6+ ♔xf6 21 ②e4+ dxe4 22 Ξxd6 ♗e7 23 Ξd2 exf3 ½-½ Sax-Bilek, Hungarian Ch (Budapest) 1973. I think White can still claim a slight advantage with 24 gxf3 ②d4 25 ♗g2; e.g., 25...②c6 26 Ξe1 ♔f6 27 f4! exf4 28 Ξxd4 ♗xg2 29 Ξxf4+ ♔g5 30 Ξf7 ♔xh6 31 Ξe2 ♗d5 32 Ξh2+ ♔g5 33 Ξfxh7 gives White a clearly better endgame. Admittedly, there is plenty of room for Black to improve earlier, and my feeling is that this line is dynamically equal.

We now return to the position after 7...♔xe7 *(D)*:

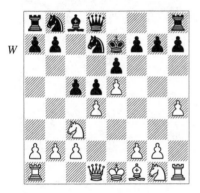

8 dxc5!?
The recent trend. Some other moves are worth noting:

a) 8 ♕d2 ②c6 9 ♕g5+ ♔f8 10 ♕xd8+ ②xd8 11 f4 b6! 12 ②f3 ②c6 13 0-0-0 ♔e7 = Situru-Hübner, Erevan OL 1996.

b) 8 ♕g4 and then:

b1) 8...♔f8 9 ②f3 cxd4 10 ②b5!? (the alternative 10 ♕xd4 ♕b6 11 ♕xb6 axb6! is fine for Black according to Psakhis) 10...②c6 11 ♕f4 ♕a5+ (or 11...f6 12 exf6 ♕xf6 13 ②c7 ②b6 14 ♕d6+ ♕e7 15 ♕xe7+ ♔xe7 16 ②xa8 ②xa8 17 ♗b5 ± Löffler-B.Schmidt, Baden-Baden 1987) 12 ♔d1 ♕b6 13 g4!? h6 (13...♔g8!?) 14 Ξg1 and the white attack looks promising, Loskutov-Chuprikov, Smolensk 2000.

b2) 8...②c6 9 dxc5 ②dxe5 10 ♕xg7 is complicated and leaves plenty of room for independent analysis. Here is something to inspire:

b21) 10...Ξg8 11 ♕xh7 ♗d7 12 0-0-0 ♕a5 13 ♕h6 Ξg6 14 ♕e3 ②g4 15 ♕e1 ♔f8 16 f3 ②f6 17 ②h3 ± Benjamin-Seirawan, USA Ch (Los Angeles) 1991.

b22) 10...♗d7!? 11 f4!? Ξg8 (this is better than 11...②g6 12 f5 ♕f8 13 f6+ ♔d8 14 ②f3 ±) 12 ♕xh7 Ξh8 13 ♕g7 Ξg8 14 ♕h6 ②g4 15 ♕h5 ②e3!? (15...②d4 16 0-0-0 ②f5 17 ②ge2 is also messy) 16 Ξc1 ♕a5 and Black has good compensation.

c) 8 f4 and then:

c1) 8...cxd4 9 ♕xd4 ♕b6 10 ♕xb6 ②xb6 11 h5 h6 12 ②f3 ♗d7 13 ②b5 ②c6 14 b3 a6 15 ②bd4 ②xd4 16 ②xd4 ②c8! 17 ♔d2 ②a7 and White retains an advantage, Nunn-Seirawan, Cannes tt rpd 1992.

c2) 8...♕b6 and then:

c21) 9 ②f3!? ♕xb2 10 ②b5 a6 11 Ξb1 ♕xa2 12 ②d6 (of course White can force a repetition with 12 Ξa1 ♕b2 13 Ξb1, as occurred in Maksimović-Ulybin, Cheliabinsk 1990) 12...♕a5+ 13 ♔f2 ②c6 14 Ξh3!? cxd4 15 ♗d3 was unclear in Matulović-Zaradić, Zagreb

1955. In practice White can expect some compensation, but objectively it may not be entirely correct.

c22) 9 ♘a4 (safer) 9...♕a5+ (9...♕c6 10 ♘xc5 ♘xc5 11 dxc5 ♕xc5 12 ♕d2 ♘c6 13 ♘f3 ♗d7 14 h5 h6 15 0-0-0 ♖ac8 16 ♔b1 ± Velimirović-Miljanić, Yugoslav Cht (Cetinje) 1992) 10 c3 b6. This is a thematic reaction, also in other classical lines. Depending on White's reply, Black will now prepare to exchange his bad bishop with ...♗a6:

c221) 11 a3 c4 12 b4 cxb3 13 ♕xb3 ♗a6 14 ♗xa6 ♘xa6 15 ♘e2 ♖hc8 was already pleasant for Black in A.Hunt-Sarkar, Witley 1999.

c222) 11 ♔f2 ♗a6 12 ♘f3 ♗xf1 13 ♖xf1 ♘c6 14 ♔g1 g6 15 b3 ♖ac8 16 a3 cxd4 17 cxd4 b5 18 ♘c5 ♘xc5 19 b4 ♕a4 20 bxc5 ♕xd1 21 ♖fxd1 ♖b8 ∓ Nataf-Ulybin, Stockholm 1999.

c223) 11 ♖h3 ♗a6 12 ♖b1 ♗xf1 13 ♔xf1 ♘c6 14 ♘e2 ±/=.

8...♘xe5 9 ♕e2 ♘bc6

9...♘ec6 10 0-0-0 ♔f8 11 f4 ♕e7 12 ♘f3 ♘d7 was Gormally-Summerscale, York 2000. Now White should play 13 ♔b1 or 13 h5 (e.g., 13...h6 14 g4 with some compensation), waiting to see how Black captures on c5.

10 0-0-0 ♔f8 11 f4 ♘d7 12 ♘f3 ♘xc5 13 ♔b1 ♕a5!

13...b5!? 14 ♕e3! (14 ♕xb5 ♕b6 =) 14...♕b6 15 ♖xd5! exd5 16 ♘xd5 ♕d8 17 ♕xc5+ ♘e7 18 ♘c3! a6 19 ♗e2 gave White plenty of compensation in Sakaev-Ulybin, Dubai 2000. Black has difficulties activating his h8-rook.

14 ♕e3 ♘a4 15 ♘xa4 ♕xa4 16 ♗d3

This is all analysis by Sakaev, who now thinks that White obtains a useful initiative in the event of 16...♘b4 17 a3 ♘xd3 18 ♖xd3, and if 16...b6 17 c3 ♗a6 18 ♗c2 ♕c4, White has the choice between repeating the position with 19 ♗d3 ♕a4 20 ♗c2 and playing for more with 19 ♖he1!?.

D)

6...♗xg5 7 hxg5 ♕xg5 *(D)*

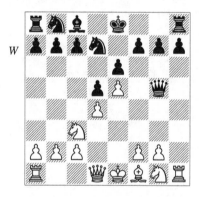

Black simply accepts the gambit; this is of course critical. Now:

D1: 8 ♘h3   131
D2: 8 ♕d3!?   133

Or:

a) 8 ♘f3 ♕e7 9 ♗d3 is too slow. Black should probably simply develop with 9...♘c6 10 ♕d2 ♘f8 followed by ...♗d7 and ...0-0-0.

b) 8 ♖h5 ♕e7 9 ♕g4 f5! 10 ♕h3 ♘f8 11 0-0-0 ♗d7 (the move-order is of importance; on 11...♘c6 White might try 12 &b5 &d7 13 &xc6! &xc6 14 &ge2 with reasonable compensation, although I am rather sceptical that it suffices for a real advantage) 12 g4 fxg4 13 ♕xg4 ♘c6 14 ♖g5 (now on 14 &b5 Black can avoid the exchange of the knight with 14...♘a5) 14...♖g8 15 ♘ge2 0-0-0, and White's compensation is not quite sufficient, Velimirović-Kovačević, Yugoslav Cht 1989.

D1)

8 ♘h3

The knight manoeuvre to f4 in conjunction with ♕g4 used to be the standard procedure in this line but White has had trouble showing real compensation against accurate defence.

8...♕e7 *(D)*

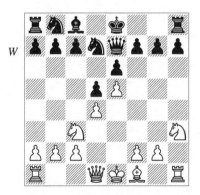

9 ♘f4

Or 9 ♕g4, and then:

a) 9...g6 10 ♘g5 h5 11 ♕f4 ♘c6 12 0-0-0 ♘b6 13 g4 &d7 14 gxh5 gxh5 15 &e2 ± Iskov-Rosell, Esbjerg 1972.

b) 9...f5!? 10 ♕g3 (10 exf6 needs to be investigated further; 10...♘xf6

11 ♕g3 ♘c6 12 0-0-0 a6 13 ♘g5 ♕d6 14 f4 &d7 15 &d3 gave White an edge in Asanov-Hernando Rodrigo, Santa Clara 1999) 10...♘f8!? 11 &e2 c6 12 0-0-0 ♘bd7 gave a solid impression in Skripchenko-Matveeva, Yugoslav wom Cht (Vrnjačka Banja) 1999.

9...♘c6

Or:

a) 9...♘f8? is of purely historical interest. The game Alekhine-Fahrni, Mannheim 1914, which served to popularize 6 h4!?, went 10 ♕g4 f5 11 exf6 gxf6 12 0-0-0 c6 13 ♖e1 ♔d8 14 ♖h6! e5 15 ♕h4 ♘bd7 16 &d3 e4 17 ♕g3! ♕f7 18 &xe4 dxe4 19 ♘xe4 ♖g8 20 ♕a3 ♕g7 21 ♘d6 ♘b6 22 ♘e8 ♕f7 23 ♕d6+ 1-0.

b) 9...a6 (to prepare ...c5) is feasible but slow.

c) The immediate 9...c5!? should be explored and is perhaps underestimated. The critical line runs 10 ♘b5 cxd4!, with two possibilities for White:

c1) 11 ♘d3 ♔d8 12 ♕g4 g6 13 ♘xd4 ♘c6 14 ♘f3 b6 15 ♕f4 &a6 16 0-0-0 ♔c7 was tenable for Black in Stefansson-Østenstad, Gausdal 1991.

c2) 11 ♘c7+ ♔d8 12 ♘xa8 ♕b4+ 13 ♔e2 (13 ♕d2 ♕xb2 14 ♖d1 ♘c6 gives Black good play as he will surely win the knight on a8) 13...♘xe5 14 ♘d3 ♘xd3 15 ♕xd3 ♕xb2 16 ♖d1 b6 with a complex position, Frolov-Matveeva, Russia Cup (Tomsk) 1998.

d) 9...g6 10 &d3! (this threatens &xg6, and is stronger than 10 ♕g4 ♘c6 – *9...♘c6 10 ♕g4 g6*) 10...♕g5 (10...♘c6 11 &xg6 fxg6 12 ♘xg6 hxg6 13 ♖xh8+ ♘f8 14 ♕g4 ♕g7 15 ♕h4 ♘e7 16 g4 ♗d7 17 0-0-0 ± Grabarczyk-Laptos, Bielsko-Biala 1991; 10...♘f8 11 ♘fxd5 exd5 12 ♘xd5 ♕d8 13 ♘f6+ ♔e7 14 ♕f3 c6 15 0-0-0 ♗e6 16 d5! cxd5 17 ♗e4 +− Ageichenko-Estrin, USSR 1967) 11 ♕d2 a6 12 ♗xg6! ♘xe5 (the alternative 12...fxg6 13 ♘xe6 ♕xd2+ 14 ♔xd2 is very good for White, Fressinet-Vallin, French Ch (Vichy) 2000) 13 ♖h5 ♘c4 14 ♖xg5 ♘xd2 15 ♗d3 ♘c4 16 ♘cxd5! exd5 17 ♘xd5 ♘b6 18 ♘xc7+ ♔f8 19 ♘xa8 ♘xa8 20 ♔d2, Velimirović-Stojanović, Yugoslav Ch (Podgorica) 1996. The ending is won for White. He already has rook and two pawns against two knights, which are both badly placed. Moreover, Black's kingside pawns are weak.

10 ♕g4 (D)

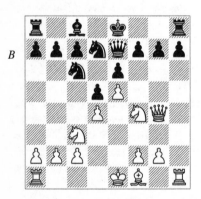

10...g6

This could also arise from the move-order *9...g6 10 ♕g4 ♘c6* but Black has avoided the dangerous possibility *10 ♗d3!*.

The alternative is 10...♘xd4 11 0-0-0 (if 11 ♕xg7, 11...♕f8 forces a relieving exchange of the queens, and Black is doing fine after 12 ♕xf8+ ♔xf8 13 0-0-0 c5) 11...♘f5 12 ♘fxd5 (12 ♘cxd5 exd5 13 ♕xf5? ♘e5! −+) 12...exd5 (12...♘xe5?! 13 ♕a4+ ♗d7 14 ♘xc7+ ♔f8 15 ♕e4 +− Garner-Harding, Dublin 1991) 13 ♘xd5, and now both captures on e5 should be examined:

a) 13...♘xe5?! 14 ♕e2! ♕d6 15 f4 ♘g3 (15...f6? 16 fxe5 fxe5 17 ♕h5+ g6 18 ♕g5 0-0 19 ♗c4 ♔g7 20 ♘f4 +−) 16 ♕e3! ♘xh1 17 fxe5 ♕d8 18 ♘f6+ gxf6 19 ♖xd8+ ♔xd8 20 ♕d4+ (20 ♕h6!?) 20...♔e8 21 ♗b5+ c6 22 exf6 ♗d7 23 ♗d3 ± Timmerman-Carleton, corr. 1992.

b) 13...♗xe5 14 ♗b5!? 0-0 15 ♗xd7 (15 f4!?) 15...♘h6!? (15...♗xd7 16 ♕h5! f6!? 17 ♘xf6+ ♕xf6 18 ♕xh7+ ♔f7 19 ♖xd7+ ♔e8 20 ♖xc7 gives White good compensation according to Gulko) 16 ♕g3!? (16 ♕h4!? is possible) 16...♘xg3 17 ♘e7+ ♔h8 18 fxg3 ♗xd7 19 ♖xd7 ± Khalifman-Gulko, Reykjavik 1991.

11 0-0-0

Now:

a) 11...♘b6 12 ♖h6 (12 ♗b5! ♗d7 13 ♗xc6! ♗xc6 14 ♖h6 poses Black some problems, Sax-Kovačević, Vinkovci 1983) 12...♗d7 13 ♗b5 ♘b4! (an excellent idea; the knight is much stronger than the bishop and hence Black doesn't allow ♗xc6) 14 ♗xd7+ ♘xd7 15 ♖dh1 ♘f8 16 a3 ♘a6 17 ♘b5 ♕d7 18 a4 ♘b4 19 ♘h5! (the only reasonable chance; after other moves White is just a pawn down) 19...gxh5 20 ♕g7 a6! 21 ♘c3 ♘g6 (21...c5!? 22 ♕xh8 cxd4 23 ♖h4! ♕e7 24 ♕f6 ♕xf6 25 ♖xf6 ♘c6 26 ♘e2 ♘xe5 27 ♘xd4 ♘fg6 28 ♖xh5 ♔e7 29 ♖xg6 ♘xg6 30 ♖xh7 ♔f6!? also looks fine for Black) 22 ♖xg6 ♖f8 23 ♖h6 c5 24 ♖h4 0-0-0 with counterplay, Loskutov-Iliushin, St Petersburg 2000.

b) 11...h5!? (this seems like a good idea) 12 ♕g3 ♘b6 13 ♗b5 ♗d7 14 ♘h3 ♘a5 15 ♘g5 ♗xb5 16 ♘xb5 a6 17 ♘c3 0-0-0 was fine for Black in Cifuentes-Agdestein, Tilburg 1993.

D2)
8 ♕d3!? *(D)*

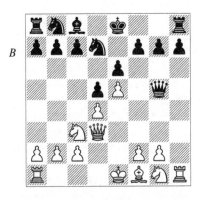

This is a relatively unexplored possibility for White and a speciality of GM Hector. All the same, I have chosen it as the main line due to White's failure to demonstrate anything impressive in the older lines. The idea of White's queen move is primarily to provoke a weakness on the kingside (...g6) and then to exert pressure on the dark squares.

8...g6
8...h5 9 ♘f3 ♕e7 10 g4 g6 (10...h4!?) 11 gxh5 gxh5 12 ♕e3 ♘b6 13 0-0-0 ♗d7 14 ♗e2 ♘c6 15 ♕f4! 0-0-0 16 ♖dg1! gave White fine compensation in Hector-Brynell, Gothenburg 1999. The weakness of the h-pawn and potential pressure against f7 fully compensate for the pawn.

9 ♘f3 ♕e7 10 ♕e3 ♘c6 11 0-0-0 ♘b6 12 ♖h6 ♗d7 13 ♕g5 ♕xg5+ 14 ♘xg5 ♔e7 15 ♘xh7 *(D)*

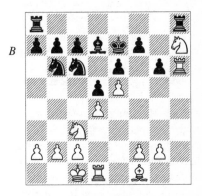

All of this is hardly forced but is very natural from both sides. White has a slight advantage. Black cannot really exploit the fact that it is difficult for White to get his knight back from h7, and indeed White has promising chances of taking control of the h-file. Hector-Brynell, Malmö 1993 went 15...♖ac8 16 f4 ♘b8 17 ♗d3 ♘a4 18 ♘xa4 ♗xa4 19 ♖dh1 c5 20 dxc5 ♖xc5 21 ♘g5 ±.

11 MacCutcheon Variation

1 e4 e6 2 d4 d5 3 ♘c3 ♘f6 4 ♗g5 ♗b4 *(D)*

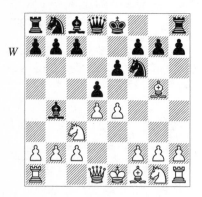

The MacCutcheon Variation is a sharp alternative to the Classical and Burn Variations. It is a strange blend between the Classical French and the Winawer. Structurally, it is closer to the type of positions arising from the Winawer. The MacCutcheon often leads to very sharp play and concrete knowledge is in most cases essential, especially some of the gambit lines such as 5 e5 h6 6 ♗e3 (or 6 ♗c1).

The lines we look at are:

A: 5 exd5 135
B: 5 e5 137

Black equalizes easily against other moves:

a) 5 ♗d3 dxe4 6 ♗xe4 ♘bd7 (6...h6 7 ♗xf6 ♕xf6 8 ♘f3 ♘d7 is also fine) 7 ♘e2 (7 ♗d3!? – Beliavsky) 7...h6 8 ♗xf6 ♘xf6 9 ♗f3 0-0 10 0-0 c6 = Romanishin-Beliavsky, Belgrade 1993.

b) 5 ♘e2 and now:

b1) 5...h6 6 ♗xf6 ♕xf6 7 a3 ♗a5 8 b4 ♗b6 9 e5 (9 exd5 0-0 gives Black excellent compensation) 9...♕e7 10 ♘a4 ♗d7 11 c3 0-0 12 ♘f4 ♗xa4 13 ♕xa4 ♘d7 14 ♗d3 a5 15 b5 ♖fc8 16 0-0 c5 17 bxc6 ♖xc6 = Kuijf-Rogulj, 2nd Bundesliga 1998/9.

b2) After 5...dxe4 6 a3 ♗e7, note the similarities to the Burn Variation. White has the extra move a3, which is not very important, but his knight is poorly placed on e2; it would normally go to f3. 7 ♗xf6 ♗xf6 (7...gxf6 8 ♘xe4 f5 9 ♘4c3 is comparable to *4...dxe4 5 ♘xe4 ♗e7 6 ♗xf6 gxf6*; here it is not that bad for White that the knight is on e2 as it fits in well with a g3 set-up, and a3 can be useful) 8 ♘xe4 0-0 (8...♗e7 9 ♘2c3 0-0 10 ♗c4 c6 11 0-0 ♘d7 = Friesen-Psakhis, Vlissingen 2000) 9 ♕d3 e5 (Black logically takes advantage of White not controlling e5) 10 ♕f3 ♘d7 11 0-0-0 (11 ♘xf6+ ♕xf6 12 ♕xf6 ♘xf6 13 dxe5 ♘g4 is just equal because 14 f4? ♖d8 gives Black a strong initiative)

11...exd4 12 ♘xf6+ ♘xf6 13 ♖xd4 ♕e7 14 h3 ♗d7 15 ♘g3 ♗c6 16 ♕d1 g6 = Zso.Polgar-M.Gurevich, Dutch Cht (Breda) 2000.

A)

5 exd5

This rather innocent-looking line is actually scoring quite well for White, so it must be taken seriously.

5...♕xd5 *(D)*

5...exd5 is a line of the Exchange Variation that White can be pleased with.

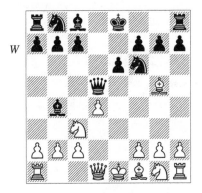

6 ♗xf6

Black equalizes easily after 6 ♘f3. One way is 6...♘e4! 7 ♗d2 ♗xc3 8 bxc3 ♘xd2 9 ♕xd2 and now either 9...♘d7 10 ♗d3 c5 =, as in Lasker – Znosko-Borovsky, St Petersburg 1909, or 9...b6 10 ♗d3 ♗a6!? 11 0-0 ♗xd3 12 cxd3 0-0 13 ♖fe1 c5, also with equal play, Mudelsee-Brynell, Berlin 1994.

6...♗xc3+

More accurate than 6...gxf6, after which White can avoid doubled pawns

by playing 7 ♘e2! with some chances of an edge:

a) 7...c5?! 8 a3! ♗xc3+ 9 ♘xc3 ♕xd4 10 ♕xd4 cxd4 11 ♘b5 ♘a6 12 ♘xd4 ♘c7 13 0-0-0 ♗d7 14 ♗d3 0-0-0 15 ♖he1 ± Chandler-Carton, Blackpool Z 1990.

b) 7...♘c6 and now:

b1) 8 a3 ♗xc3+ 9 ♘xc3 ♕xd4 10 ♕xd4 ♘xd4 11 0-0-0 c5! (11...♘c6 12 ♘b5 ±) 12 ♘e4 b6 13 c3 (13 ♘xf6+ ♔e7 14 ♘g4 ♗b7 15 c3 ♘f5 ∓) 13...♘b3+! (13...♘f5 14 g4! ♘h4 15 ♘xf6+ ♔e7 16 g5 h6 17 f4 ± Chandler-King, Hastings 1990/1) 14 ♔c2 ♘a5 15 b4 ♘b7 16 ♘xf6+ ♔e7 17 ♘e4 ♗d7 18 b5? f5 19 ♘g5 ♖hg8 20 ♘f3 ♘d6 ∓ Morozevich-Kovaliov, Moscow 1994.

b2) 8 ♕d2 ♗xc3 9 ♘xc3! (9 ♕xc3 ♗d7 10 ♕b3 ♕a5+ 11 c3 0-0-0 12 0-0-0 ♘e5!? 13 ♘g3 ♘g4 14 ♖d2 f5 15 ♗c4 ♘f6 16 ♖e1 h5 17 f3 b5 18 ♗d3 ♗c6 = Zeziulkin-Skrzypnik, Polanica Zdroj 2000) 9...♕xd4 10 ♕xd4 ♘xd4 11 0-0-0 c5 12 ♘e4 b6 13 c3 ±. Compared to 'b1' White can be content that a3 has not been played, as the option of ...♘b3+ as in Morozevich-Kovaliov is denied.

7 bxc3 gxf6 *(D)*

8 ♕d2

White stays flexible, keeping the options open of whether to develop with ♘f3, with g3 and ♗g2, with ♘e2 or with ♗e2-f3. Other moves:

a) 8 ♘f3 b6! is completely satisfactory for Black; e.g., 9 ♗e2 ♗b7 10 0-0 ♖g8 11 a4 ♘c6 12 ♕d3 0-0-0 13

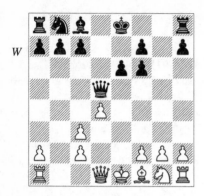

W

♖fb1 ♕h5 14 ♘e1 ♕g6 15 ♗f3 ♕xd3 16 cxd3 ♘a5 17 ♗xb7+ ♔xb7 ∓ Grigorov-Vaïsser, Cappelle la Grande 1993.

b) 8 ♕g4!? is much more dangerous, and may in fact give Black some problems equalizing:

b1) 8...♕g5 9 ♕xg5 fxg5 10 h4 g4 11 ♘e2 c5 12 ♘f4 is slightly better for White – Keres.

b2) 8...♔e7 9 ♗d3 ♘c6 10 ♘f3 e5 11 ♕e4 ♗e6 12 0-0 ♖ag8 13 ♖fe1 f5 14 ♕xd5 ♗xd5 15 ♘xe5! ♗xg2 16 f4! ♗e4+ 17 ♔f1 ± Van den Doel-Visser, Hoogeveen 1999.

b3) 8...♘d7 9 ♗d3 ♔f8 10 ♕f4!? also looks slightly awkward for Black. Turov-Glek, Korinthos 2000 saw a dramatic finish: 10...h5 11 ♕xc7 ♕xg2 12 0-0-0 ♕xh1 (12...♕xf2 13 ♘f3! ♔e8 14 ♖hf1 ♕e3+ 15 ♔b1 ±, intending to play ♖de1 followed by d5) 13 ♘e2 ♕c6? (13...♕f3 14 ♕d8+ ♔g7 15 ♖g1+ ♕g4 16 ♕c7 ±) 14 ♕d8+ 1-0. This must be one of the shortest games in recent times that a strong GM has lost.

8...♕a5 9 g3 *(D)*

9 ♘e2 is a recent idea. White intends a set-up with ♘c1-b3, f3 and ♗d3, thus restricting lots of Black's more active ideas by blocking the a8-h1 diagonal. Now:

a) 9...♗d7 10 ♘c1 ♗c6 11 ♘b3 ♕d5 12 f3 ♗b5 13 ♗d3 ♗xd3 14 cxd3 ♘d7 15 0-0 0-0 16 ♕f4 ♖ac8 17 ♖ae1 gave White a clear edge in Galkin-Lopez Martinez, Erevan 1999.

b) 9...b6 10 ♘c1 ♗b7 11 ♘b3 ♕d5 12 f3 ♘d7 13 ♗d3 ♕h5 14 0-0 f5 15 a4 ♖g8 16 ♕f4 ♕g5 17 ♕xg5 ♖xg5 18 a5 ♔e7 is roughly equal, Magem-Liogky, France 1998.

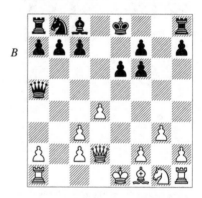

B

9...♗d7 10 ♗g2 ♗c6 11 ♘f3 ♘d7 12 0-0

Now:

a) 12...h5!? is an idea. Perhaps Black can advantageously leave out castling for a few moves.

b) After 12...0-0-0 we have:

b1) 13 ♖fd1 ♘b6 14 ♕h6 ♕xc3 15 ♕xf6 ♖hf8 16 ♘e1 ♗xg2 17 ♔xg2 ♘d5 18 ♕f3 ♖d6! was very pleasant for Black in Van der Wiel-Glek, Bundesliga 2000.

b2) 13 ♖fb1 ♘b6 14 a4 and now 14...♕h5 15 ♘e1 ♖d6 16 ♕d3 ♕g6 17 ♕f1!? e5 18 a5 ♘d5 19 ♖b3 was good for White in Lanka-Ellers, Bundesliga 1999/00, but Black should consider 14...h5!?, when 15 ♘e1 is answered by 15...♘d5.

B)

5 e5 h6 *(D)*

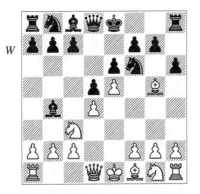

A sharp position has arisen. White's most common continuation is 6 ♗d2, preventing Black from replying with the immediate 6...♘e4, but other moves can also be considered. Of these, 6 ♗e3 and 6 ♗c1 are especially worth noting. White gambits a pawn in return for the possibility of a rapid attack on the kingside. We divide the lines into:

B1: 6 ♗e3   138
B2: 6 ♗d2   142

Other moves:

a) 6 ♗h4 g5 7 ♗g3 ♘e4 8 ♘e2 c5 9 ♕d3 ♘c6 10 a3 ♕a5 11 dxc5 ♗xc3+ 12 ♘xc3 ♗d7 13 0-0-0 ♘xc3 14 ♕xc3 ♕xc3 15 bxc3 ♖c8 16 h4 ♖g8 17 ♗e2 ♘e7 18 hxg5 hxg5 = Orlov-Sharif, Paris 1996.

b) 6 exf6 hxg5 7 fxg7 ♖g8 8 h4 ♘c6! (8...gxh4 also offers equal prospects but this recent idea of Morozevich's is better) 9 h5 (9 ♗b5 could be considered) 9...♖xg7 10 h6?! (Morozevich labels this as dubious; he gives 10 ♗b5 as White's best but thinks that Black is better after 10...♗d7 11 ♘f3 f6!? 12 ♕e2 ♕e7 13 h6 ♖h7 14 ♗d3 ♖h8 15 a3 ♗xc3+ 16 bxc3 0-0-0) 10...♖h7 11 ♗d3 (11 ♕d3 ♖h8 12 0-0-0 ♕f6 13 h7 ♗d7 ∓ Morozevich) 11...♖h8 12 ♕h5 ♕f6 13 ♘f3, Landa-Morozevich, Samara 1998, and now 13...♗d7 14 ♘xg5 0-0-0 is better for Black according to Morozevich.

c) 6 ♗c1!? ♘e4 7 ♕g4 and now Black has the choice, a standard one in the MacCutcheon, of whether to play ...♔f8 or ...g6. Here I think the king move is the worse of the two:

c1) 7...♔f8 8 ♘e2 c5 9 a3 and now Black should try 9...♗a5, as 9...♗xc3+ 10 bxc3 cxd4 11 cxd4 ♕a5+ 12 c3 ♗d7 13 f3 ♗b5 14 fxe4 ♗xe2 15 ♕h3 ♗xf1 16 ♖xf1 dxe4 looks very dangerous as White can more easily attack on the f-file.

c2) 7...g6 8 ♘e2 c5 9 a3 and now:

c21) 9...♗xc3+ should be playable but only due to a subtle tactical resource: 10 bxc3!? cxd4 11 cxd4 ♕a5+! (11...♕c7?! 12 f3 ♘c3 13 ♗d2 ♘xe2

14 ♗xe2 ♗d7 15 ♗d3 ± Hector-S.Pedersen, Oxford 1998) 12 c3 ♗d7 13 f3 ♗b5! (this is the idea that saves Black) 14 fxe4 ♗xe2 15 ♕h3 ♗xf1 16 ♖xf1 dxe4 17 ♔f2 ♘d7 18 ♔g1 ♖h7 19 ♕e3 ♕d5 20 ♖e1 ♖c8 and Black is doing very well, Rõtšagov-D.Anderton, Gausdal 2000.

c22) 9...♗a5!? 10 b4 ♘xc3 11 ♘xc3 cxd4! 12 ♘b5 ♗c7 (there are some obvious similarities to the Armenian Variation; the difference is that a pair of knights has been exchanged) 13 f4 ♘c6 14 ♗d3 a6 15 ♘xc7+ ♕xc7 16 0-0 ♗d7 with an approximately equal position, Borriss-Hübner, Bundesliga 2000/1.

B1)

6 ♗e3 ♘e4 7 ♕g4 (D)

A fairly unexplored idea here is 7 ♘e2 c5 8 dxc5! ♘c6 (perhaps 8...♕c7 is better, with the point 9 a3 ♘xc3 10 ♘xc3 ♗xc3+ 11 bxc3 ♕xe5) 9 a3 ♗xc3+ 10 ♘xc3 ♘xc3 11 bxc3 ♘xe5 12 ♗d4 ♕g5 13 h4 ♕f5 14 ♗e2 0-0 15 0-0 ♘c6 16 f4 ♘xd4 17 cxd4 ♗d7 18 g4 ♕f6 19 g5 ♕e7 20 ♗d3 ± Glek-Hoang Than Trang, Budapest 1998.

Now:

The more aggressive 7...g5 looks risky: 8 a3 h5 9 ♕f3 ♗xc3+ 10 bxc3 c5 11 ♗d3 ♘xc3 12 dxc5 (12 ♕g3 g4 13 dxc5 d4 14 ♗d2 ♕d5 gave Black good counterplay in Govedarica-Ruckschloss, Trnava 1990) 12...♘c6 13

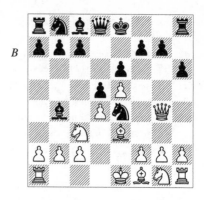

♕g3 ♕a5 14 ♔f1 and the complications look favourable to White, Veselovsky-Glek, USSR 1984.

B11)

7...g6

This has the obvious advantage compared to 7...♔f8 that Black retains the possibility of castling, but now White is also given something to attack.

8 a3 ♗xc3+ 9 bxc3 ♘xc3

9...c5 10 ♗d3 ♘xc3 is a more conventional way of countering in the centre but there is some danger in attempting to open the centre because Black is poorly developed. After 11 dxc5 ♘c6 12 ♘f3 Black has tried:

a) 12...d4 13 ♗xd4 ♘xd4 14 ♕xd4 ♕xd4 15 ♘xd4 ♗d7 16 ♔d2 ♘a4 17 c6 ♗xc6 18 ♘xc6 bxc6 19 ♖hb1 0-0-0 20 ♔e3 ♘c5 with an equal endgame, Balogh-Hoang Than Trang, Budapest 2000.

b) 12...♕a5 13 0-0 ♕a4 14 ♕xa4 (14 ♕h3!?) 14...♘xa4 15 ♗b5 ♘c3 16 a4 ♗d7 17 ♖a3 ♘e4 18 ♖b1 ♘a5!

with equality, Hraček-Vaïsser, Pula Echt 1997.

10 ♗d3 ♘c6 11 h4 ♕e7

This is safer than 11...♗d7, which after 12 h5 g5 13 ♘h3 ♕e7 transposes to the main line, but White can try Minev's suggestion, 12 ♗xg6 ♖g8 (not 12...fxg6? 13 ♕xg6+ ♔f8 14 ♖h3 +−) 13 ♗xf7+ ♔xf7 14 ♕h5+ ♖g6 15 ♘h3 with compensation.

A much more interesting alternative is 11...♘e7!?. The idea is that 12 h5 g5 13 f4 is now strongly met by 13...♘f5!. Instead, White should probably play 12 f3!? but Black seems to be doing well:

a) 12...♗d7 13 ♕f4 ♘f5 14 ♗f2 c5 15 dxc5 d4 16 ♗xf5 gxf5 17 ♗xd4 ♘d5 18 ♕d2 ± Kurajica-Dvoretsky, Wijk aan Zee 1976.

b) 12...c5!? 13 dxc5 ♘c6 14 ♗d2 d4 15 ♗xc3 dxc3 16 ♕c4 ♘xe5 17 ♕xc3 ♕f6 18 ♘e2 ♘xd3+ 19 cxd3 ♕xc3+ 20 ♘xc3 b6 21 cxb6 axb6 22 ♔e2 ♗d7 = Gi.Hernandez-Glek, Linares open 1996.

12 h5 g5 13 ♘h3 ♗d7 14 f4 gxf4 15 ♗f2 ♕f8 16 ♕xf4 0-0-0 17 ♗h4 ♖e8 *(D)*

18 0-0

This was a long series of moves without comments but the play has been very logical. White has sacrificed a pawn for an initiative and has forced open the f-file. Black has managed to castle queenside but is slightly passive. Nevertheless, he hopes to gain counterplay on the g-file, and perhaps the lonely intruder, the knight on c3,

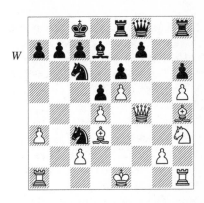

can distract White somewhat. By the way, 18 ♘f2 is worse due to 18...f5!, when 19 exf6 e5 20 dxe5 ♘xe5 is very good for Black.

18...♘e4!?

Black decides to give back the pawn in an attempt to gain control over the light squares. Alternatively:

a) 18...f5?! 19 exf6 e5 20 dxe5 ♖xe5 is dubious. White has a large advantage after 21 ♖ae1.

b) 18...♖g8!? 19 ♘f2 ♘e7 20 ♗f6 ♘f5 21 ♕d2?! (21 g4 ♗b5 22 ♔h2 ♗xd3 23 ♘xd3 ♘e2 24 ♕f2 ♘fxd4 25 c3 ♖xg4 26 cxd4 ♘xd4 27 ♖g1 is critical, but Black may be doing alright after 27...♖e4) 21...♘e4 22 ♘xe4 dxe4 23 ♗xe4 ♘g3 ∓ Cuijpers-Ree, Dutch Ch (Hilversum) 1983.

19 ♗xe4

19 ♘f2?! ♘xd4 20 ♘xe4 dxe4 21 ♕xe4 ♘f5 22 ♖ab1 was played in Iordachescu-Vysochin, Kiev 2000. Now 22...♗c6? would allow the spectacular 23 ♕xc6!! bxc6 24 ♗a6+ ♔d7 25 ♖fd1+ ♘d6 26 exd6 with a virtually decisive attack. Much stronger is

22...♕c5+ 23 ♗f2, when Finkel points out that 23...♕c6! is fine for Black.

19...dxe4 20 ♕xf7!?

Instead, 20 ♕xe4 ♘e7 21 c4 ♗c6 22 ♕f4 ♘f5 23 d5 ♗d7!? is far from clear.

20...♕xf7

20...♘xd4?! is dubious due to 21 ♕xd7+ ♔xd7 22 ♖xf8 ♖hxf8 23 ♖d1 c5 24 c3 ♔c6 25 cxd4 c4 26 ♗f6, when White has a clearly better ending, Fressinet-Vysochin, Brussels 2000.

21 ♖xf7 ♖ef8

Black has sufficient counterplay.

B12)

7...♔f8!? *(D)*

With this move, Black avoids giving White a target for attack, which he does by 7...g6. Of course the drawback is that Black's h8-rook is out of play.

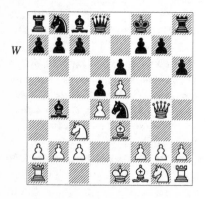

8 a3 ♗xc3+

8...♗a5 is an interesting and perhaps underestimated alternative. Then 9 ♗d3 ♘xc3 10 ♗d2 c5 (even the greedy 10...♘a4!? 11 ♗xa5 ♘xb2 might be feasible) is fine for Black. Hence, 9 ♘e2 seems like White's best but does not clearly lead to an advantage; for example, 9...c5 10 dxc5 ♘c6 11 b4 ♘xc3 12 ♘xc3 ♘xe5 13 ♕h5 ♗c7 14 ♘b5 ♗d7!? 15 ♘xc7 ♕xc7 with roughly equal chances, Iordachescu-Singh, Calcutta 2000.

9 bxc3 ♘xc3 *(D)*

9...c5 10 ♗d3 and now:

a) 10...♘xc3 – 9...♘xc3 10 ♗d3 c5.

b) 10...cxd4 11 cxd4 ♕a5+ 12 ♔f1 ♗d7 13 h4 ♘d2+ 14 ♗xd2 ♕xd2 15 ♖d1 ♕a5 16 ♖h3 ♗b5 17 ♖g3 ♖g8 18 ♘h3 ± Lanka-Dorosiev, Plovdiv 1985.

c) 10...♕a5 11 ♘e2 ♘c6 (11...♘xc3 12 ♗d2 cxd4 13 ♘xd4 ♕c7 14 0-0! ♗d7 15 ♖ae1 ♘a6 16 ♖e3 with a promising attack, Klovans-Pronold, Werfen 1991) 12 ♗xe4 cxd4 13 ♗d2 dxe4 14 cxd4 ♕d5 15 0-0 ♘xd4 16 ♘xd4 ♕xd4 17 ♖ad1 ♕xe5 18 ♗c3! ♕xc3 19 ♖d8+ ♔e7 20 ♖xh8 and White wins, Kurajica-Bednarski, Wijk aan Zee 1973.

d) 10...h5!? 11 ♕f4 ♕a5 12 ♘e2 ♘xc3 13 0-0 (13 ♗d2 ♘xe2 14 ♗xe2 ♕c7 looks OK for Black) 13...♘xe2+ 14 ♗xe2 ♘c6 15 c4 cxd4 16 ♗xd4 ♘xd4 17 ♕xd4 ♗d7 18 cxd5 exd5 19 ♗f3 ♗c6 ½-½ Kasparov-Korchnoi, Kopavogur rpd 2000.

The following is not entirely forced but clearly constitutes best play from both sides.

10 ♗d3 c5 11 dxc5 ♘c6 12 ♘f3 f5!? 13 exf6 ♕xf6 14 ♕h5!

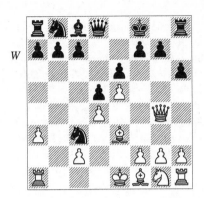

W

Black was ready to play ...e5-e4. 14 0-0?! e5 15 ♕g6 (not 15 ♕h5? e4 16 ♘h4 ♘e7! winning a piece for Black) and now:

a) 15...e4 16 ♕xf6+ gxf6 17 ♗d2 exd3! 18 ♗xc3 dxc2 is better for Black because he can support the c2-pawn with ...♗f5.

b) 15...♕xg6 16 ♗xg6 ♔e7!?, intending ...♔f6, also looks good.

14...e5 15 ♗g6 ♗e6!?

Black intends to bring the bishop to f7. The tactical justification for this lies in the fact that now 16 ♗g5?! could be met by 16...♗g4! 17 ♗xf6 ♗xh5 18 ♗xe5 ♗xg6 19 ♗xc3 ♗xc2 =.

Another line is 15...♔g8 16 0-0, and now:

a) 16...♘e2+ 17 ♔h1 ♘f4 18 ♗xf4 ♕xf4 19 h3 ♗e6 20 c3!? ♗f7 (20...e4 21 ♘d4 ±) 21 ♖ab1 ♗xg6 22 ♕xg6 ♕f7 23 ♕xf7+ (Dreev suggests 23 ♘h4!) 23...♔xf7 24 ♖xb7+ ♔f6 (Filipenko-Volkov, Moscow 1999) and now White's best chance of retaining an edge is 25 ♖d1 ♖hd8 26 ♔g1.

b) 16...♗e6 17 ♖ae1 and then:

b1) 17...♖d8 18 ♗d2 ♘e4 19 c4 (19 ♗xe4?! dxe4 20 ♖xe4 ♗f5 is a little better for Black) 19...♘xd2 20 ♘xd2 ♕g5 ½-½ Fressinet-Vallejo Pons, Mondariz 2000.

b2) 17...♗f7 18 ♘h4 ♗xg6 19 ♘xg6 ♕f7 20 f4 ♔h7 21 f5 ♖he8 gives Black good counterplay as ...d4, ...♘d5 and ...e4 is coming, Arnold-Kritz, Paks 2000.

16 0-0 ♗f7

16...♘e2+ 17 ♔h1 ♘f4 18 ♗xf4 ♕xf4 19 h3 e4 20 ♘h4 ♘e7 is a similar idea to *15...♔g8 16 0-0 ♘e2+*. Black hopes to be able to exchange a few pieces, solve the problem of his king and then exert pressure on the c-file. This is probably too much to ask, and I wouldn't be surprised if White had something good here. For example, 21 ♖ab1 ♖b8 22 c3!?, when 22...♗f7 can be met by 23 f3 e3 24 ♖fe1 ±. 22...♔g8 can be tried, after which it is not totally clear how the complications will evolve.

17 ♘h4 ♖e8 18 ♖ae1

18 f4 e4 19 f5 d4 20 ♗d2 ♘a4 21 ♗f4 ♔g8 22 ♗d6 ♘c3 was unclear in Degraeve-Vallejo Pons, Istanbul OL 2000. This type of position commonly occurs in this line and is almost impossible to assess. My feeling is that it is dynamically balanced. Black's centre is strong but there is a danger of it falling apart. Black is also playing without the h8-rook. On the other hand, White's pieces are aggressively lined up on the kingside but there is no clear way to proceed and hence they may

appear as much out of play as the h8-rook. In addition, White is fighting against the terribly strong knight on c3, which controls several important squares.

18...♔g8 19 f3 ♖e6 20 ♗xf7+ ♕xf7 21 ♕g4 ♖f6!?

Black has a slight advantage, Lanka-Morozevich, Kishinev 1998.

B2)

6 ♗d2 ♗xc3 *(D)*

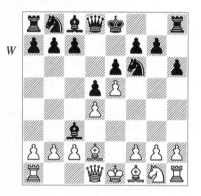

Now:

B21: 7 ♗xc3　　142
B22: 7 bxc3　　144

B21)

7 ♗xc3

This is relatively rare but has been tried occasionally in GM practice over the last few years.

7...♘e4 8 ♘e2

This is the idea White has been focusing on. There are other possibilities but none that promises White anything:

a) 8 ♗a5?! (originally one of the main ideas behind 7 ♗xc3 but since the Fischer-Petrosian game it has been regarded as dubious) 8...0-0! (8...b6 9 ♗b4 c5 10 ♗a3 is one of White's ideas – compared to the immediate 8 ♗b4 Black does not have ...♕a5 available) 9 ♗d3 ♘c6 10 ♗c3 (10 ♗xe4 dxe4 11 ♗c3 ♕g5 12 g3 ♗d7 ∓) 10...♘xc3 11 bxc3 f6! 12 f4 fxe5 13 fxe5 ♘e7 14 ♘f3 c5 15 0-0 ♕a5 16 ♕e1 ♗d7, Fischer-Petrosian, Curaçao Ct 1962. Black is slightly better as White has no real attack on the kingside and meanwhile Black keeps the better prospects on the queenside, intending ...♗a4 and ...c4.

b) 8 ♗b4 c5 9 ♗xc5 (9 dxc5? ♘xf2! 10 ♔xf2 ♕h4+ 11 g3 ♕xb4 ∓ and 9 ♗a3? ♕a5+ ∓ are not viable alternatives) 9...♘xc5 10 dxc5 ♕a5+ (10...♕c7, 10...♘c6 and 10...♘d7 are all very reasonable too) 11 ♕d2 (11 c3 ♕xc5 12 ♕d4 ♕c7! 13 ♘f3 ♘c6 = Bogoljubow-Réti, Kiel 1921) 11...♕xc5 12 ♘f3 ♘c6 13 ♗d3 ♗d7 14 0-0 b5 15 ♖fe1 ♖b8 16 ♕f4 0-0 17 ♖ad1 b4 18 ♖d2 a5 ∓ Grund-Kobaliya, Rimavska Sobota 1996.

c) 8 ♗d2 ♘xd2 (8...c5 9 ♗e3 cxd4 10 ♗xd4 ♘c6 11 f3 ♕h4+ 12 g3 ♘xg3 13 ♗f2 ♕b4+ 14 c3 ♕xb2 15 ♗xg3 ♕xc3+, as analysed by Djurić, is interesting; R.Pert-T.Wall, British League (4NCL) 1997/8 continued 16 ♔f2 ♘xe5 17 ♗xe5 ♕xe5 18 ♗b5+ ♔e7 19 ♘e2 d4! 20 ♕d3 a6 21 ♗a4 ♖d8 22 ♖ad1 b5 23 ♗b3 ♗b7 24 ♘xd4 ♖ac8 and, with three pawns and a solid position for the piece, Black was doing fine) 9 ♕xd2 c5 10 dxc5 ♘d7 11 ♗b5 0-0 12 ♗xd7 ♗xd7 = Djurić.

d) 8 ♗d3 ♘xc3 9 bxc3 c5 10 ♕g4 0-0! (the main difference compared to the main line, *7 bxc3* {Line B22}: with White's dark-squared bishop already gone, Black can safely castle) 11 dxc5 ♘c6 12 f4?! ♕a5 13 ♘e2 ♕xc5 14 h4 f6 15 ♕g6 f5 16 ♖h3 ♘e7 17 ♕g3 ♗d7 18 ♔d2 ♖ac8 ∓ Hostinsky-Vavra, Czech Cht 1995.

We now return to 8 ♘e2 *(D)*:

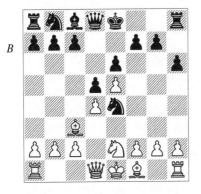

8...♘c6

This has been Glek's preference on several occasions. Rather than breaking thematically with ...c5, Black intends to complete his development with ...♕e7, ...♗d7 and ...0-0-0, while retaining the option of exchanging off White's dark-squared bishop. This seems to equalize without too much trouble, but other ideas are also worth noting:

a) 8...c5 9 dxc5 and now:

a1) 9...♘xc5 10 ♘g3 ♘c6 11 ♗b5 ♗d7 12 ♗xc6 ♗xc6 13 ♕d4 ±.

a2) 9...♘c6 10 ♗d4! ♕e7 11 ♘c3 ♘xc5 12 f4 0-0 13 ♕d2 ♗d7 14 0-0-0 ♘xd4 15 ♕xd4 ♖ac8 16 g3 ♖c7 17 ♔b1 is slightly better for White, Sutovsky-Comas Fabrego, Pamplona 1998/9.

a3) 9...♘d7 10 ♗d4 ♘exc5 11 ♘c3 b6 12 f4 a6 13 ♕g4 0-0 14 0-0-0 ± Van Riemsdijk-Giampa, La Plata 1998.

a4) 9...♘xc3! 10 ♘xc3 0-0!? 11 ♕d2 f6! 12 exf6 (12 f4 fxe5 13 fxe5 ♕h4+ 14 g3 ♕h5 gives Black a slight advantage – M.Gurevich) 12...♕xf6 13 ♗b5!? a6 14 ♗a4 ♘d7 15 ♗xd7 ♗xd7 16 0-0 ♖ac8 17 ♘d1! ♖xc5 18 c3 ♗b5 19 ♖e1 ♖c4 20 f3!? ♕g6 21 ♕e3 ♖e8 22 ♕e5 ♕f6 = Lanka-M.Gurevich, Cappelle la Grande 1999.

b) 8...0-0 9 ♗b4 (9 ♕d3 c5 10 dxc5 ♕c7 =) 9...c5 10 ♗a3 and now:

b1) 10...cxd4? 11 ♗xf8 ♕xf8 is objectively a rather speculative sacrifice but looks fun, which, I believe, was the main reason that Morozevich went for it: 12 f3 (12 a3!?) 12...d3!? (or 12...♕b4+ 13 c3 dxc3 14 a3! ♕xb2 15 fxe4 c2 16 ♕c1 ♕xe5 17 ♖a2 ±) 13 fxe4! (13 ♕xd3 ♕b4+ 14 c3 ♕xb2 15 ♖b1?! ♘c5! was probably Black's main idea; unfortunately White doesn't go for it) 13...dxe2 14 ♕xe2! ♘c6 15 exd5 exd5 16 0-0-0 and Black's experiment has obviously gone wrong, Galkin-Morozevich, Novgorod 1997.

b2) 10...♘c6! (this leads to complicated play in which Black is doing alright because he is better developed) 11 f3 b5! 12 fxe4 (the alternative 12 c3 b4 13 ♗xb4 cxb4 14 fxe4 bxc3 15 bxc3 dxe4 16 ♘g3 may be worth investigating) 12...b4 13 ♗xb4 ♘xb4 14 c3 ♘c6 15 exd5 ♕xd5 16 dxc5 ♕xc5 17 ♘c1 (17 ♕d6 ♕b6!, intending ...♖d8, is good for Black) 17...♕xe5+ 18 ♕e2 ♕c7 ∓ Svidler-Morozevich, Frankfurt rpd 1999.

9 ♘f4 ♕e7 10 ♗d3 ♘xc3 11 bxc3 *(D)*

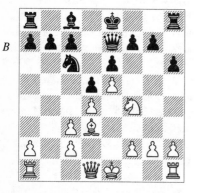

11...♗d7

Psakhis mentions 11...g6 12 ♗xg6 fxg6 (12...♕g5? loses to 13 h4! ♕xf4 14 g3) 13 ♘xg6 ♕g7 14 ♘xh8 ♕xh8 15 ♕h5+ ♔d8, after which Black has a few problems to solve before he can feel completely safe.

12 ♘h5 ♖g8!

12...♕g5? loses to 13 h4!, because 13...♕xg2? 14 ♘g3 followed by ♗f1 traps the queen.

13 ♗h7

13 ♕g4 0-0-0 14 ♗h7 ♖h8 15 ♕xg7 would be good for White if only he had time for ♘f6, but Black has enough defensive resources. Psakhis proposes

15...♕a3 16 ♔d2 (16 0-0 ♕xc3 17 ♘f6 ♘xd4 with counterplay) 16...♕a5 17 ♘f6 ♘xd4 18 ♘xd7 ♔xd7, which might be OK for Black, but 15...f5! 16 ♕xe7 ♘xe7 17 ♘f6 ♖df8 intending ...♖f7 looks the simplest.

13...♖h8 14 ♗d3

14 ♘xg7+? ♔f8 −+.

14...♖g8 15 0-0 0-0-0 16 a4

White has few chances to make progress on the queenside, so possibly this is a bad plan. 16 f4!? appears more logical, when Black can choose from 16...♕a3!?, 16...♘a5 and 16...f5!?, all of which look very reasonable.

16...♘a5! 17 f4 c5 18 ♗b5 ♔b8 19 ♗xd7 ♕xd7 20 ♕d3 ♕c7!

Sutovsky-Psakhis, Tel-Aviv 1999. Black has a comfortable position as ...♖c8 is coming next with strong pressure on the c-file, while White is far from achieving anything tangible on the kingside.

B22)

7 bxc3 ♘e4 8 ♕g4 *(D)*

This is White's only chance for an advantage. 8 ♘f3 c5 9 ♗d3 ♘c6 10 0-0 ♘xd2 11 ♕xd2 ♕a5 is fine for Black, and the same goes for 8 ♗d3 ♘xd2 9 ♕xd2 c5 10 f4 ♘c6 11 ♘f3 ♕a5.

Now Black has a choice:

B221: 8...g6   145
B222: 8...♔f8   148

The first line is the most common as Black keeps the option of castling. However, the latter is a Korchnoi favourite and also has a lot to be said for

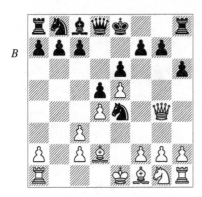

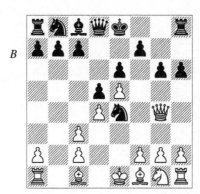

it, since Black avoids weakening his kingside.

B221)
8...g6
Now:
B2211: 9 &c1   145
B2212: 9 &d3   146

White has also continued 9 h4 or 9 ♘f3 but these moves usually transpose to variations covered inside the 9 &d3 complex.

B2211)
9 &c1 (D)
This is a rather tricky variation and requires very careful play from Black. The main point is that White avoids having his dark-squared bishop exchanged for Black's knight. At the moment the e4-knight lacks support and is almost surrounded by white pawns.
9...c5
Black could also play the immediate 9...♘xc3, which usually transposes to the main line after 10 &d3 c5.

10 &d3
10 ♘e2 is far from convincing and allows Black an easy game: 10...cxd4 11 f3 h5 12 ♕h3 ♘xc3 13 ♘xd4 ♘c6 14 ♘xc6 bxc6, with the better game for Black, Penrose-O'Kelly de Galway, Hastings 1950.
10...♘xc3
10...cxd4 is risky:

a) Black is doing OK after 11 &xe4 dxe4 12 ♕xe4 ♕a5 13 ♘e2 ♘c6.

b) 11 ♘e2! is more critical:

b1) 11...♘c5 12 cxd4 (12 &xg6 fxg6 13 ♕xg6+ ♔d7 14 cxd4 {14 ♕f7+!?} 14...♘ca6 15 &xh6 ♕g8 should be alright for Black) 12...♘xd3+ 13 cxd3 b6 14 h4 h5 15 ♕f3 favours White, Bronstein-Goldenov, Kiev 1944.

b2) 11...♕a5 12 0-0 dxc3 13 &xe4 dxe4 14 ♘g3! ♘c6 15 ♘xe4 ♘xe5 16 ♕g3 &d7 17 ♘d6+ ♔f8 18 ♘xb7 ♕d5 19 &a3+ ♔g8 20 ♘c5 ± Boleslavsky-Lisitsyn, USSR Ch (Moscow) 1944.

b3) 11...♘c6 12 &xe4 dxe4 13 cxd4 ♘xd4 14 ♕xe4 ♘xe2 15 ♕xe2 &d7 16 0-0 ♕c7 17 &a3 0-0-0 18 &d6

♕c6 19 ♖ab1 ± Liberzon-Faibisovich, Moscow-Leningrad 1967.

b4) 11...dxc3 12 ♗xe4 dxe4 13 ♘xc3 ♕d4?! (13...♘c6!?) 14 ♗b2 ♗d7 15 ♖b1 ♗c6 16 0-0 ♕c4 17 ♕g3! ♘d7 18 ♗a3 ♘c5 19 ♘d1 ♘a4 (19...♕xa2? 20 ♘b2! +–) 20 ♕f4! ± De Vreugt-Glek, Wijk aan Zee 1999.

11 dxc5 ♕a5!

Black has to be very careful that his knight on c3 doesn't end up getting trapped. The e4-square is the only secure retreat but at the moment this costs a pawn. The following manoeuvre is, if not essential, at least the best way to rescue the knight.

12 ♗d2 ♕a4

This move is in my opinion the safest. However, an experimental idea is 12...♕xc5!?. Now:

a) 13 ♘f3 ♘c6 14 ♕f4 ♗d7 15 ♕f6 ♖h7 16 0-0 (Keller-Kinlay, Hastings 1975/6) 16...♘e4 is fine for Black; e.g., 17 ♕f4 ♘xd2 18 ♕xd2 ♘d4.

b) 13 ♗xg6!? is a more critical idea. 13...d4 14 ♘f3! is good for White but 13...♘e4 14 ♗xe4 ♕d4! might be OK for Black.

13 h3 h5

At once 13...♘e4 is also feasible. Then 14 ♗xe4 ♕d4!? 15 ♖b1 ♕xe5 is fine for Black, while 14 ♘e2 ♘xc5 15 ♕f3 ♕d7!? 16 0-0 b6, intending ....♗a6, is also reasonable for Black, Arbakov-D.Gurevich, USSR 1978.

14 ♕f3 ♘e4 15 ♗xe4 ♕xe4+ 16 ♕xe4 dxe4 17 ♘e2 ♗d7

= Voitsekhovsky-Alavkin, St Petersburg 1999.

B2212)
9 ♗d3 ♘xd2 10 ♔xd2 c5 *(D)*

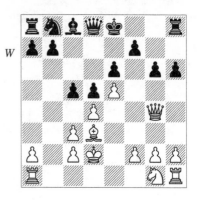

11 h4

White usually continues with something like h4, ♘f3, ♕f4 and possibly dxc5, but the order in which the moves are played varies. The text-move is perhaps the most aggressive since White hasn't blockaded the f-pawn and thus if a later h5 is met by ...g5, he has the option of playing f4. Additionally, h4 has the advantage, in some lines, of preventing Black from exchanging queens with ...♕g5+.

We shall look briefly at alternatives:

a) 11 ♘f3 and now:

a1) 11...♘c6 and then:

a11) 12 h4 – *11 h4 ♘c6 12 ♘f3*.

a12) 12 ♕f4 ♕e7 13 h4 c4!? 14 ♗e2 ♗d7 15 h5 (maybe the wrong plan; 15 ♘h2 is perhaps better) 15...g5 16 ♕f6 0-0-0! 17 ♕xe7 ♘xe7 18 ♘h2 ♘g8! 19 ♘g4 f5 20 exf6 ♖f8 = Bryson-Daly, Rotherham 1997.

a13) 12 ♖hb1 c4 13 ♗e2 b6 14 h4 ♗d7 15 ♘h2 ♕e7 16 h5?! (this seems premature; 16 ♕g3 is better, with perhaps an edge for White) 16...0-0-0 17 hxg6 f6! (a strong temporary pawn sacrifice; it is clear that White cannot hope to keep the g6-pawn) 18 ♘f3 fxe5 19 ♘xe5 ♘xe5 20 dxe5 (Sutovsky-Daly, Port Erin 1999) and Black is doing well after 20...♖dg8 followed by ...♗e8.

a2) 11...♗d7 12 dxc5 (12 h4 – *11 h4 ♗d7 12 ♘f3*; 12 ♕f4 – *11 ♕f4 ♗d7 12 ♘f3*) 12...♘c6 13 ♖hb1 (13 ♖ab1 ♕e7 14 h4 ♘d7 15 ♖he1 ♘xc5 16 ♘d4 ♖c8 17 ♘xc6 bxc6 18 ♖b4 a5 19 ♖bb1 0-0! ∓ Spassky-Relange, French Cht 1991) 13...♕e7 14 a4 ♘d7 15 a5 ♘xc5 16 ♔e1 ♘e4 17 ♖b3 a6 ∓ King-K.Müller, Bundesliga 2000/1.

b) 11 ♕f4 ♗d7 (11...♘c6 12 ♘f3 – *11 ♘f3 ♘c6 12 ♕f4*) 12 ♘f3 ♗c6 13 h4 ♘d7 14 ♖h3?! (this is too optimistic; 14 dxc5 ♕e7 15 ♘d4 looks right) 14...♕e7 15 dxc5 0-0-0 16 ♘d4 ♘xc5! 17 ♖b1 ♕c7! ∓ Spraggett-Glek, Cappelle la Grande 1998.

We now return to the position after 11 h4 *(D)*:

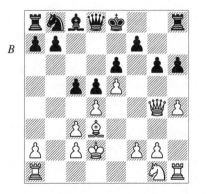

11...♗d7

This is a popular plan: Black's idea is to continue ...♗c6 and ...♘d7. This would be a good set-up since on c6, the bishop defends b7 and the d7-knight supports the c5-pawn. The queen usually goes to e7, and Black is then ready to castle queenside, away from the danger on the kingside.

11...♘c6 is a more active continuation:

a) 12 ♖h3 ♕a5!? (a little provocative, since this is one of the things White's last move tries to prevent) 13 ♗xg6 (this move is known from the game Euwe-Bogoljubow, Budapest 1921 but Black then reacted poorly with 13...♖f8) 13...♘xd4! 14 ♖g3 (or 14 ♕h5 ♖f8 15 ♗h7 ♗d7 16 ♕xh6 0-0-0 ∓) 14...♖f8 15 ♗d3 ♗d7 ∓ Phillippe-Goczo, Budapest 2001.

b) 12 h5!? g5 13 f4 cxd4 14 cxd4 ♘xd4 15 fxg5 and now 15...♕xg5+ 16 ♕xg5 hxg5 17 g4 gave White good compensation for the pawn in Dworakowska-Hoang Than Trang, Calicut girls U-20 Wch 1998. Instead, the alternative 15...♕a5+ leads to a dynamically balanced position after 16 c3 ♘c6 17 gxh6 d4 or 16 ♔d1 ♘f5 17 ♗xf5 exf5 18 ♕f4.

c) 12 ♕f4 cxd4!? 13 cxd4 ♕a5+ 14 c3 b5! 15 ♕f6 ♖f8 16 ♘e2 b4 17 ♖hc1 ♗a6 (a critical position) 18 ♗xa6 ♕xa6 19 cxb4 (or 19 h5!? gxh5 20 ♕xh6 bxc3+ 21 ♖xc3 ♖b8 with counterplay) 19...♘xb4 20 ♕f3 ♘c6 (Glek suggests 20...♔d7!?) 21 ♖c5 ♘a5 22 ♖ac1 ♖b8 23 ♔e1 ♘c4 with an unclear but probably balanced position, Sutovsky-Glek, Essen 2000.

d) 12 ♘f3 and then:

d1) 12...♕a5 13 ♕f4 cxd4 14 h5!? (White goes for a counterattack, rather than 14 ♘xd4 ♘xd4 15 ♕xd4 ♗d7 with roughly equal chances) 14...dxc3+ 15 ♔e2 g5 16 ♕f6 ♖g8 17 ♕xh6 g4 18 ♘g5 ♕c7? (18...♘xe5 19 ♕f6 ♕d8 20 ♕xe5 ♕xg5 looks more critical) 19 ♘xf7! ♕xf7 20 ♗g6 ♖xg6 21 hxg6 +– A.Horvath-Naiditsch, Paks 1998.

d2) 12...cxd4 13 cxd4 ♕a5+ 14 c3 b6 15 h5 g5 16 ♘h2 ♗a6 with approximately equal chances, Milos-Cichocki, Koszalin 1997.

We now return to 11...♗d7 (D):

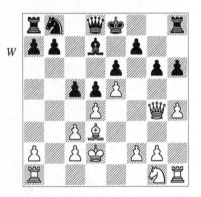

12 ♘f3

A critical alternative is 12 h5!? g5 13 f4, which demands accurate play from Black:

a) 13...♕a5 14 fxg5 ♘c6 leads to a very unclear position; for example, 15 g6 0-0-0!? 16 ♘f3 cxd4 17 ♔e2 ♕xc3 18 gxf7 ♖df8 19 ♕f4 ♘d8 20 ♕xd4 ♕xd4 21 ♘xd4 ♘xf7 22 ♘f3 ♖hg8

and Black was much better in Gaponenko-Grabuzova, Timisoara wom 1994.

b) 13...♘c6 14 fxg5 ♕xg5+ 15 ♕xg5 hxg5 16 ♔e3 g4! 17 ♖f1 (17 ♗e2!? ♖c8 18 ♖b1 ♘a5 19 ♗d3 with perhaps an edge for White) 17...♔e7 18 ♖h4 ♖ag8 19 ♖b1 (19 ♗e2!? ♖c8 20 ♖xg4 cxd4+ 21 cxd4 ♘d8! 22 ♖gf4 ♖xc2 is unclear according to Leko) 19...b6 20 ♗e2 cxd4+ 21 cxd4 f5 22 exf6+ ♔xf6 23 ♖f1+ ♔e7 = Leko-Short, Batumi Echt 1999.

12...♕e7 13 ♕f4

13 dxc5 ♗c6 14 ♘d4 ♘d7 15 f4 0-0-0 16 ♖ab1 ♕xc5 17 ♕e2 ♘b6 ∓ Gdanski-Bromann, Stockholm 2001.

13...♗c6 14 ♘h2 ♘d7

14...h5!? prevents ♘g4 but fatally weakens g5: 15 ♘f3 ♘d7 16 ♘g5 ±.

15 ♘g4 0-0-0!?

15...♕f8 16 ♘f6+ ♘xf6 17 ♕xf6 ± V.Werner-Bohnenblust, Berne 1999. Black has an inferior bishop and difficulties on the kingside. Sacrificing the h-pawn is a dynamic way of avoiding this type of problem.

16 ♘xh6 f5! 17 exf6 ♘xf6 18 ♘g4 ♘e4+ 19 ♗xe4 dxe4 20 ♘e5 cxd4 21 ♘xc6 bxc6 22 ♖ab1 dxc3+ 23 ♔e1 ♕d6

The position is equal, Sutovsky-Zifroni, Israeli League 2000.

B222)
8...♔f8 (D)

This has become more popular over the years. Korchnoi favours it, which of course counts for something. Black's

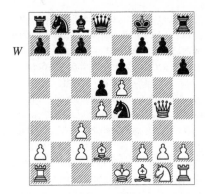

idea is to avoid weakening the kingside too much, advance on the queenside and at a suitable moment try to rescue his king, which also frees the h8-rook.

9 h4!?

I am not sure what is White's most exact move. Much depends on the set-up White is aiming for, since he has a number of slightly different attacking schemes. With the text-move, White introduces the idea of bringing the rook onto the third rank via h3. Apart from the possibility of attacking the black king from g3 or f3, the rook has another useful purpose in defending c3.

Two of the alternatives are important:

a) 9 ♗c1 is not so dangerous here, since after 9...c5 10 ♗d3 ♘xc3 11 dxc5 ♕a5 12 ♗d2, Black can safely play 12...♕xc5, although 12...♕a4 (as in the 8...g6 line) is also possible.

b) 9 ♗d3 (this is the most natural) 9...♘xd2 10 ♔xd2 ♕g5+!? (this is the main argument against White's 9th

move; 10...c5 11 ♘f3 – 9 ♘f3 c5 10 ♗d3 ♘xd2 11 ♔xd2) 11 ♕xg5 hxg5 and now:

b1) 12 ♘h3 f6 (12...g4 13 ♘f4 g5 14 ♘e2 c5 15 ♘g3 ♘c6 16 ♔e3 b6 =) 13 f4 g4 14 ♘f2 f5 15 g3 ♘c6 16 h3 gxh3 17 ♘xh3 ± McDonald-Maduekwe, London 1994.

b2) 12 g4!? f6 13 h4! fxe5 14 dxe5 ♘c6 15 ♘f3 gxh4 16 ♖ae1 h3 17 ♖h2 ♔e7 18 ♖eh1 ♗d7 19 ♖xh3 ♖xh3 20 ♖xh3 ± Gdanski-P.Dittmar, Saint Vincent Ech 2000.

c) 9 ♘f3 (this prevents the ...♕g5+ idea, but renounces plans of a direct attack against f7) 9...c5 10 ♗d3 ♘xd2 11 ♔xd2 and here:

c1) 11...♘c6 and then:

c11) 12 h4 c4 13 ♗e2 b5 14 a3 ♗d7 15 ♕f4 ♔e7!? 16 h5 ♗e8 17 ♘h4 a5 gives Black counterplay, J.Polgar-Korchnoi, Wijk aan Zee 2000.

c12) 12 dxc5!? ♕a5 13 ♕f4 ♕xc5 14 ♘d4 ♗d7 15 ♖hb1 b6 16 a4 ♘a5 17 ♗a6 ± Leko-Hübner, Dortmund 2000.

c2) It is possible that Black should play 11...c4 12 ♗e2 and only then 12...♘c6. Korchnoi played this recently, and there doesn't seem to be any clear way for White to exploit it.

9...c5 10 ♗d3 ♘xd2 11 ♔xd2 (D)
11...c4

I am not sure whether the move-order is of any significant importance. I suppose you could argue that 11...♘c6 is slightly more flexible. Then:

a) In the event of 12 ♖h3 Black can transpose to the main line with 12...c4 13 ♗e2. 12...♕a5?! 13 ♖g3 g5 has

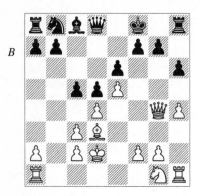

been played a few times but is not good. Instead, 12...cxd4 13 cxd4 ♕a5+ is an experimental idea, with the point 14 c3 ♕a3!?.

b) 12 ♕f4 c4 (12...♕a5!? could be considered) 13 ♗g6!? ♕e7 14 ♘e2 ♗d7 15 ♗h5 and now Talla thinks that Black should play 15...♗e8! (rather than 15...♘d8?! 16 g4 with a strong attack for White, Gdanski-Talla, Ostrava 1998) 16 g4 f6! 17 exf6 (17 ♗xe8 ♖xe8 18 exf6 ♕xf6 19 h5 ♔f7 =) 17...♕xf6 18 ♕xf6+ gxf6 19 ♘f4 ♗xh5 20 ♘xh5 (20 gxh5 ♔f7 21 ♖ae1 ♖ae8 22 ♖hg1 e5 is even better for Black) 20...♔f7, when Black is doing fine.

12 ♗e2 ♘c6 13 ♖h3

This is slightly better for White according to Anand but Korchnoi tends to like this type of position for Black.

13...♖g8 (D)

Korchnoi's move. Covering the g-pawn in advance makes it possible to evacuate the king to the queenside before things get too hot on the kingside.

13...b5 has been seen more frequently. It is clear that Black will have excellent chances if he can open the queenside. The question is whether White will be able to make progress on the kingside before that. Now:

a) 14 ♕f4 ♗d7 15 ♗h5 ♗e8 16 ♘e2 (White could consider playing 16 g4 first, just to deny Black the possibility of 16...f5) 16...a5 (16...f5!?) 17 g4 b4 18 ♖ah1 ♖a7 19 g5 ♘e7 20 ♗g4 and now 20...♕b6 21 h5 gave White a strong attack in Kindermann-Reefschläger, Altenkirchen 1999. Instead, 20...h5! is correct, when Black succeeds in blockading the kingside since 21 ♗xe6 can be met by 21...♖a6!? or 21...♔g8.

b) 14 ♖f3 is another set-up for White. Now something like 14...♗d7 15 ♘h3 ♘e7 16 ♕f4 ♗e8 17 h5 a5 18 a3 would be natural. It is difficult for either side to break through. White's attack looks somewhat more intimidating but as long as Black doesn't panic, his position remains solid. His worst problem is that he is playing without the h8-rook, but this problem can sometimes be solved by ...♔g8-h7.

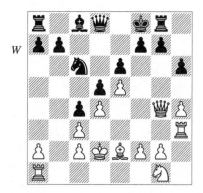

14 ♕f4 ♗d7

14...♚e7 is met by 15 ♗h5, and Black is not allowed his ideal set-up, which would be to get the bishop to e8.

15 ♗h5 ♗e8 16 ♘e2 f5!? *(D)*

An interesting defensive idea, which White should look out for in this line. Black is happy to gain space but it is double-edged since White gets a new target.

17 g4

Here, Anand suggests 17 ♗xe8! ♚xe8 18 g4 ♘e7 19 ♖g1 as a better way to attack. The position still seems fairly unclear after 19...♚d7.

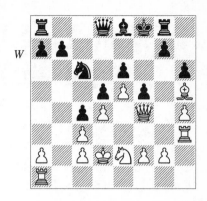

17...♘e7 18 ♖g1 ♗xh5 19 gxh5

Anand-Korchnoi, Dos Hermanas 1999. Anand now gives 19...♖c8! 20 ♕f3 ♚f7 as a good defence.

12 Main Line Winawer: 7 ♕g4 ♕c7

1 e4 e6 2 d4 d5 3 ♘c3 ♗b4 4 e5 c5 5 a3 ♗xc3+ 6 bxc3 ♘e7 7 ♕g4 ♕c7 *(D)*

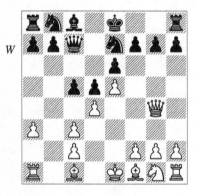

This is the sharpest of the Winawer variations and has long been considered the main line. Black offers two pawns on the kingside in return for counterplay against White's centre. There are arguments for and against this way of playing. Strategically, this is somewhat illogical since the doubled c-pawns are a long-term disadvantage for White, but it is also of crucial importance that Black quickly mixes things up, as otherwise White will have good chances of exploiting the positional advantage of the bishop-pair and his spatial advantage.

In this chapter, our two main lines are:

A: 8 ♗d3   152
B: 8 ♕xg7   154

The majority of weight is on the latter, but the former has lately been seen as an attempt to side-step masses of theory and ensure that the bishop is developed before being blocked by ♘e2.

A)

8 ♗d3

Israeli GM Emil Sutovsky has experimented with this move lately.

8...cxd4

This leads to complex play, similar to the main line. Another option is to keep the position closed with 8...c4 9 ♗e2, and then Black must decide whether to throw in ...♕a5. This looks like a matter of taste:

a) 9...♕a5 10 ♗d2 ♘f5 11 ♘f3 ♘c6 12 ♕h5 h6 13 0-0 ♗d7 14 ♖fb1 0-0-0!? looks like a good practical option. After 15 ♕xf7 g5 Black had definite compensation in Z.Almasi-Beliavsky, Hungary 1996.

b) 9...♘f5 10 ♘f3 ♘c6 11 ♕h5 h6 12 g4 (White could also castle first but why not go ahead with the plan?)

12...♘fe7 13 ♘g5 ♖f8! 14 ♘h3 (after 14 ♘h7, 14...♖h8 15 ♘g5 ♖f8 is just a repetition but Black can even continue 14...♕a5! 15 ♗d2 ♖g8, when it is not clear how the knight ever escapes from h7) 14...♕a5 15 ♗d2 ♗d7 16 f4 0-0-0. According to Lautier, Black has equalized as the knight is poorly placed on h3.

9 ♘e2 *(D)*

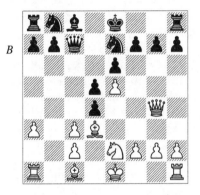

9...dxc3

Other moves are also possible. In particular, 9...♕xe5 looks worth investigating as Black grabs a further central pawn and protects g7, but he also exposes his own queen and further neglects his development. After 10 ♗f4 ♕f6, 11 ♗g5 ♕e5 12 cxd4 h5 13 ♕h4 ♕c7 14 ♗f4 ♕a5+ 15 ♗d2 gave White an edge in J.Polgar-Knaak, Cologne 1990 but I also like the simple 11 cxd4 h5 12 ♕g3 ♘bc6 13 ♗g5 h4 14 ♗xf6 hxg3 15 ♗xg7 ♖xh2 16 ♖xh2 gxh2 17 ♔d2, when White regains the pawn on h2, with the better position.

10 ♕xg7 ♖g8 11 ♕xh7 ♕xe5!?

This has for some time been underestimated, and it looks like a more accurate way of grabbing the e5-pawn, for there is now the possibility of exchanging queens by ...♕h8. The resulting position is quite typical of the Winawer. White has the bishop-pair and an outside passed h-pawn, but Black has the better, more compact, pawn-structure, good piece-play and prospective chances on the semi-open c-file.

As an alternative, Black can try to complete his development and hide his king on the queenside. This also looks like a sensible plan. 11...♘bc6 12 ♗f4! (because the bishop has left f1, compared to the main line, this looks like a better way of protecting e5 than 12 f4, which opens the possibility of Black taking on g2) 12...♗d7 (of course, the rook is now trapped by ♗g3 if Black takes on g2, and 12...♘xe5? ends up in an annoying pin after 13 ♔f1!) 13 0-0 0-0-0 14 ♗g3!? (now White contemplates the possibility of taking on f7; 14 ♕xf7 ♖df8 15 ♕h5 ♘d4!? looks fine for Black) and now Black may consider various strategies:

a) 14...♘xe5 15 ♕h4! ♘7c6 16 ♘xc3 a6 17 ♕f6 ♖df8 18 ♖ae1 ♘g4 19 ♗xc7 ♘xf6 20 ♗d6 ♖e8 21 f4 ± Montheard-Holcman, Paris 1999.

b) 14...d4!? 15 ♖fe1 ♖h8 16 ♕xf7 ♖df8 17 ♕g7 ♖fg8 18 ♕f6 ♘d5 19 ♕f3 ♗e8 with an equal position, Acs-Riazantsev, Oropesa del Mar U-18 Wch 1998.

c) 14...♖df8!? 15 ♖fe1 d4!? (the alternative 15...♕a5 16 ♕h4 ♕c5 17 ♖eb1 a6 18 ♖b3 d4 19 ♖ab1 b5 also looked fine for Black in I.Rogers-Webster, London Lloyds Bank 1990) 16 ♕h4 ♖h8 17 ♕f4 f6! 18 exf6 e5 19 ♕f3 ♖h6 20 f7 ♗e6 21 ♗e4 ♖xf7 22 ♕d3 ♗f5 ∓ Krakops-Poldauf, Groningen 1995.

12 ♗f4 (D)

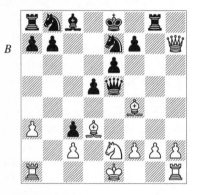

12...♕f6

It would be premature to attempt to exchange queens since after 12...♕g7 or 12...♕h8, White exchanges and follows with up 14 ♗e5!, after which the bishop obtains a dominant role on the a1-h8 diagonal, which can be a lethal factor in combination with the passed h-pawn.

13 h4 ♘d7!

Black should control the f6-square. This is important as White was threatening 14 ♗g5 and after 14...♕g7 or 14...♕h8, White's bishop would take up a place on the a1-h8 diagonal after a queen exchange.

Other moves:

a) 13...♖h8? 14 ♗g5! ♕e5 15 f4 ♖xh7 16 fxe5 ♖h8 17 ♗f6 ♖g8 18 h5 ♘d7 19 h6 ♘xf6 20 exf6 ♘c6 21 h7 ♖h8 22 ♘xc3 +−.

b) 13...♘bc6 14 ♗g5 ♕e5 (alternatively, 14...♕h8 15 ♕xh8 ♖xh8 16 ♗f6 ±) 15 f4! ♕c7 16 h5 looks very dangerous for Black. Izeta-Vella, Cordoba 1991 finished abruptly: 16...e5? 17 h6 e4 18 ♕xg8+! 1-0. 16...♗d7 is best but 17 h6 0-0-0 18 ♕xf7 is good for White.

c) 13...♖xg2?! 14 ♔f1! and now:

c1) 14...♖g8?! 15 ♗g5 ♕h8 (not 15...♕f3? 16 ♘g3 ± Rodriguez Talavera-Sanchez Jimenez, Granada 1991) 16 ♕xh8 ♖xh8 17 ♗f6 is much better for White.

c2) 14...e5 15 ♔xg2 exf4 16 ♕h5 ♘bc6 17 f3!? ♗f5 18 ♕g5 ♕xg5+ 19 hxg5 0-0-0 20 ♔f2 ± Apicella-Gerard, Avoine 1993.

14 ♗g5 ♕h8 15 ♕xh8 ♖xh8 16 ♘xc3 a6 17 0-0-0 f6 18 ♗e3

Now 18...e5? 19 ♘xd5 1-0 was an embarrassing end for Black in Am.Rodriguez-Matamoros, Bayamo 1989. Am.Rodriguez suggests 18...♘e5 as an improvement. This was tried out successfully in Engsner-Nygren, Swedish League 1993/4, when Black had plenty of play after 19 h5 ♗d7 20 ♗d4 ♘xd3+ 21 ♖xd3 ♔f7 22 f3 e5. It is the typical case of whether White's h-pawn is strong or weak.

B)

8 ♕xg7 ♖g8 9 ♕xh7 cxd4 (D)

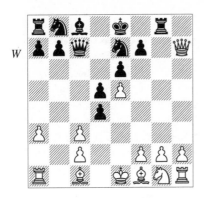

Now:

B1: 10 ♔d1   155
B2: 10 ♘e2   157

B1)

10 ♔d1

This is a fairly rare but very complex line which Black needs to be prepared for.

10...♘bc6 11 ♘f3 dxc3

Another, obviously critical, continuation is 11...♘xe5 12 ♗f4 ♕xc3 13 ♘xe5 ♕xa1+ 14 ♗c1 *(D)*.

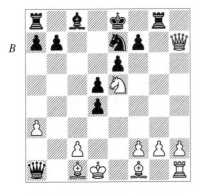

Now Black has two options:

a) 14...♖f8?! is a risky attempt to avoid a draw. White has:

a1) 15 ♗b5+?! ♘c6 16 ♘xc6 ♗d7 is given as clearly better for Black by most sources. 17 ♘e5 ♗xb5 18 ♘xf7 ♖xf7 19 ♕g8+ ♔e7 20 ♕xa8 ♗a6 is critical in verifying that assessment. Black is probably better, though I am not sure by how much. White has good chances of getting in lots of checks.

a2) 15 ♗d3 ♗d7 and then:

a21) 16 ♔e2?! ♘c6 and now:

a211) 17 ♘xf7 ♖xf7 18 ♕g8+ ♖f8 19 ♗g6+ ♔e7 20 ♕g7+ ♔d6 21 ♗f4+ ♖xf4 22 ♖xa1 ♖g4 23 ♕h6 ♘e5 24 ♗d3 ♖xg2 is given as unclear by Uhlmann. Black has more pieces to play with but the white queen and passed h-pawn are a constant worry for Black.

a212) 17 ♘g6 0-0-0 18 ♘xf8 ♖xf8 19 ♕g7 ♖e8 20 h4 e5 gives Black more than enough counterplay.

a213) 17 ♗g5 ♕xa3 and now 18 ♖a1 ♕d6 19 ♘g4 ♘e7 looks fine for Black, as does 18 ♘g6 ♕d6 19 ♕g7 e5 20 ♗e7 ♕xe7 21 ♘xe7 ♔xe7.

a22) 16 ♖e1! ♘c6 17 ♘xf7 ♖xf7 18 ♗g6 0-0-0 19 ♕xf7 e5 20 ♔e2 e4 21 ♔f1 ♕c3 22 ♗g5 ±.

b) 14...d3 15 ♕xf7+ ♔d8 16 ♕f6 dxc2+ and then:

b1) 17 ♔xc2 ♕a2+ 18 ♗b2 ♗d7 19 ♘f7+ ♔e8 20 ♘d6+ ♔d8 (White doesn't have more than a perpetual) 21 ♗d3?! ♗a4+ 22 ♔d2 ♔d7 23 ♖e1 ♘c6 24 ♘xb7? ♖af8 25 ♘c5+ ♔d6 26 ♕c3 ♖xf2+ 27 ♖e2 (Grabarczyk-Spiess, 2nd Bundesliga 1994/5) 27...d4! 28 ♕c1 ♖f1 −+.

b2) 17 ♔d2 ♕d4+ 18 ♗d3 ♕c5! 19 ♔e2 ♗d7 and here:

b21) 20 ♗e3, B.Stein-Beliavsky, London Lloyds Bank 1985, and now Stein considers 20...♕xa3! 21 ♖a1 ♕b4 to be unclear.

b22) 20 ♘f7+ ♔e8 (20...♔c8 looks risky due to 21 ♗f4) 21 ♗f4 is a tempting alternative, but 21...♘f5 22 ♗xf5 ♗b5+ 23 ♗d3 ♗xd3+ 24 ♔xd3 ♕xa3+ 25 ♔d2 ♕a5+ 26 ♔c1 ♕a3+ 27 ♔d2 ♕b4+ 28 ♔c1 ♕b1+ 29 ♔d2 ♕b4+ is just a draw. Neither side can afford to avoid the repetition.

We now return to the position after 11...dxc3 *(D)*:

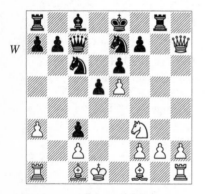

12 ♘g5

There are a few minor alternatives:

a) 12 ♗f4 ♕b6 13 ♗e3 and then:

a1) 13...♕b2 14 ♖c1 ♗d7 and now 15 h4?! 0-0-0 16 ♗d3 ♘f5 was very good for Black in Steil-Farago, Budapest 1986. White should play 15 ♗d3 at once, intending to meet 15...0-0-0 with 16 ♔e2. Black looks fine in this line though.

a2) 13...d4!? 14 ♗g5 ♕b2 15 ♖c1 ♗d7 16 ♗d3 0-0-0 17 ♔e2 ♕xa3 is an additional possibility.

b) 12 h4!? ♕b6 13 ♗e3 (13 ♔e1!?) 13...d4 14 ♗g5 ♕b2 15 ♖c1 ♗d7 16 ♗d3 0-0-0 17 ♔e2 is an improved version of line 'a2', because White has a tempo more (h4). Korchnoi continues the analysis with 17...♕xa3 18 ♖a1 ♕c5 19 ♖hb1 ♘b4 20 ♕xf7 ♘bd5, with unclear play.

c) 12 ♖b1 ♗d7 13 ♗g5 0-0-0 14 ♕d3 (Minić-Ivkov, Yugoslav Ch (Titograd) 1965) 14...d4 doesn't look bad for Black.

12...♘xe5

A recent, and possibly better, idea is 12...♕xe5!? 13 ♕xf7+ ♔d7 14 ♗f4 (14 h4 might be better, but the response is the same: Black plays 14...♕d4+ 15 ♔e1 and now 15...e5 or McDonald's suggestion, 15...♕e5+ 16 ♗e3 ♖g7 17 ♕f4 ♕xf4 18 ♗xf4 e5) 14...♕d4+ 15 ♔e1 e5 16 ♗e3 ♕g4 17 ♗e2 ♕f5, and Black was better in Busquets-Se.Ivanov, Irvine 1997.

13 ♗f4!

This is stronger than 13 f4, when Black has a choice of two viable lines: 13...♖xg5 14 fxg5 ♘5g6 and 13...f6!? 14 fxe5 fxg5.

13...♕b6 14 ♗xe5 ♖xg5 15 ♕h4!

White's latest attempt, and a good one. Since it is clear that Black is not going to be knocked over just like that, White tries a more positional approach.

15...♖g8

Of course, Black cannot continue 15...♖xe5?, owing to 16 ♕h8+.

16 ♕d4! ♕xd4+ 17 ♗xd4 *(D)*

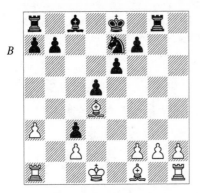

The endgame will favour White, if he is allowed to consolidate and complete his development. Hence the assessment depends on whether Black can quickly generate counterplay by advancing his central pawns. Now:

a) 17...♘c6 18 ♗xc3 e5 19 ♔d2 d4 20 ♗b2 ♗f5 21 ♖e1 ♔f8 22 f3! ♖c8 23 g4 ♗g6 24 ♗d3 ± Kagan-B.Martin, Canberra 1999.

b) 17...♘f5 18 ♗xc3 ♗d7 19 h4 ♖c8 20 ♔d2 d4 21 ♗b2 ♗c6 22 ♖h2 ♖h8 23 g3 e5 was given as equal by Watson but McDonald disagrees on the basis of 24 ♗d3! ♘e7 (another point is 24...e4 25 ♖e1 e3+ 26 ♔c1, when Black's position falls apart) 25 ♖e1 f6 26 f4.

In both these lines, White successfully accomplishes a blockade of the pawns, after which the bishop-pair promises him an advantage.

B2)
10 ♘e2 ♘bc6 11 f4 ♗d7

11...dxc3 12 ♕d3 d4 is an independent line that deserves a mention. Then:

a) 13 ♖b1 ♗d7 14 ♖g1 0-0-0 15 g4 ♗e8 16 ♖g3 is slightly better for White, Rodriguez-Pecorelli Garcia, Matanzas 1994.

b) 13 ♘xd4 ♘xd4 14 ♕xd4 ♗d7 15 ♖g1!? ♘f5 16 ♕f2 ♕c6 (throwing in 16...♖h8 17 h3, as in Wang Zili-Kuijf, Lucerne Wcht 1989, is not superior since Black takes off the pressure against g2, and thus after 17...♕c6 18 ♗d3 ♕d5 19 ♖b1 ♗c6 White even has 20 ♖b4!, intending ♗e4; if then 20...♖d8, White plays 21 ♖c4 ♘h4 22 ♖c5! and picks up the c-pawn) 17 ♗d3 ♕d5 18 ♖b1 ♗c6 19 ♖b3 0-0-0 20 ♖xc3 ♔b8 21 g4 ♘d4 22 ♖g3 ♕a2 23 ♗e3 ♕a1+ 24 ♔d2 ♘b5 25 ♖b3 ± Wach-Cech, Germany 1997/8.

12 ♕d3 dxc3 *(D)*

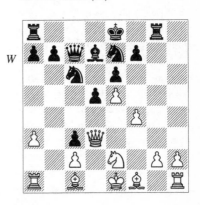

Now:

Another interesting and important alternative is 13 h4. There is a fairly small number of practical games with this line but it is interesting that Norwegian GM Djurhuus, who is himself a devoted French player, prefers this. After 13...♘f5 14 ♖b1 0-0-0 15 h5, Black has:

a) 15...d4?! 16 ♖g1 ♘h6 17 ♘xd4 ♘xd4 18 ♕xd4 b6 19 ♖b3 +− Djurhuus-Johannessen, Norwegian Ch (Alta) 1996.

b) 15...♘a5 16 ♖g1 ♘c4 17 g4 ♕c5 18 ♕xc3 a5 19 ♖g2 ♘h6 20 g5 ♘f5 21 ♘g3, Djurhuus-Antonsen, Torshavn 1997, and now Djurhuus recommends 21...♗c6 22 ♘xf5 exf5 23 ♕d3 with an unclear position.

B21)
13 ♗e3
White aims to complete his development rather than wasting time on capturing the c3-pawn. 13 ♗e3 has enjoyed a brief moment of popularity lately but is not dangerous for Black. On the contrary, Black may even be able to keep his pawn on c3 and maintain his dynamic possibilities without risking nearly as much as in other lines.

13...0-0-0!
This is simple and strong. Other moves:

a) 13...d4 and then:

a1) 14 ♗f2 0-0-0 15 ♘xd4 ♘xd4 16 ♕xd4 b6 17 ♗h4 ♗b5 with equality, Spassky-Korchnoi, Belgrade Ct (2) 1977.

a2) 14 ♘xd4 is better: 14...♘xd4 15 ♕xd4 ♘f5 16 ♕c5 gives White a slight advantage, Sievers-Heyken, Bundesliga 1990/1.

b) 13...♘f5 14 ♗f2 *(D)* and now:

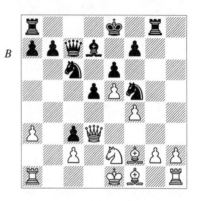

b1) 14...f6 15 exf6 0-0-0 16 h3 e5 17 f7 ♖gf8 18 g4 e4 19 ♕xc3 d4 20 ♕c5 e3 21 ♗g1 ♘h4 22 0-0-0 ♗e6 23 f5 ♗d5 24 ♗h2 ♕xf7 25 ♘f4 ♗xh1 26 ♗c4 ♕c7 27 ♖xh1 ± Shmuter-Kaplun, Kherson 1990.

b2) 14...0-0-0 15 h3! d4 16 g4 ♘fe7 17 ♗g2 ♘g6 (17...♗e8!?) 18 0-0 a6?! 19 ♖ab1 ± David-Ranieri, Turin 1998.

b3) 14...d4!? and then:

b31) 15 h3? ♕a5! 16 ♖b1 ♕xa3 17 ♕c4 b5! 18 ♕b3 ♕xb3 19 ♖xb3 b4 20 g4 a5! ∓ Esser-Arounopoulos, corr. 1992.

b32) 15 ♘xd4 ♘cxd4 16 ♗xd4 0-0-0! 17 ♕xc3? (17 ♗xa7 is necessary) 17...♘xd4 18 ♕xd4 – *13...0-0-0! 14 ♕xc3 d4 15 ♘xd4? ♘d5 16 ♕d2 ♘xe3 17 ♕xe3 ♘xd4 18 ♕xd4 −+*.

b33) 15 ♗xd4 ♘cxd4 16 ♘xd4 0-0-0 gives Black compensation.

b34) 15 ♘g3 0-0-0 16 ♘xf5 exf5 ∓
Cobo Arteaga-Ivkov, Havana 1963.

c) 13...♖c8 14 g3 ♘f5 15 ♗f2 ♕a5
16 ♗h3 d4! 17 0-0 (17 ♗xf5 exf5 18
♘xd4 ♘xd4 19 ♗xd4 ♗c6 with compensation) 17...♖d8 18 ♖fd1 ♘xe5!
(even now, when fully developed, White
cannot feel safe; with this piece sacrifice Black takes over the a8-h1 diagonal) 19 fxe5 ♗b5 20 ♕e4 ♗c6 21 ♕f4
♕d5 22 ♔f1 ♕h1+ 23 ♘g1 ♕xh2 and
now 24 ♖d3? ♘e3+ 25 ♔e2 ♗b5 left
White in big trouble in Almasi-
Timman, Ubeda 1997. Instead, 24
♗xf5! seems to draw; e.g., 24...♕g2+
25 ♔e1 (25 ♔e2?! exf5 26 ♖xd4?!
♗b5+ 27 ♔d1 ♕f1+ 28 ♗e1 ♕xf4 ∓)
25...exf5 26 ♖xd4 (26 e6 ♖g6! 27
exf7+ ♔xf7 28 ♕xf5+ ♖f6 29 ♕h7+
♔f8 30 ♕h8+ also leads to a perpetual
– Yusupov) 26...♕g4 27 ♖xd8+ ♔xd8
28 ♖d1+ ♔e8 29 ♕h6 ♖e4+ 30 ♘e2
♖xe2+ 31 ♔xe2 ♗f3+ 32 ♔e1 ♗xd1
33 ♕h8+ ♔e7 34 ♕f6+ = Yusupov.

We now return to 13...0-0-0 (D):

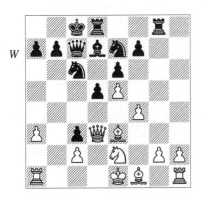

14 g3

This is a sensible attempt to finish
development but is not very energetic.
Other moves come into consideration
but none of them look very promising:

a) 14 ♘d4 ♘xd4 15 ♗xd4 ♘f5
looks good for Black.

b) 14 ♕xc3 and now:

b1) 14...d4 is tempting but White
can probably just reply 15 ♗xd4 (15
♘xd4? ♘d5 16 ♕d2 ♘xe3 17 ♕xe3
♘xd4 18 ♕xd4 ♗b5! and then, for example, 19 ♕e3 ♗xf1 20 ♔xf1 ♕xc2 21
g3 ♖d2 22 ♖e1 ♖gd8 wins for Black)
15...♘d5 16 ♕c5.

b2) Black should prefer 14...♘f5
15 ♗f2 d4 16 ♕d2, when the thematic
16...f6! 17 exf6 e5! looks attractive.

c) 14 ♗f2 could be considered.

d) 14 h3, preparing to meet 14...♘f5
15 ♗f2 d4 with 16 g4, is interesting,
and might even be best.

14...d4!

14...♘f5 15 ♗f2 ♔b8 (15...d4
should be considered) 16 ♗h3 ♘ce7
17 g4 ♘h6 18 ♖g1 ♖c8 19 ♘d4 ♘g6
20 ♕e3! b6 21 a4 ♔a8 and after 22
♗f1 f6! Black obtained counterplay in
Sax-Shulman, Pula Echt 1997, but 22
a5!? b5 23 g5 ♘f5 24 ♘xf5 (24 ♗xf5
exf5 25 h4) 24...exf5 25 ♕d4 ♗e6 26
♗g2 maintains a solid advantage.

15 ♗f2

15 ♘xd4? ♘xd4 16 ♗xd4 ♗c6
wins for Black.

15...♘g6!?

Black threatens a cruel knight sacrifice on e5. 15...♘f5 is a good alternative.

16 ♕c4

This was given a '?' by Rõtšagov but is actually White's best. However, White does seem to be in difficulties. Rõtšagov's line 16 ♗g2 ♘gxe5 17 fxe5 ♘xe5 18 ♕d1 (18 ♕xd4 ♗c6 19 ♕xa7 ♗xg2 20 ♗b6 ♕d6 21 ♖f1 ♗xf1 22 ♔xf1 ♖d7 23 ♘xc3 ♘c4 ∓) 18...♗c6 19 ♘f4, when he continues 19...♗xg2 20 ♘xg2 ♕c6 21 0-0 ♘f3+ 22 ♔h1 ♘h4 (22...e5!? gives Black compensation, and can be considered) 23 ♖g1 ♘f3 24 ♖f1 =, leaves much to be answered. I think, for example, 19...d3! 20 0-0 ♗a4 looks very good for Black.

16...f6! 17 exf6

17 ♘xd4 puts up more resistance. With accurate play, Black is still better though: 17...♘xd4 (17...fxe5? 18 ♘b5 ♕a5 19 ♖b1 ±) 18 ♗xd4 ♗c6 19 ♗h3 ♔b8 20 ♖f1 ♖h8!? 21 ♗xe6 fxe5 22 fxe5 ♘xe5 23 ♕c5 ♖xd4 24 ♕xd4 ♗f3! ∓.

17...e5 18 ♗g2 exf4 19 ♗xd4 ♘xd4 20 ♕xc7+ ♔xc7 21 ♘xd4 ♖ge8+ 22 ♔f2 ♗g4!

Black is better, Rõtšagov-Djurhuus, Oslo 1997.

B22)

13 ♖b1 *(D)*

This is rather a popular move-order. It may transpose to just about every other line since White usually plays ♖b1 at some point, no matter which line he chooses, but playing it immediately has a few subtleties. First of all, black-players who think too much about its real virtue will probably get very confused trying to measure the

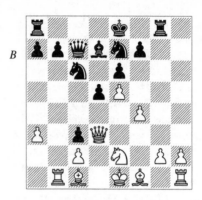

B

ups and downs of every single line. Indeed, the move is an attempt to get the best of everything!

13...0-0-0

13...♘f5 (13...d4 – *11...dxc3 12 ♕d3 d4 13 ♖b1 ♗d7* ±) is the only other reasonable move and has the sensible point that both captures on c3 transpose to better-known lines. However, White has a third option in 14 h3! (14 h4!? – *13 h4 ♘f5 14 ♖b1* ∞). Then:

a) 14...♖c8 15 g4 ♘fe7 16 ♗e3!? (or 16 ♕xc3) looks good for White.

b) 14...d4 15 g4 ♘h4 (15...♘fe7 16 ♘xd4 ±) 16 ♕h7 ♘f3+ 17 ♔f2 0-0-0 18 ♗xf3 ♘xe5+ 19 fxe5 ♗c6+ 20 ♔f2 ♗xh1 21 ♖b4! ± J.Horvath-Uhlmann, Szirak 1985.

c) 14...0-0-0!? 15 g4 ♘fe7 16 ♘xc3 ± must be an improved version of the main line since White has achieved h3 and g4 for free and White often takes his time to prepare these, but it may be worth looking deeper into this.

14 ♘xc3

14 ♕xc3 – *13 ♕xc3 0-0-0 14 ♖b1* ±/=.

14...♘a5 *(D)*

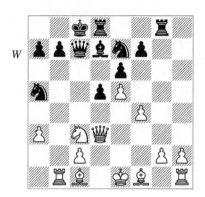

15 ♖g1!?

White prepares to advance his g-pawn to g4, where it would not only prevent Black from playing ...♘f5 (if the g1-rook is protected) but also make room for ♖g3, which can defend the c3-knight and perhaps even swing over to the queenside at some point. Other moves:

a) 15 g3 ♔b8 16 ♘e2 ♗a4 and now:

a1) 17 c3?! ♘f5 18 ♗h3 d4! 19 ♗d2 ♘b3 20 ♗xf5 dxc3 21 ♕xc3 ♘xd2! 22 ♕xc7+ ♔xc7 23 ♖c1+ ♗c6 was very good for Black in Svidler-Ivanchuk, Linares 1999.

a2) It is difficult to say what prevented Svidler from playing the very obvious 17 ♘d4. He might have been worried about something like 17...♘f5 18 ♗e3 b6 19 c3 ♘xd4 20 ♗xd4 ♘c4, when White has an extra pawn but Black has excellent counterplay.

b) 15 ♘b5 ♗xb5 16 ♖xb5 ♘c4 17 g3 ♕c6 18 ♖b3 ♔b8 19 ♗g2 ♕c5 and

Black had counterplay in Heidenfeld-Hillermann, Württemberg 1992.

c) 15 h3 has been met by 15...a6 a few times, with Black close to equalizing. However, this was before Black's ...♔b8 idea was discovered. Thus, here too Black should play 15...♔b8, when h3 looks rather slow compared to the other lines.

15...♔b8 16 g4 ♘g6

16...♖c8 17 ♖g3 is probably a useful insertion for White. The rook is now defended and is usefully placed, guarding the third rank.

17 ♕d4

Instead Mitkov-Shulman, Erevan OL 1996 continued 17 ♘e2 ♖c8 18 ♘d4 and now Shulman and Kapengut suggest 18...f6!? 19 exf6 ♘xf4 20 ♗xf4 ♕xf4 21 ♕g3 ♕xg3+ 22 ♖xg3 e5, with an unclear game.

17...f6!? 18 ♗e3 b6

18...♘c6 19 ♕c5 fxe5 20 ♘b5 ♕a5+ 21 ♗d2 ♕b6 might be an idea.

19 exf6 e5 20 fxe5 ♘c6 21 ♕c5 ♗e6

Lutz-Feygin, Bundesliga 2000/1. The position is rather messy. White seems to have a promising attack but should it fail his own king could be in danger. My feeling is that the position is good for White. The game would have provided clearer evidence for this, if only White had not blundered: 22 ♘a4 ♘cxe5 23 ♘xb6 ♕xc5 24 ♘d7+ ♔a8 25 ♘xc5 ♗xg4 26 ♗a6 ♗c8 27 ♗e2 ♖d6, and now Lutz's move, 28 ♗d4, might still be OK, but 28 ♗f4! or 28 h4! looks strong; e.g.,

28...♖xf6 29 h5 ♖e8 30 hxg6 ♘f3+ 31 ♗xf3 ♖xf3 32 g7 ♖fxe3+ 33 ♔d2 ♖e2+ 34 ♔d1 +−, or 28...♖e8 29 h5 ♘h4 30 ♗f4 +−.

B23)

13 ♕xc3 (D)

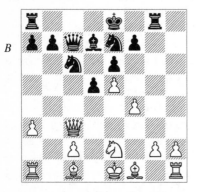

For a long time this has been considered the main line. However, it seems that White is in need of something new in order to prove a real advantage. The current assessment is that the line is almost a forced draw! The variations are lengthy and the theory goes up to around move 30. This might sound a chore, but the moves flow very naturally.

13...♘f5

Black's play is centred around the ...d4 push, queenside castling and a quick ...f6 break to blow up the centre before White gets time to consolidate his position.

Alternatively, Black may go for 13...0-0-0, immediately connecting his rooks and perhaps maintaining more flexibility in his choice of plan. Then 14 ♖b1 is probably still best, after which Black has a choice:

a) 14...♘f5 – *13...♘f5 14 ♖b1 0-0-0*.

b) 14...♔b8 prepares to play ...♖c8, or possibly ...♗c8 followed by ...b6 and ...♗b7/a6. This may look slow, but White has weaknesses and is struggling with his development so Black can afford some time to improve his position further. 15 ♗d2 (15 g3 ♗c8 16 ♗g2 b6 17 0-0 ♗a6 18 ♖e1 ♘f5 gives Black fine counterplay according to John Watson; as an illustrative line, Watson gives 19 ♗d2 ♖c8 20 ♘c1 ♕e7 21 ♕b2 ♕c5+) 15...d4 16 ♕c4 ♗c8 17 g3 b6 18 ♗g2 ♗b7 19 0-0 ♘f5 20 ♕d3 ♕c8! with good counterplay for Black, Riemersma-Sisniega, Seville 1987.

14 ♖b1

This is well established as 'best'. Against most other moves ...♕b6, planning ...♖c8, would be annoying for White.

14...0-0-0

Black's other main plan is 14...♖c8, which logically aims for counterplay on the c-file. The drawback is that the king has to remain in the centre. 15 ♗d2! (discouraging ...♘cd4), and then:

a) 15...♘cd4 16 ♘xd4 ♕xc3 17 ♗xc3 ♖xc3 18 ♘xf5 exf5 19 ♖xb7 is clearly better for White.

b) 15...♕d8 16 ♕d3! ♘a5 17 g3 ♗a4 (17...♘c4 18 ♗h3 ♕c7 19 ♗xf5 exf5 20 ♘d4 with a clear advantage for White, Borg-Skalkotas, Kavala 1985)

18 ♘c3 ♗c6 19 ♗h3 d4 20 ♘e4 ♖g6 (Röttig-Perdekamp, Konstanz 1983) 21 ♗g2 ♔f8 22 0-0 ±.

c) 15...♘ce7 16 ♕xc7 ♖xc7 17 c3 ♗a4 18 ♖b2 ♘c6 19 h3, intending g4, favours White, Mestel-Depasquale, British Ch (Southampton) 1986.

d) 15...d4 16 ♕d3 ♘ce7 17 ♘xd4 ♘xd4 18 ♕xd4 ± Karpov-Agdestein, Oslo 1984.

e) 15...b6?! 16 g3! ♕b7 17 ♕d3 ♘ce7 18 ♖g1 ♖c4 19 g4 ♘h4 20 ♖g3 ♕c8 21 ♖b2 ♘hg6 22 ♖f3! ♘c6 23 ♖f2 ♖h8 24 h3 ♕d8 25 ♕g3! with a slight advantage for White, Karpov-Farago, Wijk aan Zee 1988.

f) 15...a6! 16 ♖g1! ♕d8 (16...b5 17 g4 ♘h4 18 ♖g3 ± Short-Kosten, Hastings 1988/9) 17 ♕h3 b5 18 g4 ♘h4 has been mentioned by Korchnoi and tried in a few games between lesser-known players. White looks better after, for example, 19 ♕d3 ♖h8 20 ♖g3 ♘g6 21 ♖h3, Pineault-Anton, corr. 1992.

15 ♖g1

This is the sharpest approach. White is planning to harass the f5-knight with g4. Quieter continuations don't seem particularly threatening to Black, whose pieces work splendidly together. The knight tandem on c6 and f5 is especially irritating.

15...d4 *(D)*

Or 15...f6 16 g4 (White should play this before he captures on f6; otherwise Black has d6 available for the knight) 16...♘h6 17 exf6 ♖xg4 18 ♖xg4 ♘xg4 19 f7, and now:

a) 19...♕a5? 20 ♕xa5 ♘xa5 21 ♗h3 e5 22 f5! +– Cladouras-Wiedenkeller, Liechtenstein 1988.

b) 19...♕d6? 20 ♕g7! e5 21 ♗h3 ♕f8 22 ♕g6 ± Hellers-Østenstad, Oslo 1991.

c) 19...e5!? 20 ♗h3 (20 ♕c5!?) 20...♖f8 21 ♕g3 ♘f6 22 ♕g7 ♕d8 23 ♗xd7+ ♘xd7 24 ♖b5 ♕e7 25 ♖xd5 ♖xf7 gives Black counterplay.

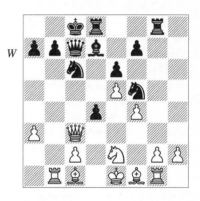

16 ♕d3

This brings us to an important position. White has won a pawn but his pieces are very disorganized, almost randomly placed. Hence it is logical for Black to attempt to stir up some trouble before White is able to consolidate. The first thing that springs to mind is how to improve the position of the bishop. There are two ideas:

1) Sacrifice another pawn with ...f6. This clears a route via e8 to squares like g6. If White captures on f6, Black can continue aggressively with ...e5. Then the bishop doesn't need re-routing as it is already on a fine diagonal.

2) Remove the knight from c6, thus preparing ...♗a4/c6.

Instead of putting the queen on d3, 16 ♕c5!? is an important alternative. Then after 16...♖e8!? 17 g4 ♖d5 18 ♕c4, Black has two options:

a) 18...♘h4 19 ♖g3 ♕a5+ 20 ♗d2 ♖c5 21 ♕d3 ± Dizdarević-Gehlert, Bavaria 1995/6.

b) 18...♘e3!? 19 ♗xe3 dxe3 20 ♕c3 ♘d4 21 ♕xc7+ ♔xc7 22 ♘xd4 ♖xd4 23 ♖b4 ♖d2 and Black has good counterplay, Ankerst-Uhlmann, Bundesliga 1995/6.

16...f6!?

This has been analysed in depth. Black's counterplay is sufficient but probably no more than that. However, White must tread very carefully indeed. Other interesting ideas worth noting are:

a) 16...♗e8 17 g4 ♘h4 18 ♖g3 f6 19 exf6 – *16...f6 17 g4 ♘h4 18 exf6 ♗e8 19 ♖g3* ±.

b) 16...♘a5!? 17 ♖b4!? ♗c6 (White can meet 17...♘c6 by 18 ♖b2, and if 18...♘a5 White plays 19 g4, because Black doesn't have ...♗a4, which is one point if White plays 17 g4 immediately) 18 ♘g3 ♘xg3 19 hxg3 ♖g6 20 ♗e2 ± Antoszkiewicz-Eisenacher, corr. 1990-1.

c) 16...♘ce7 17 g4 (17 ♖b4?! is the right reaction against *16...♘a5* but here Black obtains a promising position with 17...♘d5 18 ♖c4 ♗c6, Renet-Hübner, Germany Cup 1989) 17...♗a4!? 18 ♗g2!? (18 ♖b2 is the alternative) 18...♘d5 19 c4 dxc3 20 gxf5 ♖xg2 21

♖xg2 c2 22 ♖b2 ♘xf4 23 ♕xd8+ ♕xd8 24 ♗xf4 ♕d1+ 25 ♔f2 ♗c6 26 ♖g3 exf5 27 ♖c3 1-0 Diani-Dorner, 1995.

17 g4

17 exf6? is a mistake, since Black has the d6-square available for the knight. Black plays 17...e5! and then when White plays g4, Black can put his knight on d6.

17...♘h4

17...♘h6? 18 exf6 ♖xg4 19 ♖xg4 ♘xg4 20 f7 ± Balashov-Kosten, Minsk 1986.

18 exf6 (D)

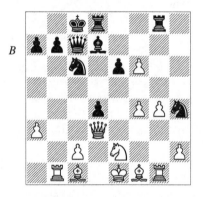

18...e5

This is the most direct. Another interesting idea is 18...♗e8 19 ♖g3, and now:

a) 19...e5!? 20 g5! ♗f7! 21 ♗h3+ (21 ♖h3 ♗g6 22 ♕c4 ♗f7 23 ♕a4 is unclear – Nogueiras) 21...♔b8 22 f5 (22 fxe5? ♘xe5 23 ♕e4 ♖ge8!! gave Black a strong attack in Sznapik-Nogueiras, Thessaloniki OL 1988) 22...♗d5 23 g6 e4 24 ♕b5 ♘e5 25

♗f4 ♘hf3+ 26 ♖xf3 exf3 27 f7 and White is better – Neven.

b) 19...♗f7 20 ♗h3 ♖ge8 21 g5 ♗g6 22 ♕c4 ♘f5 23 ♖gb3 ♘d6 24 ♗xe6+! ♔b8 and now 25 ♖xb7+! ♘xb7 26 f5 wins for White.

c) 19...♗g6 20 f5! exf5 21 ♗f4! ♕d7 (21...♕a5+ 22 ♔f2 fxg4 23 ♕b3! b6 24 ♖xg4 ±) 22 g5 ♗h5 23 ♕b5! ♖ge8 24 ♔f2 ♖e4 25 ♗d2 ♖e5 26 ♕d3 ♘g6 27 ♘f4 ± Polzin-Poldauf, Austrian League 1999/00.

19 f7

At least this will distract Black somewhat from the issue in the centre and on the kingside. Other moves that come into consideration are:

a) 19 g5?! e4! 20 ♕xe4 ♗f5 21 ♕h1 ♖ge8 is much better for Black, Galov-Lenhardt, corr. 1993.

b) 19 h3 ♗e6!? is Watson's suggestion, intending ...♗d5 and ...♘f3+.

c) 19 ♗h3 ♖ge8 20 ♕g3 d3! (another idea is 20...♘g6!?) 21 f7 ♖e7 22 ♕xh4 dxe2 was messy in Přibyl-Kolcak, corr. 1992.

19...♖xg4 20 ♖xg4 ♗xg4 21 ♗h3 ♕d7 22 ♗xg4 ♕xg4 23 ♕g3 ♕h5 24 ♖b3! e4! *(D)*

After an almost forced sequence of moves, we have arrived at a dynamically balanced position. White's only trump card (though a good one) is his pawn on f7, while Black has attacking possibilities against the unsafe white king. Now:

a) 25 ♕g7 d3! 26 cxd3 ♘f3+ 27 ♔f2 ♕xh2+ 28 ♕g2 (28 ♔e3?! ♘cd4! 29 ♘xd4 ♘xd4 30 ♕g4+ ♔b8 31 f8♕

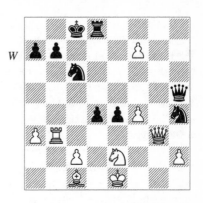

♘c2+ 32 ♔xe4 ♕h1+ 33 ♕f3 gives Black a choice between 33...♕h7+ 34 f5 ♖xf8, with some attacking chances, and 33...♕e1+, which forces a draw) 28...♕xg2+ 29 ♔xg2 exd3 30 ♔xf3 dxe2 31 ♖e3 ♖f8 = Hellers-Djurhuus, Gausdal 1992.

b) 25 ♕g8!? ♕d5! 26 ♕g7!? ♘f3+ (26...♕c5 27 ♕g4+! ♘f5 28 c4!! ± Tatar Kis-Seres, Szeged 1998) 27 ♔f2 ♕h5 28 f8♕ ♕xh2+ 29 ♔f1 ½-½ Brenke-Rümmele, corr. 1994.

B24)

13 ♘xc3 *(D)*

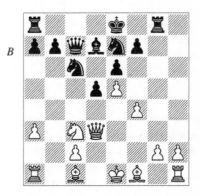

13...a6

This is not altogether forced but it is clearly the best way to prevent White's threat of 14 ♘b5. The move also has a positional purpose since sometimes the manoeuvre ...♘a7 followed by ...♘b5 or ...♗b5 comes into consideration.

Other moves:

a) 13...0-0-0? 14 ♘b5 ♘xe5 15 ♘xc7 ♘xd3+ 16 ♗xd3 ♔xc7 17 ♗b2!? ♖xg2 18 ♗f6 gave White more than enough compensation for the pawn in Feigin-Poldauf, Dortmund 1998.

b) 13...♘a5 14 ♘b5 ♗xb5 15 ♕xb5+ ♘ac6 16 g3 0-0-0 17 ♕c5 ♔b8 18 ♗d3 d4 19 ♗d2 ♖d5 20 ♕c4 ♖c8 21 0-0 ♕d8 22 ♕b3 ♕c7 23 ♖ab1 ± Smagin-Naumkin, Palma de Mallorca 1989.

c) 13...♘f5 and now:

c1) Note that 14 g4?! ♖xg4 15 ♗h3 ♘xe5 16 fxe5 ♕xe5+ is a clearly improved version for Black of note 'b' to Black's 14th move, because the a1-rook is attacked. Hence after 17 ♘e2 ♖h4 Black is ready to play 18...♘d4, with a strong attack.

c2) 14 ♘b5 ♕d8 15 ♖b1! a6 16 ♘d6+ ♘xd6 17 exd6 ♘a5 18 ♕h7 ♖f8 19 ♗d3 ± Lau-Negele, Dresden open 1998.

14 ♖b1 *(D)*

This is by far the most common move. It is very useful for White in many lines that he is attacking b7. There are also advantages in removing the rook from a1 as in some lines Black sacrifices a knight on e5 and then the rook wouldn't come under

attack. Furthermore, White prevents 14...0-0-0 due to 15 ♕xa6!.

14 ♘e2!? is a very reasonable alternative. White has won a pawn and made ...0-0-0 a risky affair for Black, and now anticipates that in order to make his pieces work more efficiently together, Black will have to move his knight from c6, after which White can take possession of the d4-square. However, this is where ...a6 actually comes in conveniently for Black as it is possible to fight for d4 from b5, via a7. Ideally, Black might even solve the problem of his 'bad' bishop before that. A few lines:

a) 14...♖c8 15 ♖b1 ♘a7! 16 ♗e3 ♘b5 17 ♘g3 ♘c3 18 ♗b6 ♕c6 19 ♖b4 ♘e4 ∓ Vescovi-De Toledo, Schahin Cury 1997.

b) 14...♘f5 15 ♖b1 ♘a7! 16 ♕c3 ♗c6 17 ♘d4 ♘xd4 18 ♕xd4 ♘b5 19 ♕c5 d4 20 ♖b3 ♕d8! and Black had excellent counterplay in Ehlvest-P.Nikolić, Reykjavik 1991.

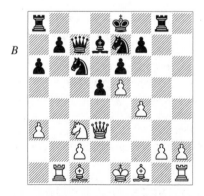

14...♘a5

Black keeps his options open regarding whether he wants to castle or play ...♖c8. Two important alternatives are:

a) 14...♖c8 was a popular line in the 1980s but Black has now switched to the more flexible text-move, since practice has shown that Black has a difficult time coping with a rushing h-pawn. 15 h4! ♘f5 16 ♖h3 ♘ce7! (this has superseded the older 16...♘a5; the knights are needed to cover each other) 17 ♗d2 ♗c6 18 h5 ♘h6 19 ♖g3! ♖xg3 20 ♕xg3 ♘ef5 (20...d4 21 ♘d1 ♗e4 22 ♕g5 ♘eg8 23 ♖b4 ±) 21 ♕h3 d4 22 ♘d1 ♕d8 and now:

a1) 23 ♘f2!? ('?' – Uhlmann, but this looks far from clear) 23...♘e3 (a good chance to mix things up, but the sacrifice doesn't look that convincing) 24 ♗xe3 dxe3 25 ♕xe3 ♘f5 and now, rather than 26 ♕d3 ½-½ Psakhis-Uhlmann, Tallinn 1987, Psakhis later suggested that White has a fairly sizeable advantage after 26 ♕d2! ♕h4 27 ♖b3 ♘g3 28 h6!; e.g., 28...♕h2 29 h7! ♘xf1 30 ♖h3! +–, or 28...♘xf1 29 ♔xf1 ♕xh6 (29...♕h2 30 ♘h3) 30 ♖h3 ±.

a2) 23 g4!? ♘h4 (not 23...♕h4+? 24 ♘f2 ♕xh3 25 ♗xh3 ± Korchnoi-Nogueiras, Brussels 1988) 24 ♖b3! ♗e4 (Molnar-Berkes, Pecs 1998; after 24...♗a4, 25 ♗d3!? is a promising exchange sacrifice suggested by Tal) 25 ♘f2! ♗xc2 26 ♖b2 b5 27 f5 ♕d5!? 28 ♕xh4 ♕xe5+ 29 ♗e2 d3 30 ♘xd3 ♗xd3 31 ♗xh6 ♕xb2 32 ♗xd3 ± Uhlmann.

b) 14...♘f5 is met by the thematic and strong 15 g4! *(D)*:

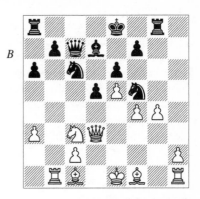

b1) 15...♘xe5 16 fxe5 ♕xe5+ 17 ♘e2 ♖xg4 18 ♗h3 – *15...♖xg4 16 ♗h3 ♘xe5 17 fxe5 ♕xe5+ 18 ♘e2 ±.*

b2) 15...♘fd4?! 16 h3 ♖c8 17 ♗d2 ♘xe5 (17...b5 18 ♔d1 ♕b6 19 ♗e3 ♕c5 20 ♘e2 ♕xc2+ 21 ♕xc2 ♘xc2 22 ♔xc2 d4 23 ♗f2 ♘xe5+ 24 ♔d1 ♗c6 25 ♖g1 ♗e4 26 ♖c1 and White emerged a piece up in Landa-Kaminski, Cappelle la Grande 1999) 18 fxe5 ♕xe5+ 19 ♔d1 ♘xc2 (Hasurdzić-Hari Kos, Patras 1999) 20 ♔xc2 d4 21 ♔b2! ♗c6 22 ♖g1 dxc3+ 23 ♕xc3 +– McDonald.

b3) 15...♘h4 16 ♖g1 ♘a5 17 ♖g3 0-0-0 18 ♔f2 ♗c6 19 ♕d4 ± Nijboer-Poldauf, Leeuwarden 1994.

b4) 15...♖xg4 16 ♗h3 ♘xe5 (or 16...♖g6 17 ♗xf5 exf5 18 ♘xd5 ±) 17 fxe5 ♕xe5+ 18 ♘e2 ♖e4 19 ♗xf5! exf5 20 ♖xb7 ♗b5 21 ♖xb5 axb5 22 ♕xb5+ ♔f8 23 ♖g1 ♕xh2 24 ♕c5+ ♖e7 25 ♕f2 ± Skripchenko-Poldauf, Groningen 1994.

b5) 15...♘fe7 (this retreat seems best but since it is not uncommon for White to prepare g4 in these positions, it cannot be bad to have it for free) 16 ♖g1 (16 h3!?) 16...♖c8?! (according to Farago, this is an inaccurate move-order; Black should first play 16...♖h8) 17 ♖g3 (17 ♘e2!?) 17...♘a5 18 ♕d4 (White can probably take advantage of Black's imprecise move-order with 18 ♕h7!?) 18...♖h8 19 h3 b5 20 ♗d2 ♘c4 21 ♗xc4 ♕xc4 22 ♕xc4 ♖xc4 23 ♔d1 (23 ♖b4!?) 23...♘c6 24 ♘e2 is slightly better for White, Leko-Far-ago, Budapest 1995.

15 h4

Passed pawns must be pushed. Well, White hardly has any hopes of queen-ing the pawn just like that, but there are realistic thoughts that when the pawn gets closer to h8 it will divert Black's attention, and with that White will be able finish his development without too much interference. We will see on the next move that advancing the pawn is not the only idea of 15 h4. The move also makes way for the rook, which can join the action from h3, where it is very useful in guarding the third rank, particularly the c3-knight, which needs protection in the event of Black stepping up the pres-sure on the c-file.

15...♘f5 16 ♖h3 0-0-0 17 h5 *(D)*

A very critical position. Black has to take measures against White's very simple plan of h6-h7, after which if Black is forced to reply with ...♖h8, White is able to follow with g4. Hence, whenever White plays h6, Black should be able to respond with something like ...♖g6, thus keeping one rook on the

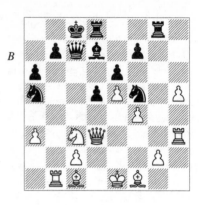

g-file and the other defending against the h-pawn.

17...♘c4

This move is the best established of Black's options, and this is the only reason why I have chosen it as the main line. There are certainly other ideas that look worth testing:

a) 17...♖g4!? and now:

a1) 18 h6?! ♖h8 19 h7 ♖g7 ∓ is Black's primary idea.

a2) 18 ♕f3!? used to be the recom-mendation for White and might still be best; e.g., 18...♖dg8 19 h6 ♖4g6 20 h7 ♖h8 21 g4 ♘e7 22 ♘d1! (better than the formerly played 22 a4) 22...♖g7 23 ♗d3 ♘g6 24 ♕h1 ♘c4 25 ♘f2 ± Fuentes-Moreno, Lima 1999.

a3) 18 ♘d1 ♗a4 19 ♕c3 ♕xc3+ 20 ♖xc3+ ♘c4 21 ♘b2 ♗c6 22 ♘xc4 dxc4 23 ♖xc4 ♔d7 gave Black com-pensation in Lutz-Uhlmann, Dresden Z 1998.

b) 17...♕c5!? worked fine for Black in Moutousis-B.Martin, Tunja jr Wch 1989 but hasn't been tested since: 18 ♘d1 ♗b5 19 ♕c3 ♘c4 20 h6 ♖g6 21 h7 ♖h8 22 ♕f3 ♖g7 23 g4 ♘e7 with good counterplay for Black.

18 ♖b4 *(D)*

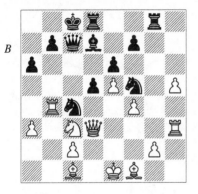

B

Now:

a) 18...b5 (reinforcing the c4-knight and preparing ...♕c5, ...♗c6, etc.) 19 h6 ♖g6 20 h7 ♖h8 21 ♘e2 ♕c5 22 c3 ♖g7 23 ♘d4 ± Malmgren-Kalveus, Stockholm 1994.

b) 18...♕c5!? 19 ♘e4 ♕g1 20 ♘g5 ♗b5 21 ♖xb5! axb5 22 h6 ♖g6 23 h7 ♖h8 24 g4! (24 ♘xf7 ♖xg2) 24...♖xg5 25 fxg5 ♕xg4 26 ♕e2 ♕d4 27 c3 ♕xe5 = Groszpeter-Hagara, Pardubice 1999.

c) 18...♗c6!? 19 ♘e2 ♗b5 20 a4 ♕c5 21 ♗a3 ♗c6 was unclear in Hort-Nogueiras, Biel 1988.

13 Main Line Winawer: 7 ♕g4 0-0

1 e4 e6 2 d4 d5 3 ♘c3 ♗b4 4 e5 c5 5 a3 ♗xc3+ 6 bxc3 ♘e7 7 ♕g4 0-0 *(D)*

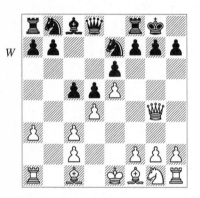

This simple method of preventing ♕xg7 has now become more popular than 7...♕c7. Not long ago, one could have this as a useful sideline to avoid masses of theory but the last 10-15 years have seen a vast investigation of this line. Black seems to be castling straight into a menacing-looking attack but his counterchances (usually based on ...f6 or ...f5, or counterplay against White's centre) shouldn't be underestimated.

We shall look at:

A: 8 ♘f3 170
B: 8 ♗d3 173

In the 'early' days White usually chose 8 ♘f3 but the verdict is now that 8 ♗d3 is a more precise move-order.

A)

8 ♘f3

This has almost disappeared from tournament practice and is clearly superseded by the modern and more accurate 8 ♗d3. It is fairly well established that 8 ♗d3 is more flexible, avoids key defences from Black and is, well, ... just better.

8...♘bc6

A few alternatives deserve a mention:

a) 8...♕a5 9 ♗d2 ♕a4 10 ♗d3 c4 11 ♗xh7+ ♔xh7 12 ♕h4+ ♔g8 13 ♕xe7 ♘c6 14 ♕g5 ♕xc2 15 h4 f6 16 exf6 ♖xf6 17 h5 ♗d7 18 ♖c1 ♕e4+, Lputian-Psakhis, Kharkov 1985, and now Psakhis gives 19 ♗e3 as better for White.

b) 8...f5 9 exf6 ♖xf6 10 ♗g5 *(D)* and now:

b1) 10...♖f8 11 ♕h4 ♘bc6 12 ♗d3 is good for White. Black's rook would have been much better placed on f7.

b2) 10...e5!? 11 ♕g3 ♖e6 is untested but may be feasible.

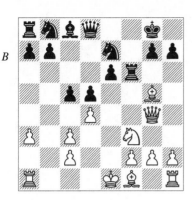

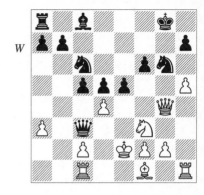

b3) 10...♘d7 is interesting:

b31) Now, accepting the exchange gives Black a terrific initiative after 11 ♗xf6 ♘xf6 12 ♕f4 ♕a5, and then if 13 ♕e3? Black has 13...♘f5 and ...♘e4.

b32) One critical line is 11 ♗b5!? ♕a5 (11...e5 is also interesting; e.g., 12 dxc5 ♖g6 13 ♕h4 ♘f6 14 ♘xe5 ♘f5 with compensation for Black, Rogers-Arencibia, Calcutta 1988) 12 ♗xd7 ♕xc3+ 13 ♔e2 h5 14 ♕g3 (14 ♕xh5!?) 14...♗xd7 15 ♗xf6 ♘f5 16 ♕g5 ♗b5+ 17 ♔d1 ♕xa1+ 18 ♔d2, and now Stoinev gives 18...♕xa3! 19 ♘h4 ♕a5+ 20 ♔c1 ♕c7 as better for Black.

b4) 10...♕a5 11 ♗xf6 ♕xc3+ 12 ♔e2! (12 ♔d1 ♕xa1+ 13 ♔d2 ♘g6 14 ♗d3 ♕xh1 15 ♗xg6 gxf6 16 ♕h4 hxg6 17 ♕xf6 ♕xg2! 18 ♘g5 ♕xg5+ 19 ♕xg5 ♔f7 20 ♕f4+ ♔g7 21 ♕e5+ ♔f7 22 ♕c7+ ♘d7 23 dxc5 g5! 24 f3 ♔g6 was about equal in Balashov-Bareev, Voronezh 1987) 12...♘g6 13 ♖c1 gxf6 14 h4 ♘c6 15 h5 e5 *(D)*.

The position is extremely messy and has arisen in several games. It is something that can turn upside down – and indeed has! – if one of the sides makes a single mistake. The position also makes a good exercise in the training of your tactical skills. 16 ♕g3 e4 17 hxg6 exf3+ 18 ♔d1 ♗f5! 19 ♖xh7 and now:

b41) 19...♗xc2+!? 20 ♖xc2 ♕xd4+ 21 ♔c1 ♕a1+ 22 ♔d2 ♕d4+ 23 ♗d3 ♘e5 24 ♖c3 fxg2 25 ♔c2! ♘xd3! 26 ♖xd3 (26 ♖h8+ ♔g7 27 ♕c7+ ♔xg6 28 ♕h7+ ♔g5 is a draw) 26...♕c4+ 27 ♔b2 ♕b5+ 28 ♔a2 (28 ♔a1 ♕xd3!) 28...♕c4+ 29 ♖b3 ♕e2+ 30 ♖b2 ♕c4+ 31 ♔a1 ♕c1+ 32 ♖b1 g1♕ =.

b42) 19...♕xd4+ 20 ♗d3 ♘e5 (not 20...♗xd3? 21 ♖h8+ ♔g7 22 ♕c7+ ♔xg6 23 ♕h7+ ♔g5 24 ♕h5+ ♔f4 25 g3+ ♔e4 26 ♕g4+ ♔e5 27 ♕xd4+ ♔xd4 28 ♖xa8 +−) 21 ♖h4 ♗g4 22 gxf3 ♗xf3+! (22...♘xd3? 23 ♖h8+! +− Lau-Hertneck, Bundesliga 1986/7) and now:

b421) 23 ♔d2!? is worth considering. Hertneck gives 23...♗g4(?) 24 ♖h8+ ♔xh8 25 ♕h4+ ♔g7 26 ♕h7+ ♔f8 27 g7+ ♔e7 28 g8♕+ ♔d6 29

♕xa8 ♘f3+ 30 ♔e2 ♘h2+ 31 f3
♕e5+, and continues 32 ♔f2(?) ♕d4+
33 ♔g3 ♕e5+ with perpetual check,
missing 32 ♔d1! ♗xf3+ 33 ♔d2 +−.
Therefore 23...♘c4+! is necessary.

b422) 23 ♔e1 ♕b2 24 ♖d1 ♘xd3+
25 ♔f1 ♗xd1! (25...♘e5 26 ♖h8+ ♔g7
27 ♖h7+ ♔g8 28 ♕h4 +− Korchnoi)
and now:

b4221) Korchnoi gives 26 ♕c7 as
winning for White but this is wrong:
26...♗e2+! 27 ♔g2 (27 ♔g1? ♕a1+!)
27...♗f3+! 28 ♔xf3 ♘e1+ 29 ♔e2
♕xc2+ (29...♕e5+ 30 ♕xe5 fxe5 31
♔xe1 ♔g7 32 ♖h7+ ♔xg6) 30 ♔xe1
♖e8+ 31 ♔f1 ♕d3+ 32 ♔g2 ♕xg6+
33 ♔h3 ♕d3+ 34 ♔g2. Black is better
but it is unclear whether he can win
due to his unsafe king.

b4222) 26 ♖h8+ ♔g7 27 ♖h7+
♔g8 28 ♖h8+ =.

9 ♗d3 f5 10 exf6

This is of course the principal continuation but recently White has also
experimented with other moves. If
White moves the queen away, the position remains closed, which at first
sight seems in Black's favour but White
may have ideas of breaking up the
kingside with g4. However, with a quick
attack against White's centre, there
doesn't seem to be time for this; e.g.,
10 ♕h3 ♕a5 11 ♗d2 ♕a4! 12 dxc5
♘g6 13 ♕g3 ♕g4!? 14 0-0 ♕xg3 15
hxg3 ♘cxe5 16 ♘xe5 ♘xe5 17 ♖fe1
♘xd3 18 cxd3 ♗d7 19 ♖ab1 b6 20
cxb6 axb6 21 ♖xb6 ♖xa3 = Mitkov-
Kasimdzhanov, Istanbul OL 2000.

10...♖xf6 11 ♗g5 (D)

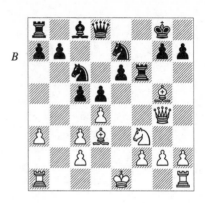

11...e5!

This move is considered to give
Black excellent dynamic play for a
very small material investment.

The main line used to be 11...♖f7.
A brief survey:

a) 12 ♕h3 h6 13 ♗g6 ♖f8 14 ♘e5
has been played several times but
14...cxd4! 15 cxd4 (15 ♗xe7 ♕xe7 16
cxd4 ♕f6 17 ♕g3 ♘xd4 ∓) 15...♕a5+
16 ♗d2 ♕b6 looks very good for Black.

b) 12 ♕h4 h6 13 ♗xe7 ♕xe7 14
♕xe7 ♖xe7 15 dxc5 e5 16 ♘d2 e4 17
♗b5 ♘e5 18 ♘b3 ♗g4 with counterplay, Meshkov-Dokhoian, USSR Cht
(Naberezhnye Chelny) 1988.

c) 12 ♕h5!? g6 (on 12...h6?, Kova-
čević gives 13 ♗h7+! ♔xh7 14 ♕xf7
hxg5 15 g4 ♘g6 16 h4 gxh4 17 ♘xh4
♘xh4 18 ♕h5+ ♔g8 19 ♖xh4, intending g5 ±) 13 ♕h4 c4 14 ♗e2 ♕a5 15
♗d2 ♘f5 16 ♕g5 ♗d7 17 g4 ♘d6 18
h4 ♘e4 19 ♕e3 e5!? 20 h5 exd4 21
♘xd4 ♖e8 22 hxg6 hxg6 23 ♖h6 ♖g7
with an unclear but probably balanced
position, Ernst-L.B.Hansen, Östersund
Z 1992.

d) 12 ♗xe7 ♖xe7 13 ♕h4 g6 (better than 13...h6 14 0-0 c4 15 ♗g6 ♗d7 16 ♖fe1 ♗e8 17 ♗xe8 ♕xe8 18 ♘e5 ♘xe5 19 ♖xe5 with an edge for White, Hjartarson-Yusupov, Linares 1988) 14 0-0 c4 15 ♗e2 ♗d7 16 ♖fe1 ♕f8 17 ♗d1 ♖ae8 18 ♘e5 ♘xe5 19 ♖xe5 ♔g7! 20 ♕g5 ♖f7 21 ♕e3 ♖f5 with roughly equal chances, Kindermann-Hübner, Bundesliga 1987/8.

12 ♕g3

Or:

a) 12 ♕h4 e4 13 ♗xf6 gxf6 14 ♕xf6 exd3 15 cxd3 ♗f5!? 16 0-0 ♗xd3 17 ♖fe1 ♘g6 18 ♕e6+ ♔h8 was unclear in Groszpeter-Sergienko, Zalakaros 1996.

b) 12 ♗xh7+ ♔xh7 13 ♕h5+ ♔g8 14 ♗xf6 gxf6 15 dxe5 ♕f8! 16 exf6 ♕xf6 17 ♕g5+ ♔g7 18 0-0-0 ♗g4 19 ♖d3 ♖f8 ∓ Enders-Hübner, Bundesliga 1998/9.

12...♖xf3 13 gxf3 c4 14 ♗e2 ♕a5 15 ♗d2 ♘f5 16 ♕g5 ♗d7

Black has very good compensation for the exchange, Szalanczy-Hertneck, Vienna 1996.

B)

8 ♗d3 *(D)*

Now we investigate four main lines for Black:

B1)

8...♘d7

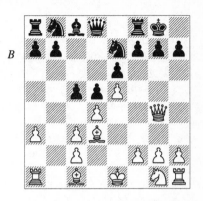

Over the years this has been viewed rather differently. Its current reputation is poor but this is not necessarily justified. It is right that the knight has less influence from d7 but instead the manoeuvre ...♘b6-c4 becomes available.

9 ♘f3

Many alternatives been tried here but this natural development is best.

9...f5

9...f6 10 ♕xe6+ ♔h8 11 ♕h3 g6 is a suspicious-looking gambit tried a few times by the Finnish player Norri. Although it is not easy to refute, White does seem to get a clear advantage with 12 e6 c4 13 ♗xg6!? ♘xg6 14 exd7 ♗xd7 15 ♕g3, as in Luther-Norri, Arnhem jr Ech 1989.

10 ♕h3

With Black's knight on d7 there is no pressure against d4 and thus White's centre is very secure. That explains this retreat, as White now has time to open the kingside by other means, i.e. by ♖g1 and g4, in one order or the other.

10...♛a5

Alternatively:

a) 10...♛e8?! 11 ♘g5 h6 (11...♛g6? 12 ♗e2!, intending ♗h5 +−) 12 ♘xe6 ♘xe5 13 ♘xf8 ♘xd3+ 14 ♛xd3 ♘g6+ 15 ♛e2 ♛xf8 16 0-0 ± Lau-Zysk, Budapest 1988.

b) 10...♖e8 11 ♖g1! ♘f8 12 g4 ♛c7 13 ♗d2 ♗d7 14 ♛g3 ♗a4 15 ♔d1 cxd4 16 cxd4 ♘fg6 17 h4 ♖ac8 18 ♖c1 ♘f8 19 h5 ± Raaste-Renman, Sweden-Finland 1989.

c) 10...♘b6 11 a4 and then:

c1) 11...♗d7 12 a5 ♘c4 13 g4 ♘xa5 14 gxf5 ♘xf5 15 ♖g1 c4 16 ♘g5 h6 17 ♗xf5 ♖xf5 18 ♘f3 ± Sax.

c2) 11...c4 12 ♗e2 a5 13 ♖g1 ♛e8 14 g4 ♘xa4 (14...♗d7 15 gxf5 ♖xf5 16 ♘h4 ♛f7 17 ♖b1 ♖a6 18 ♘xf5 ♘xf5 19 ♗g5 ♗e8 20 ♗g4 +− Ehlvest-Vaganian, Skellefteå 1989) 15 gxf5 ♘xf5 16 ♘g5 h6 17 ♗h5 ♛c6 18 ♗g6 ♘e7 19 ♘h7! ♖xg6 20 ♘xf8 ♔xf8 (20...♘xf8 21 ♗xh6 g6 22 ♗xf8 +−) 21 ♖xg6 ♛e8 22 ♛g3 1-0 Sax-Dolmatov, Clermont Ferrand 1989.

11 ♗d2

11 0-0 deserves attention:

a) If 11...c4 12 ♗e2 ♘b6, White has 13 a4!, with the idea that White wins in the event of 13...♘xa4? 14 ♗a3 ♖e8 15 ♘g5 h6 16 ♛h5 (Korchnoi).

b) Black's best is 11...♘b6 12 dxc5, and then:

b1) 12...♛xc5?! 13 a4! ♛xc3 14 ♗a3 ♖e8 15 ♘g5 h6 16 ♛h5 ♗d7 17 ♛f7+ ♔h8 18 ♗xe7 hxg5 19 ♗f6! 1-0 Rõtšagov-Norri, Helsinki 1990.

b2) 12...♘c4 (±) is mentioned by Rõtšagov and Oll.

b3) 12...♘a4 could be Black's best; e.g., 13 ♛h4 ♘c6 14 c4 ♘xc5 15 cxd5 exd5 with counterplay.

11...♘b6 *(D)*

11...c4? would be strategically incorrect because Black has no counterplay against White's coming attack on the kingside. 12 ♗e2 ♘b6 13 0-0 ♛a4 14 ♖a2 ♛e8 15 ♔h1! and now:

a) 15...h6? 16 ♖g1 ♛g6 17 g4 fxg4 18 ♖xg4 ♛h7 19 ♖a1 ♘f5 20 ♖ag1 ♗d7 21 ♘h4 gave White a decisive attack in Kindermann-L.B.Hansen, Munich 1989.

b) 15...♗d7 16 ♖g1 ♘g6 is a better defence, with the idea of answering 17 g4?! with 17...f4. Instead, White should either provoke ...h6 with 17 ♘g5 h6 18 ♘f3, intending g4, or play 17 ♛g3!?, with the idea of h4-h5.

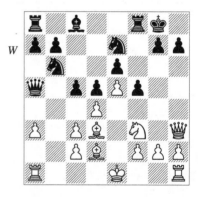

12 g4!?

This is stronger than 12 c4?! ♛a4 13 cxd5 c4! (13...exd5?! 14 dxc5 ♘c4 15 ♛h4 ♘g6 16 ♛d4 ± Izeta-Norri,

Haifa Echt 1989) 14 d6 ♘ed5 15 ♗e2 ♕xc2 with an unclear position according to Kindermann. Black's counterplay looks sufficient if we take this a little further: 16 0-0 c3 17 ♖fc1 ♕b2 18 ♖cb1 ♕c2 and White has nothing better than 19 ♖c1 with a repetition of moves.

12...♘c4 13 ♖g1 ♘xd2!

13...cxd4 14 gxf5 ♘xf5 allows the spectacular 15 ♗h6!!. Black's threats on the queenside are harmless, while White's attack smashes through on the kingside: 15...♖f7 (15...♕xc3+ 16 ♔e2 only improves White's position) and now:

a) 16 ♗xg7 (good, but not best) 16...♖xg7 17 ♖xg7+ ♔xg7 18 ♔e2 ♕d8 19 ♖g1+ ♔h8 20 ♘g5 (Minasian-Oll, Lvov Z 1990) 20...♕e7 21 ♗xc4 ♗d7 (21...dxc4 22 ♕h5 +−) 22 ♗d3 ± Minasian.

b) The calm 16 ♔e2! (Minasian) is stronger; e.g., 16...g6 17 ♖xg6+ hxg6 18 ♖g1, with a winning attack.

14 ♔xd2 cxd4

Other moves are too slow; e.g., 14...c4? 15 gxf5! ♘xf5 16 ♗xf5 ♖xf5 17 ♖g2 with a winning attack.

15 ♘xd4 ♗d7

Minasian gives the line 15...♘c6? 16 gxf5! ♘xd4 17 ♖xg7+ ♔xg7 18 f6+ +−.

16 gxf5 exf5 17 e6?!

This move may be premature. 17 ♕h4!? ♘g6 18 ♖xg6! hxg6 19 e6, Werner-Giemsa, Bundesliga 1990/1, is worth investigating. If Black moves the bishop to e8 or a4, White has

attacking ideas such as ♖g1-g3-h3 or ♘f3-g5.

17...♗e8 18 ♘xf5 ♘xf5 19 e7 ♖f6 20 ♗xf5 g6

Luther-Rausch, Seefeld 1996. The position is complicated, but since White is not winning with a direct attack, Black should not be worse.

B2)

8...♘bc6 *(D)*

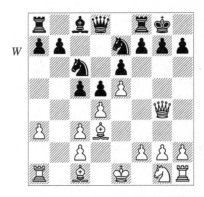

9 ♕h5

Otherwise:

a) 9 ♘f3 – *8 ♘f3 ♘bc6 9 ♗d3*.

b) 9 ♕h4 ♘g6 10 ♕xd8 ♖xd8 11 ♗e3 ♗d7 12 h4 ♘ge7 13 g4 cxd4 14 cxd4 ♘a5! was roughly equal in Bezgodov-Riazantsev, St Petersburg 2000.

c) 9 ♗g5 (this is more dangerous and deserves to be taken seriously) 9...♕a5 10 ♘e2. Now:

c1) 10...cxd4 11 f4! requires accurate defence from Black:

c11) 11...♘f5 12 0-0 (12 ♗f6 is interesting; e.g., 12...♘ce7 13 ♗xe7 ♘xe7 14 ♗xh7+ ♔xh7 15 ♕h4+ ♔g8

16 ♕xe7 dxc3 17 h4 with better prospects for White) 12...♔h8 13 ♕h5 f6 14 ♗xf5 exf5 15 exf6 gxf6 16 ♕h6 ♕d8 17 ♗h4 dxc3, Luther-Hertneck, Bundesliga 1992/3, and now 18 ♘xc3 looks good for White.

c12) 11...dxc3 12 0-0 ♘g6 13 ♕h5 ♕c5+ 14 ♔h1 ♘ce7 15 ♖f3 f6 16 exf6 gxf6 17 ♖h3 ♗f7 18 ♗xf6 ♖xf6 19 ♕xh7+ ♔f8 20 ♖g3 with a strong attack, Hertneck-Uhlmann, Bundesliga 1992/3.

c2) 10...♕a4!? 11 0-0 (11 ♗xh7+!? ♔xh7 12 ♗xe7 ♘xe7 13 ♕h4+ ♔g8 14 ♕xe7 and now both 14...♕xc2 15 ♕xc5 and 14...cxd4 15 ♘xd4 appear slightly better for White) 11...♘xe5 and now:

c21) 12 ♗xh7+?! ♔xh7 13 ♕h5+ ♔g8 14 ♗xe7 ♖e8 15 dxe5 ♖xe7 led to an unclear position in Orlov-Se.Ivanov, St Petersburg 1992.

c22) 12 ♕h5 ♘xd3 13 ♗xe7 ♖e8 14 ♗f6! gxf6 15 cxd3 appears very strong. There are ideas such as f4, followed by a rook-lift to the third rank or ♕h6, intending ♘g3-h5.

c3) 10...♘g6! *(D)* is best. Then:

c31) 11 h4?! ♘xd4! 12 ♕g3 ♘xe2 13 ♗xe2 ♕c7! 14 f4 ♘e7 15 ♗d3 ♔h8 and White's attack is neutralized, Wallace-P.H.Nielsen, Gausdal 1996.

c32) 11 0-0 ♕a4 (11...c4!? 12 ♗xg6 fxg6 13 h4 ♕c7 = Renet-Dolmatov, Cannes 1994) 12 f4 c4 13 ♗xg6 fxg6 14 ♖a2 ♗d7 (14...♔f7!? 15 h4 h5 16 ♕f3 ♖h8 is unclear according to Apicella) 15 h4 ♖f5 (15...h5?! 16 ♕f3! intending 17 g4 ±). Now:

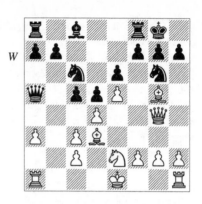

c321) 16 ♘g3 and then:

c3211) 16...♗e8 17 ♘xf5 gxf5 18 ♕f3 (if 18 ♕g3, then 18...♗h5 comes to rescue, with the point 19 ♗f6 ♗g4! ∓) 18...h6, Shaposhnikov-Se.Ivanov, Russia 2000, and now 19 ♗f6! is critical; e.g., 19...gxf6 20 exf6 ♔f7 21 ♕h5+ ♔xf6 22 ♕xh6+ ♔e7 23 ♕g5+ ♔d7 24 h5 ± Psakhis.

c3212) 16...♕a5!? 17 ♘xf5 gxf5 18 ♕g3 ♗e8 (with compensation) was first given by Apicella and then played in I.Almasi-Galyas, Budapest 2000. Indeed, Black should be fine because White's bishop is out of play.

c322) 16 h5! gxh5 (16...h6? 17 hxg6 hxg5 18 ♕h5 +−) 17 ♕xh5 h6 18 g4 ♖f7 19 ♔g2! (19 ♗xh6 gxh6 20 f5 gives White an attack according to Se.Ivanov, but this appears somewhat suspicious in view of 20...exf5! when both 21 e6 ♖g7 22 exd7 ♘e7 and 21 gxf5 ♖g7+ 22 ♔h2 ♖f8 look very acceptable for Black) 19...♗e8 20 ♕h3 hxg5 21 f5, Koch-Apicella, Chambéry 1994. According to Apicella, White has a strong attack.

9...♘g6

Other moves have been virtually refuted:

a) 9...h6? 10 ♗xh6! gxh6 11 ♕xh6 ♘f5 12 ♗xf5 exf5 13 0-0-0! (13 ♘h3 is probably also good, but the text-move gives White a decisive advantage; the threat is 14 ♖d3 f4 15 ♖g3+! fxg3 16 hxg3 +−) 13...c4 (13...f4 14 ♘h3 ♗f5 15 ♘xf4 f6 16 ♘g6 fxe5 17 dxe5 ♕a5 18 ♕h8+ ♔f7 19 ♕h7+ ♔e8 20 e6 +− Kindermann-Psakhis, Dortmund 1989) 14 ♘h3 (14 ♖e1!?) 14...f6 15 ♕g6+ ♔h8 16 ♖he1 fxe5 17 dxe5 f4 18 ♕h6+ ♔g8 19 ♘xf4 ♕e7 20 ♖e3 +− Vogt-Uhlmann, Berlin 1989.

b) 9...♘f5?! 10 ♘f3 f6 (10...c4 11 g4! cxd3 12 gxf5 exf5 13 ♖g1 f6 – *10...f6 11 g4! c4 12 gxf5 cxd3 13 ♖g1! exf5 +−*) 11 g4! c4 (11...g6 12 ♕h3 ♘g7 13 ♕h6! looks very dangerous) 12 gxf5 (there is no point in mentioning alternatives; this is simply best) 12...cxd3 13 ♖g1! gives White a very powerful attack, which is illustrated by the following lines:

b1) 13...♕a5? 14 ♖xg7+! ♔xg7 15 ♗h6+ ♔h8 16 ♗xf8 ♕xc3+ 17 ♔f1 ♕xa1+ 18 ♔g2 +− Se.Ivanov.

b2) 13...♕e8 14 ♕xe8 ♖xe8 15 exf6 exf5+ 16 ♘e5! ♘xe5 17 ♖xg7+ ± Se.Ivanov.

b3) 13...♘e7 14 exf6 ♖xf6 15 ♖xg7+! ♔xg7 16 ♕g5+ ♘g6 17 fxg6 hxg6 18 ♗f4 dxc2 19 ♗e5 ♗d7 20 h4! with a decisive attack, Kruppa-Komarov, Kherson 1991.

b4) 13...dxc2 14 ♗h6 ♖f7 15 ♔d2 ♗d7 16 ♗xg7! (16 ♕xf7+!? ♔xf7 17 ♖xg7+ ♔e8 18 ♖ag1 exf5 19 ♖xh7 ♗e6 20 ♖gg7 is a nice alternative win pointed out by Stohl) 16...♖xg7 17 ♕h6 ♕f8 18 ♖xg7+ ♕xg7 19 ♖g1 ♕xg1 20 ♘xg1 fxe5 21 f6 1-0 Palac-Kovačević, Vinkovci 1995.

b5) 13...exf5 14 ♗h6 ♖f7 15 ♔d2! ♗e6 16 ♗xg7! ♖xg7 17 ♖xg7+ ♔xg7 18 ♖g1+ 1-0 Khalifman-P.Nikolić, Moscow 1990. The point is 18...♔h8 19 ♘h4 +−.

10 ♘f3

10 ♘h3 is a recent idea but based on the practical evidence it doesn't look stronger than the more common text-move; e.g., 10...♕c7 11 ♗e3 ♘ce7!? 12 f4 ♕a5 13 ♗d2 ♕a4 ("a typical move in these positions" – Psakhis) 14 g4 (this is very aggressive – maybe even too aggressive, but 14 dxc5 b6! 15 cxb6 axb6 also looks fine for Black) 14...c4 15 ♗e2 ♕xc2 16 ♖c1 ♕b2 17 ♘g5 h6 18 ♘h3 f6! 19 g5 hxg5 20 exf6 ♖xf6 21 ♘xg5 ♘f8 and Black was better in J.Polgar-Hillarp Persson, Malmö 2000.

10...♕c7 *(D)*

Now Black threatens to take on d4. Note that 10...c4? is bad owing to 11 ♘g5 h6 12 ♘xf7 +−.

11 ♗e3

Or:

a) 11 ♘g5 h6 12 ♘xf7 ♕xf7 13 ♕xg6 ♕xg6 14 ♗xg6 cxd4 15 cxd4 ♘xd4 16 ♗d3 ♗d7 = Gelfand-Hübner, Wijk aan Zee 1992.

b) 11 0-0 c4 12 ♗e2 f6 13 exf6 ♖xf6 14 ♗g5 ♘f4! 15 ♗xf4 ♕xf4 16 g3 ♕d6 17 ♕g5 ♗d7 18 ♕e3 ♗e8 19

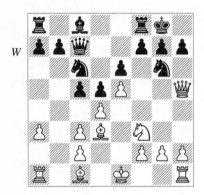

♘e5 ♗g6 = Oll-Dolmatov, Groningen PCA 1993.

c) 11 h4!? is more dangerous, especially if Black isn't prepared for it. The critical line is 11...cxd4 (11...c4 12 ♘g5 h6 13 ♗xg6 fxg6 14 ♕xg6 hxg5 15 hxg5 ♘xe5 16 ♕h5! gave White excellent compensation in Morozevich-Dolmatov, Moscow 1996) 12 ♔d1!? (12 cxd4? ♘xd4! ∓) 12...dxc3, which actually might be good for Black: 13 ♖h3!? (White brings more heavy artillery into the attack; the immediate 13 ♘g5 h6 gets him nowhere) 13...♘ce7!? (13...f6!? could be considered but opening the side where White is attacking would require some courage) 14 ♘g5 h6 15 ♘f3 (15 ♘xf7?! ♖xf7 16 ♗xg6 ♘xg6 17 ♕xg6 ♕xe5 and White's position falls apart) 15...f5!? 16 exf6 ♖xf6 17 ♖g3 ♘f8 and White was soon pushed back in Barsky-Se.Ivanov, Russian Ch (Oriol) 1992. Note that on 18 ♗xh6? Black has the response 18...♖xh6 19 ♕xh6 ♕xg3!.

11...♘ce7!?

The other main line is 11...c4 12 ♗xg6 fxg6 13 ♕g4 but Black has experienced some problems in this line recently:

a) 13...♕f7!? 14 ♘g5 ♕e8 (alternatively, 14...♕f5 15 ♕e2 ±) 15 h4 ♘e7 16 ♕e2 ♘f5 17 g4 ♘xe3 18 ♕xe3 h6 19 ♘h3 ♕e7 20 ♕g3 ♗d7 21 f4 and White is slowly building up an impressive position, Nijboer-Harikrishna, Wijk aan Zee 2001.

b) 13...♗d7 14 h4 ♖f5 15 h5 gxh5 16 ♖xh5 gives Black two options:

b1) 16...♖xh5 17 ♕xh5 ♖f8 18 ♔d2 ♗e8 19 ♕h3! ± Macieja-Novković, Presov 2000.

b2) 16...♖af8 17 ♖h3!? ♗e8, Rowson-Barsov, York 2000, and now Psakhis mentions 18 ♘g5 ♕a5 19 ♔d2 ♖xg5! 20 ♕xg5 ♗g6 with some compensation for the exchange, as the critical line.

12 h4 ♗d7 13 ♕g5!?

This might represent an improvement over Anand-Lputian, New Delhi FIDE 2000, which went 13 a4 f5 14 exf6 ♖xf6 15 0-0 c4 16 ♗xg6 ♘xg6 17 ♕g5 e5!? (17...h6 18 ♕g3 ♕xg3 19 fxg3 h5 is suggested by Psakhis as a safer line for Black, while Black could also consider 17...♖af8) 18 dxe5 ♖xf3! 19 gxf3 ♖f8 20 ♕g3 ♕xe5 21 ♕xe5 ♘xe5 22 ♖fd1 ♘xf3+ 23 ♔f1. Lputian has gone for a typical exchange sacrifice, and clearly has some compensation, but objectively White is probably slightly better, and Anand also went on to win after a few inaccuracies by Black.

13...f6

Psakhis suggests 13...h6 14 ♕g4 ♘f5, which slightly weakens the kingside but actually looks quite solid.

14 exf6 gxf6

Thus far Rowson-Hillarp Persson, York 2000. Now Psakhis considers 15 ♕h6!? to be critical and gives 15...cxd4 16 h5 (16 ♗xd4 e5 17 h5 ♘f5 18 ♗xf5 ♗xf5 19 hxg6 ♗xg6! with counterplay) 16...♕xc3+ 17 ♔e2 ♘f5 18 ♗xf5 ♗b5+ 19 ♔d1 dxe3 20 ♖a2! as much better for White.

B3)

8...♕a5 (D)

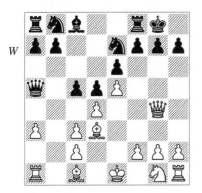

This move has been heavily popularized by Russian GM Alexander Rustemov. The main idea should be seen in the context of the line *8...♘bc6 9 ♕h5 h6?*, when *10 ♗xh6!* seems to win for White. Black intends first to entice White's dark-squared bishop to d2, after which the above sacrifice wouldn't work.

9 ♗d2

This is by far the most common. 9 ♘e2 deserves serious attention though. Black's best would be to transpose to Line B2 with 9...♘bc6 10 ♗g5 ♘g6!. Instead in Shabalov-Rustemov, Bad Wiessee 1999, Black was quickly punished after trying the more ambitious 9...cxd4 (9...f5?! is now bad due to 10 exf6 ♖xf6 11 ♗g5 ♘d7 12 ♕h3 h6 13 ♗xf6 ♘xf6 14 ♕g3 ±) 10 ♗g5 ♘g6 11 f4 ♘d7?! (McDonald recommends 11...f5 12 exf6 e5 but I prefer White after 13 ♗f5 ♗xf5 14 ♕xf5) 12 ♗xg6 hxg6 13 h4 f5 14 ♕h3 ♘c5 15 h5 with a devastating attack.

9...♘bc6

This move of Rustemov's is much stronger than 9...f5 10 exf6 ♖xf6 11 ♕h5 ♘f5 12 dxc5!, when White good chances; e.g.:

a) 12...g6 is possible, with the point that after 13 ♕h3 ♕xc5 14 ♘f3 ♕c7!? the queen defends h7. White should prefer 13 ♕e2 ♕xc5 14 ♘f3 ±.

b) 12...♘d7 13 g4!? (at first I was very tempted by 13 ♕e8+ but 13...♘f8 14 g4 ♘h4 15 g5 ♖g6! 16 ♗xg6 ♘hxg6 17 h4 ♕xc5 18 h5 ♘e5 is actually far from clear; perhaps Black can even claim some sort of compensation after 13...♖f8!? 14 ♕xe6+ ♔h8 15 ♕xd5 ♘xc5) 13...g6 14 ♕h3 ♘e7 15 ♘f3 ♕xc5 16 ♘g5! ♘f8 (16...♕xf2+? 17 ♔d1 ♘f8 18 ♗e3 +−) 17 f4! ♘c6 18 ♕g3 ♗d7 19 ♔d1! (an excellent move; rather typically for the French, White aims for control of the e5-square) 19...♖e8 20 ♖e1 ♘a5 21 ♘f3 ♗a4 22 g5 ♖f7 23 ♘e5 and White was better in Sakaev-Rustemov, St Petersburg 1997.

10 ♘f3

This seems White's best try for an advantage. The older 10 ♕h5 h6 is not a problem for Black. White must either allow ...c4, which forces the bishop back to a worse square, or he is faced with a dynamic pawn sacrifice if he captures on c5:

a) 11 c4? opens the position prematurely; Black is better after 11...♕c7 (Rustemov). The sacrifice on h6 doesn't work (12 ♗xh6 gxh6 13 ♕xh6 ♘g6 14 ♘f3 ♘xd4 and Black defends) and if 12 cxd5, 12...exd5 gives Black a good position since there is no problem with the bishop.

b) 11 ♘f3 c4 12 ♗e2 (Se.Ivanov notes that 12 ♗xh6? doesn't work owing to 12...♕xc3+ 13 ♗d2 ♕xa1+ 14 ♔e2 cxd3+ 15 cxd3 ♕xh1 16 ♘g5 ♘xd4+ 17 ♔e3 ♘ef5+ 18 ♔f4 ♘h6 −+) 12...f6 (a thematic break; Black intends to develop his bishop with ...♗d7-e8-g6) 13 exf6 ♖xf6 14 ♘e5 ♕a4 15 ♖a2 ♘xe5 16 ♕xe5 ♘c6 17 ♕e3 ♗d7 18 0-0 ♖af8 19 f3 ♗e8 20 ♗e1 ♘e7 21 g4 (Se.Ivanov's 21 ♕d2 = is better) 21...♘g6 22 ♗g3 ♕d7 23 ♖e1 ♘f4 24 ♗d1 g5 and Black stands better, Solozhenkin-Se.Ivanov, St Petersburg 2000.

c) 11 dxc5 b6! (a thematic idea that solves the problem with the development of the bishop and intends to destroy one of White's most powerful attackers) 12 cxb6 ♗a6!? (12...axb6 should also be considered, if only to

deprive White of the possibility of 13 bxa7). Now:

c1) 13 bxa7 is possible, but Black secures excellent compensation after 13...♖xa7 due to his strong queenside pressure and the large number of weak white pawns.

c2) 13 ♘f3 ♕xb6 14 0-0 ♗xd3 15 cxd3 ♕b5 16 d4 (Rustemov thinks that White should strive for an equal position with 16 c4! dxc4 17 ♖fb1 ♕d5 18 dxc4 ♕xc4 19 ♗b4) 16...♕d3 17 ♕g4 ♕h7! ∓ Madl-Rustemov, Budapest 1999. From h7, the queen can be used in the defence as well as for attacking purposes due to Black's control of the entire h7-b1 diagonal. Control of b1 is of primary importance as Black is then able to seize the b-file.

c3) 13 ♕e2 ♗xd3 14 cxd3 axb6 15 ♘f3 ♕c5 16 0-0 ♖xa3 17 ♖xa3 ♕xa3 18 ♖b1 ♖b8 gives Black a minimal advantage, Shaposhnikov-Rustemov, St Petersburg 1998.

10...f5

10...c4? would be desirable from a positional point of view but fails tactically to 11 ♗xh7+! ♔xh7 12 ♕h5+ ♔g8 13 ♘g5 ♖d8 14 ♕h7+ ♔f8 15 ♕h8+ ♘g8 16 ♘h7+ ♔e7 17 ♕xg7 with a huge attack for White.

11 exf6 ♖xf6 12 ♕h5 ♘f5 (D)

12...g6 13 ♕g5 ♖f7 (Psakhis mentions 13...♖xf3 14 gxf3 c4 15 ♗e2 ♗d7 16 h4!, when "White's chances are better") 14 h4! c4 15 ♗e2 ♗d7 16 h5 ♖af8 17 hxg6 ♘xg6 18 ♕h6 ± Timoshenko-Schmidt, Koszalin 1999.

13 c4

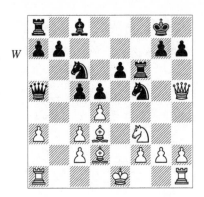

This received high marks after Svidler used it in a rapid game to defeat Psakhis. However, Black seems to have good counterplay if he replies accurately. Other moves:

a) 13 0-0 c4 14 ♗e2 ♘d6 15 ♕h4 ♗d7 16 ♘e5 ♘xe5 17 dxe5 ♘f5 = Nguyen Anh Dung-Andrienko, Budapest 1994.

b) 13 dxc5!? ♕xc5 14 g4 (14 0-0 g6 15 ♕g5 ♖f7 16 ♖fe1 ♗d7 looks fine for Black; an important finesse is 17 h4 ♖af8 18 h5? h6! 19 ♕xg6+? ♖g7 –+) 14...♘h6 15 g5 g6! 16 ♕h3 e5 17 ♕g2 ♖xf3 18 ♕xf3 e4 is unclear – Kindermann.

c) 13 g4!? c4! is a critical continuation, but the tactics seem to work well for Black:

c1) 14 ♗xf5?! exf5 15 g5 ♖e6+ 16 ♔d1 g6! 17 ♕h3 (17 ♕h6 f4! is very good for Black because White has no time to open the h-file as 18 h4?? is met by 18...♘e7 or 18...♘d8, trapping the queen on the next move) 17...f4! 18 ♕h4 ♖e4 ∓ Cuijpers-Rustemov, Pamplona 1998/9.

c2) 14 ♗e2 ♘fe7 (14...♘d6!?) 15 ♘g5 h6 16 ♘f3 ♖f7! is unclear according to Rustemov. Note that 17 g5? is met by 17...g6!.

c3) 14 gxf5! (this is the only move that can trouble Black) 14...cxd3 15 ♖g1 ♗d7 (15...♕c7 16 ♗h6 ♖xf5 17 ♕e8+ ♖f8 18 ♗xg7! ♖xe8 19 ♗e5+ ♔f8 20 ♗xc7 ± Paramos Dominguez-Oms Pallise, Spanish Cht (Cala Galdana) 1999) 16 c4 (16 ♕g5 ♖f7 17 f6 ♕d8 ∓ Kovačević-Dimitrov, Lazarevac 1999) 16...♕c7 17 ♗h6 ♗e8! 18 ♕h4 ♖xh6! 19 ♕xh6 dxc4! (this is getting rather complicated; Black could also investigate the line 19...♗g6 20 ♕e3 ♗xf5 21 cxd3 ♕b6!, which is rather messy) 20 cxd3 cxd3 21 ♖d1 ♗g6! 22 ♖xg6 hxg6 23 ♕xg6 ♕a5+ 24 ♔f1 ♕xf5 25 ♕xf5 exf5 26 ♖xd3 ♖d8 = Sax-Goloshchapov, Montecatini Terme 1999.

13...♕a4 14 cxd5 ♘cxd4!

This improvement was found soon after the game Svidler-Psakhis, Haifa rpd 2000, which had gone 14...exd5?! 15 dxc5 ♗d7 16 0-0 ♗e8 17 ♕h3 ♗g6 18 ♗c3! d4 19 ♗d2 ±.

15 ♘g5 h6 16 ♘e4 ♖f8 17 0-0

17 ♘xc5 ♘xc2+ 18 ♗xc2 ♕xc2 19 ♖c1 ♕a2 ∓ Kindermann.

17...b6! 18 ♘c3 ♕e8 19 ♕xe8 ♖xe8

Now Kindermann gives two lines:

a) 20 ♖fe1 ♗b7 21 dxe6 ♘h4 with no assessment, but probably implying that Black is better.

b) 20 ♘b5!? ♖d8 (20...♗a6 21 ♘c7 ♗xd3 22 cxd3 exd5 23 ♘xa8 ♖xa8 24 ♖ae1, again with no assessment, but in this case White should be better) 21 ♘c7 ♖b8 22 dxe6 ♘xe6 23 ♗xf5 (23 ♘xe6 ♗xe6 24 ♗f4 ♖b7 25 ♖fe1 ♘d4 also looks roughly equal) 23...♘xc7 24 ♗f4 ♖b7 =.

B4)
8...f5 9 exf6
The other idea is 9 ♕h3, aiming to play g4 at a suitable moment. Black has three ways to counter this:

a) 9...♘bc6 10 ♘f3 – *8 ♘f3 ♘bc6 9 ♗d3 f5 10 ♕h3 =.*

b) 9...♕a5 10 ♗d2 ♕a4 11 dxc5 ♘d7 12 ♕e3 ♕c6 13 ♘f3 ♘xc5 14 ♘d4 ♘xd3+ 15 cxd3 ♕a4 16 0-0 ♘c6 = Khachian-V.Grigorian, Erevan open 1996.

c) 9...♕e8!? 10 ♘f3 ♕g6 (an interesting idea) 11 dxc5 (11 0-0?! ♕g4! leads to favourable simplifications for Black) 11...♘d7 12 ♗e3 ♘c6 (12...b6!? may be more flexible) 13 ♗d4 b6 14 cxb6 axb6 15 0-0 ♗a6 16 ♕g3 ♕xg3 17 hxg3 h6, Mitkov-Farago, Salsomaggiore Terme 1998. Black has adequate counterplay for the pawn due to White's queenside weaknesses.

9...♖xf6 (D)
10 ♗g5
10 ♕h5 has fallen into disuse, mainly because Black has worked out a reliable defence after 10...h6!. Black would usually prefer to weaken the light squares around his king if he is forced to make a concession on the kingside. First of all it is very likely that he will get an opportunity to coerce White's bishop away from the

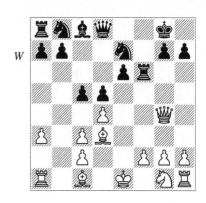

b1-h7 diagonal, while he can also sometimes bring his own bishop to the defence via d7 and e8. White has tried:

a) 11 ♘f3 ♘bc6 12 0-0 c4 13 ♗e2 ♕a5 14 ♗d2 ♗d7 15 ♘e5 ♗e8 16 ♕g4 ♘g6 17 ♘xc6 ♗xc6 18 ♕g3 ♖af8 19 ♗g4 ♕a4 20 ♖a2 ♗d7 = Gallagher-Farago, Hastings 1990.

b) 11 h4 can be met by 11...♘bc6 – *8 ♘f3 ♘bc6 9 ♗d3 f5 10 exf6 ♖xf6 11 ♕h5 h6 =.* 11...c4 is also a good reply.

c) 11 g4! is critical; White aims for a direct assault. Then:

c1) 11...c4 12 g5 g6! (you will quickly notice that this is a thematic defence; 12...♖f8?! 13 gxh6! cxd3 14 hxg7 ♔xg7 15 ♗h6+ wins for White) 13 ♕d1 (13 ♕xh6?! ♖f7 14 ♗xg6 ♖g7 15 ♗h5 ♖h7 ∓) 13...♖f7? (13...♖f8 is better according to Kishnev; I assume that against the similar sacrifice, 14 ♗xg6 ♘xg6 15 ♕h5, Kishnev has in mind the defence 15...♕e8!) 14 ♗xg6! (a bold idea but Black would have no worries if he were allowed to blockade the position with 14 ♗e2 h5) 14...♘xg6 15 ♕h5 ♘f8!? 16 ♘h3 e5 17 gxh6

♕f6 18 ♖g1+ ♔h8 19 dxe5 ♕f5 20 ♖g5 ♕f3 21 ♖xf3 ♖xf3 22 ♘f4 with an unclear position, Spiriev-Kishnev, Budapest 1991.

c2) 11...♕f8 12 g5 g6 13 ♕h4 (perhaps 13 ♕xh6 ♖xf2 14 ♘h3 gives White an edge) 13...♘f5 14 ♗xf5 ♖xf5 15 gxh6 e5! 16 h7+ (16 ♕g3!? is possible) 16...♔h8 17 ♗h6 ♕e8 18 0-0-0 ♘d7 19 ♖e1! cxd4 20 cxd4 e4 ± Korchnoi.

c3) 11...♘bc6 12 g5 g6 (D) and now:

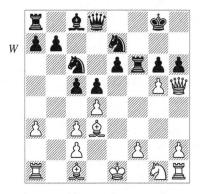

c31) 13 ♕h4 ♘f5 14 ♕h3 (14 ♗xf5?! ♖xf5 15 ♕xh6 ♘e7 16 ♘e2? ♖f7 17 ♕h3 e5 18 ♕g2 ♗f5 19 f3 ♘c6 is much better for Black, Tischbierek-Vladimirov, Berlin 1989) 14...♖f8 15 gxh6 e5 16 ♕g2 ♕e8! 17 dxc5 (17 ♕xd5+ ♗e6 18 ♕xc5 b6 19 ♕b5 a6 20 ♕xb6 ♗d5 ∓) 17...e4 18 ♗b5 ♗d7 19 ♘e2 ♘e5 20 ♗xd7 ♕xd7 gives Black excellent compensation, Aseev-Vladimirov, Leningrad 1989.

c32) 13 ♕xh6 ♖f7 14 ♗xg6 (14 ♕h4?! c4 15 ♗e2 ♘f5 16 ♕f4 ♘fxd4

17 ♕d2 ♘xe2 18 ♘xe2 e5 ∓ Isoev-Se.Ivanov, USSR Cht (Azov) 1991) 14...♖g7 15 ♗d3 e5 16 dxe5 ♘xe5 17 ♕h4 ♘f5 (the immediate 17...♕e8! looks even stronger, then on 18 ♗e2, 18...♗f5! is very good) 18 ♕f4 ♕e8 (Tischbierek gives 18...♘g6 19 ♕d2 ♘gh4 ∓) 19 ♗e2 ♘g6 20 ♕f3 ♕e5 and Black has good compensation, David-Kindermann, Frankfurt rpd 1998.

10...♖f7 (D)

There are two interesting sacrifices worth noting. Though both are probably not entirely correct, White should be prepared against them:

a) 10...e5 11 ♕h4 e4 12 ♗xf6 gxf6 13 ♗e2 ♘f5 14 ♕f4 cxd4 (Emunds-Piskov, Münster 1991) and now Veličković gives 15 ♗g4! ±, which is correct, but we ought to analyse further to verify this: 15...♘g7 16 cxd4 ♕a5+ 17 ♔f1 ♕c3 18 ♖e1!? ♗xg4 19 ♕xg4 ♕xc2 20 ♘e2 f5 21 ♕g3 ♘c6 22 h4!, intending to bring the other rook into play.

b) 10...♘d7 (this is similar to the line *8 ♘f3 f5 9 exf6 ♖xf6 10 ♗g5 ♘d7* but having the bishop on d3 rather than the knight on f3 makes a significant difference) 11 ♕h4 (this is definitely a useful move to make before taking the rook; not only does White oblige Black to weaken his kingside but he also avoids ...♘xf6 gaining a tempo by hitting the queen) 11...h6 12 ♗xf6 ♘xf6 13 dxc5 (as we have seen repeatedly, it is worth preventing Black from playing ...c4, which would force the bishop away from d3 and thus obtain good squares for the knights) 13...e5 14 f3!? and then:

b1) 14...e4!? 15 fxe4 dxe4!? 16 ♗xe4!? (16 ♗c4+ ♔h7 17 ♘e2 ♕a5 18 ♕f2 ♗g4 19 0-0 ♖c8 20 ♖ab1, as mentioned by Glek, should also be favourable for White) 16...g5 17 ♕xh6 ♘xe4 18 ♘f3 ± Kiseliov-Piskov, Berlin 1990.

b2) 14...♕c7 15 ♕f2 ♗e6 (McDonald suggests 15...e4!?) 16 ♘e2 e4 17 fxe4 dxe4 18 ♕f4 ♘ed5 19 ♕xc7 ♘xc7 20 ♖b1 exd3 21 cxd3 ♗d5 22 0-0 ± Gallagher-McDonald, Hastings 1993/4.

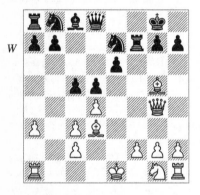

11 ♕h5

This is now the most common. The idea is to make ...h6 less appealing.

Other moves:

a) 11 ♘f3 e5 (11...♘bc6 – *8 ♘f3 ♘bc6 9 ♗d3 f5 10 exf6 ♖xf6 11 ♗g5 ♖f7 =*) 12 ♗xh7+ ♔xh7 13 ♕h4+ (13 ♕h5+ ♔g8 14 ♘xe5 ♖f5 15 g4 ♖xg5 16 ♕xg5 ♘bc6 should be satisfactory for Black) 13...♔g8 14 ♘xe5 ♕e8 (14...♘bc6 allows the pretty 15 ♕h8+!

♔xh8 16 ♘xf7+ ♔h7 17 ♘xd8 +–) 15 0-0 ♘f5 (15...♘bc6 16 ♖ae1!? ♗e6 17 ♘xf7 ♕xf7 18 ♗xe7 ♘xe7 is roughly equal) 16 ♕h5 ♖e7 17 ♕f3 ♖c7 18 ♖ae1 with compensation for the piece.

b) 11 ♕h4 has for some reason declined in popularity, even though it doesn't look worse than the main line. It is quite similar to *8 ♘f3 ♘bc6 9 ♗d3 f5 10 exf6 ♖xf6 11 ♗g5 ♖f7 12 ♕h4 =*, but with the knight not committed to f3 White has some extra options. 11...h6 and then:

b1) 12 ♘f3 and now 12...hxg5 13 ♕h7+ ♔f8 14 ♕h8+ ♘g8 15 ♗h7 ♔e7 16 ♗xg8 is dangerous for Black but there is a safe reply in 12...♘bc6 – *8 ♘f3 ♘bc6 9 ♗d3 f5 10 exf6 ♖xf6 11 ♗g5 ♖f7 12 ♕h4 h6 =*.

b2) 12 ♗xe7 ♖xe7 (12...♕xe7 13 ♕xe7 ♖xe7 14 f4! gave White an advantage due to his strong bind on the e5-square in Z.Almasi-Uhlmann, Dresden rpd 1997 and a number of other games; the option of playing f4 is one major advantage of not yet having committed the knight to f3). Now White has a choice:

b21) The idea of setting up a bind with 13 f4 does not work here owing to 13...e5!.

b22) 13 ♘f3 e5 (13...♘c6 – *8 ♘f3 ♘bc6 9 ♗d3 f5 10 exf6 ♖xf6 11 ♗g5 ♖f7 12 ♗xe7 ♖xe7 13 ♕h4 h6 ±*) 14 dxe5 ♖xe5+ 15 ♔d2 ♕xh4 16 ♘xh4 ♘c6 17 ♘g6 ♖e6! 18 ♖he1 c4 = Šibarević-Draško, Yugoslavia 1999.

b23) 13 ♕g3!? ♕a5!? (13...cxd4 14 cxd4 e5!? 15 dxe5 ♕c7 16 ♘e2

♕xe5 17 ♕xe5 ♖xe5 ± Korchnoi) 14
♘e2 c4 (14...cxd4! looks more consistent with the ...♕a5 idea; e.g., 15 ♕g6
♘d7 16 ♕h7+ ♔f7 17 ♗g6+ ♔f6 18
♗h5 ♘f8 19 ♕d3 g6! 20 ♕xd4+ e5 21
♕h4+ ♔f7 ∓) 15 ♗g6 ♘c6 16 f4 ♗d7
17 0-0 ± Gdanski-Farago, Haifa Echt
1989.

b24) 13 ♘e2 ♘c6 (13...♘d7!? is
worth contemplating; the knight can
then go to f8 or f6 depending on the
situation that arises) 14 0-0 c4 15 ♗g6
♗d7 (15...e5 16 f4! is promising for
White, who may well seek to play f5-
f6) 16 f4 ♗e8 17 ♗xe8 ♕xe8 18 ♕g4
♔h7 19 ♖ae1 ± Z.Almasi-I.Farago,
Hungarian Ch 1993.

We now return to 11 ♕h5 *(D)*:

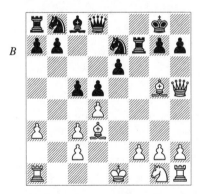

11...g6

11...h6 is risky now:

a) 12 ♗h7+ ♔xh7 (12...♔f8? 13
♗g6! +−) 13 ♕xf7 hxg5 14 ♘f3 ♘f5
15 h4 g4 16 ♘g5+ ♔h6 17 ♕xf5 exf5
18 ♘f7+ ♔g6 19 ♘xd8 ♔f6 20 h5!?
♔e7 21 h6 gxh6 22 ♖xh6 ♔xd8 23
dxc5 gives White an initiative in the
endgame but it is difficult to assess at
this stage. I will leave it as an idea.

b) 12 ♗g6 ♖f8 13 ♘f3 ♘bc6 14
0-0 (14 ♗xh6 gxh6 15 ♕xh6 ♘xg6 16
♕xg6+ ♔h8 and now 17 ♕h6+ forces
a draw, while Korchnoi has suggested
17 ♘g5 ♕e7 18 0-0-0 c4 19 ♖de1 intending ♖e3, but I am not sure I trust
it for White) 14...♗d7 (in J.Polgar-
Uhlmann, Amsterdam OHRA 1990
White obtained the better chances after 14...♕c7?! 15 ♗xe7 ♕xe7 16 ♖ae1)
15 ♖ae1 (15 dxc5 ♗e8 16 ♗xe8 ♕xe8
17 ♕xe8 ♖axe8 18 ♗xe7 ♖xe7 is
level) 15...♗e8 16 ♗xe8 ♕xe8 17 ♕xe8
♖axe8 18 ♗xe7 ♖xe7 19 dxc5 ♖f4!?
and Black has good counterplay.

12 ♕d1!

White has succeeded in weakening
Black's kingside and now retreats the
queen, intending to develop normally.

12 ♕h4 ♘bc6 13 ♘f3 – *8 ♘f3
♘bc6 9 ♗d3 f5 10 exf6 ♖xf6 11 ♗g5
♖f7 12 ♕h5 g6 13 ♕h4 =*.

12...♘bc6 13 ♘f3 *(D)*

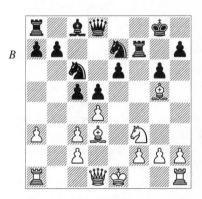

Now we shall divide the lines into:

B41: 13...♕a5 186
B42: 13...♕f8 187

A few alternatives are worth mentioning:

a) 13...c4 14 ♗e2 ♕f8 is noted by McDonald as "a significant error in move-order". I wonder what prompted Timman to insert ...c4 before ...♕f8. While Black's position is still difficult to overrun, there is no doubt that White's options are increased here. Now:

a1) 15 ♕d2 would invite a possible ...♘f5-d6-e4 manoeuvre, as it would gain a tempo against the queen.

a2) 15 ♕c1! is a high-class move, since compared to *13...♕f8* there is no ...♖xf3 sacrifice to worry about, so White can concentrate on taking control of the dark squares. 15...♘f5 16 h4!? h6 17 ♗f4 ♗d7 18 ♘e5 ♘xe5 19 ♗xe5 ♘e7 20 ♕e3 ♘c6 21 ♗g3 ♖e8 (Black is very close to creating counterplay with ...♕g7 and ...e5) 22 h5! g5 23 0-0 (intending 24 f4) 23...♘e7 (23...♕g7 24 f4 g4 25 ♗h4! ±) 24 ♗e5! ♘c6 25 ♗h2 ♖g7 (25...♘e7 26 g4! ±) 26 ♗g4 ± Anand-Timman, Dortmund 1999.

b) 13...♕c7 14 0-0 c4 (14...e5!? is worth considering) 15 ♗e2 ♘f5 16 ♕c1 ♗d7 looks like a respectable attempt to equalize. It has been employed in a couple of games by Farago. Of course White would like to establish total domination of the e5-square – the question is how. 17 ♗f4? is a tactical blunder due to 17...♘fxd4!. My suggestion is

17 ♖e1!, when 17...♖af8 can be met by 18 ♗f4 ♕a5 19 ♗d2 intending 20 ♘g5 followed by 21 f4. If White can establish control over e5, he has a fantastic position.

B41)
13...♕a5 14 ♗d2 *(D)*

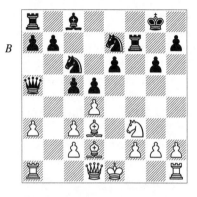

This position may also arise via *12...♕a5 13 ♗d2 ♘bc6 14 ♘f3*.

14...c4

Another very interesting idea is 14...♕c7 15 0-0 e5!, and now:

a) 16 ♘g5 ♖f8 17 c4!? exd4 (17...e4 18 cxd5 exd3 19 dxc6 ♕xc6 20 cxd3 ± Ernst-Schmidt, Vienna 1991) 18 ♖e1 ♗f5 19 cxd5 ♘xd5 20 ♗c4 ♖ad8 21 ♕f3 ♕d6 22 ♕b3 b6 23 ♘e4 ♗xe4 24 ♖xe4 and White had compensation for the pawn (but not more) in Hraček-Kindermann, Bad Homburg 1997.

b) 16 ♘xe5 ♘xe5 17 dxe5 ♕xe5 18 c4 ♗f5 (18...d4 also looks equal) 19 ♖e1 ♕f6 20 ♕f3 ♗xd3 21 ♕xf6 ♖xf6 22 cxd3 ♘f5 23 ♖e5 dxc4 24 dxc4 ♖d6 = Lutz-Kindermann, Porz 1997.

15 ♗e2 ♗d7 16 0-0

16 h4 ♘f5 17 h5 and now 17...e5 18 hxg6 hxg6 19 dxe5 was very good for White in Ernst-Giddins, Gausdal 1994, but 17...gxh5! is much stronger. Then after 18 ♖xh5 ♖g7 19 g3 ♖f8 Black is fine.

16...♘f5

16...♗g7?! 17 ♕c1! ♘g8 18 ♗f4 ♖af8 19 ♗d6, Topalov-Yusupov, Dortmund 1997, is good for White, who has successfully infiltrated on the dark squares.

17 ♕c1 ♖af8 18 a4 ♘d6

The position is approximately equal, Vehi Bach-Alvarez Ibarra, San Sebastian 1994. White has excellent control over the dark squares but Black is ready to create counterplay with ...♘e4.

B42)

13...♕f8 *(D)*

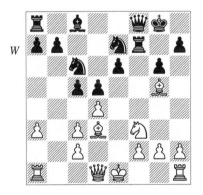

A strategically complex position arises after this. It is worth noting that the queen is well placed on the kingside. For example, from g7 it supports an ...h6, ...g5 advance and controls the e5-square.

14 0-0

On 14 ♕d2 (or 14 ♕c1 for that matter) Black has a pleasant choice between 14...♖xf3 15 gxf3 cxd4 and 14...cxd4.

14...c4

Korchnoi mentions 14...♖xf3 15 ♕xf3 cxd4 16 cxd4 ♘xd4 17 ♕d1 with better chances for White, but sacrificing the exchange at this point looks too desperate.

15 ♗e2 h6 *(D)*

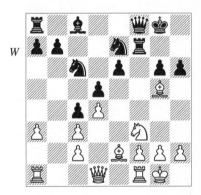

16 ♗c1 *(D)*

White prepares a4, redeploying the bishop to the a3-f8 diagonal. The assessment of this position has changed over the years. The view now is that Black has fair chances of equality. A few alternatives are:

a) 16 ♗h4 ♘f5 17 ♗g3 ♗d7 18 ♕d2 ♔h7 = ½-½ Kovačević-Draško, Vrnjačka Banja 1999.

b) 16 ♗xe7!? is actually not a bad idea, as Black's knight is just as strong as White's bishop. After 16...♕xe7 17 ♖e1 ♗d7 18 ♗f1 ♖af8 19 ♖e3 g5 20 h3 ♖f6 the position was roughly equal in Gabrielsen-Zifroni, Siofok 1996.

c) 16 ♗d2 ♘f5 and now:

c1) 17 ♕c1 g5? (this is too risky; 17...♔h7, with roughly equal chances, is correct) 18 ♘e5 ♘xe5 19 dxe5 ♕c5 20 g4! ♘e7 21 ♗e3 ♕a5 22 f4 ♕xc3 23 fxg5 ♖xf1+ 24 ♗xf1 ♘g6 25 gxh6 and White is much better, Khachian-Rõtšagov, Moscow 1996.

c2) 17 g3 ♗d7 18 h4 ♘d6 19 ♘e5 ♘xe5 20 dxe5 ♘f5 21 ♕e1 ♗a4 22 ♖c1 ♕g7 23 h5 ♖af8 with a slight advantage for Black, Baklan-Berelovich, Ordzhonikidze 2000.

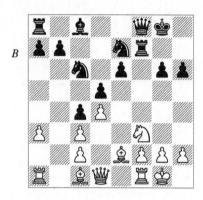

B

16...♕g7 17 ♕d2 ♔h7 18 a4 ♗d7 19 ♗a3 g5 20 ♗d6 ♘f5 21 ♗e5 ♕g6

The chances are roughly equal, Sutovsky-Kindermann, Bad Homburg 1997.

14 Modern Main Lines: 7 ♘f3, 7 a4 and 7 h4

1 e4 e6 2 d4 d5 3 ♘c3 ♗b4 4 e5 c5 5 a3 ♗xc3+ 6 bxc3 ♘e7 *(D)*

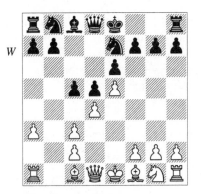

Of course, White doesn't have to embark on the sharp 7 ♕g4, which we discussed in the two previous chapters. There are other, more positional, approaches. 7 ♘f3 and 7 a4 have been on the map for a long time but during the last 10 years a third option has been added: 7 h4. Since there are transpositions between especially the first two and similar ideas that occur in all three lines, I will take a little time to discuss the main differences between these moves.

To take them in the order they are presented here, 7 ♘f3 is perhaps the least flexible of them all but it is a natural and sensible developing move. White simply wants to get on with development and has no desire to look for a 'refutation' of the black set-up. There may be times, though, where White ventures ♘g5 followed by ♕h5, creating weaknesses on Black's kingside. However, I must admit that of the three it is the move that is easiest to equalize against. Therefore, I have better thoughts of 7 a4. There are two, perhaps three, main ideas with this move. The two most important are that it supports ♗b5 in some lines and that it denies Black the option of a blockade on the a4-square. The latter is, in my opinion, of prime significance. Additionally, with 7 a4, White may sometimes benefit from the possibility of being able to advance the pawn even further.

With 7 h4, White shares ideas with 7 ♘f3 and 7 a4 but wants to create weaknesses on the black kingside while at the same time staying very flexible. There are even possibilities of adopting a ♕g4 set-up because the knight hasn't gone to f3 yet.

On to the specifics...

A: 7 ♘f3   190
B: 7 a4   198
C: 7 h4   202

A)

7 ♘f3 *(D)*

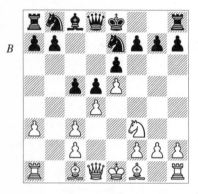

Now:

A1: 7...♘bc6   190
A2: 7...♕a5   191
A3: 7...♗d7   192
A4: 7...b6   194

7...♕c7 will just transpose to lines covered later, depending on whether White wants an a4 or an h4 set-up. If White continues 8 ♗e2 or 8 ♗d3 instead, I will just say that the ...b6 idea (as in Line A4) gains in strength. If 8 h4 we have Line C2.

A1)

7...♘bc6 8 ♖b1!? *(D)*

This slightly unusual move intends to lure Black into positions he rather wouldn't play. Alternatively, moves such as 8 ♗d3, 8 ♗e2 and 8 a4 would

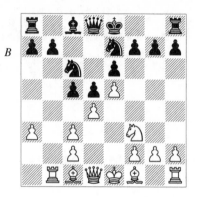

transpose to other lines. Rather than guide you through every single transposition, I advise you to skim through the other lines to look for the sort of position which can arise.

8...♕c7

The point of a ...b6 set-up has disappeared at this stage as Black does not have the option of exchanging bishops. Other moves:

a) 8...♕a5 9 ♖b5!? (9 ♕d2 c4 10 h4 also looked quite promising for White in Socko-Bartel, Warsaw 2001, while 9 ♗d2 c4 10 ♕c1, Borriss-Enders, Bundesliga 1999/00, is another idea) 9...♕xc3+ 10 ♗d2 ♕xa3 11 ♖b3 ♕a2 12 dxc5 gives White good compensation according to Bologan.

b) 8...a6 9 ♗e2 ♕a5 was Lanka-Kindermann, Bundesliga 1995/6. Now Lanka sacrificed the pawn on c3 for a lead in development with 10 0-0, and obtained a degree of compensation after 10...♕xc3 11 ♖b3 ♕a5 12 dxc5 ♘g6 13 ♖e1 ♕xc5 14 ♗d3 b5 15 ♗d2 but whether this is really enough is hard to say. Alternatively, both 10 ♗d2 and 10

♕d2 are sensible moves, after which
...a6 doesn't fit in too well with Black's
plans.

9 h4! h6 10 h5 ♗d7 11 ♗d3

11 ♗e2 0-0-0 12 0-0 f6 13 ♗f4 also
gave White an advantage in Bologan-
Nadero, Manila OL 1992.

**11...0-0-0 12 g3 f5 13 ♔f1 c4 14
♗e2 ♕a5 15 ♕e1**

± A.Sokolov-Blauert, Berne 1992.

A2)

7...♕a5 (D)

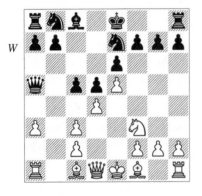

W

8 ♗d2

A seemingly innocuous line is 8
♕d2 b6 9 c4 (9 dxc5 bxc5 10 c4 ♕c7!
11 cxd5 exd5 12 ♕c3 leads to equality
– Bareev) 9...♕xd2+ 10 ♗xd2 ♗a6 11
cxd5 ♗xf1 12 ♖xf1 exd5 13 dxc5 bxc5
14 0-0-0 (14 ♖b1!? ♘d7 15 ♖b7 0-0-0!
16 ♖xa7 ♘c6 17 ♖a8+ ♔b7 18 ♖xd8
♖xd8 gives Black compensation –
Nogueiras) 14...♘bc6 15 ♖fe1 0-0 16
e6 d4! = Short-Nogueiras, Wijk aan
Zee 1987.

8...♘bc6

Or:

a) 8...♗d7 9 a4 ♘bc6 – 7 a4 ♕a5 8
♗d2 ♘bc6 9 ♘f3 ♗d7.

b) 8...♕c7 has also been played.
Black's point is that a4 set-ups are not
very dangerous since the bishop cannot go to a3. In fact, the bishop would
often rather be on c1 to have this possibility. In comparison with Line A1,
Black also has the option of a ...b6
idea. Fedorov-J.Sørensen, Saint Vincent Ech 2000 continued 9 h4 h6 10 h5
b6 11 ♗b5+ ♗d7 12 ♗d3 ♗a4 13 0-0
♘bc6 14 ♖e1 c4 15 ♗f1 0-0-0 16 g3
♕d7 17 ♗h3 ♕e8 18 ♘h4 ♕g8 19
♘g2 ♔b7 20 ♘e3 and White was only
very slightly better.

9 ♗e2

Otherwise:

a) Since Black often voluntarily
closes the position with ...c4, there
seems little reason to invite this with 9
♗d3, which actually just transposes to
another line; viz. 9...c4 10 ♗f1 (10
♗e2 is just the main line a tempo down
for White) – 7...♗d7 8 ♗d3 c4 9 ♗f1
♕a5 10 ♗d2 =.

b) Another idea for White is 9 h4,
which of course closely resembles 7
h4. Then we have:

b1) 9...cxd4 10 cxd4 ♕a4 11 h5 – 7
h4 ♘bc6 8 h5 ♕a5 9 ♗d2 cxd4 10
cxd4 ♕a4 11 ♘f3 ±/=.

b2) 9...♗d7 10 h5 0-0-0 11 h6 gxh6
– 7 h4 ♘bc6 8 h5 ♕a5 9 ♗d2 ♗d7 10
h6 gxh6 11 ♘f3 0-0-0 =/∓.

b3) 9...f6!? 10 exf6 (10 c4 ♕a4 11
cxd5 exd5 12 exf6 gxf6 ∓ Shirov)
10...gxf6 11 ♘h2 ♕a4 12 ♖b1 c4 13

♕h5+ ♚d8 14 ♘g4, Shirov-Plaskett, Reykjavik 1992, and now Shirov suggests 14...♕xc2! 15 ♖c1 ♕e4+ 16 ♗e3 ♕f5 17 ♕xf5 ♘xf5 18 ♘xf6 ♘xe3 19 fxe3 ♚e7 20 ♘g4 h5 21 ♘h2 e5 with a slight advantage for Black.

9...♗d7

9...cxd4 10 cxd4 ♕a4 was a popular line in the late 1980s but is now rarely seen. It is generally agreed that White is better after 11 ♖b1! ♘xd4 12 ♗d3 ♘dc6 (12...♘ec6 13 ♗b4! ♘f5 14 ♕c1 b6 15 c4 ♘xb4 16 ♖xb4 ♕c6 17 0-0 0-0 18 ♕f4 favoured White in Timman-Hübner, Tilburg 1988) 13 ♖b3! ♘f5 14 0-0, Dolmatov-Oll, USSR Ch (Odessa) 1989. White has a strong bishop-pair and generally very active pieces as compensation for the pawn, and Black is struggling to find a reasonable way to save his queen.

10 0-0 *(D)*

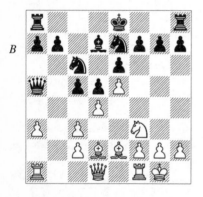

10...c4

Just in case White should be thinking of opening the position with c4. Black could also bring his queen back to c7 first, but he would probably need to close the position at some point anyway. This type of position arises more frequently in the 7 a4 line, and actually 11 a4 would now transpose to *7 a4 ♘bc6 8 ♘f3 ♕a5 9 ♗d2 ♗d7 10 ♗e2 c4 11 0-0*. We should make a close comparison with those lines, but in general White can be happy to have an extra tempo for his development, rather than have it spent on a4. In Dolmatov-Draško, Tallinn 1985 Black tried to manage without ...c4 but also looked worse after 10...♕c7 11 ♖e1 b6 12 g3 ♘a5 13 ♗d3 ♘c4 14 ♗c1 h6 15 h4.

11 ♘g5!?

11 ♖e1 0-0-0 12 ♗f1 is worth considering. Then after 12...f6 13 g3 ♘g6 14 h4 fxe5 15 dxe5 ♖hf8 16 ♗h3 ♖de8 (Spassky-Dückstein, Zurich 1984), Spassky recommends 17 ♗g4! ♘h8 18 ♖e2 ♘f7 19 ♕e1 with an edge for White.

11...h6 12 ♘h3 ♘g6!?

This cleverly prevents ♘f4.

13 ♗h5 0-0-0

Now White usually plays a4 at some point, thus transposing to similar positions to the line *7 a4 ♘bc6 8 ♘f3 ♕a5 9 ♗d2 ♗d7 10 ♗e2 c4* (Line B22), etc. I advise a comparison with those lines. Black should respond by planning ...f6, with, for example, ...♖df8 and ...♘ge7. The position is roughly equal.

A3)

7...♗d7 *(D)*

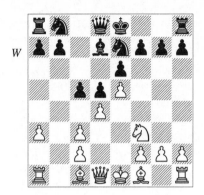

Black wants to set up a blockade with the bishop on a4. This also has the useful purpose of attacking c2.

8 dxc5!?

This became popular after the 1977 Spassky-Korchnoi match. White ruins his pawn-structure but more importantly maintains his space advantage and gets active piece-play. Other moves:

a) 8 a4 ♕a5 9 ♗d2 ♘bc6 – *7 a4 ♕a5 8 ♗d2 ♘c6 9 ♘f3 ♗d7*.

b) 8 ♗e2 ♗a4 9 0-0 ♕c7 10 ♖a2 ♘d7 11 ♖e1 h6 12 ♖b2 0-0-0 13 dxc5 ♘xc5 with an approximately equal position, Short-Beliavsky, Madrid 1995.

c) 8 ♗d3 and now 8...c4 9 ♗f1!? ♕a5 10 ♗d2 ♘bc6 11 g3 0-0-0 12 ♗h3 f6 13 exf6 gxf6 14 0-0 e5 was roughly equal in Abramović-P.Nikolić, Yugoslav Ch (Vakuf) 1980, but 8...♗a4 might be more precise; e.g., 9 0-0 c4 10 ♗e2 ♘bc6 11 ♖e1 h6 12 ♗f1 ♕a5 13 ♕d2 0-0-0 14 g3 g5!? with equality, Gutierrez-Farago, Kikinda 1978.

8...♘g6
Or:

a) 8...♗a4!? 9 ♖b1 ♕c7 (in *Play the French*, Watson recommended 9...♘d7 10 ♖xb7 ♘xc5 11 ♖b4 ♕a5 as an interesting gambit) 10 ♗d3 ♘d7 11 0-0 ♘xc5 12 ♖b4 a6 13 ♕e2 ± Ehlvest-Timman, Rotterdam 1989.

b) 8...♕c7 9 ♗d3 (the alternative move-order, 9 ♖b1!?, could be considered) and then:

b1) 9...♗a4 10 ♖b1 ♘ec6 (10...♘d7 might be inaccurate in view of 11 ♖b4 ♗c6 12 0-0 ♘xc5 13 ♖g4 ♘g6 14 ♘d4 0-0-0 15 f4 and White was better in Spassky-Korchnoi, Belgrade Ct (10) 1977) 11 0-0 ♘d7 12 ♗e3 h6 13 ♖e1 ±/± Shirov-Zsu.Polgar, Pardubice 1994.

b2) 9...♘bc6 10 ♗f4 ♘g6 11 ♗g3 ♕a5 12 ♕d2 ♕xc5 13 h4 d4 14 ♗xg6 hxg6 15 cxd4 ♕c4 16 ♖b1 b6 gives Black enough compensation. In Nunn-Korchnoi, Brussels 1986 White opted to repeat the position with 17 ♕e2 ♕c3+ 18 ♕d2 ♕c4.

9 ♗d3 ♘c6 10 ♖b1 ♘cxe5 11 h4!?

This aggressive continuation was first played in Anand-P.Nikolić, Monaco Amber blindfold 1995. Another idea is 11 ♘xe5 ♘xe5 12 ♖xb7 but then 12...♕c8 13 ♖b4 ♕xc5 equalized in the game Mokry-Farago, Prague 1985.

11...♕c7 12 0-0 *(D)*

12...♕xc5

In the aforementioned Anand-P.Nikolić game, Black went wrong with 12...♘xf3+?! 13 ♕xf3 ♘h4 14 ♕g3 ♕xg3 15 fxg3 ♘g6 16 ♖xb7 ±.

13 h5 ♘xf3+ 14 ♕xf3 ♘e5 15 ♕g3 ♘xd3 16 cxd3

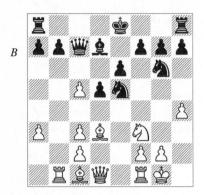

White stands better in spite of having a pawn less, Galkin-Zakharov, Kolontaevo 1997. The opposite-coloured bishops clearly favour White, because Black's king is unsafe.

A4)
7...b6 *(D)*

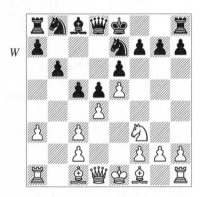

If I had to point to a specific drawback of 7 ♘f3 compared to 7 a4 it would have to be 7...b6. The usual reaction to ...b6 ideas is 8 ♗b5+ ♗d7, after which White retreats his bishop to d3, arguing that Black's bishop is poorly placed on d7. However, here it has a useful function of taking up the role as a blockader on a4. This is one main reason why I think 7 a4 is actually more accurate than 7 ♘f3.

8 ♗b5+

Because Black wishes to exchange light-squared bishops with ...♗a6, White first intends to make Black's bishop go to d7, so he loses the option of playing ...♗a6. Other moves are:

a) 8 ♖b1!? has, as far as I am aware, only been played in Ljubojević-Hort, Montreal 1979. Black can then play 8...♕c7 9 ♗d3 ♗a6 as Hort did, but 8...♗a6 is also not bad. Then 9 dxc5!? (the main idea of White's 8th move) 9...♗xf1 (9...bxc5? 10 ♖xb8) 10 cxb6 axb6 gives Black plenty of compensation, with play against White's many weak pawns.

b) 8 ♘g5 h6 9 ♕h5 g6 10 ♕h3 is an attempt to deny Black the option of castling kingside but it is very time-consuming. If White gets time to develop and protect his centre he will undoubtedly be better. However, the line has gone out of fashion as it has been proved that Black comes first with his counter-attack. For example:

b1) 10...♔f8 (this is the solid approach but there really is no reason to reject 'b2') 11 ♗d3 ♔g7 12 ♘f3 ♗a6 13 dxc5 (13 0-0 ♗xd3 14 cxd3 c4! ∓ Gulko; this is an instructive way of seizing control of the light squares) 13...♗xd3! (this is possibly the simplest equalizer, though 13...bxc5 looks viable, while 13...♕c7!? 14 0-0 ♕xc5

15 ♗d2 ♘ec6 16 ♕h4 ♕e7 17 ♕f4, Gulko-Panno, Vina del Mar 1988, 17...♗xd3! 18 cxd3 ♘d7 is also OK for Black) 14 cxd3 bxc5 15 0-0 ♘d7 16 ♖b1 ♖b8 17 ♗d2 ♖b6 18 ♕h4 ♘c6 ½-½ Nunn-P.Nikolić, Skellefteå 1989.

b2) 10...♕c7 11 ♗d2 (11 a4 has the idea that White gets good compensation for a pawn after 11...cxd4 12 cxd4 ♕xc2 13 ♗b5+ ♗d7 14 0-0, but simply 11...♔f8! gave Black a clearly superior version of 'b1' above in the game A.Sokolov-Yusupov, Riga Ct (13) 1986) 11...cxd4 12 cxd4 ♕xc2! 13 ♖c1 ♕b2 14 ♘f3 (14 ♗d3? ♕xd4 is much better for Black, Nunn-Hertneck, Munich 1991) 14...♘bc6 15 ♗d3 ♕xa3 (White may be able to claim some compensation after 15...♘xd4 16 ♘xd4 ♕xd4 17 0-0 as Black's king is caught dangerously in the middle of the board and the exchange of knights has greatly helped White) 16 ♖c3 ♕a2!? 17 0-0 ♗a6 18 ♗xa6 ♕xa6 19 ♗g5 ♔d7! 20 ♗f6 ♖hc8 and Black is better according to Hertneck. Note the trick 21 ♕xh6? ♘xd4! ∓.

c) 8 h4 may be compared to Line C (7 h4), but whereas early ...b6 ideas are rarely a good idea against the immediate 7 h4, White's options have here been greatly reduced owing to the knight's early commitment to f3. Hence, Black has no real problems here: 8...♗a6 9 ♗xa6 ♘xa6 10 h5 h6 11 ♕d3 ♘b8 12 dxc5 bxc5 (12...♕c7!?) 13 c4 ♘bc6 14 0-0 0-0 15 ♗e3 ♕a5 16 ♖ab1 ♖fd8 17 ♖b5 dxc4 18 ♕xc4 ♕xa3 19 ♖xc5 ♖ac8 with an equal

position, Benjamin-Gulko, Saint John 1988.

d) 8 a4 ♗a6 (D) with two options for White:

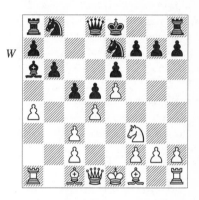

d1) 9 ♗xa6 ♘xa6 and then:

d11) 10 ♕e2 ♘b8 11 dxc5 ♕c7! (it is striking how often this thematic reply turns out to be better than the simple recapture; after 11...bxc5 12 0-0, 12...0-0 13 c4 ♕c7 14 cxd5 ♘xd5 15 ♕e4 h6 16 ♕g4 ♔h7 17 ♖a3 gave White a promising attacking position in Galkin-Rõtšagov, Russia 1997, but perhaps Black castled prematurely; McDonald suggests 12...h6 as more solid) 12 0-0 ♕xc5 13 ♕d2 ♘bc6 14 ♗a3 ♕c4 15 ♘d4 h6 16 f4 ♘xd4 17 cxd4 ♘f5 18 c3 h5 19 a5 b5 20 a6 ♔d7 21 ♗b4 ½-½ Galkin-Najer, St Petersburg 1998.

d12) On 10 0-0 I would prefer 10...♕c7, as in Reeh-Kindermann, Hamburg 1993, or perhaps 10...h6!?. It is difficult to see a better set-up for White than that in 'd11'. 10...0-0 is also natural but then White may be able to use a similar set-up as in Gal-kin-Rõtšagov above. It is also worth pointing out that 10...♘b8 11 ♘g5 is more than just a random blow in the wind. In Karpov-Short, London 1982 White was clearly better after 11...h6 12 ♕h5 g6 13 ♕h3 cxd4?! (13...♘bc6 is more accurate) 14 cxd4 ♘bc6 15 ♘f3 ♔d7?! 16 c3 ♖c8 17 ♘d2 ♘a5 18 ♕f3 ♖h7 19 ♗a3. One should always remain alert to the idea of ♘g5 followed by ♕h5 in these lines.

d2) 9 ♗b5+ ♗xb5 10 axb5 *(D)* and then:

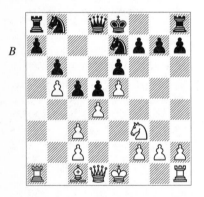

d21) 10...♕d7 11 ♕e2 c4 12 ♗a3 ♕xb5 (12...h6!?) 13 ♘g5 ♕d7 14 ♕h5 ♘g6 15 0-0 ♘c6 16 f4 0-0-0 17 ♖ae1 was unclear in Gulko-Eingorn, USSR 1983 but White probably has good compensation for the pawn.

d22) 10...0-0 11 0-0 ♕c7 12 ♗g5!? h6? (12...♘g6 is better) 13 ♗xe7 ♕xe7 14 c4! dxc4 15 d5 ♕d7 16 dxe6 ♕xe6 17 ♕d6 gives White a strong initiative for the pawn, Mortensen-Antonsen, Danish Ch (Ringsted) 1995.

d23) 10...h6 11 0-0 0-0 12 ♕e2 ♘d7 13 ♗a3 a6 14 bxa6 ♕c8 = Apicella-Hertneck, Uzes 1990.

8...♗d7 9 ♗d3 *(D)*

Or 9 a4 ♗xb5 – *8 a4 ♗a6 9 ♗b5+ ♗xb5*.

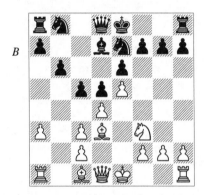

9...c4

The beginning of an interesting strategy. Black wishes to blockade the queenside by ...♗a4. Then, for the duration of the middlegame, there is effectively only one side to play on, the kingside, which at first sight may seem favourable for White because he has a space advantage there. However, Black may restrain this somewhat by playing ...h6. Then his plan is to transfer the queen to h7 (!) by playing ...♔d7 and ...♕g8-h7, attacking c2 and thus tying White's pieces up a bit. There is an interesting strategic struggle ahead.

Note also that I prefer the text-move, which defines the structure immediately, to 9...♗a4, when White can still keep the queenside open if he wishes, while it is not clear that Black can extract any benefit from his extra flex-ibility if White carries on as normal:

a) 10 dxc5!? (I am not sure if this is a real problem for Black but I see no reason why Black should allow White this possibility) 10...bxc5 (we have become familiar with 10...♕c7? as a common reaction to captures on c5 but here is an example where it is not ad-visable: 11 0-0 ♕xc5 12 ♘g5! h6 13 ♕h5 g6 14 ♕h4 b5 15 ♘xf7! ♔xf7 16 ♕f6+ ♔g8 17 ♗xg6 +– Lautier; if Black wishes to sacrifice a pawn it is better done with 10...♘d7!? 11 cxb6 axb6) 11 0-0 c4 12 ♗e2 ♘g6?! (this is inaccurate; instead 12...♘bc6 is OK for Black after 13 ♗e3 ♕a5! or 13 ♗f4 ♘g6 14 ♗g3 0-0 15 ♕d2 f5 16 exf6 ♕xf6 – Nunn) 13 ♘g5! ♘xe5 (13...h6 14 ♘xe6 fxe6 15 ♗h5 ±) 14 f4 ♘d3!? 15 ♗xd3 cxd3 16 f5! with a dangerous attack for White, Nunn-P.Nikolić, Belgrade 1991.

b) 10 h4!? (White instead gets on with the standard plans; Black can now delay or omit ...c4 entirely, but has not demonstrated any clear-cut benefits from this) 10...♕c7 (of course 10...c4 would reach positions similar to those in the main line) 11 0-0 (this is the most accurate because 11 h5 cxd4! obliged White to sacrifice a couple of pawns for speculative compensation in Shirov-Casper, Bundesliga 1994/5, for 12 cxd4 ♕c3+ 13 ♗d2 would be met by 13...♕xd3! with a very com-fortable position for Black) 11...h6 (now Black shouldn't close the centre as he does not have the ...♕g8-h7

manoeuvre available) 12 h5 ♘d7 13 ♖e1 ♕c6 14 ♖b1 a6 (Black consis-tently plays for an exchange of the light-squared bishops but he should probably have played ...0-0-0 here or on the last move) 15 ♘d2 cxd4 16 cxd4 ♗b5 17 ♖xb5! (an ingenious positional sacrifice after which White's bishops will have no opposition) 17...axb5 18 ♕e2 ♖a4!? 19 ♘b3 (19 ♗xb5 ♕xc2 is rather unclear) 19...♖c4 20 ♗d2 ♘f5 21 ♗b4! ♘xd4 22 ♘xd4 ♖xd4 23 ♗xb5 and White's bishops completely dominated the game in Topalov-Gulko, Dos Hermanas 1994.

10 ♗f1

Alternatively, there is 10 ♗e2 ♗a4 11 0-0 (11 h4 is also possible, when play resembles that of the main line) 11...h6, when Black intends ...♔d7 followed by ...♕g8-h7. I think it is im-portant in these lines that Black delays the development of the b8-knight, so that he can later choose between ...♘c6, ...♘a6-c7 and ...♘d7. If White plays slowly and puts the knight on h5, Black's knight should go to d7. If White instead plays more aggressively with a quick f-pawn thrust, Black should defend e6 with ...♘a6-c7. 12 g3 ♔d7 13 ♘h4 ♕g8 14 f4!? (this is more dangerous for Black than 14 ♘g2 ♕h7 15 ♖a2 ♔c7 16 ♘f4 ♘d7 17 ♘h5 ♖af8, which is approximately equal as long as Black does not attempt to open the position prematurely) 14...♕h7 15 f5 ♘a6! (it is best to reinforce the de-fence of the e6-pawn; 15...exf5 16 ♘xf5 ♘xf5 17 ♖xf5 is bad for Black,

while 15...g5 is risky due to 16 fxg6
fxg6 17 ♖f6!) 16 ♗g4 ♘c7 17 ♖f2 g5!
18 fxg6 fxg6 19 ♕f1 ♖ag8 20 ♘g2
♘f5 = Hamdouchi-Kosten, Montpellier 1998.

10...♗a4 *(D)*

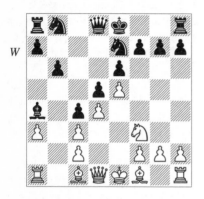

11 h4

This space-gaining move is White's
most common set-up. If White instead
plays 11 g3 h6 12 ♘h4 ♔d7 13 ♗h3
♕g8 14 f4 it is important that Black
does not panic. The best defence is to
play 14...♕h7 15 ♖a2 ♘a6!, intending
...♘c7. It is very hard for White to
breach that type of set-up.

**11...h6 12 h5 ♔d7 13 g3 ♕g8 14
♗f4**

White intends to defend his c-pawn
with ♖c1 but it is now very unlikely
that White is ever going to be able to
advance the f-pawn.

14...♕h7 15 ♖c1 ♘bc6

With White's knight being unable
to get to h5, and an f5 thrust unlikely,
the knight definitely belongs on c6.

16 ♗g2 a5 17 ♘h2 b5

= Shirov-Yusupov, Moscow OL
1994.

B)

7 a4 *(D)*

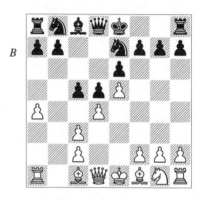

We shall now look at:

B1: 7...♕c7   199
B2: 7...♕a5   200

7...♘bc6 8 ♘f3 ♕a5 is also logical,
but possibly less precise than putting
the queen on a5 immediately:

a) 9 ♗d2 – 7...♕a5 8 ♗d2 ♘bc6 9
♘f3.

b) 9 ♕d2 ♗d7 and now:

b1) 10 ♗a3!? cxd4 11 cxd4 ♕xd2+
12 ♔xd2 ♘f5 13 ♖b1 b6 14 c3 ♘a5 15
♗b4 ♘c4+ 16 ♗xc4 dxc4 = Kan-Bot-
vinnik, Sverdlovsk 1943 and Moro-
vić-Shaked, Groningen FIDE 1997.

b2) 10 ♗d3 f6! 11 0-0 (11 exf6
gxf6 12 dxc5 e5 gives Black good
counterplay) 11...fxe5 12 dxe5 0-0 13
♖e1 h6 is roughly equal, and has been
seen in several games, including Smys-
lov-Uhlmann, Havana 1964.

b3) 10 ♗e2 ♖c8!? (on 10...f6 11 exf6 gxf6, 12 dxc5 is a better version for White than after 10 ♗d3) 11 ♗a3 cxd4 12 cxd4 ♕xd2+ 13 ♔xd2 ♘f5 14 c3 ♘a5 15 ♖hb1 h5 16 ♗b4 ♘c4+ 17 ♔e1 f6 = Gi.Hernandez-Vilela, Santa Clara 1991.

B1)
7...♕c7 8 ♘f3 (D)

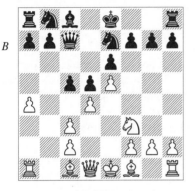

8...h6!

This little move has the very subtle point of meeting White's most logical move, 9 ♗d3, with 9...b6!, when Black has an improved version of Line A4, since Black will force an exchange of the bishops with ...♗a6.

The main line used to be 8...b6 9 ♗b5+ ♗d7 10 ♗d3 ♘bc6 11 0-0 h6 (11...0-0?? 12 ♗xh7+! +−) 12 ♖e1 0-0, when White has a difficult choice of how to develop his bishop:

a) 13 ♗f4 ♘g6 14 ♗g3 cxd4 15 ♘xd4 (15 cxd4?! ♘b4 ∓) 15...♘a5 16 ♕g4!? (16 ♖e3 ♘c4 17 ♗xc4 ♕xc4 18 h4 ♗xa4! 19 h5 ♘e7 20 ♗f4 ♘f5

was unclear in Nunn-P.Nikolić, Amsterdam 1988) 16...♕xc3 17 ♘e2 (17 ♘b5!? might be worth considering) 17...♕c7 18 ♗xg6 ½-½ Galkin-Se.Ivanov, Stockholm 1999.

b) 13 ♗a3! ♘a5 14 dxc5 bxc5 15 ♘d2 ♗xa4 16 ♕g4! (16 ♗xc5 ♕xc5 17 ♖xa4 ♕xc3 18 ♖e3 ♔h8!, Nunn-Yusupov, Linares 1988, and now Yusupov suggests 19 ♘f3 ♖ab8 20 h3 with compensation for White) 16...♗d7 17 ♘f3 ♖ab8 (17...♘c4 18 ♗c1 f5 19 exf6 ♖xf6 20 ♗xc4 dxc4 21 ♕xc4 was very good for White in Nunn-P.Nikolić, Wijk aan Zee 1992) 18 ♗c1 ♔h8 and now:

b1) 19 ♕h4 ♘g8 is unclear, Chandler-Hertneck, Bundesliga 1993/4. White could then try 20 g4!?.

b2) McDonald suggests that 19 ♕h3!? ♘g8 20 g4! is more accurate. His main line runs 20...c4 21 g5! cxd3 22 gxh6 g6 23 h7 ♘e7 24 ♗g5 f6 25 ♗xf6+ ♖xf6 26 exf6 e5 27 ♕h6 ♘f5 28 ♕xg6, with "serious threats" such as 29 ♘xe5 and 29 ♘g5. In fact, this looks completely winning for White.

9 ♗b5+

9 h4!? is also feasible, although White rarely combines a4 and h4.

9...♗d7 10 ♗d3 ♘bc6 11 0-0

Knaak thinks that White should prevent the exchange on d4 followed by a ...♘b4 sortie with 11 ♕d2 but then Black has a good version of the line examined in the note to Black's 8th move.

11...cxd4!?
Or:

a) 11...b6 – 8...b6 9 ♗b5+ ♗d7 10 ♗d3 ♘bc6 11 0-0 h6.

b) 11...f5 is another idea: 12 ♗a3 c4 13 ♗e2 g5!? 14 h4 (14 ♘d2? ♕a5 ∓ Z.Almasi-Knaak, Altensteig 1993) 14...g4 15 ♘e1 h5 is unclear – Knaak.

12 cxd4 ♘b4 13 ♗a3 ♘xd3 14 cxd3 ♗c6

Black may have a tiny edge, Sherzer-Yermolinsky, New York 1993.

B2)

7...♕a5

It was Uhlmann who pointed out that if Black wants to play a line with ...♕a5, then it is most precise to play the queen move immediately. After 7...♘bc6 8 ♘f3 ♕a5, White has the additional important option of playing 9 ♕d2. We shall see that this is not so strong after the immediate 7...♕a5.

8 ♗d2

If 8 ♕d2 Black has the strong reply 8...b6!, when White has two options:

a) 9 ♗b5+ ♗d7 10 ♗d3 looks like a speculative sacrifice. I think Black can actually take on a4; for example, 10...♗xa4 11 ♘f3 h6 12 0-0 ♘d7 13 ♗a3 c4 14 ♗e2 b5 and White has some practical chances but honestly I don't think his compensation is adequate. Another continuation for Black is 10...♘bc6 11 ♘f3 f6!?, Borkowski-Draško, Polanica Zdroj 1988, which doesn't look bad either.

b) 9 ♘f3 ♗a6 10 ♗xa6 ♕xa6 11 ♕e2 ♕xe2+ 12 ♔xe2 ♘d7 13 a5 b5 gave Black a pleasant endgame in Pelikov-Uhlmann, Szombathely 1966.

8...♘bc6 9 ♘f3 ♗d7 (D)

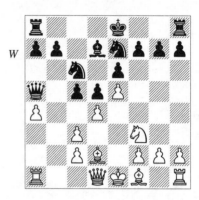

This position has occurred hundreds of times. Now White has two ways of developing his bishop:

Again 10 ♗d3 would most likely just be a waste of time. Black often closes the position voluntarily with ...c4, so there is no reason to invite this.

B21)

10 ♗b5

White's idea is to provoke ...a6, and to prove that this is a weakness.

10...♕c7

This is the most solid continuation. Black retreats the queen before c4 becomes a real threat, and now he will slowly prepare a ...f6 break. There are other lines that Black should consider. First of all, he can try the immediate ...f6 break, while there is also the possibility of shutting White's bishop out with ...c4:

a) Usually Black avoids 10...a6 11 ♗e2, accepting the view that ...a6 is weakening. However, it is yet to be established whether this is really the case. In view of *10 ♗e2 f6!* (Line B22) being generally accepted as OK for Black, it may in the future be worth looking further into 11...f6.

b) 10...f6 11 exf6 gxf6 12 dxc5!? (12 0-0) 12...a6 (12...♕c7 13 ♘d4!? ♕e5+ 14 ♗e3 a6 15 ♗d3 h5 16 0-0 ♕c7 17 c4 was good for White in Zhang Zhong-Harikrishna, Udaipur 2000) 13 c4 ♕c7 14 cxd5 ♘xd5 15 ♗d3 ♘cb4 (Sznapik-Holzke, Biel 1991) and now I like 16 ♗e2 ♕xc5 17 c4 ♘e7 18 0-0 for White.

c) 10...c4 11 0-0 f6 12 ♗c1! 0-0-0 (12...♘xe5? 13 dxe5 ♗xb5 14 exf6 gxf6 15 ♕d4 ±) 13 ♗a3 ♖he8 14 ♖e1 ♘f5 15 ♕d2 h5 16 h3 h4 17 ♗c5 ♕c7 18 ♗xc6! ♗xc6 19 a5 ♔b8 20 ♖eb1 is much better for White, Chandler-Timman, Reykjavik 1991.

11 0-0 0-0 12 ♖e1

12 ♗c1!? b6 13 ♗a3 ♘a5 and now:

a) 14 dxc5 ♗xb5 15 cxb6 axb6 16 axb5 ♖fc8 17 ♗b4 ♘c4 gave Black good compensation in, amongst others, Nunn-Yusupov, Belgrade 1991.

b) It is interesting that in the event of 14 ♗d3 h6, White is a tempo down on the line *7 a4 ♕c7 8 ♘f3 b6 9 ♗b5+ ♗d7 10 ♗d3 ♘bc6 11 0-0 h6 12 ♖e1 0-0 13 ♗a3 ♘a5*. The reason is that here Black has spent two moves moving his queen to c7 (...♕a5-c7) compared to one move in the 7 a4 line, while White has spent two moves

bringing his bishop back to c1 and only then positioned it on a3 (♗d2-c1-a3). In the 7 a4 line this took a single move because the bishop was already on c1.

12...b6 13 ♗d3 h6 14 ♕c1!? c4 15 ♗f1 f6

This position has occurred several times, and it is generally agreed that Black has no problems. The critical line is 16 g3 fxe5 17 ♘xe5 ♘xe5 18 ♖xe5 ♘g6 19 ♖e3 e5, when after 20 ♗g2 e4 Black was doing fine in Hellsten-Wiedenkeller, Swedish Ch (Borlange) 1992.

B22)

10 ♗e2 *(D)*

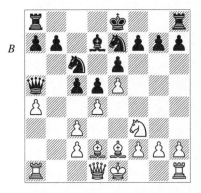

10...f6!?

10...c4 is an important alternative:

a) 11 0-0 f6 12 ♖e1 fxe5 13 dxe5 0-0 14 ♗f1 ♖f5 15 g3 ♖af8 16 ♖e3 h6 with roughly equal chances, Pein-Plaskett, British Ch (Swansea) 1987.

b) 11 ♘g5 h6 12 ♘h3 ♘g6 13 ♗h5 0-0-0 14 0-0 ♖df8 15 ♕e1 ♘ge7 16

♗c1 f6 with equality, Galkin-Bunz-mann, Saint Vincent Ech 2000.

11 c4

This looks like the critical test. Other moves:

a) 11 exf6 gxf6 12 0-0 c4! 13 ♘h4 0-0-0 14 f4 = Shaked.

b) 11 ♖b1 ♕c7 12 ♗f4 ♘g6 13 ♗g3 fxe5 14 0-0 0-0 (14...c4!?) 15 ♗b5 cxd4 16 cxd4 ♘f4 17 ♗xc6 ♗xc6 18 ♘xe5 ♗xa4 19 ♖b4 b5 20 ♕d2 ♘h5 ∓ Kostić-Ulybin, Munich 1991/2.

11...♕c7 12 exf6 gxf6 13 cxd5 ♘xd5 14 c4

14 c3 0-0-0 15 0-0 ♖hg8 16 ♖e1 e5 17 c4 ♗h3 18 ♗f1 ♘b6 19 d5 ♘xc4! 20 dxc6 ♕xc6 21 g3 ♗xf1 22 ♖xf1 e4 23 ♕b3 ♕d5 24 ♖ac1 ♘xd2 25 ♘xd2 ♕xd2 26 ♖xc5+ ♔b8 = Spassky-Korchnoi, Belgrade Ct (4) 1977.

14...♘de7 15 dxc5 0-0-0 16 ♗c3 e5 17 ♕d6 ♘f5 18 ♕xc7+ ♔xc7

The endgame is roughly equal, as White's extra pawn is obviously not important, Timman-Korchnoi, Leeuwarden 1976.

C)

7 h4 *(D)*

Now:

C1: 7...♕a5   202
C2: 7...♕c7   203
C3: 7...♘bc6   205

C1)

7...♕a5 8 ♗d2 cxd4

This is the most common but Black might also play 8...♕a4 immediately. This has one advantage of avoiding

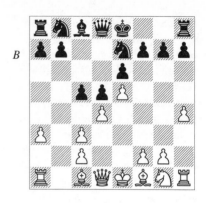

Milos's idea *10 c3!?* (after *8...cxd4 9 cxd4 ♕a4*). Then:

a) 9 ♘f3 and here:

a1) 9...♘bc6 10 h5 h6 11 ♖h4 (11 ♕b1 – *7...♘bc6 8 h5 ♕a5 9 ♗d2 ♕a4 10 ♕b1 h6 11 ♘f3 ∞*) 11...c4 12 ♖g4 ♖g8 13 ♖f4 ± Renet-Apicella, French Ch (Strasbourg) 1992.

a2) 9...b6 has its logic. Then after 10 h5 h6 11 ♖h4 ♘f5 (11...♕d7!? is an idea) 12 ♖f4, Black can close the centre with 12...c4 (probably slightly in White's favour) or insist on the idea of exchanging bishops with 12...♕d7!?.

b) White can probably force Black to close the centre with 9 ♕b1!? but the queen is not that well placed on the queenside and will probably have to return to the centre later. To be fair, however, this is not worse than losing the tempi with the bishop after, say a ♗d3 c4, ♗e2/f1 sequence. Milos-Palmisaro, Buenos Aires 1998 continued 9...c4 10 h5 h6 11 ♘f3 ♘bc6 12 g3 ♗d7 13 ♗h3 0-0-0 14 0-0 ♖df8 15 ♕d1 with perhaps a slight plus for White.

9 cxd4 ♕a4 *(D)*

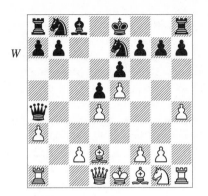

10 c3!?

Or:

a) 10 h5 ♘bc6 – 7...♘bc6 8 h5 ♕a5 9 ♗d2 cxd4 10 cxd4 ♕a4 ±.

b) 10 ♘f3 and then:

b1) 10...♘bc6 11 h5 – 7...♘bc6 8 h5 ♕a5 9 ♗d2 cxd4 10 cxd4 ♕a4 11 ♘f3!? ±.

b2) 10...b6 is logical, and seems to lead to fairly equal chances; e.g., 11 h5 h6 12 ♕b1 ♗a6 13 ♕b3 ♕xb3 14 cxb3 ♗xf1 15 ♔xf1 ♘bc6 16 ♔e2 ♔d7 = Werner-Poldauf, Bundesliga 1994/5.

10...♕xd1+ 11 ♖xd1 ♘bc6

11...b6 looks a little more accurate. Then 12 h5 h6 13 ♗b5+ ♗d7 14 ♗d3 ♘bc6 15 ♘e2 is a tempo better for Black than the main line.

12 h5 h6 13 ♗d3 ♗d7 14 ♘e2

The knight is much better here than on f3, as it doesn't block the f-pawn and serves the useful purpose of defending c3. It may also be convenient to have the opportunity of going to f4 if Black breaks with ...f6.

14...♘a5 15 ♖b1 b6 16 g4 ♘c4 17 ♗c1 ♖c8 18 f3!

This is a very good move. If 18 f4, Black replies 18...f6 with a roughly equal position, whereas now 18...f6 can be met by 19 exf6 gxf6 20 ♘f4 with a considerable advantage to White. White is now slightly better because he can slowly prepare to open the g-file after playing ♔f2, so in the event of a ...hxg5, ♗xg5 sequence, White's b1-rook can come over to the g-file.

C2)
7...♕c7 8 h5

I can't figure out whether this move is played just to tempt Black into grabbing the d4-pawn (see the next note). Personally, I would prefer 8 ♘f3 and only then h5, which leads to the main line without allowing the pawn-grab.

Another idea is 8 ♖h3, which keeps an eye on c3 but also makes it possible to bring the rook into the attack. A further point is that White keeps open the option of playing ♕g4. However, I don't think that Black need fear this, and 8...♘bc6 9 h5 h6 10 ♕g4 ♘f5 11 ♕f4 f6 12 exf6 ♕xf4 13 ♗xf4 gxf6 14 dxc5 e5 15 ♗d2 ♗e6 was fine for Black in Steinbacher-Short, Bundesliga 1990/1.

8...h6

8...cxd4 9 cxd4 ♕c3+ 10 ♗d2 ♕xd4 leads to a rather unclear position after 11 ♘f3 ♕e4+ 12 ♗e2 ♘f5 13 0-0 b6 14 ♗b5+ ♗d7 15 ♗d3 ♕g4 16 h6 gxh6!, which has happened in a few games by Rustemov.

9 ♘f3 *(D)*
9...b6

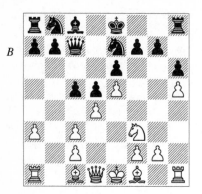

The other main line is 9...♗d7. The main difference between this and the main line is that Black intends to keep the b6-square free. This could increase his possibilities on the queenside later on. On the other hand, White gets a chance to sharpen the game by taking on c5. Thus after 10 ♗d3 (10 a4 ♘bc6 11 ♗b5 cxd4 12 cxd4 ♘b4 13 0-0 ♕xc2 14 ♕e1, Kuczynski-Gdanski, Polish Cht (Mikolajki) 1991, 14...a5 15 ♗a3 ♗xb5 16 axb5 0-0 17 ♗xb4 axb4 18 ♕xb4 ♖xa1 19 ♖xa1 ♘f5 = Kuczynski) 10...♗a4, White's best is probably 11 dxc5!? ♘d7 12 ♖h4:

a) 12...♕a5? 13 ♗e3! ♖c8 14 ♖b1 ♗c6 15 ♕d2 ♕xa3 16 ♖g4 ♔f8 17 ♖bb4!? ♘f5 18 ♗xf5 exf5 19 ♖gf4 ♕a1+ 20 ♕d1! ♕xd1+ (20...♕xc3+ 21 ♗d2 ♕a3 22 ♖xf5 followed by ♖bf4 gives White a strong attack) 21 ♔xd1 ♖e8 22 ♖xf5 ♔g8 23 ♖g4 ± Short-Ivanchuk, Horgen 1995.

b) 12...♗c6 13 ♗f4 0-0-0 14 ♖g4 ♖dg8 15 ♖b1 ♘xc5 with a complicated position, J.Polgar-P.Nikolić, Monaco Amber blindfold 1996.

10 ♗b5+

10 a4 ♗a6 11 ♗b5+ ♗xb5 12 axb5 is a type of position I believe should be fine for Black. 12...a5 is feasible, but Black must then reckon with 13 dxc5! bxc5 14 c4, which gives White some initiative, as in Iordachescu-Martin Blanco, Linares 2000. 12...♘d7 13 0-0 0-0 is safer, when 14 ♖e1 ♖fc8 15 ♖e2 a6! 16 bxa6 ♘b8 17 dxc5 ♖xa6 18 ♖xa6 ♘xa6 19 cxb6 ♕xb6 20 ♗e3 ♕a5 was fine for Black in Rechel-De Jong, Groningen 1999.

10...♗d7 11 ♗d3 ♘bc6

11...♗a4 is another logical option. Then after 12 0-0 we have:

a) It is probably premature to close the position with 12...c4 13 ♗e2 ♘bc6. Ehlvest-Yusupov, USSR Ch (Moscow) 1988 saw White achieve his optimal set-up in this type of position with 14 g3 0-0-0 15 ♘h4 ♖dg8 16 ♗g4 ♘d8 17 ♖e1 ♕d7 18 ♘g2. If White can make ...f6 unattractive, then Black is deprived of most of his counterplay, and White can then slowly improve his position and prepare a breakthrough on the kingside.

b) 12...♘d7 13 ♖e1 a6!? (13...0-0-0 14 ♘h4 ♔b7 15 ♖a2 ♕c6 16 ♕g4 ♖dg8 was roughly balanced in Dolmatov-P.Nikolić, Moscow 1990) 14 ♘h4 ♗b5 15 ♕g4 ♗xd3 16 cxd3 ♖g8 17 ♕e2 (Kuczynski-Hertneck, Bundesliga 1994/5) and now Hertneck gives 17...c4! 18 a4 ♖c8 19 ♗a3 cxd3 20 ♕xd3 ♕c4 with an unclear position.

12 0-0

White has also tried 12 ♔f1!?, which intends to use the rook more actively via h4, but Short made this look very unimpressive with 12...♘a5 13 ♖h4 0-0-0!? 14 dxc5 bxc5 15 ♔g1 ♔b8 16 ♖g4 ♖dg8 17 ♕e1 ♔a8 18 ♗d2 c4 19 ♗e2 ♘ac6 ∓ in Milos-Short, Buenos Aires 2000.

12...0-0

12...c4 13 ♗e2 0-0-0 should be considered.

13 ♗e3 c4

Dolmatov gives 13...f6 as a better try for Black; e.g., 14 exf6 ♖xf6 15 c4 cxd4 16 ♘xd4 ♘xd4 17 ♗xd4 e5 18 ♗b2 d4 19 c3 ♘c6 with an edge for White.

14 ♗e2 f6 15 exf6 ♖xf6 16 g3!

Accurate. 16 ♘h4?! is answered by 16...♘f5!.

16...♖af8 17 ♘h4

Now 17...♘f5 is met by 18 ♗f4.

17...♗e8 18 ♕d2 ♘c8 19 ♘g2

White is slightly better, Dolmatov-Hertneck, Tilburg 1992.

C3)

7...♘bc6 8 h5 *(D)*
8...♕a5

If 8...h6 White has the dangerous 9 ♕g4 ♕a5 10 ♗d2. Then 9...cxd4 is met by 11 ♕xg7 ♖g8 12 ♕f6! dxc3 13 ♗xh6 ±. Black should prefer 10...♗d7 11 ♕xg7 0-0-0 12 ♘f3 ♕a4 but White is better after 13 dxc5 ♕xc2 14 ♕f6 ♕b2 15 ♖c1.

9 ♗d2 ♗d7!?

With this Black decides that he will have to live with the weaknesses on

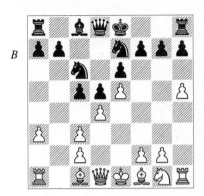

the kingside created by White playing h6, and simply carries on with development. A few other important lines:

a) 9...♕a4 10 ♕b1!? h6 (the move-order of Ljubojević-Hübner was actually 10...♗d7?! but this allows 11 h6!, which Hübner assesses as ±; for example, 11...gxh6 12 ♘f3 0-0-0 13 ♖xh6 ♘f5 14 ♖f6 cxd4 15 ♗b5 ♕a5 16 cxd4 +−) 11 ♘f3 ♗d7 12 ♖h4, and now rather than 12...0-0-0?! 13 dxc5! ♕a5 14 c4, which gave White the better game in Ljubojević-Hübner, Tilburg 1987, Black should play 12...c4, when Hübner gives 13 ♖f4 ♖f8 14 g4 0-0-0 15 ♗h3 f6 16 exf6 gxf6 17 ♘h4 ♘g8 with an unclear position.

b) 9...cxd4 10 cxd4 ♕a4 11 ♘f3!? (better than 11 ♗c3 b6, when 12 h6 gxh6 13 ♕d3 a5 14 ♕d2 ♘f5 gave Black a good game in Short-Korchnoi, Wijk aan Zee 1987, while after 12 ♘f3 ♗a6 13 ♗xa6 ♕xa6 14 a4 ♖c8 Black should have no problems, Short-Ivanchuk, Tilburg 1990) 11...♘xd4 12 ♗d3 ♘ec6 (12...h6 is well met by 13 ♗b4!, while 12...♘xf3+ 13 ♕xf3 ♕d4 14

0-0 ♕xe5 15 ♖fe1 ♕f6 16 ♕g3 gives White good compensation according to Kasparov) 13 ♔f1 and now:

b1) 13...♘xf3?! 14 ♕xf3 b6 (the alternative 14...♕d4 15 ♖e1 ♘xe5 16 ♕g3 ♘xd3 17 cxd3 is very good for White according to Kasparov) 15 h6! ♗a6 16 hxg7 ♖g8 17 ♗xa6 ♕xa6+ 18 ♔g1 ♖xg7 19 ♕f6 ± Kasparov-Anand, Linares 1992.

b2) 13...♘f5! 14 ♔g1 (on 14 ♗xf5 exf5 15 h6 Black has the very strong 15...♖g8! 16 ♗g5 ♗e6 17 ♖h4 ♕a6+ 18 ♔g1 gxh6 19 ♗f6 ♖g4, which favoured Black in Hellers-Gulko, Biel IZ 1993) 14...♕g4 15 ♕e2 f6!? 16 h6 fxe5 (16...♖g8!? is worth considering) 17 hxg7 ♖g8 18 ♖xh7 is unclear, Fedorov-Gulko, Las Vegas FIDE 1999.

10 h6 gxh6 (D)

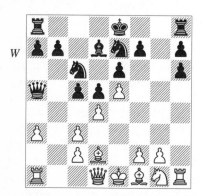

This is not such a big decision, as anything else is just bad. Meanwhile, Black hopes that his lead in development will compensate for the ruin of his kingside, and there are even small hopes of counterplay on the g-file.

11 ♘f3 0-0-0 12 ♗d3

The alternative 12 ♖xh6 ♖dg8 looks fine for Black.

12...c4

I don't think Black has any problems in this position. 12...♖hg8 13 ♔f1 ♘f5 14 ♗xf5 exf5 15 ♖xh6 ♖g4 also appeared quite reasonable for Black in Hall-Karlsson, Malmö 1999. Black has counterplay on the g-file and against d4. 12...♖dg8 is also possible.

13 ♗e2 ♘g8!?

Protecting h6 but also preparing to break up White's centre with ...f6.

14 ♔f1

Instead, the game Hector-Hillarp Persson, York 1999 went 14 a4 ♖f8 15 ♕c1 f6 16 ♕a3 ♖f7 17 ♗f4 ♘ge7 18 exf6 ♖xf6 19 ♗xh6 ♖g8 20 ♔f1 ♘f5 21 ♗d2 ♖fg6 22 g3 and now the well-timed 22...e5! gave Black excellent dynamic play. One point is that 23 ♘xe5 ♘xe5 24 dxe5 is met by 24...♖xg3!, with the idea that 25 fxg3 ♘xg3+ 26 ♔f2 ♕b6+ 27 ♗e3 ♘e4+ wins for Black.

14...f6 15 ♕e1 fxe5 16 dxe5

16 ♘xe5 ♘xe5 17 dxe5 ♘e7 18 ♗xh6 ♖hg8 19 ♗f3 ♗e8! 20 a4 ♗g6 21 ♖a2 ♖d7 was very comfortable for Black in Short-Psakhis, Isle of Man 1999.

16...♖f8 17 g3

This was the game Tischbierek-Uhlmann, Baden-Baden 1992. Now rather than 17...♗e8? 18 ♘d4 ± Black should play 17...♕c7! (Uhlmann) 18 ♗f4 ♘ce7 19 ♘d4 ♘g6 with a good position.

15 Armenian Variation (5...♗a5)

1 e4 e6 2 d4 d5 3 ♘c3 ♗b4 4 e5 c5 5 a3 ♗a5 *(D)*

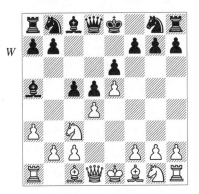

Retreating the bishop to a5 rather than giving it up for the knight on c3 is an attractive idea. Both approaches have sound positional ideas but I like the idea of keeping the bishop – as long as it works tactically.

It has been dubbed the Armenian Variation due to the great impact Grandmasters Vaganian and Lputian have had in developing this line. Although Botvinnik used it three times in his 1954 World Championship match against Smyslov (+1, =1, −1) there didn't seem to be a great deal of interest in the variation until Vaganian and Lputian began playing it in the mid-1980s.

The sharp 6 b4 was for long considered White's best reply but nowadays some other ideas are taken just as seriously. For example, Kasparov tried 6 ♗d2 ♘c6 7 ♕g4 against Khalifman, while the continuation 6 ♕g4 ♘e7 7 dxc5 ♗xc3+ 8 bxc3 is very fashionable at the moment of writing.

Hence our main lines are:

A: 6 ♗d2   207
B: 6 ♕g4   209
C: 6 b4   212

A)

6 ♗d2 ♘c6

More accurate than 6...cxd4 7 ♘b5, after which Black doesn't appear to equalize:

a) 7...♗xd2+ 8 ♕xd2 ♘c6 9 f4 ♘h6 10 ♘d6+ ♔f8 11 ♘f3 f6 12 ♗b5! ♘f7 13 ♗xc6 bxc6 14 ♘xf7 ♔xf7 15 0-0 ± Sax-Korchnoi, Lugano 1986. Note that 15...c5 is met by 16 b4!, when White recovers his pawn and gains control over d4.

b) 7...♗c7 can be compared with *6 b4 cxd4 7 ♘b5 ♗c7*. White has played ♗d2 rather than b4, which is surely favourable for White: 8 f4 ♘c6 9 ♘f3 ♘ge7 10 ♗d3 a6 11 ♘bxd4, Stefansson-Bjarnason, Icelandic Ch 1993 (and others).

c) 7...♘c6 and then:

c1) 8 ♘d6+? ♔f8 9 f4 ♗c7 ∓.

c2) 8 ♘f3 f6 (8...♘ge7 9 ♗d3 ♘g6 10 ♗xg6 hxg6 11 0-0 ♗c7 12 ♗g5 ♕d7 13 ♘xc7+ ♕xc7 14 ♖e1 ♗d7 15 ♘xd4 ♘xd4 16 ♕xd4 ± Kurajica-Enklaar, Amsterdam 1971) 9 ♘bxd4 ♘xd4 10 ♘xd4 ♗xd2+ 11 ♕xd2 fxe5 12 ♗b5+ ♔f8 13 ♘f3 ♕d6 14 ♕g5 e4 15 ♘e5 ♕e7 16 ♕e3 ♘h6 17 0-0-0 ♘f5 18 ♕c3 a6 19 ♗e2 ♗d7 20 ♗g4 ♖c8 (A.Sokolov-Vaganian, Minsk Ct (4) 1986) 21 ♘xd7+ ♕xd7 22 ♕e5 ♕c7 23 ♕xc7 ♖xc7 24 ♗xf5 exf5 25 ♖xd5 ±.

c3) 8 f4!? ♘ge7 9 ♘d6+ ♔f8 10 ♗xa5 ♕xa5+ 11 b4 ♕b6 12 ♕h5 ♘g6 13 ♗d3 and White has an initiative – Tyomkin. In fact, this sort of position looks very good for White. It is going to be very difficult for Black to break up the centre, while White can develop in peace with ♘ge2 and 0-0, preparing to attack on the kingside. Meanwhile, Black is struggling to find a role for the passive rook on h8.

c4) 8 ♗xa5!? ♕xa5+ 9 b4!? is perhaps the critical test; for example, 9...♕b6 (9...♕d8 10 f4 ♘h6 11 ♘d6+ ♔f8 12 ♘f3 f6 13 ♗d3 fxe5 14 fxe5 ♘xe5 15 ♘xe5 ♕xd6 16 ♕h5 ♔g8 17 0-0 was extremely good for White in Milos-Se.Ivanov, Cappelle la Grande 2000) 10 f4! a5 11 ♘d6+ ♔f8 12 b5 ♘ce7 13 ♘f3 ♘g6 14 ♕d2 ♘8e7 15

♘xd4 ♗d7 and White has the advantage – Tyomkin. Again, I think this sort of position is very good for White.

We now return to the position after 6...♘c6 (D):

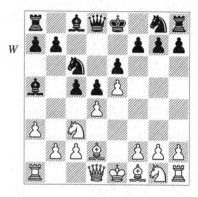

7 ♕g4

This dangerous move was prepared by Kasparov for his game against Khalifman at Linares 2000. White has not achieved anything from 7 ♘b5 ♘xd4! 8 ♘xd4 cxd4 (this is more accurate than 8...♗xd2+ 9 ♕xd2 cxd4 10 ♘f3, when White has a slight plus, Nunn-Hug, Biel 1986) 9 ♗b5+ (9 ♘f3 ♘e7 10 ♘xd4 ♘c6 and 9 ♗xa5 ♕xa5+ 10 b4 ♕b6 11 ♘f3 ♘e7 12 ♕xd4 ♕xd4 13 ♘xd4 ♘g6 14 ♘f3 ♗d7, Wegener-Nijboer, Bundesliga 1999/00, are both fine for Black) 9...♗d7 10 ♗xd7+ ♔xd7 11 ♘f3 ♗b6!, and Black is doing fine; for example, 12 c3 dxc3 13 ♕a4+ ♔e7 14 bxc3 ♔f8! 15 c4 ♘e7 16 ♗b4 ♔g8 17 ♗xe7 ♕xe7 18 cxd5 exd5 19 0-0 g6 ∓ De Vreugt-Barsov, Dieren 1999.

7...♔f8

In general, Black is not afraid of sacrificing the g7-pawn, so of course 7...♘ge7 suggests itself as an alternative. Then 8 dxc5 (8 ♕xg7 ♖g8 9 ♕xh7 cxd4 10 ♘b5 ♗xd2+ 11 ♔xd2 ♘xe5 is not a problem for Black) 8...0-0 9 ♘f3 f6 10 exf6 ♖xf6 11 0-0-0 e5 12 ♕a4 gave White an advantage in Brodsky-Berelovich, Ordzhonikidze 2000.

8 dxc5! ♘xe5 9 ♕g3 ♘g6 10 0-0-0

10 ♗d3 ♗c7 11 f4 ♘f6 12 ♘ge2 ♗d7 13 h3 ♗c6 14 ♕f2 b6 15 ♘d4 ♘e7 16 ♘xc6 ♘xc6 17 ♘b5 ♘d7 18 ♗e3 d4 19 ♘xd4 ♘xd4 20 ♗xd4 bxc5 21 ♗e3 ♗b6 22 ♖d1 was better for White in Mitkov-Zaja, Pula Z 2000 but there is plenty of room for improvement here.

10...♘f6 11 f3 ♗d7 12 ♘ge2 ♗c7 13 ♕f2 b6! 14 ♗e3 ♘e7 15 g4 bxc5 16 ♗xc5 ♗b6 17 h4 ♗xc5 18 ♕xc5 ♕b6 19 ♕xb6 axb6 20 ♗h3

So far Kasparov-Khalifman, Linares 2000. Now Kasparov recommends 20...h6! with the idea of meeting 21 f4 with 21...h5 22 g5 ♘g4, with roughly equal chances.

B)

6 ♕g4 ♘e7 (D)
7 dxc5

Critical. Alternatives are:

a) 7 b4? (this is much worse than the immediate *6 b4*) 7...cxb4 8 ♘b5 b3+! 9 c3 (this is very good for White without ♕g4 and ...♘e7 inserted but here it favours Black) 9...♘f5 10 ♗d2 0-0 11 ♕h3 a6 12 g4 ♕h4 ∓ Timman-Vaganian, Horgen 1995.

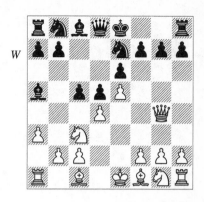

b) 7 ♕xg7 ♖g8 8 ♕xh7 cxd4 9 b4 and now:

b1) 9...dxc3 10 bxa5 – *6 b4 cxd4 7 ♕g4 ♘e7 8 bxa5 dxc3 9 ♕xg7 ♖g8 10 ♕xh7 ±/=*.

b2) 9...♗c7 10 ♘b5 – *6 b4 cxd4 7 ♕g4 ♘e7 8 ♘b5 ♗c7 9 ♕xg7 ♖g8 10 ♕xh7 =*.

7...♗xc3+ 8 bxc3 ♘g6

This has been the most popular move lately. Other moves also deserve consideration:

a) 8...♕c7?! 9 ♕xg7 ♖g8 10 ♕xh7 ♕xe5+ 11 ♘e2 ♘bc6 12 ♖b1 ♕f6 13 h4 ♖h8 14 ♗g5 ♕e5 15 ♕d3 ± Filipenko-Shomoev, Tula 1999.

b) 8...♘f5 9 ♗d3 h5 10 ♕f4 ♘c6 11 ♖b1 ♕a5 12 ♘e2 ♕xc5 13 0-0 a6 14 ♗xf5 exf5 15 ♕g5 0-0 16 ♘f4 ♘xe5 17 ♘xh5 ♘g6 18 ♖e1 ± Coleman-Fant, Gausdal 1991.

c) 8...0-0!? (curiously, Neil McDonald, in his *French Winawer* calls this move "untried", even though it has been played several times) 9 ♗d3 (D).

This is similar to another Winawer line, *5...♗xc3+ 6 bxc3 ♘e7 7 ♕g4 0-0*

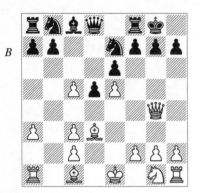

B

(Chapter 13). Here White has the move dxc5 for free. The question is who this change favours:

c1) 9...♘d7 10 ♘f3 f5 11 exf6 ♘xf6 12 ♕h4 ♕c7 13 ♗f4 ♕xc5 14 ♗e5 ♘f5 (King-Lputian, Dortmund 1988) 15 ♕b4! ±.

c2) 9...♘bc6 10 ♘f3 (10 ♕h5 can be considered; compare with *5...♗xc3+ 6 bxc3 ♘e7 7 ♕g4 0-0 8 ♗d3 ♘bc6 9 ♕h5*) 10...f5 11 exf6 ♖xf6 12 ♗g5 e5 (12...♖f7 13 ♕h4 h6 14 ♗xe7 ♕xe7 15 ♕xe7 ♖xe7 leaves White a tempo up on the line *5...♗xc3+ 6 bxc3 ♘e7 7 ♕g4 0-0 8 ♘f3 ♘bc6 9 ♗d3 f5 10 exf6 ♖xf6 11 ♗g5 ♖f7 12 ♕h4 h6 13 ♗xe7 ♕xe7 14 ♕xe7 ♖xe7*) 13 ♕h4 (13 ♕g3 ♖e6 ∓) 13...e4 14 ♗xf6 gxf6 15 ♕xf6 exd3 and now, rather than 16 ♕g5+ ♔h8 17 ♕f6+ ♔g8 18 ♕g5+ ♔f8 19 ♕f6+ ½-½ Karayannis-Khalkias, Agios Nikolaos 2000, the critical line is 16 cxd3 ♗f5.

c3) 9...♘g6!? 10 ♘f3 f5 11 exf6 ♕xf6 12 ♕d4 ♘c6! (12...e5? 13 ♕xd5+ ♗e6 14 ♕xb7! is much better for White, Savon-Liogky, Odessa 1989)

13 ♕xf6 gxf6 14 c4 d4 15 ♗e4 ♖d8 with unclear play – Savon.

d) 8...♘d7!? was employed successfully by Botvinnik more than 50 years ago, but for some reason it has never been very popular. White has:

d1) 9 ♕xg7?! (here it seems favourable for Black to trade his g-pawn for White's e-pawn) 9...♖g8 10 ♕xh7 ♘xe5 11 ♗e2 (11 ♘f3 ♘xf3+ 12 gxf3 might be better, but personally I would find it very difficult to accept such weakened pawns) 11...♕a5! (not, of course, 11...♖xg2? 12 ♕h8+ ♖g8 13 ♕xe5 +−) 12 ♗d2 ♕xc5 13 ♘f3 ♘xf3+ 14 ♗xf3 e5! is good for Black because of his strong centre, Reshevsky-Botvinnik, USSR-USA (Moscow) 1946.

d2) 9 ♘f3 ♕c7 10 ♕xg7 ♖g8 11 ♕xh7 ♘xe5 and now:

d21) 12 ♗e3!? ♘g4 (12...♘xf3+ 13 gxf3 ♗d7 14 ♖b1! ±) 13 ♗b5+ ♗d7 14 ♗xd7+ ♔xd7 15 ♕d3 ♘xe3 16 ♕xe3 ♘f5 17 ♕e5 (Baklan-Zhao Zong, Istanbul OL 2000) 17...♕xc5 =.

d22) 12 ♕h5 ♘xf3+ 13 ♕xf3 ♗d7 14 ♗f4 ± Shamkovich-Gipslis, USSR Ch (Baku) 1961.

e) 8...♕a5 9 ♗d2 ♘g6 and then:

e1) 10 h4!? h5 11 ♕g5 ♘d7 12 c4 (12 ♘f3 ♘xc5 13 ♗d3 ♘e4 14 ♕e3 ♗d7! is fine for Black) 12...♕xc5! (12...♕a4 13 cxd5 ♘dxe5!? 14 ♗e2 ♕e4!? 15 0-0-0 ± Short-Timman, Amsterdam 1991) 13 ♘f3 dxc4 14 ♗b4 ♕d5 (much stronger than 14...♕c7? 15 0-0-0! with good attacking chances for White) 15 ♖d1 ♕e4+ 16 ♗e2 f6!

17 exf6 gxf6 18 ♕e3 ♕xe3 19 fxe3 ♘b6 20 ♘d2! with roughly balanced chances, Kruppa-Lputian, USSR Ch (Moscow) 1991.

e2) 10 ♘f3 ♘d7 (10...♘c6?! is worse; then White continues 11 ♗d3 intending h4-h5) 11 c4 ♕a4. Now White has two options:

e21) 12 ♕d4!? dxc4 13 ♗xc4 0-0 14 ♗b4 (14 ♗c3! may offer better prospects of obtaining an advantage) 14...a5 15 0-0 ♕c6 16 ♗d2 ♘xc5 17 ♗e3 b6 = Rowson-Vaganian, Istanbul OL 2000.

e22) 12 h4!? ♕xc2!? (12...0-0 13 ♕d4 ♕xc2 14 cxd5 exd5 was played in Saravanan-B.Lalić, Andorra 2000, and now White should try 15 h5 ♘e7 16 h6 with an attack) 13 cxd5 ♕b2! (13...exd5?! 14 e6! is dangerous for Black) 14 ♖c1!? ♘gxe5 15 ♘xe5 ♕xe5+ 16 ♗e2 h5 with approximately equal chances, Short-Vaganian, Rotterdam 1989.

9 ♘f3

9 h4 h5 10 ♕g3 ♕a5!? 11 ♗d2 ♘d7! 12 ♘f3 ♘xc5 and Black has a good position. Note by the way that d7 is often the best square for Black's queen's knight.

9...♘d7

9...♕a5 10 ♗d2 – 8...♕a5 9 ♗d2 ♘g6 10 ♘f3 =.

10 ♗d3

10 h4 h5 11 ♕g3 ♘xc5 is again fine for Black since White is denied time for ♗d3.

10...♕c7 11 0-0 (D)

11...♘xc5

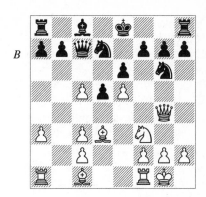

B

11...♘dxe5 is more ambitious but even though Black is doing well from a structural point of view after 12 ♘xe5 ♕xe5 13 ♗b5+ ♗d7 14 ♗xd7+ ♔xd7, there is a big drawback in the insecurity of his king. In Leko-Khalifman, Linares 2000, this was skilfully exploited by Leko: 15 ♕a4+! (a major improvement upon 15 ♖b1 ♖hb8 16 c4 ♕e4 = Fogarasi-Atalik, Budapest 1998) 15...♔e7 (15...♔c7, as mentioned by Atalik, may be better) 16 ♕b4 ♖ab8 17 f4! ♕e4 18 f5 ♕xb4 (18...exf5 19 ♗g5+ ♔f8 20 c6+!? ♕xb4 21 axb4 bxc6 22 ♖xa7 ±) 19 axb4 exf5 20 ♖xf5 and although Khalifman later managed to make a draw, there is no doubt about White's advantage.

12 ♗e3

12 a4 0-0 (12...♘xd3? 13 cxd3 ♕xc3 is obviously too risky owing to 14 ♗a3, when Black's king is caught in the centre) 13 ♗a3 b6 14 ♖fe1 f5! 15 exf6 ♘xd3! (an important interpolation; 15...♖xf6 16 ♗xc5! would have been good for White) 16 cxd3 ♖xf6 17 ♕g3!?, Leko-Khalifman, Istanbul OL

2000, and now Black should have tried 17...♕xc3 18 ♕d6 ♗a6! 19 ♖ac1 ♕xd3 20 ♖xe6, when "White has compensation but no more" – Leko.

12...♗d7! 13 ♗xc5 ♕xc5 14 h4 ♕xc3 15 ♕g3 0-0-0

The position is roughly balanced. Leko-Vaganian, Istanbul OL 2000 was quickly drawn after 16 ♖ab1 f6! 17 ♖fe1 ♘xe5 18 ♘xe5 fxe5 19 ♕xg7 ♖dg8 20 ♕xe5 ♕xe5 21 ♖xe5 ♔c7 22 c4 ½-½.

C)

6 b4 *(D)*

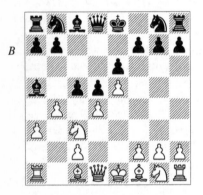

For a long time, this has been considered the critical move.

6...cxd4

The other capture, 6...cxb4, has a dubious reputation owing to 7 ♘b5. Then:

a) 7...b3+ 8 c3 and White regains the b-pawn with a clear advantage.

b) 7...bxa3+ 8 c3 ♘e7 9 ♘d6+ ♔d7 (9...♔f8 10 ♕b3 is also good for White) 10 ♖xa3 ♖f8 11 ♘f3 ♘bc6 12 ♗e2

♘f5 13 ♘xf5 exf5 14 0-0 ± Anand-Lodhi, Dubai OL 1986.

c) 7...♗c7 8 f4 ♗d7 9 ♘xc7+ ♕xc7 10 ♗d3 ♗a4 11 ♗b2 ♘h6 12 ♘f3 ♘c6 13 0-0 ♘f5 14 ♕e2 ± Yagupov-Hedman, Aars 1999.

d) 7...♘c6 8 axb4 (8 ♗d2!? is possible) 8...♗xb4+ 9 c3 ♗e7 10 ♗a3! ♘h6 11 ♗xe7 ♕xe7 12 ♘d6+ ♔f8 13 ♗b5! f6! (13...f5? 14 ♗xc6 bxc6 15 ♕a4 ♗d7 16 ♖b1 ♘f7 17 ♕a3! ± Topalov-Ermenkov, Burgas 1994) 14 f4 (14 ♗xc6 bxc6 15 ♕a4 ♗d7 16 ♕a3 should be considered) 14...♘f7 15 ♗xc6 bxc6 16 ♘xc8 ♖xc8 17 ♘f3 fxe5 18 fxe5 g6 19 ♖a6 ♖c7 20 ♕a4 ♔g7 21 0-0 with good compensation for the pawn, Salm-Zagorovsky, corr. Wch 1962-5.

After the text-move (6...cxd4) White has the following options:

C1: 7 ♘b5   212
C2: 7 ♕g4   216

C1)

7 ♘b5 ♗c7

7...♗b6!? is a provocative alternative which is rarely seen. White should not be tempted into playing ♘d6+ but rather concentrate on developing and regaining the d4-pawn at an appropriate moment. However, getting a real advantage is not so easy. Best seems 8 ♕g4 ♔f8 9 ♘f3 ♘c6 10 ♕f4 with an edge for White.

8 f4 *(D)*

The other way to defend the e5-pawn is with minor pieces, viz. 8 ♘f3 ♘c6 9 ♗f4. The drawback of this approach is that the e5-pawn can easily become vulnerable. After 9...♘ge7 White has two options, but neither seems to cause Black many headaches:

a) 10 ♘xc7+ ♕xc7 11 ♗d3 ♘g6 12 ♗g3 ♘gxe5 (12...a5 13 h4 axb4 14 axb4 ♖xa1 15 ♕xa1 0-0?! 16 0-0 ♘xb4 17 h5! ♘e7 18 h6 gxh6 was unclear in J.Horvath-Lputian, Sochi 1985) 13 ♘xe5 ♘xe5 14 ♗b5+ ♗d7 15 ♗xd7+ ♔xd7 16 ♕xd4 f6 17 0-0 and White has compensation – Lputian.

b) 10 ♘bxd4!? ♗d7 11 ♘xc6 ♘xc6 12 b5 ♘e7 13 ♗d3 ♘g6 14 ♗g3 ♗a5+ 15 ♔f1, Uhlmann-Knaak, Dresden 1995, and now simply 15...0-0 is fine for Black.

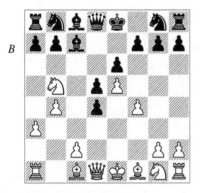

8...♗d7!

There is a large choice for Black at this point, but the main 5...♗a5 experts, Lputian and Vaganian, seem to have arrived at the conclusion that this move is best. Black intends to exchange his 'bad' bishop for the knight on b5. Of course White can avoid this by simply capturing on c7 but then

Black can quickly generate counterplay on the queenside.

First, a summary of the alternatives:

a) 8...♘h6 9 ♘f3 ♗d7 10 ♘xc7+ ♕xc7 11 ♗d3 a6 12 a4 ♘f5 – 8...♘e7 9 ♘f3 ♗d7 10 ♘xc7+ ♕xc7 11 ♗d3 a6 12 a4 ♘f5 ±/=.

b) 8...♘e7 (I could cite a great many games featuring this move, but since it has lost much of its former popularity, I have concentrated on giving only what seems really relevant at the moment) 9 ♘f3 and now there are two principal options for Black:

b1) 9...♘bc6 10 ♗d3 ♗b8!? (of course Black can also simply continue 10...a6 but the insertion of ...♘bc6 has prevented him from executing one of his main ideas, namely the attempt to exchange light-squared bishops) 11 ♘bxd4 ♘xd4 12 ♘xd4 a6 13 ♗e3 ♗a7 14 ♕d2 0-0 15 0-0 ± Ghinda-Lechtynsky, Bratislava 1983.

b2) 9...♗d7 10 ♘xc7+ ♕xc7 11 ♗d3 a6 12 a4 (White should prevent ...♗b5; Khachian-Lputian, Armenian Ch (Erevan) 1999 continued 12 0-0 ♗b5 13 ♘xd4 ♗xd3 14 cxd3 ♘bc6 15 ♗e3 0-0 16 ♖c1 ♕b6! 17 ♖c5 a5 18 ♘c2 axb4 19 axb4 d4! with a good game for Black) 12...♘f5. Now we have:

b21) 13 ♕d2 ♘c6 (13...♘e3!? and 13...♕c3 are both reasonable but still untested alternatives) 14 ♗b2 0-0!? (14...♕b6 15 b5 axb5 16 axb5 ♖xa1+ 17 ♗xa1 ♕a5, Atlas-Kindermann, Ptuj Z 1995, 18 ♔e2! ♕xd2+ 19 ♔xd2 ♘a5 20 ♘xd4 ♘xd4 21 ♗xd4 ♘c4+ 22

♗xc4 dxc4 23 ♖b1 0-0 24 ♔c3 ♖c8 25 ♔b4 ♔f8 26 ♖a1 ± Kindermann) 15 ♗xf5 exf5 16 ♗xd4 ♘xd4 17 ♘xd4 ± Z.Almasi-Lputian, Pula Echt 1997.

b22) 13 0-0 ♘c6 14 ♕e1 ♕b6 15 ♖b1 ♘ce7 16 b5 axb5 17 axb5 ♘e3 18 ♖f2 ♘c4 ∞ Anand-Lputian, Wijk aan Zee 2000.

c) 8...a5!? *(D)* and now:

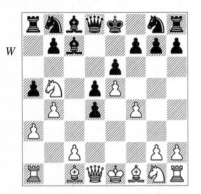

c1) 9 ♘f3 axb4 10 ♘fxd4 ♗d7 11 ♗b2 bxa3 12 ♗xa3 (12 ♖xa3!? is another idea) 12...♘e7 13 ♗d6 (13 ♗xe7 ♗a5+ 14 ♔f2 ♔xe7 ∓) 13...♗a5+ 14 c3 ♗xb5 15 ♗xb5+ ♘bc6 16 ♕b3 0-0 is slightly better for Black, Golubev-Korchnoi, Münster 1996.

c2) 9 ♗b2 axb4 10 axb4 ♖xa1 11 ♗xa1 ♘c6 12 ♘xc7+ ♕xc7 13 ♕d2 ♘h6 14 ♘f3 ♘f5 15 ♗d3 0-0 16 0-0 ♗d7 has occurred twice but doesn't seem to cause Black too much trouble. White may hope for a slight pull in a knight vs 'bad' bishop type of position but this implies exchanges of two minor pieces and allowing Black counterplay on the queenside:

c21) 17 ♖b1 ♖a8 18 b5 ♘a5 19 b6?! (this only makes c6 available for Black's minor pieces; 19 ♕f2! is superior) 19...♕d8 20 g4 (too sharp; again 20 ♕f2 is preferable) 20...♘h4! 21 ♘xd4 ♘c6 22 ♗e2 h5! ∓ Leko-Lputian, Ljubljana 1995.

c22) 17 ♗xf5 exf5 18 ♗xd4 ♘xd4 (Black should probably eliminate this bishop when he has the chance; a funny line is 18...♖a8?! 19 ♕c3! ♖a4 20 ♖b1 ♕c8 21 e6 ♗xe6 22 ♗xg7, when 22...♘xb4? loses to 23 ♕f6! ♕xc2 24 ♕g5! and White forces mate, but 22...♖xb4! keeps the game unclear) 19 ♘xd4 ♖a8 20 h3 h6 21 ♖b1 ♕c4 22 ♔f2 ♖a2 and Black has good counterplay, Gi.Hernandez-Korchnoi, Merida (4) 1996.

c3) 9 ♗d2! (this move looks best) 9...♘h6 10 ♘f3 ♘f5 (or 10...axb4 11 axb4 ♖xa1 12 ♕xa1 0-0 13 ♘xc7 ♕xc7 14 ♘xd4 ♘f5 15 ♘xf5 exf5 16 ♕c3 ± Svidler-Se.Ivanov, St Petersburg 1997) 11 ♗d3. Now Black has tried:

c31) 11...♗d7?! 12 ♘xc7+ ♕xc7 13 b5! (a very strong move; White not only prevents Black from getting counterplay by opening up the queenside with ...axb4 but also severely restricts the b8-knight) 13...♕c5 14 ♕e2 0-0 15 a4 f6 16 0-0 ♘e3 17 ♖fe1 ♘c4 18 ♗c1 b6 19 exf6 ♖xf6 20 ♘e5 with a slight advantage for White, Z.Almasi-Korchnoi, Budapest 1996.

c32) 11...0-0 12 0-0 (in order to avoid 12...♗b6, White might consider 12 ♘xc7 ♕xc7 and only then 13 0-0) 12...♘c6 (the alternative 12...♗b6 is worth considering; e.g., 13 bxa5 ♗xa5 14 ♗xf5 exf5 15 ♗xa5 ♕xa5 16 ♘fxd4 ♘c6 17 ♕d3 ♘xd4 18 ♘xd4 ♕c5 =) 13 ♘xc7 ♕xc7 14 b5 ♘ce7 15 ♕e2 ♗d7 16 g4!? ♘e3 17 ♗xe3 dxe3 18 ♕xe3 f5 19 exf6 ♖xf6 20 ♘e5 ♗e8 21 ♖ae1 ± Leko-Se.Ivanov, Budapest 1996.

9 ♘f3

Or:

a) 9 ♕g4 g6 (9...♔f8 may also be worth testing) 10 ♘f3 ♘h6 11 ♕g5 ♘f5 12 ♕xd8+ ♗xd8 13 g4 ♘h4! 14 ♘d6+ ♔f8 15 ♘xh4 ♗xh4+ 16 ♔d1 is unclear according to Benjamin.

b) 9 ♘xc7+ ♕xc7 10 ♘f3 and then:

b1) 10...a6 11 a4!? ♘e7 12 ♗d3 ♘f5 13 0-0 ♘c6 14 ♕e1 ♕b6 15 ♖b1 ♘ce7 16 b5 axb5 17 axb5 ♘e3 18 ♖f2 ♘c4 was unclear in Anand-Lputian, Wijk aan Zee 2000.

b2) I like 10...♗a4! 11 ♗d3. Then both 11...♘c6 12 0-0 a6 13 ♗b2 ♘ge7 14 ♘xd4 ♖c8 15 ♘f3 ♗b5, del Rio de Angeles-Romero, Linares 1998 and 11...♕c3+ 12 ♗d2 ♕xd3 13 cxd3 ♗xd1 14 ♔xd1 ♘e7 15 ♘xd4 ♔d8!? 16 ♔e2 ♘bc6, Van Delft-Barsov, Vlissingen 2000, are equal.

9...♗xb5 10 ♗xb5+ *(D)*

10...♘d7!?

With this move Black aims for a future ...♘b6-c4.

10...♘c6 is an alternative:

a) 11 ♘xd4 ♘ge7 and now:

a1) 12 ♕h5 g6 13 ♕h6 is very ambitious but White is overreaching: 13...♗b6 14 ♘xc6 bxc6 15 ♕g7 ♖f8 16 ♗a4 ♗d4 17 ♖b1 ♕b6 is much

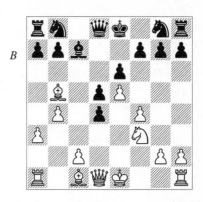

B

better for Black, De Vreugt-Nijboer, Wijk aan Zee 1999.

a2) 12 c3 ♗b6 13 ♗e3 0-0 14 ♕d2 ♗xd4! (a very notable decision; Black gives up another bishop for counterplay on the queenside) 15 cxd4 a5! (now White's bishop on b5 is just getting in the way, and hence Black obtains strong pressure) 16 0-0?! (this is not an entirely correct pawn sacrifice but Black would also have a good position after 16 bxa5 ♘xa5) 16...axb4 17 a4!? (17 axb4 ♕b6 ∓) 17...b3! ∓ Bologan-Vaganian, Groningen FIDE 1997.

b) 11 ♗b2 ♘ge7 12 ♗d3 ♗b6 13 0-0 ♘g6 14 g3 ♕d7 15 ♔g2 0-0 16 ♕e2 a6 = Balcerak-Luther, Senden 1999.

c) 11 0-0! (White's best chance seems to be to treat the position as a temporary gambit; regaining the pawn on d4 leads to more trouble than good) 11...♘ge7 12 ♗d3 ♗b6 13 ♔h1 ♘f5 14 ♗xf5 exf5 15 ♗b2 ♕d7 16 ♘xd4 (16 ♕d3!?) 16...0-0 17 ♘f3! ♖fd8 18 ♕d3 ♖ac8 19 ♖ad1 ♘e7 20 ♗d4 and

White is slightly better, Socko-Vaganian, Belgrade ECC 1999.

11 0-0 ♘e7 12 ♘xd4

Van den Doel-Lputian, Wijk aan Zee 1999 saw the much too aggressive 12 g4?!, the idea of which is rather uncertain to me. White's king is now too exposed and Black exploited this splendidly with 12...a6 13 ♗d3 h5! 14 h3 hxg4 15 hxg4 ♘b6 16 b5 (16 ♘xd4 ♘c6 17 ♘f3 ♘c4, though probably the lesser evil, is also good for Black) 16...♘c4 17 bxa6 ♖xa6 ∓.

12...0-0 13 ♗d3 g6

Black has a pleasant position. Gallagher-Lputian, Lucerne Wcht 1997 now continued 14 ♗b2?! ♘b6 15 ♕f3 ♘a4 16 ♗c1 ♗b6 17 ♗e3 ♘b2!, when the best White can hope for is an equal game. Obviously, the bishop is badly placed on b2 and 14 ♗e3 is a natural improvement. However, I would be surprised if Black turned out to have any real difficulties after 14...♘b6 with the idea of ...♘c4. There is also the possibility of playing 14...♗b6 followed by ...♘c6.

C2)

7 ♕g4 *(D)*

7...♘e7 8 bxa5

8 ♘b5 ♗c7 9 ♕xg7 ♖g8 10 ♕xh7 is a mixture of the ♕g4 and ♘b5 variations. It should not worry Black, but it is tried once in a while. Black has two main options:

a) 10...♗xe5 11 ♘f3 ♖h8 12 ♕d3 ♗g7 has a bad reputation in view of 13 ♗f4 ♘g6 14 ♘c7+ ♔f8 15 ♗g3 e5 16

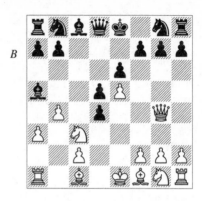

♘xa8. Black has some compensation for the sacrificed material but not quite enough.

b) 10...a6! 11 ♘xc7+ ♕xc7 12 ♘e2 ♕xe5 13 ♗b2 and now:

b1) 13...♕f6 14 f4 (14 ♗xd4 e5 15 ♗c5 ♘bc6 16 ♕d3 ♘f5 17 ♕xd5 ♗e6 18 ♕e4 0-0-0 gives Black a strong attack) 14...♘bc6 15 ♕d3 ♘f5 16 0-0-0 ♕h6! is generally agreed upon as fine for Black but is far from clear. The key continuation is 17 ♔b1 ♗d7 18 ♖e1 ♖c8 19 g3 ♔f8! (19...♘e3 20 ♘xd4 ♘xd4 was M.Müller-Vaganian, Bundesliga 1993/4, but now 21 ♖xe3! ♘xc2 22 ♖e5 doesn't look bad for White) 20 h4!? ♘ce7 21 ♘xd4 ♘xg3 22 ♖h2 ♕xf4 23 ♗c1! ♕d6 24 ♕h7 and White has some compensation for the pawn, Yudasin-Lputian, USSR Ch (Kiev) 1986.

b2) 13...♕c7!? and then:

b21) 14 ♘g3?! e5 15 ♗e2 ♗e6 and now in Timman-Khalifman, Sanur 2000, Timman went for the overly aggressive 16 f4? and was in bad shape after 16...exf4 17 ♘h5 ♕e5!. Khalifman analysed instead 16 0-0 ♘bc6 17 f4 exf4 18 ♘h5 0-0-0 19 ♘xf4 ♖h8 20 ♕d3 ♘f5!? 21 b5 ♘e5 22 ♕b3 axb5 23 ♕xb5 ♘g6, when Black has an attack to compensate for his positional defects.

b22) 14 f4 ♘bc6 15 ♕d3 ♘f5 16 0-0-0 ♗d7 with a complicated position, Nunn-Kinsman, London Lloyds Bank 1993.

8...dxc3 9 ♕xg7 ♖g8 10 ♕xh7 ♘bc6 (D)

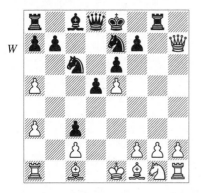

11 f4

This safeguards the e5-pawn in a very natural way but there are a few negative aspects of the move too. The most noteworthy is that the move seriously inhibits the dark-squared bishop.

White has also played 11 ♘f3!? ♕c7 12 ♗f4 (White can hope for no more than an equal position after 12 ♗b5 ♗d7 13 0-0 ♘xe5 14 ♘xe5 ♕xe5 15 ♗xd7+ ♔xd7 16 ♕d3 ♖ac8 17 ♖b1 ♖c7, Wach-Enders, Ptuj Z 1995) 12...♗d7 13 ♗d3 (it is also interesting to throw in 13 a6!?) 13...0-0-0 14 ♗g3

♕xa5 15 0-0. There are now two options for Black:

a) 15...♕c5 16 ♕h4 (16 ♕xf7 ♖df8 17 ♕h7 ♖xf3 18 gxf3 ♘xe5 was Shirov-Akopian, Merida 2000, and now Shirov suggests 19 ♔h1 ♘xf3 20 ♕h5 ±) 16...♖g7 (16...♘f5 17 ♗xf5 exf5 18 h3!? ±) 17 ♖fb1 a6 18 h3 ♖dg8 19 ♔h2 d4 20 ♗e4 and White is better, Lutz-K.Müller, Altenkirchen 1999.

b) 15...♖h8! is the recent trend. Now:

b1) 16 ♕g7 d4 17 ♕g4 ♘f5! 18 ♖fb1?! (18 ♗xf5 exf5 19 ♕f4 ♗e6, intending ...♕a4, leads to approximate equality) 18...♘xg3 19 ♕xg3 ♕c7! 20 ♔f1 ♖hg8 21 ♕f4 f5!, and Black already has a pleasant position, J.Polgar-Khalifman, Hoogeveen 2000.

b2) 16 ♕xf7 ♖df8 17 ♕g7 ♖hg8 18 ♕h6 ♖xf3! (a strong positional sacrifice; an important defender of the king and the e5-pawn is removed, and in return Black obtains promising piece-play in the centre) 19 gxf3 ♘d4 20 ♕f4 ♘ef5 21 ♔h1 (21 a4 ♘h4!? 22 ♔h1 ♘hxf3 23 ♖fd1 ♕c5 with counterplay) 21...♗b5! 22 ♖fd1 ♗xd3 23 ♖xd3 ♕c5 24 ♕c1 ♔b8 25 ♕d1 ♖c8 ∓ Galkin-Khalifman, Hoogeveen 2000.

11...♕xa5 12 ♘f3

12 ♖b1 attempts to tease a little but Black can play 12...♗d7 anyway. Then Black has strong counterplay after 13 ♖xb7 ♘d4! 14 ♕d3 ♘ef5 15 ♘f3 ♕c5! 16 ♘xd4 ♘xd4, intending ...♗c6, ...♘f5 and ...d4, Dolmatov-Lputian, Irkutsk 1986.

12...♗d7 13 ♖b1

After 13 ♘g5?!, 13...♖xg5 14 fxg5 0-0-0 15 ♕xf7 ♘f5 gives Black excellent compensation, while 13...0-0-0!? 14 ♘xf7 ♘f5 15 ♘xd8 ♕xd8 16 ♕h3 ♘cd4 17 ♕xc3+ ♔b8 also appeared promising for Black in Ernst-Kinsman, Gausdal 1995.

13...0-0-0 14 ♕d3 *(D)*

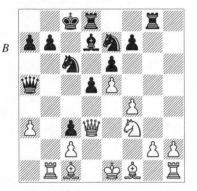

14...d4!?

This is the critical position for this line. Black usually advances the d-pawn sooner or later but it is not imperative to do it immediately. Other moves:

a) 14...♗e8 is untested.

b) 14...♘f5 15 ♖g1! (15 ♖b5?! ♕a4 16 ♕xc3?! ♖xg2 17 ♗xg2 ♕xb5 18 ♗h3 d4 19 ♕d3 ♕c5 ∓ Rudolf-Vaganian, German Team Cup 2000) and now:

b1) 15...d4 16 g4! ♘fe7 17 ♖g3 ♗e8 18 h4 ± Anand-Khalifman, Linares 2000.

b2) 15...f6 is untried. It is an idea I have been labouring over for some time, but unfortunately I don't think it works: 16 g4 (16 exf6 ♘d6!? gives Black compensation; he is toying with an ...e5 break) 16...♘h6 (16...fxe5 17 gxf5 e4 18 ♕e3 exf5 19 ♖xg8 ♖xg8 20 ♘d4 is insufficient for Black) 17 exf6 (17 h3 fxe5 18 fxe5 ♘f7 19 ♗f4 can also be considered) 17...♖xg4 18 ♖xg4 ♘xg4 19 ♕g6 e5 20 h3 e4 21 hxg4 exf3 22 ♖b5 ♕c7 23 f7 ±.

c) 14...a6 is Khalifman's latest idea. Black wants to play ...♕c5 without having to worry about ♖b5. Now:

c1) 15 ♘g5?! ♖xg5 (more or less a standard reaction) 16 fxg5 ♘f5 17 ♗f4 ♕xa3 18 ♖b3 ♕a4! 19 g3 d4 ∓ Anand-Khalifman, Dortmund 2000.

c2) 15 ♖b3 d4! 16 ♘xd4 ♘xd4 17 ♕xd4 ♗c6 18 ♕xc3 ♕d5 19 ♕d3 and now 19...♕a5+ forces a repetition by 20 ♕c3 ♕d5, since 20 ♗d2 ♕a4 gives White a strong attack according to Ivanchuk.

c3) 15 g3 d4!? (15...♘f5 is also possible) 16 ♗g2 ♕d5 (not 16...♕c5 17 ♘g5! ±, but 16...♘f5 or 16...♘d5 should still be considered) 17 0-0 (after 17 ♖a1 ♕c5, 18 ♘g5 is met by 18...♖xg5; with the rook on b1 this would be much less clear since White would have an attack against b7) 17...♕a2 18 ♖b3 ♗e8 19 ♖d1 ♔b8 20 a4! ♕xa4 21 ♗a3 ♘f5 22 ♖a1 ♔c8 23 ♗b2 ♘b4 24 ♕c4+ ♕c6 25 ♕xb4 cxb2 26 ♖b1 ±.

c4) 15 ♖g1 and now:

c41) 15...d4 16 ♘xd4 ♘xd4 (alternatively, 16...♗e8 17 ♘b3!) 17 ♕xd4 ♗c6 18 ♕b4 ♕d5 19 ♔f2! ± Anand.

c42) Black should probably play 15...♗e8 and only then ...d4. If White plays g4 at some stage then Black has at least saved the two tempi he wasted on ...♘f5 and ...♘fe7 in Anand-Khalifman in line 'b1'.

We now return to the position after 14...d4!? *(D)*:

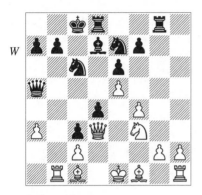

15 ♖b5!?

If Black can hold his centre he will be guaranteed excellent play because White is playing with a vulnerable king and bad development. This is a logical way to put pressure on Black's centre.

Other moves:

a) 15 ♘xd4?! ♘xd4 16 ♕xd4 ♗c6 17 ♕b4 ♕d5 ∓ Gretner-Bonne, Zurich 1962.

b) 15 ♘g5?! ♖xg5 16 fxg5 ♕xe5+ gives Black plenty of compensation.

c) 15 g3!? ♘f5 (15...♘d5 16 ♗g2 ♕c5 17 0-0 a6 with an unclear position – Kindermann) 16 ♗g2 ♕c7 17 0-0 was Shirov-Romero, Spanish Cht (Salamanca) 1998, and now Shirov

gives 17...♘ce7! 18 ♘g5 ♗c6 19 ♘xf7 ♗xg2 20 ♔xg2 ♖d5 with compensation for Black.

15...♕c7 *(D)*

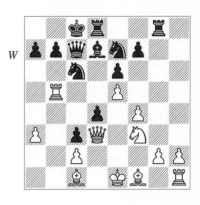

16 a4

Another try is 16 ♕c4 ♘f5 17 ♖g1 a6 18 ♖b1 ♕a5 19 g4 ♘e3 20 ♗xe3 dxe3 21 ♖b3, when White is better. There is a likelihood that Black can improve on this but since White is not really getting anything clear out of 16 a4, this could be a way to improve White's play.

16...a6 17 ♖b1 ♕a5 18 ♕c4 ♕d5!

Now in Arakhamia-Kindermann, Vienna 1996, White went for the bait on a6 but after 19 ♕xa6 ♘b4! 20 ♕e2 ♘ec6 Black seized the initiative. Instead, Kindermann suggests 19 ♔f2! ♕xc4 20 ♗xc4 ♘f5 (20...♘a5?! 21 ♗d3 ♗xa4 22 ♖a1 b5 23 ♘g5 ♖g7 24 h4 ±) 21 ♖g1 ♘ce7 with an unclear position.

16 Winawer: Early Deviations

1 e4 e6 2 d4 d5 3 ♘c3 ♗b4 *(D)*

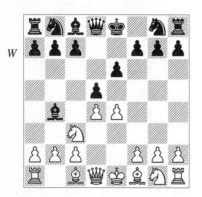

In this chapter we shall consider a large number of early deviations from both White's and Black's side. Rather than naming a number of different chapters "Rare 4th moves for White", "Rare 4th moves for Black" and the like, I have chosen to collect it all together in one big chapter. It is a massive bunch of different types of systems, so I will just get on with it...

A: **4 ♕d3** 220
B: **4 ♕g4** 222
C: **4 ♗d3** 224
D: **4 ♘e2** 225
E: **4 ♗d2** 227
F: **4 a3** 229
G: **4 exd5** 231
H: **4 e5** 233

Line H is of course the main line; in this chapter we only consider lines that have not already been dealt with in previous chapters.

A)

4 ♕d3 *(D)*

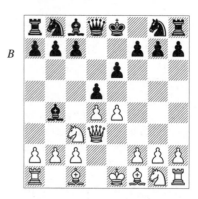

I am surprised by the large number of strong players who have played this early queen move. The idea is to transfer it to the kingside after 4...dxe4 5 ♕xe4 ♘f6 6 ♕h4. This may give White some sort of a promising attacking position if Black is not careful, but clearly shouldn't give Black any worries either.

4...♘e7!?

This seems the most annoying for White. The queen is not particularly well placed on d3 so it is very logical to avoid forcing it to a better square and instead just to continue developing. For the record, there isn't anything wrong with 4...dxe4. Then after 5 ♕xe4 ♘f6 6 ♕h4, Black's best is 6...♕d5!, intending to simplify the position with ...♕e4(+). The logical continuation is 7 ♗d2 ♗xc3 8 ♗xc3, and then Black should decide whether he wants to exchange queens:

a) 8...♕e4+ 9 ♕xe4 ♘xe4 10 ♗a5 (! – Berelovich) 10...♘c6 (10...b6 is dubious according to Berelovich owing to 11 f3 but I don't see anything particularly wrong with Black's position after 11...♘f6 12 ♗d2 ♗b7 13 0-0-0 ♘bd7; White has the bishop-pair but Black is solid and well developed) 11 ♗xc7 ♘xd4 12 ♗d3 ♘c5 13 0-0-0 – Berelovich. No assessment is attached so I assume he thinks White has a small advantage.

b) 8...♘e4 and then:

b1) 9 ♗c4?! ♕xc4 10 ♕xe4 ♘d7 (10...♕d5 =) 11 ♘f3 ♘f6 12 ♕h4 0-0 13 ♘e5 and now 13...♕d5 14 0-0 ♕e4 was equal in Kekelidze-Berelovich, Cappelle la Grande 1998 but Black could also try to play for an advantage with 13...♕a6!?, keeping White's king in the centre for a while.

b2) 9 ♗d3 ♘xc3 10 bxc3 ♕xg2 11 ♗e4 g5 12 ♗xg2 (12 ♕xh7 ♖xh7 13 ♗xg2 ♘c6 14 ♖b1 ♗d7 15 ♖xb7 0-0-0 gives Black good compensation for the pawn) 12...gxh4 was given by Berelovich as more testing, though he also seems to imply that Black is fine in

this last line after 13 ♘f3 h3 14 ♗xh3 b6.

b3) 9 ♘f3 ♘xc3 10 bxc3 ♕a5 11 ♔d2 was suggested by Berelovich.

We now return to the position after 4...♘e7 (D):

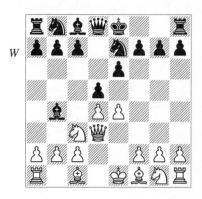

5 ♗d2

This is relatively best but doesn't promise anything. Other moves:

a) 5 ♘e2 c5!? 6 ♗g5 f6 7 ♗d2 ♘bc6 8 a3 ♗xc3 9 ♗xc3, Schmittdiel-Jolles, Groningen 1990, and now Watson recommends 9...cxd4 10 ♘xd4 e5 11 ♘xc6 bxc6, when Black is fine due to his strong centre.

b) 5 ♗g5 0-0 6 ♘f3 ♗xc3+ (6...f6 7 ♗d2 c5 also seems playable) 7 bxc3 f6 8 ♗d2 b6 9 ♕e3 ♗b7 10 ♗d3 dxe4 11 ♗xe4 ♘f5 12 ♕e2 ♗xe4 13 ♕xe4 ♕d5 ∓ Smirin-Vaganian, USSR Cht (Naberezhnye Chelny) 1988.

5...0-0

I agree with McDonald that the text-move is more flexible (and thus better) than the immediate 5...c5, when 6 a3 c4 (6...♗xc3 7 ♗xc3 ±) 7 ♕g3

♗xc3 8 ♗xc3 0-0 9 e5 might promise White a little something.

6 ♘ge2

Or:

a) 6 0-0-0 c5 7 dxc5 ♘bc6 8 ♘f3 ♗xc5 was approximately equal in the game Ribeiro-Russek, Maringa U-26 Wcht 1991.

b) 6 a3 ♗xc3 7 ♗xc3 b6! is also fine for Black, as the attempt to stop ...♗a6 with 8 b4 meets with the strong response 8...♗d7! (intending ...dxe4 followed by ...♗c6) 9 e5 a6 =/∓, when White cannot really prevent Black from exchanging the light-squared bishop in any case, Hector-Dokhoian, Århus 1991.

6...c5 7 a3

7 dxc5 ♘bc6 is not a problem for Black either.

7...♗xc3 8 ♗xc3 c4 9 ♕f3 dxe4 10 ♕xe4 ♘d5

The position is roughly equal, Heidenfeld-Knott, York 2000.

B)

4 ♕g4 (D)

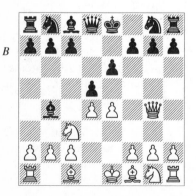

This is a very tactical line where White tries to punish Black immediately for the early bishop development by omitting a3 and not even taking time to secure his centre with e5. Indeed, the instability of the centre is the drawback of this line.

4...♘f6

After this the position quickly becomes very sharp but there is no reason for Black to avoid these complications. An attempt to simplify with 4...dxe4 5 ♕xg7 (5 ♕xe4 – *4 ♕d3 dxe4 5 ♕xe4*) 5...♕f6 was met by 6 ♕g3! ♘c6 7 ♗b5 ♘e7 8 ♘e2, leaving White better, in Miladinović-Rozentalis, Montreal 2000.

5 ♕xg7 ♖g8 6 ♕h6 ♖g6

Or:

a) 6...dxe4 7 ♘e2 b6 8 ♗g5 ♘bd7 9 ♘g3 ♗b7 10 ♗b5 ♖g6 11 ♕h4 h6 12 ♗xh6 a6 13 ♗e2 ♕e7 14 ♗d2 is slightly better for White, Planinc-Andersson, Amsterdam 1973.

b) 6...♘xe4!? has been criticized by some sources. White's best may be 7 ♘e2!?. However, after the natural 7 ♕xh7?!, Minev points to the little-known game Bonsdorff-Liipola, Helsinki 1957, which continued 7...♖g6! 8 ♕h8+ ♔d7 9 ♕xd8+ ♔xd8 10 ♗d2 (10 ♘e2 might be better) 10...♘xd2 11 ♔xd2 c5 12 a3, and now simply 12...♗a5! 13 ♘f3 ♘c6 would have been good for Black.

c) 6...c5!? is an attempt to be more accurate than in the main line. Then:

c1) White can try to force a transposition with 7 ♘e2:

c11) 7...♖g6 8 ♕e3 ♘c6 9 ♗d2 ♘g4 10 ♕d3 – *6...♖g6 7 ♕e3 c5 8 ♗d2 ♘g4 9 ♕d3 ♘c6 10 ♘ge2 =*.

c12) Black can try 7...cxd4 but it is not obviously favourable for him to exchange so early on d4.

c2) Of course, White may also play differently: 7 e5 cxd4 8 a3 ♗f8 (simple and good) 9 ♕xf6 ♕xf6 10 exf6 dxc3 11 ♘e2 ♘d7 12 ♘xc3 ♗d6 13 g3 ♘xf6 14 ♗g2 ♗d7 15 0-0 0-0-0 16 ♗e3 ♔b8 is equal, Antoniewski-Shaked, Zagan jr Wch 1997.

7 ♕e3 *(D)*

7 ♕h4?! ♖g4 ∓.

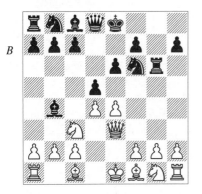

7...c5!

The natural 7...♘xe4 proves risky: 8 ♗d3! f5 (8...♘xc3? 9 ♗xg6 ♘xa2+ 10 c3 ♘xc1 11 ♗xf7+ ♔xf7 12 cxb4 ±) 9 ♘ge2 c5 10 ♗xe4! fxe4 (10...dxe4 11 ♕h3 cxd4 12 ♕xh7 ♕f6 13 ♘xd4 ♖xg2 14 ♘db5!? ±) 11 ♕h3! ♘c6 12 ♕xh7 ♕f6 13 ♘f4! cxd4 14 ♘xg6 dxc3 15 b3 ± Alekhine-Euwe, Amsterdam Wch (9) 1935.

8 ♗d2

After 8 a3 ♗a5! 9 ♗d2, there are a few nuances to be aware of with the moves a3 and ...♗a5 inserted:

a) 9...♘g4 10 ♕d3 (Velcheva-Bobrowska, Ostrava wom Z 1999) 10...♘c6 is analogous to the recommended move-order in the line without a3 and ...♗a5. However, it fails here due to 11 dxc5, as Black does not have the possibility of taking back with the bishop.

b) Hence, Black should continue 9...♘c6. Then:

b1) 10 ♗b5? (again, analogous to the treatment in the line without a3 and ...♗a5) is inaccurate here due to 10...cxd4 11 ♕xd4 ♗b6! (a great advantage of having had the bishop pushed to a5).

b2) Therefore, White has nothing better than playing similarly to the main line but also here it is to Black's advantage that the bishop is on a5 instead of b4: 10 ♘f3 ♘g4 11 ♕d3 cxd4 12 ♘xd4 ♘xf2!? 13 ♔xf2 ♗b6 14 ♗e3 ♕f6+ 15 ♔e1 ♘xd4 and Black is "at least equal" – McDonald. The key point compared with the main line is that with Black's bishop on b6 rather than on c5, White does not have 16 ♘b5?! owing to 16...♘xb5 17 ♗xb6 ♗d7, when Black is attacking b6 and b2 simultaneously.

8...♘g4

8...♘c6?! is an inaccurate move-order because of 9 ♗b5! ♗d7 10 ♗xc6 ♗xc6 11 ♘ge2 dxe4 12 dxc5 ± Planinc-Byrne, Moscow 1975.

9 ♕d3

9 ♗b5+?! ♔f8! ∓.

9...♘c6 10 ♘ge2 cxd4

Incidentally, 10...♕f6 also appears playable: 11 ♗e3 cxd4 12 ♘xd4 ♘xe3 13 fxe3 ♗xc3+ (13...♕h4+? 14 g3 ♖xg3 15 hxg3 ♕xh1 16 exd5 ±) 14 ♕xc3 ♘xd4 15 ♕xd4 ♕xd4 16 exd4 dxe4 and the endgame is only very slightly in White's favour, Magem-Jerez Perez, Barcelona 2000.

11 ♘xd4 ♘xf2!?

11...♕b6!? is still untested but it doesn't look bad for Black.

12 ♔xf2 ♗c5 13 ♗e3 ♕f6+

Alekhine gave this as clearly better for Black. This is an overstatement but Black doesn't have anything to complain about.

14 ♔e1!

14 ♘f5? is much worse: 14...d4! (14...exf5? 15 exd5 ♗xe3+ 16 ♕xe3+ ♘e7 17 ♗b5+ ±) 15 ♔g1 dxe3 16 ♘xe3 ♘d4! –+.

14...♗xd4

Not 14...♘xd4? 15 ♘b5! (note the difference from the line where 8 a3 ♗a5 was inserted; here 15...♘xb5 is not an option because the c5-bishop is hanging after 16 ♕xb5+) 15...dxe4 16 ♗xd4 ±.

15 ♗xd4 ♕xd4

15...♘xd4 16 ♖d1 ± Zlotnik.

16 ♕xd4 ♘xd4 17 ♔d2 dxe4 18 ♘xe4 e5!?

The endgame is equal.

C)

4 ♗d3

This is a rare line, but it shouldn't be underestimated.

4...dxe4

4...c5 leads to sharper play; e.g., 5 exd5 ♕xd5 6 ♗d2 ♗xc3 (6...♕xd4 looks very risky, while 6...♕xg2?? is certainly out of the question since the queen is trapped after 7 ♗e4) 7 ♗xc3 cxd4 (7...♕xg2? 8 ♕f3! ♗xf3 9 ♘xf3 cxd4 10 ♘xd4 is known to give White more than enough compensation for the pawn) 8 ♗xd4, and now:

a) 8...♕xg2?! (this is a better moment to grab the pawn but it still involves a great deal of risk) 9 ♕f3 (the very sharp 9 ♕d2!? ♕xh1 10 0-0-0 f6 11 f3 ♘c6 12 ♗c5 is best parried by 12...♘ge7!, when Black survived the storm and eventually capitalized on his material advantage in Groszpeter-F.Portisch, Budapest 1978) 9...♕xf3 10 ♘xf3 f6 11 ♖g1 ♔f7 12 0-0-0 ♘c6 13 ♗c5! ♘ge7 14 ♘d2 g6 15 ♘c4 ♘d5 16 ♗e4 ♔g7 17 ♘d6 ♖d8 18 c4 ♘f4 19 ♖d2 e5 20 ♖gd1 ± Vaïsser-Bauer, French Ch (Vichy) 2000.

b) 8...e5 9 ♗c3 ♘c6 (9...♘f6!? 10 ♕e2 ♕xg2 11 0-0-0 0-0! was very complicated in Flückiger-Cochet, Berne 1989) 10 ♕e2 ♘ge7 11 f4 exf4 12 ♗xg7 ♖g8 13 ♗e4 ♕g5 14 ♗c3 with a slight advantage for White, Lejlić-Tonning, Copenhagen 1996.

5 ♗xe4 ♘f6 (D)

6 ♗d3

Or:

a) 6 ♗g5 – 3...♘f6 4 ♗g5 ♗b4 5 ♗d3 dxe4 6 ♗xe4 =.

b) 6 ♗f3 c5 and then:

b1) 7 ♘e2 ♘c6 8 ♗e3 cxd4 9 ♗xc6+ (9 ♘xd4 can be answered by

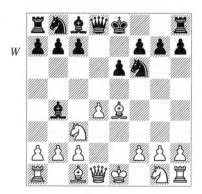

W

9...♗xc3+ 10 bxc3 ♘e5, Van Dop-Zuidema, Leeuwarden 1972, or the immediate 9...♘e5, as Uhlmann has played; Black is fine in either case) 9...bxc6 10 ♕xd4 ♕xd4 11 ♗xd4 0-0 12 0-0-0 ♖e8 13 ♗xf6 gxf6 14 ♘e4 ♗e7 15 ♘d6 ♖d8 16 ♘xc8 ♖axc8 with equality, Khavsky-Liogky, Simferopol 1990.

b2) 7 a3 ♗xc3+ 8 bxc3 ♘c6 9 ♘e2 e5!? 10 ♗g5 (10 ♗xc6+ bxc6 11 dxe5 ♕xd1+ 12 ♔xd1 ♘g4 =) 10...exd4 11 ♗xc6+ bxc6 12 cxd4 cxd4 13 ♕xd4 ♕a5+! 14 ♗d2 ♕d5 was roughly equal in Hort-Pietzsch, Kecskemet 1964 and Al.Hernandez-M.Gurevich, Havana 1986.

6...c5 7 ♘f3

This is the favourite move of Yugoslav GM Stefan Djurić. Another possibility is 7 a3 but the simple 7...♗xc3+ 8 bxc3 ♕c7 is fine for Black. One point is 9 ♘f3?! c4! 10 ♗e2 ♘d5 which gave Black a very pleasant position in V.Scherbakov-Petrosian, USSR Ch (Moscow) 1955.

7...cxd4 8 ♘xd4 e5 9 ♘de2 0-0

Black has also tried to delay this but I see no point in doing so, because the king really belongs on the kingside.

a) 9...♗e6 10 0-0 ♘c6 11 a3 ♗c5 12 ♗g5 h6 13 ♗xf6 ♕xf6 14 ♘e4 ♕e7 15 ♘xc5 ♕xc5 16 b4 ♕d6 17 ♘g3 ♖d8 18 ♖e1 0-0 19 ♕h5 ± Djurić-Khuzman, Erevan OL 1996.

b) 9...e4 10 ♗b5+ ♗d7 11 0-0 ♕a5 12 ♗xd7+ ♘bxd7 13 a3 ♗xc3 14 ♘xc3 ♕e5 15 ♖e1 ♘c5 16 ♗e3 ♘e6 17 ♕e2 and White has a slight advantage, Djurić-Villamayor, Manila 1997.

10 0-0 ♗g4 11 f3 ♗h5

11...♗e6 12 a3 ♗e7 looks very solid for Black.

12 a3 ♗c5+ 13 ♔h1 ♗g6 14 ♗xg6 hxg6 15 ♗g5 ♘c6 16 ♕e1 ♕d7 17 ♕h4

± Djurić-Draško, Yugoslav Cht (Nikšić) 1996.

D)

4 ♘e2 (D)

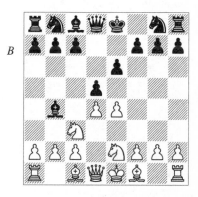

B

This is a fairly popular alternative to the main lines, especially at club level, where many players prefer to avoid doubled pawns on the c-file.

4...dxe4

After this White will temporarily be a pawn down. In most lines he will regain it quickly though. A reasonable alternative for Black is 4...♘c6!? 5 a3 ♗a5; e.g., 6 b4 (6 e5 f6!? 7 f4 fxe5 8 dxe5 ♘h6 is unclear – Kindermann) 6...♗b6 7 ♗b2 ♘ge7 8 g3 e5!? 9 exd5 ♘xd4 10 ♗g2 ♗g4 11 0-0 0-0 with equality, Volokitin-Stellwagen, Groningen 1999.

5 a3 ♗xc3+

Surrendering the bishop-pair may not be to everybody's taste but by doing so Black gains time for a quick attack against d4 and might in some lines even hope to keep the e4-pawn.

5...♗e7 is a solid alternative, after which the main line runs 6 ♘xe4 ♘f6 (6...♘c6 is another option) 7 ♘2g3; e.g., 7...0-0 8 c3 ♘c6 9 ♗d3 e5 10 ♘xf6+ ♗xf6 11 d5 ♘e7 12 c4 g6 was roughly equal in Zeller-P.Schlosser, Stuttgart 2001.

6 ♘xc3 *(D)*

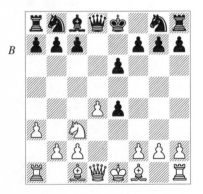

6...♘c6

Clearly best. Black counterattacks the d4-pawn.

a) 6...♘f6?! would run into an annoying pin after 7 ♗g5.

b) 6...f5? has for a very long time been known to be too risky: 7 f3! exf3 8 ♕xf3 and then:

b1) 8...♕h4+ 9 g3 ♕xd4 10 ♗f4! (10 ♘b5 {Alekhine} is also good for White) 10...c6 11 ♕h5+ g6 12 ♕e2 ♕g7 13 0-0-0 ± Larsen.

b2) 8...♕xd4 9 ♕g3!? (9 ♘b5 and 9 ♗f4 again deserve attention) 9...♘f6 10 ♕xg7 ♕e5+?! (10...♖g8 11 ♕xc7 ♘c6 is more resilient, although White gets an advantage by 12 ♗f4! – Alekhine) 11 ♗e2 ♖g8 12 ♕h6 ♖g6 13 ♕h4 ♗d7 14 ♗g5! ♗c6? (14...♘c6, intending ...0-0-0, may be better) 15 0-0-0 +– Alekhine-Nimzowitsch, Bled 1931.

b3) 8...♘c6 9 d5 ♘d4 10 ♕f2 e5 11 ♗e3 ♕e7? (11...♘f6 12 ♗xd4 exd4 13 ♕xd4 0-0 14 0-0-0 ♘e8! 15 ♗d3 ♘d6 16 ♖de1 ±) 12 0-0-0 ± Vallejo Pons-E.Berg, Mamaia U-10 Wch 1991.

b4) 8...♘f6 9 ♗f4 0-0 10 0-0-0 ♘bd7 (Sisniega-Skalkotas, Lucerne OL 1982) 11 ♗c4 ♘b6 12 ♗b3 gives White good compensation for the pawn due to his control of e5 and the possibility of breaking up the kingside with g4.

7 d5

With this White hopes to exploit a very slight initiative, although in reality the position is very likely to end up pretty equal. The alternatives see White not aiming to regain the pawn but rather embarking on rapid development and attempting to increase the pressure immediately:

a) 7 ♗e3 ♞f6 (Black may also fortify the e4-pawn with 7...f5 but since White cannot easily increase the pressure on that pawn, there is no need to weaken his position; alternatively, 7...♞ge7 will end up in a position very similar to that after *7 ♗b5 ♞e7* but with White having the option of not playing ♗b5) 8 ♕d2 ♗d7!? (an original idea; other options are 8...b6 or 8...h6, to rule out ♗g5; Korchnoi's move intends to improve on the probably less accurate move-order 8...♞e7 9 ♗g5, when Black is not ready to protect his e4-pawn) 9 0-0-0 ♞e7 10 ♗g5 ♗c6 11 ♗c4 ♕d6 12 ♖he1 0-0-0 13 g3 ♞ed5 14 ♞xe4 ♞xe4 15 ♖xe4 ♞b6 16 d5 ♞xc4 17 ♖xc4 ♕xd5 18 ♖d4 ♕xd4 19 ♕xd4 ♖xd4 20 ♖xd4 e5 21 ♖d1 f6 with an extra pawn for Black, which is, however, difficult to exploit, Van Mil-Korchnoi, Dutch Cht 1993.

b) 7 ♗b5 ♞e7 and then:

b1) 8 ♗e3 0-0 9 ♕d2 e5! 10 d5 (10 dxe5 is better; then 10...♕xd2+ 11 ♗xd2 ♗f5! 12 0-0-0 ♞xe5 13 ♖he1 ♞g4 14 ♞xe4 ♞g6 15 ♞g3 ♗e6 is approximately equal) 10...♞d4 was good for Black in Garcia Martinez-Uhlmann, Leipzig 1983.

b2) 8 ♞xe4 seems to give Black several ways to equalize, including 8...0-0 9 c3 e5, or the immediate 8...e5. Another interesting idea is 8...♕d5 9 ♕e2 0-0 (9...f5 10 ♞g3 0-0 11 c3

♕xg2 12 f4! ♕xe2+ 13 ♔xe2 gives White reasonable compensation for the pawn, Koglin-Ehrke, Bundesliga wom 1992/3) 10 c3 e5 11 dxe5 (11 ♗c4 ♕d8 and now either 12 ♞g5 or 12 ♗g5, intending to sacrifice a pawn for development and initiative, looks a lot more critical) 11...♞xe5 12 ♗g5 f6 13 ♖d1 ♕f7 14 ♗f4 ♞7g6 15 ♗g3 a6 16 ♗d3 ♞xd3+ 17 ♖xd3 ♗d7 ∓ Storland-L.Johannessen, Oslo 2000.

b3) 8 ♗g5 f6 9 ♗e3 0-0 10 ♕d2 with two options for Black:

b31) 10...e5 11 d5 (11 dxe5 ♕xd2+ 12 ♗xd2 ♞xe5 13 ♞xe4 ♗f5 14 f3 ♗xe4 15 fxe4 c6 16 ♗e2 ♖fe8 =) 11...♞d4 12 ♗xd4 exd4 13 ♕xd4 ♞f5 14 ♕xe4 c6 15 ♗e2 ♖e8 16 ♕d3 cxd5 = K.Müller-Holzke, Hamburg 1990.

b32) 10...f5 11 0-0-0 a6 12 ♗xc6 ♞xc6 13 f3 e5! 14 d5 ♞a5 = Hartmann-Hertneck, Bundesliga 1988/9.

7...exd5 8 ♕xd5 ♞ge7

This is Black's most solid move.

9 ♕xd8+ ♞xd8 10 ♞xe4 ♗f5 11 ♗d3 ♞e6 12 ♗d2 0-0-0 13 0-0-0 ♞d4

The position is equal, Zelčić-Psakhis, Batumi Echt 1999.

E)

4 ♗d2 *(D)*

The Keres Gambit. White avoids doubled pawns on the c-file but leaves the d4-pawn unprotected, and hence White often has to gambit this pawn in order to develop an initiative. The variations arising are very complicated, so Black should be well prepared against this line when playing

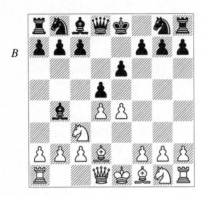

the Winawer; otherwise he can suffer a quick defeat.

4...dxe4

This is most consistent. There are various alternatives, but there is really no need to side-step the main line.

5 ♕g4

5 ♘xe4?! ♕xd4 6 ♗d3 ♗xd2+ 7 ♕xd2 is a highly speculative gambit:

a) The passive 7...♕d8? was played in Alekhine-Flohr, Nottingham 1936, which was brilliantly won by Alekhine.

b) 7...♕xb2 8 ♖d1 and now Black can choose either 8...♘d7 or 8...♘c6. My preference is for the latter, because it then looks easier for Black to complete his development by ...♗d7 and ...0-0-0.

5...♘f6

A safe alternative is 5...♕xd4 6 ♘f3 ♘h6! 7 ♕f4 (7 ♗xh6? ♗xc3+ −+) 7...e5 8 ♕xe5+ (8 ♕xh6 gxh6 9 ♘xd4 exd4 10 ♘xe4 ♗xd2+ 11 ♔xd2 =) 8...♕xe5 9 ♘xe5 ♘g4 =.

6 ♕xg7 ♖g8 7 ♕h6 ♕xd4

Black greedily goes pawn-grabbing and thus accepts lagging development

for material gains. This is the cutting-edge line of the entire variation, and unless White can somehow show compensation here, the variation may be regarded as dead and buried. If instead 7...♖g6 White hangs on to his d-pawn with 8 ♕e3 ♘c6 9 ♘ge2 ±, and 7...♘c6 8 0-0-0! ♖g6 9 ♕h4 is not simple equality either, although Black comes close with 9...♗xc3! 10 ♗xc3 ♕d5.

8 0-0-0!? *(D)*

8 ♘ge2 ♕e5! 9 0-0-0 is a less investigated continuation. White avoids losing the f-pawn and is already threatening to win back the lost pawn with ♗f4. However, I think Black is doing well after 9...♘bd7 10 ♗f4 ♕f5 (or 10...♕a5).

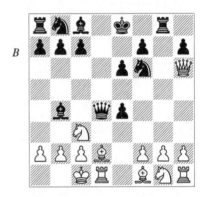

8...♗f8!?

We shall compare this closely to the alternative, 8...♖g6, since the position arising after the 10th move also occurs after 8...♖g6 9 ♕h4 ♖g4 10 ♕h3 ♕xf2 with the difference that here Black's bishop is still on b4. This has some advantages but also some drawbacks.

Let us have a look at the possible replies:

a) 11 &e2 罝h4 12 營xh4 營xh4 13 g3 &xc3 14 gxh4 (14 bxc3 營g4 15 &xg4 ②xg4 ∓) 14...&xd2+ 15 罝xd2 &d7 16 ②h3 &c6 = Rantanen-Brynell, Sweden-Finland 1989.

b) 11 &e3 is one place where it is appropriate to draw a comparison to our main line. With the bishop on f8 Black could play 11...營h4 12 營xh4 罝xh4 because 13 &g5 can be met by 13...&h6. Here, 11...營h4 just loses material, so 11...營f5 is forced, when 12 &b5+ c6 13 罝f1! 營e5 14 罝xf6 營xf6 (14...h5?! leads to trouble for Black after 15 罝h6 &xc3 16 bxc3 and 17 罝xh5) 15 營xg4 cxb5 16 營g8+ &f8 17 ②xe4! and now 17...營g7 (rather than 17...營e5? 18 營xh7 +− Drill-Masternak, Berlin 1998) keeps Black in the game.

9 營h4

9 營e3 營xe3 10 &xe3 ②g4 ∓ Keres.

9...罝g4 10 營h3 營xf2 11 &e2

The famous game Boleslavsky-Bronstein, Moscow Ct playoff (14) 1950 went 11 ②b5? ②a6 12 ⬡b1 &d7 13 &e3 營f5 14 ②d4 營g6 15 ②b3 ②b4 −+.

11 &e3 is an alternative for White but even then 11...營h4 is feasible because on 12 營xh4 罝xh4 13 &g5 Black has 13...&h6.

11...罝h4

Or:

a) 11...罝xg2?? 12 &e3 +−.

b) 11...營xg2 12 &xg4 營xg4 13 營xg4 ②xg4 14 ②xe4 &d7 15 h3 &c6

16 hxg4 &xe4 17 罝h3 ②d7 18 罝e1 &g6 was roughly equal in Redolfi-Idigoras Guisasola, Mar del Plata 1956.

c) 11...罝g6 is a solid alternative, when after 12 g4 營c5 White has nothing better than 13 &e3 營e5 (13...營a5 14 g5 罝xg5 15 營h4 罝g6 16 ②h3 is less clear) 14 &d4 營f4+ 15 &e3 with a repetition.

12 營xh4! 營xh4 13 g3 *(D)*

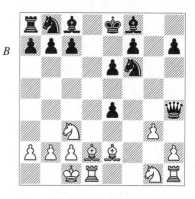

An amazing position. Black's queen is trapped.

13...營h6!

13...e3 14 gxh4 exd2+ was for some time considered Black's best continuation since 15 ⬡xd2 &h6+ 16 ⬡e1 &d7 gives him a fair amount of compensation, but 15 ⬡b1! &h6 16 ②h3 is now rightly considered good for White.

14 &xh6 &xh6+ 15 ⬡b1 e5 16 h3 c6

Perhaps Black even has an edge, Escalona-Bronstein, Oviedo rpd 1993.

F)

4 a3

White forces Black to part with his bishop. It is seen from time to time but shouldn't really worry Black if he is prepared for it.

4...♗xc3+ 5 bxc3 *(D)*

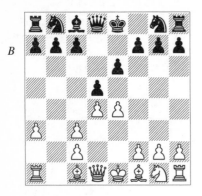

5...dxe4

I don't see a reason for delaying this, although 5...♘e7 is also seen. Then after 6 ♗d3 Black has usually gone 6...c5, but 7 ♕g4 dxe4 8 ♕xe4 ♗d7 9 ♘e2 ♗c6 10 ♕g4 favoured White in Wojtkiewicz-Chernin, Polanica Zdroj. Instead, Wojtkiewicz suggests the wild 6...0-0 7 ♘f3 e5!? aiming to open lines before White is fully developed. I am not sure I really trust it though. It is worth noting that White can also play 6 e5 with a likely transposition to the Winawer Main Lines, but then why play 4 a3 in the first place?

6 ♕g4

6 f3 is a notorious gambit, but I don't believe in it. Black can accept the pawn but psychologically this would probably be a mistake since it gives White what he wants. 6...c5!? is a

good and interesting reply but Hübner recommendation, 6...e5!, looks even better. Then: 7 fxe4? loses to 7...♕h4+; 7 ♗b5+?! c6 8 ♗c4 ♕a5 is good for Black; 7 ♗e3 exd4 ∓ 8 cxd4?! ♘h6! gave Black an excellent position in Grabarczyk-Gdanski, Polish Cht (Lubniewice) 1993; 7 a4 might be White's best, but Black has several good continuations: 7...exd4 8 cxd4 c5, or even 7...c5!?.

6...♘f6 7 ♕xg7 ♖g8 8 ♕h6 ♘bd7

This flexible continuation appears best. Instead, Black can immediately drive White's queen back or strike against White's centre:

a) 8...c5 9 ♘e2 ♖g6 (9...♘bd7 – 8...♘bd7 9 ♘e2 c5) 10 ♕d2 ♘bd7 11 g3 b6 12 ♗g2 ♗b7 13 0-0 ♕c7 14 a4 a6 with approximately equal play, Mora-Naumkin, Toscolano 1996.

b) 8...♖g6 9 ♕d2 b6 (9...c5 10 ♘e2 – 8...c5 9 ♘e2 ♖g6 10 ♕d2) 10 ♘h3 ♗b7 11 ♘f4 ♖g8 12 c4 ♘bd7 13 ♗b2 ♕e7 14 0-0-0 0-0-0 = Balashov-Bunzmann, Schwäbisch Gmünd 1998.

9 ♘e2

White could take his knight in another direction with 9 ♘h3, when the knight has a further option of moving forward to g5, but 9...b6 10 ♘g5 ♖g6 11 ♕h4 ♗b7 12 ♘xh7 ♘xh7 13 ♕xh7 ♕f6 gives Black good compensation. One point is 14 h4?! 0-0-0 15 ♗g5 ♖h8! 16 ♗xf6 ♖xh7 17 ♗e5 ♘xe5 18 dxe5 ♖g5!, when Black has the advantage, Degraeve-Djurhuus, Arnhem jr Ech 1988/9.

9...b6

Another option is 9...c5, and now 10 g3 b6 11 ♗g2 ♗b7 12 0-0 ♕e7 13 a4 ♘g4! 14 ♕f4 f5 looked fine for Black in Ki.Georgiev-Psakhis, Sarajevo 1986.

10 ♗g5!? ♕e7 11 ♕h4 ♗b7 12 ♘g3

If 12 ♘f4 h6 13 ♕xh6 0-0-0 14 ♕h4 Black obtains counterplay by 14...e3!? 15 f3 ♖h8 16 ♘h5 ♕d6! 17 ♗xf6 ♘xf6 18 ♕xf6 ♖xh5 19 ♗d3!, Estevez-Vilela, Havana 1991, and now Vilela recommends 19...♖g8!, with the point that 20 ♕xf7 ♖hg5 gives Black compensation.

12...h6! 13 ♗d2

White must be a little careful. 13 ♗xh6 might be feasible but looks risky. 13 ♕xh6?? is, however, a blunder. It is amusing that White's bishop is trapped after 13...♘g4 14 ♗xe7 ♘xh6 15 ♗b4 (or 15 ♗h4 ♖g4) 15...a5.

13...♖g4!? 14 ♕xh6 0-0-0 15 c4 ♘g8 16 ♕e3 f5

Black has good compensation, Romero-Matamoros, Elgoibar 1997.

G)

4 exd5 exd5 *(D)*

4...♕xd5?! – 3...dxe4 4 ♘xe4 ♕d5 5 ♘c3 ♗b4 ±.

The Exchange Winawer is a solid line for White, for those who want to avoid too much theory. It is a favourite of French GM Igor-Alexandre Nataf. It shouldn't cause Black that many problems if he knows what to do.

5 ♗d3

5 ♕f3 used to be a pet line of Larsen's but it has now been established

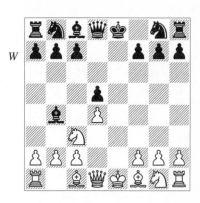

that Black has no problems at all after the accurate 5...♕e7+! 6 ♗e3 ♘f6.

5...♘c6

Other options are:

a) 5...♘e7 6 ♕h5 and now:

a1) 6...♘bc6 7 a3 ♗xc3+ 8 bxc3 – *5...♘c6 6 a3 ♗xc3+ 7 bxc3 ♘ge7 8 ♕h5! ±.*

a2) 6...c5 7 dxc5! d4 8 a3 ♕a5 9 axb4! ♕xa1 10 ♘ce2 ♘bc6 11 ♘f3 ♘xb4 12 ♗b5+ ♘bc6 13 0-0 gave White a strong attack in Glek-Hochstrasser, Zurich 1999.

b) 5...c6 6 ♗f4 ♘f6 7 ♘ge2 0-0 8 a3 ♗d6 = Ivanisević-Draško, Yugoslav Ch (Nikšić) 1997.

c) 5...♘f6 6 ♗g5 h6 7 ♗h4 0-0 8 ♘ge2 ♖e8 9 0-0 c6 10 f3 ♘bd7 11 ♔h1 ♘f8 intending ...♘g6 =, Ulybin-Prokopchuk, Koszalin 1999.

6 a3 ♗xc3+

Retreating the bishop is solid but slightly passive. Black can also maintain the pin with 6...♗a5 but the bishop may then end up out of play after a subsequent b4.

7 bxc3 ♘f6

Some time ago this was lightly assessed as inferior because White could simply pin the knight, with the recommended method for Black being to neutralize White's d3-bishop by preparing ...♗f5. However, it has since become clear that this isn't so easily done:

a) 7...♘ge7 8 ♕h5! ♗e6 9 ♖b1 b6 10 ♘f3 ♕d6 11 ♘g5 h6 12 ♘xe6 ♕xe6+ 13 ♗e3 0-0 14 0-0 ♘a5 15 ♖be1 ♕f6 16 ♗c1 c6 17 ♖e3 gave White a strong attack in Glek-Naumkin, Bad Wörishofen 2001.

b) 7...♕f6 8 ♕h5 ♘ge7 9 ♗g5 ♕e6+ 10 ♘e2 ♕g4!? 11 ♘g3! (11 ♕xg4 ♗xg4 12 f3 ♗f5 was equal in Fressinet-Bricard, Saint Affrique 2000) 11...h6 12 ♗xe7 ♘xe7 13 0-0 ♕xh5 14 ♘xh5 0-0 15 ♖ae1 ♖e8 16 ♖e3 ♔f8 17 ♖fe1 ♗e6 18 f4 with an edge for White, Annageldiev-P.Nikolić, Istanbul OL 2000.

8 ♘e2 (D)

8 ♗g5 is quite logical once Black has parted with his dark-squared bishop, but is completely innocuous. Black has no trouble unpinning the knight and hence the bishop might turn out to be developed prematurely. Black's simplest is 8...h6 9 ♗h4 (9 ♗xf6 ♕xf6 is equal, Casper-Kindermann, Bundesliga 1996/7) 9...0-0 10 ♘e2 ♘a5 11 0-0 ♕d6 12 ♖b1 (if 12 ♗g3 ♕c6 13 ♕d2 ♘c4 14 ♕f4 Black defends with 14...♘d6) 12...b6 and Black is doing fine, Vorotnikov-Zakharov, Moscow 1995. White's most natural development has been spoiled since ♘g3 is

not an option with the bishop on h4. Black is also ready to play ...♘c4 or ...♘e4.

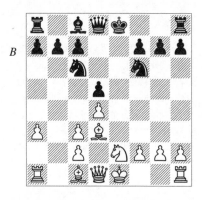

8...♘a5

Black shouldn't hurry with the development of the light-squared bishop. The type of position which arises after 8...♗g4 (Black can also castle first) 9 f3 ♗h5 10 ♘f4 ♗g6 11 ♘xg6 is better for White due to his bishop-pair and because Black's knights are restricted by the pawns.

With the text-move, Black is planning to play ...♕d6 as after ♗f4 the queen can step aside to c6. Besides, the knight may hop into c4 at a later point.

Indeed, 8...0-0 has often been Black's choice, and now 9 0-0 ♖e8 was Nataf-Short, New Delhi FIDE 2000. Black's last move is very natural but probably not very useful. White was now able to dig out a little something from the opening: 10 ♗g5 h6 11 ♗h4 ♘a5 12 ♕d2! ♕d6 13 ♗g3 ♕c6 14 ♕f4! ♖e7 15 ♗h4 ±.

9 0-0 0-0 10 ♘g3

10 ♗g5 h6 11 ♗h4 – *8 ♗g5 h6 9 ♗h4 0-0 10 ♘e2 ♘a5 11 0-0 =.*

10...♗g4!?

Black faces some minor difficulties after other moves:

a) 10...♖e8 11 ♖e1! (11 ♕f3 is also interesting; then after 11...♗g4 12 ♕f4 h6 13 h3 ♗e6 14 ♕f3 ♘c4 15 ♗f4 ♘d6, Rabiega-Kindermann, Austria 1998, White obtains a slight advantage with 16 ♗e5) 11...♖xe1+ 12 ♕xe1 ♗e6 13 ♕e5! ♘c6 14 ♕e2! ♕d6 15 ♗g5 ± Nataf-Degraeve, Mondariz Z 2000.

b) 10...♘c4 11 ♖e1 ♗g4 12 f3 ♗e6 13 ♗g5 (13 ♗f4!?) 13...h6 14 ♗xf6 ♕xf6 15 ♗xc4 dxc4 16 ♖e5 c6 17 ♕e2 ♕d8 18 f4 ♗d5 19 ♕g4 ♔h7 20 ♖ae1 ± Neubauer-Kindermann, Baden 1999.

11 f3 ♗d7 12 ♖e1

If ♕h4 were legal White would have a very promising attack, so I was toying with the idea of bringing the queen there. However, on 12 ♕d2 ♘c4 13 ♕g5 (Black is also fine after 13 ♕f4 h6!) 13...h6 14 ♕h4, 14...♘e8 looks like a well-timed neutralizer.

12...♖e8

12...♘c4 13 ♗f4 ♖e8 also looked very reasonable for Black in Spraggett-Eingorn, Metz 1997, but this allowed White to decide whether to exchange rooks. In the game White opted for 14 ♗e5 but possibly 14 ♖xe8+ is a slightly better version for White of what we see in the main line below.

13 ♗f4 ♖xe1+ 14 ♕xe1 ♘c4 15 ♗xc4 dxc4 16 ♕e5 ♕e8!

An excellent defensive resource. Black shouldn't worry too much about his c7-pawn as there will always be splendid compensation if White takes it.

17 ♕c5

17 ♕xc7 ♘d5 18 ♕d6 ♘xc3 19 ♗d2 ♘b5 20 ♕f4 c3 21 ♗e3 ♘c7 is roughly equal.

17...♗e6 18 ♗g5 b6!? 19 ♕xc7 ♘d5 20 ♕xc4 ♖c8 21 ♕e2 ♕c6 22 ♗d2 ♘xc3 23 ♕d3 ♕c4

Black has enough compensation for the pawn but it is not enough for a real advantage. The position is balanced, and in Blehm-Lputian, New Delhi FIDE 2000, White rightly went for the endgame after 24 ♕xc4 ♖xc4 25 ♗xc3 ♖xc3 26 ♖c1 ♔f8 27 ♘e4 ♖xa3 28 c4, and the game was soon drawn.

H)

4 e5 *(D)*

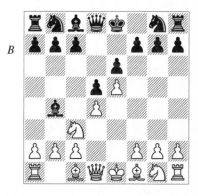

Now:

H3: 4...♘e7   238
H4: 4...c5   239

The four lines are related in pairs. H1 and H2 are very similar. Usually ...b6 and ...♕d7 sit together but one advantage of 4...♕d7 over 4...b6 is that White's 5 ♕g4 can be met with 5...f5, although even this might be better for White.

Line H4 is Black's most frequent move-order but 4...♘e7 has some merit as a way of trying to avoid some of White's 5th move alternatives in Lines H41, H42 and H43.

H1)
4...♕d7

With this peculiar queen move, Black aims for a ...b6 set-up but he first attempts to take some of the sting out of ♕g4 or ♗b5 ideas. The move ♕g4 is often annoying for Black but after the text-move he can meet it with ...f5.

5 a3 *(D)*

White also has:

a) 5 ♗d2 (White avoids doubled pawns and this time it is not a sacrifice, like *4 ♗d2*; it is a solid idea which seems to promise White a slight advantage) 5...b6 and now:

a1) 6 ♘f3 ♘e7 7 ♘e2! ♗xd2+ 8 ♕xd2 ♗a6 9 h4 c5 10 c3 ♘bc6 11 ♘f4 ♗xf1 12 ♔xf1 h5 13 g3 cxd4 14 cxd4 g6 15 ♔g2 ± Psakhis-Short, Hastings 1987/8.

a2) 6 ♗b5!? c6 7 ♗a4 (this is a common manoeuvre; White wants to avoid an exchange of the light-squared bishops and later intends to bring it back to a better position with c3 and ♗c2) 7...a5 8 a3 ♗xc3 (8...♗f8 9 ♘ce2! intending c3 ±) 9 ♗xc3 ♗a6 10 ♗d2 ♗b5 (10...♘e7 11 c3 ♘f5 12 ♘e2 ± Nunn-Lutz, Krefeld 1986) 11 ♗xb5 cxb5 12 ♕g4 f5 13 ♕h5+ g6 14 ♕e2 ♕c6 15 h4 h6 16 ♖h3 ± Khalifman-Brynell, Leningrad 1989.

b) 5 ♕g4 f5 6 ♕g3 b6 7 ♘h3 ♗a6 8 ♗xa6 ♘xa6 9 0-0 c6 10 ♘f4 ♘c7 11 ♘ce2 ♕f7 12 b3, intending c4, gave White the better position in Hjartarson-Adams, Reykjavik tt 1990.

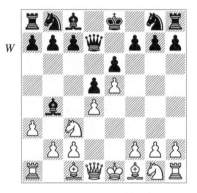

5...♗xc3+

5...♗f8 is feasible but I don't believe in it. I should probably speak a little about the ...♗f8 idea as it occurs quite often in the ...♕d7/...b6 systems. Black insists on keeping the bishop-pair but if he is not ready to give it up, in my opinion, he probably shouldn't be playing the Winawer! Black's position is solid enough so he wouldn't be overrun immediately, despite the loss of two tempi, but I don't think he deserves to equalize. The only thing that justifies the retreat is that on c3 the knight is slightly misplaced. Imagine if White plays 6 ♘b1: then we have an Advance Variation which has been met by 3...♕d7 and White replying 4 a3! Hmm, which is more useful? Not clear when you think of it in the first time but I am sure it is ...♕d7, as long as Black does not rush with ...c5. However, White can of course find better things to do than 6 ♘b1?:

a) 6 ♘f3 b6 – *4...b6 5 a3 ♗f8 6 ♘f3 ♕d7* ±.

b) 6 ♘ce2!? b6 7 ♘f4 c5 (7...♗a6 8 ♗xa6 ♘xa6 9 ♕d3 ±) 8 dxc5! (8 c3 ♗a6 is now OK for Black since after the bishops are exchanged Black can bring his knight to c7) 8...bxc5 9 c4 ♘e7 10 ♘f3 ♗b7 11 ♗e2 d4 12 ♘d3 ♕c7 13 ♗f4 ♘d7 14 h4 a5 15 h5 a4 16 ♔f1 ♘c6 17 ♖c1 ♗e7 18 ♖h3 ± Fedorowicz-Seirawan, USA Ch (Estes Park) 1986.

6 bxc3 b6 7 ♕g4

This is far from White's only option. Other things have been tried too and most lead to a slightly better position for White. In fact, 7 a4 might be the most accurate. Then after 7...♗a6 8 ♗xa6 ♘xa6 9 ♕g4 f5, White has the option of playing 10 ♕g3, which transposes to the main line, or putting the queen on e2, after, for example, 10 ♕h5+ g6 11 ♕e2.

7...f5 8 ♕g3

8 ♕h5+ g6 9 ♕d1 ♗a6 10 ♗xa6 ♘xa6 11 h4 also looks promising for White.

8...♗a6 9 ♗xa6 ♘xa6 10 a4

10 ♘e2 is seen more frequently, and is also good. Then if 10...0-0-0, 11 a4 ♘b8 12 a5 ♘c6 13 ♕d3! ♘ge7 14 ♗g5 was good for White in Ashley-Karatorossian, New York Open 2000.

10...♘b8 11 a5 ♘c6 12 axb6 cxb6 13 ♘e2

White has opened files on the queenside, which may be useful later, but right now he should now just concentrate on improving his position on the kingside. Fedorov-Dizdar, Dubai 2001 went 13...♔f7 14 h4 ♘ge7 15 h5 h6 16 ♘f4 ♖he8 17 ♕h3 ♔g8 18 ♖g1 ♖f8 19 ♗a3 ♖f7 20 ♕d3 ♖c8 21 ♔e2 ♘a5 22 ♘g6! ±.

H2)
4...b6 (D)

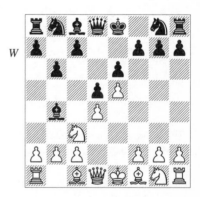

5 a3

Around here White must decide which he finds more useful: a3 or ♕g4. The aggressive-minded player would probably prefer the latter but it is not totally clear how useful the queen is on g4. White has a third choice in ♗d2, but again this appears a bit tame. Thus, the alternatives are:

a) 5 ♗d2 and now:

a1) 5...♕d7 – 4...♕d7 5 ♗d2 b6 ±.

a2) 5...♘e7 – 4...♘e7 5 ♗d2 b6 =.

b) 5 ♕g4 and then:

b1) Sacrificing a pawn in the usual Winawer fashion with 5...♘e7 is a bit optimistic since there is no counterplay against White's centre.

b2) 5...♔f8 is the only real alternative to retreating the bishop, but then simply 6 ♗d2 is good for White.

b3) 5...♗f8 *(D)*.

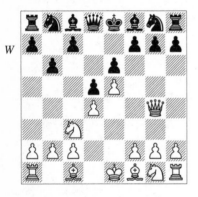

Black doesn't want to weaken his kingside. His plan is clear: he wants to exchange the light-squared bishops, so White usually seeks to avoid this. For that purpose, White would like to see a sequence such as ♗b5+ c6 and then ♗a4. Later White might then move the knight away from c3 and bring the bishop back with c3 and ♗c2. Thus:

b31) 6 ♘h3 (ideas of ♘f4-h5 may be annoying for Black) 6...♗a6 7 ♘b5!?

(7 ♗xa6 ♘xa6 8 ♘f4 ♘b4! 9 ♕e2 ♘e7 10 a3 ♘bc6 11 ♗e3 ♘f5 12 0-0-0 ♗e7 did not cause Black any real problems in Kovaliov-Vaganian, Tilburg 1992, although White later won the game) 7...♕d7 8 a4 ♘e7 (Rogulj-Dizdar, Pula 1998 ended in a quick draw after 8...♗b7 9 ♘f4 a6 10 ♘c3 ♘c6; this looks like a fairly simple solution for Black) 9 ♘f4 ♘g6 10 ♘h5 (Roser-Karatorossian, Budapest 1997) 10...c6 should be fine for Black: 11 ♘d6+ ♗xd6 12 exd6 (after 12 ♘xg7+, 12...♔f8 13 ♗h6 ♗e7 14 ♗xa6 ♘xa6 is perhaps not so clear, but White still needs to prove there is enough for the piece; even the unnatural 12...♔d8!? 13 exd6 ♕xd6 isn't necessarily that terrible for Black) 12...f5 (12...0-0?! 13 ♗xa6 ♘xa6 14 ♕e2 ♘b8? 15 ♗h6 ±) 13 ♕g3 ♗xf1 14 ♖xf1 0-0 with equality.

b32) 6 ♘f3 ♗a6 (6...♕d7 7 ♗b5 c6 8 ♗e2 ♗a6 9 0-0 ♘e7 10 ♖d1 ♘f5 11 a3 ± Mokry-Ravikumar, Dieren 1990) 7 ♘b5!? ♕d7 8 a4 ♘e7 9 ♗d3 ♘f5 =.

b33) 6 ♗b5+ ♗d7! (6...c6 7 ♗a4 a5 8 a3 ♘e7 9 ♘ce2! ♗a6 10 c3 ♘d7 11 ♘h3 ♕c7 12 0-0 ♘f5 13 ♖e1 h6 14 ♘ef4 0-0-0 15 ♗c2 ± David-Conquest, Amsterdam 1996) 7 ♗g5 (7 ♗d3 ♘c6!? 8 a3 f5! =) 7...♕c8 8 ♗e2 c5 9 ♘f3 c4! =.

b34) 6 ♗g5 (this aims to rule out ...♗d7 as a reply to ♗b5) 6...♕d7 7 ♗b5 ♘c6!? (7...c6 8 ♗a4 ±) 8 ♘f3 h6 9 ♗d2 ♗b7 10 0-0 a6 11 ♗a4 ♘ge7 12 ♘e2 g6 13 c3 ♘f5 14 h4 h5 15 ♕f4

♗h6 16 ♘g5 ± Sulskis-Hjartarson, Groningen FIDE 1997.

5...♗f8 *(D)*

5...♗xc3+ 6 bxc3 ♕d7 – *4...♕d7 5 a3 ♗xc3+ 6 bxc3 b6 ±.*

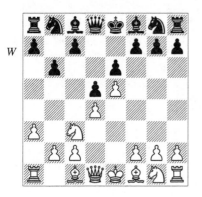

W

6 ♘f3

6 ♗b5+ is a good alternative (in this position a3 appears more useful than ♕g4): 6...♗d7 (6...c6 7 ♗a4 ♗a6 8 ♘ce2 ♗b5 9 ♗b3 c5 10 c3 ♘c6 11 ♘f3 ♘ge7 12 0-0 ♘f5 13 ♖e1 ♗e7 14 ♗c2 ± Čabrilo-Arencibia, Manila IZ 1990) 7 ♗d3 c5 8 ♘f3 ♘c6 9 0-0 (this concept is what makes White's a3 much more useful than ♕g4: it is easier for White to defend his centre and there is no risk of 'losing' the bishop to ...♘b4) 9...♘ge7 (9...a6 10 dxc5! bxc5 11 b3 ♘ge7 12 ♖e1 ♘g6 13 ♘a4 ♕c7 14 ♕e2 ♘b8 15 ♘b2 ♗e7 16 ♗d2 ♗c6 17 c4 and White was better in Knaak-Portisch, Dresden 1995) 10 ♘b5 ♘g6 11 c3 c4 12 ♗xg6 hxg6 13 ♗g5 ♕b8 14 a4, *Deep Junior*-Illescas, KasparovChess GP 2000, and now 14...♘a5 looks fine for Black.

6...♘e7

The other option is 6...♕d7 but the text-move seems more logical, as ...♕d7 is often played with the intention of being able to meet ♕g4 with ...f5. Here ♕g4 is not available and thus ...♕d7 makes less sense. Even so, 6...♕d7 is seen quite frequently. White's most natural reply is 7 ♗b5, and then:

a) 7...♘c6 8 ♘e2 ♗b7 9 ♘f4 a6 10 ♗a4 0-0-0 11 0-0 h6 12 c3 ♔b8 13 b4 ± Psakhis-Karlsson, Tallinn 1987.

b) 7...c6 8 ♗a4 ♗a6 9 ♘e2 ♗b5 10 ♗b3 c5 11 c3 ♘c6 12 0-0 ♘ge7 13 ♖e1 ♗xe2!? 14 ♖xe2 c4 15 ♗c2 b5 16 ♖e3!? h6 17 ♘d2 ♘c8 18 ♕g4 with the better position for White in Atalik-M.Gurevich, New York Open 1998.

7 h4!? *(D)*

This is a typically modern interpretation of the white plan in many Winawer positions. White seizes space on the kingside before anything else is undertaken.

7 ♗b5+ ♗d7 8 ♗d3 c5 9 0-0 ♘bc6 – *6 ♗b5+ ♗d7 7 ♗d3 c5 8 ♘f3 ♘c6 9 0-0 ♘ge7 =.*

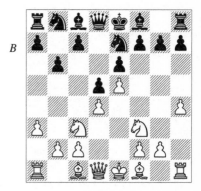

B

7...h6 8 h5 a5

8...c5 9 ♘e2 ♗a6 10 c3 ♘ec6 11 b4! gave White an advantage in Dolmatov-Gulko, USSR 1985.

9 ♗b5+ c6 10 ♗a4

The thematic way of avoiding the exchange of bishops. Now White just needs to play ♘e2 and c3, whereupon the bishop can come back to a more natural place. This type of set-up usually gives White a pleasant space advantage.

10...♘d7 11 ♘e2 b5 12 ♗b3 c5 13 c3 ♘c6 14 0-0 ♕c7 15 ♖e1

Another idea would be 15 ♘h2 followed by f4, which also looks good for White.

15...c4 16 ♗c2 ♘b6 17 ♗f4

White is slightly better, Kasparov-Ivanchuk, Horgen 1995.

H3)

4...♘e7 *(D)*

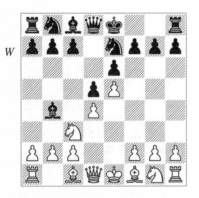

This may just lead to the Main Line Winawer after, for example, 5 a3 ♗xc3+ 6 bxc3 c5, but Black has then avoided some of White's normal 5th move alternatives (Lines H41-H43). The question is whether White can exploit the fact that Black doesn't attack White's centre immediately.

5 ♗d2

Since Black hasn't attacked White's centre, White can take his time to avoid doubled pawns. Otherwise:

a) 5 ♕g4 ♘f5 6 ♘f3 ♘c6!? 7 ♗d3 h5 8 ♕f4 ♘ce7!? 9 ♘h4 ♘xh4 10 ♕xh4 c5 11 a3 ♗xc3+ 12 bxc3 c4 13 ♗e2 ♘f5 = Delekta-Eingorn, Berlin 1994.

b) 5 a3 ♗xc3+ 6 bxc3 b6 (6...c5 – *4...c5 5 a3 ♗xc3+ 6 bxc3 ♘e7*) 7 ♕g4 and now:

b1) 7...0-0?! 8 ♗g5! ♘d7 9 ♗d3 has given White promising attacking chances in several games.

b2) 7...♔f8 is fairly solid but White is better; e.g., 8 ♘h3 (intending ♘f4-h5) 8...♘g6 9 a4 c5 10 a5 ♗a6 11 ♗xa6 ♘xa6 12 axb6 axb6 13 0-0 ± Spassky-Rødgaard, Thessaloniki OL 1984.

b3) 7...♘f5 8 ♗b5+ c6 9 ♗d3 h5 10 ♕h3 (threatening g4) 10...c5 11 ♘f3 c4 (11...♘c6 12 g4 ♘fe7 is probably better but I prefer White) 12 ♗xf5 exf5 13 ♕g3 ♔f8 14 h4 ± Unzicker-Herzog, Graz 1984.

b4) 7...♘g6 8 h4 h5 9 ♕d1 ♗a6 (9...♘xh4 10 g3 ♘g6 11 ♖xh5 ±) 10 ♗xa6 ♘xa6 11 ♗g5 ♕d7 12 ♘e2 with a critical position. Black needs just a few moves of peace and quiet to set up a fairly acceptable position. White would like to open the position quickly, since right now Black's pieces are not coordinating well, and Black has problems with his badly-placed knight on a6 and potentially weak h-pawn. Black has chosen between:

b41) 12...♕a4 13 ♖h3!? ♘e7 14 ♘f4 g6 15 ♕d2 ♔d7 (on 15...♘f5 White might try 16 f3 intending g4) 16 ♗xe7! (a key idea in this line; White removes the black knight before it has a chance to become superior to White's bishop) 16...♔xe7 17 ♖f3 ♖af8 18 ♘h3 c5 19 ♘g5 ± Ivkov-R.Byrne, Varna OL 1962.

b42) 12...♕c6 13 0-0 ♘e7 (13...♘f8 14 ♕d3 ♘b8 15 ♕f3!? ♘bd7 16 a4 a5 17 ♘g3 g6 18 ♖fe1 ♕c4 19 ♘f1 ♘h7 20 ♗d2 ♕a6 21 ♘e3 ± Sadvakasov-Zaja, Istanbul OL 2000) 14 ♗xe7!? ♔xe7 15 a4 ♘b8 16 ♕d2 ♔f8 17 a5 ♔g8 18 ♖fe1 ♘d7 19 ♘f4 ♘f8 20 ♖e3 is much better for White, Groszpeter-Kelečević, Lenk 2000.

b43) 12...♘b8 13 0-0! ♘e7 14 ♘f4 g6 15 ♗xe7 ♕xe7 16 c4 ± Khalifman.

b44) 12...♘e7 13 ♘f4 g6 14 ♗xe7! ♕xe7 15 ♕d3 ♘b8 16 c4 and White is better, Adorjan-Farago, Hungarian Ch (Budapest) 1968.

5...b6

5...c5 – 4...c5 5 ♗d2 ♘e7.

6 ♕g4

This is White's most aggressive move. The more positional 6 ♘ce2 ♗xd2+ 7 ♕xd2 offers White very little; e.g., 7...c5 8 ♘f3 ♗a6 9 g3 ♘bc6 10 c3 ♖c8 with roughly equal play in Hector-Timman, Malmö 1999.

6...♘f5

6...♘g6 7 h4 h5 8 ♕g3 ♗a6 9 ♗xa6 ♘xa6 10 ♘f3 ♗e7 11 ♗g5 ♘b4 12 0-0-0 ± I.Sokolov-Farago, Portorož/Rogaška Slatina 1993.

7 ♗d3 h5 8 ♕f4 g5!?

Or:

a) Black also has the option of playing a queenless middlegame with 8...♕h4 9 ♕xh4 ♘xh4, but 10 g3 ♘f5 11 ♘b5 ♗xd2+ 12 ♔xd2 ♘a6 13 ♘e2 gave White an edge in Leko-Panno, Buenos Aires 1994.

b) 8...♘c6 9 ♘f3 ♘ce7 10 ♕g5 ♗xc3 11 ♗xc3 a5 (Lutz-Dizdar, Austrian Cht 1999) 12 0-0 ♗a6 13 ♗xa6 ♖xa6 14 ♗d2 intending h3 and g4 ought to be a bit better for White.

9 ♕xg5 ♕xg5 10 ♗xg5 ♘xd4 11 0-0-0 ♗e7 12 h4 c5

The chances are roughly equal, Martinez Gonzales-Psakhis, Benasque 1995.

H4)

4...c5 (D)

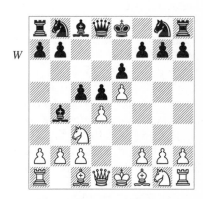

We now have:

H41: 5 ♕g4   240
H42: 5 dxc5   240
H43: 5 ♗d2   241
H44: 5 a3   244

There are lots of transpositions between lines H41, H42 and H43, and it is not an easy job to categorize them as they may arise from various move-orders. I have tried to point out the different move-orders in the notes.

5 ♘f3 ♘c6 usually transposes to H41 after 6 dxc5. Acs-Bunzmann, Budapest 1998 took a similar yet slightly different course: 6 ♗b5 ♘ge7 7 dxc5 ♗xc5 8 0-0 ♘g6 9 ♘a4 ♗e7 10 ♗e3 ♗d7 11 ♗xc6 ♗xc6 12 ♘c3 0-0 13 ♖e1 ♕c7 14 ♗d4 ♖ae8!? 15 ♖e3 f5, and Black was doing well.

H41)

5 ♕g4

Compared to the sharp main lines with 7 ♕g4 (Chapters 12 and 13) this early queen sally is riskier for White with the unsettled centre.

5...♘e7 6 ♘f3 *(D)*

6 dxc5 ♘bc6 7 ♗d2 – 5 ♗d2 ♘e7 6 dxc5 ♘bc6 7 ♕g4.

6...cxd4

This is the simplest way to equalize (at least). Another possibility for Black is 6...♘bc6 7 ♗b5 ♗xc3+!? 8 bxc3 ♕a5 9 ♗xc6+ bxc6 10 0-0 ♗a6 which led to a slight advantage for Black in Zelčić-Kindermann, Bad Wörishofen 1994.

7 ♘xd4 ♘g6 8 ♗d2 0-0 9 ♘f3 ♘c6 10 0-0-0 f5 11 exf6 ♕xf6

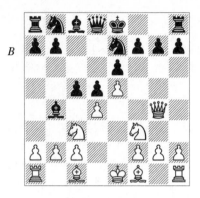

=/∓ Movsesian-Shaked, Zagan jr Wch 1997.

H42)

5 dxc5 ♘c6 6 ♘f3

6 ♕g4 ♘ge7 7 ♗d2 – 5 ♗d2 ♘e7 6 dxc5 ♘bc6 7 ♕g4.

6...♘ge7

6...d4 might be premature; e.g., 7 a3 ♗a5 8 b4 ♘xb4 (8...dxc3 9 bxa5 ♕xd1+ 10 ♔xd1, as in Gallagher-Knott, London GLC 1986, is probably better but I would prefer White owing to the bishop-pair) 9 axb4 ♗xb4 10 ♗b5+! ♗d7 11 0-0 ♗xc3 12 ♖b1 and White was better in Soltis-Cappello, Reggio Emilia 1971/2.

7 ♗d3 *(D)*

7...d4

7...♘g6 allowed White an advantage in Hodgson-Adams, Haringey 1989 after 8 ♗xg6! fxg6!? 9 ♗e3 0-0 10 0-0 ♗xc3 11 bxc3 ♕c7 12 ♖b1 ♘a5 13 ♖e1 ♗d7 14 ♗d4 ±.

8 a3 ♗a5

Not 8...♕a5? 9 axb4 ♕xa1 10 ♘b5 ±.

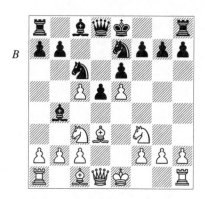

9 b4 ♘xb4 10 axb4 ♗xb4 11 0-0 ♗xc3 12 ♖b1

This position has occurred several times. One example is 12...h6!? 13 ♘d2 ♗xd2 14 ♗xd2 ♗d7!? 15 ♖xb7 ♗c6 with counterplay, Gomez Baillo-Giaccio, Trelew 1995.

H43)
5 ♗d2 *(D)*

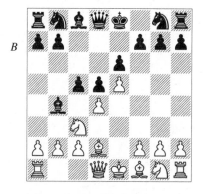

This is the most popular of White's alternatives to 5 a3.

5...♘e7

Black has three alternatives:

a) 5...♘c6 6 ♘b5 ♗xd2+ 7 ♕xd2 ♘xd4 8 ♘xd4 cxd4 9 f4 is slightly better for White; e.g., 9...♘e7 10 ♘f3 ♕b6 11 0-0-0 ♘c6 12 h4 h5 13 ♖h3 g6 14 ♔b1 ♗d7 15 ♘g5! a6 16 ♖b3 ♕a7 17 a4!? ± Movsesian-Hochgräfe, Hamburg 1997.

b) 5...cxd4 6 ♘b5 ♗e7 7 ♕g4 ♔f8 8 ♘f3 ♘c6 9 ♘bxd4 ♕b6 10 ♘b3 f5 11 ♕f4 ♘h6 12 ♗d3 ± Al Modiahki-Barua, Balaguer 1997.

c) 5...♘h6!? 6 ♗d3!? ♘c6 7 ♘f3 and now:

c1) 7...cxd4 8 ♘e2! ♗xd2+ 9 ♕xd2 0-0 10 ♘exd4 f6 11 ♘xc6 bxc6 12 ♕e2 ± Leko.

c2) 7...c4 8 ♗f1! ♘f5 9 ♘e2 ♗e7 10 c3 h5 11 g3 b5 12 ♗g2 a6 13 h3 ♗b7 14 ♕c1! with a slight advantage for White, Leko-A.Rabinovich, Szeged U-16 Wch 1994.

c3) 7...f6!? 8 exf6 ♕xf6 and now 9 a3 ♗xc3 10 bxc3 c4 11 ♗g5 ♕f7 12 ♗xh6 cxd3 13 ♗e3 dxc2 14 ♕xc2 0-0 was fine for Black in de la Villa-Al Modiahki, Ubeda 1998, but 9 dxc5 looks more critical.

After the text-move (5...♘e7), we shall look at two main lines for White:
H431: 6 ♘b5   242
H432: 6 dxc5   243

White has two other ideas:

a) 6 a3 ♗xc3 7 ♗xc3 b6!? (intending ...♗a6) 8 ♗b5+ ♘bc6 9 f4 ♗d7 10 ♗d3!? cxd4 11 ♗d2 0-0 12 ♘f3 f6 13 0-0?! (13 ♕e2 fxe5 14 fxe5 ♘f5 15 0-0-0 is probably better, with an unclear position) 13...h6!? 14 ♕e2 ♕c7 15

♖fe1 fxe5 16 fxe5 ♘f5 ∓ Costantini-Naumkin, Montecatini Terme 2000.

b) 6 f4 ♘ec6!? (this is slightly unusual; 6...♘f5 is more common) 7 dxc5 (7 ♘b5 ♗xd2+ 8 ♕xd2 0-0 9 ♘f3 could be tried; one point of Black's last move is that after 7 ♘f3 cxd4 8 ♘b5 ♗c5 White would have 9 b4 if the black knight were on f5, but not now) 7...♘d7 8 ♘f3 0-0 9 ♗d3 f6 10 ♕e2 ♘xc5 and Black was doing well in Prasad-Harikrishna, Indian Ch (Mumbai) 2000.

H431)
6 ♘b5 (D)

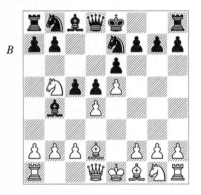

A consistent continuation. White exchanges the dark-squared bishops and intends to bring the knight in on the dark squares.

6...♗xd2+ 7 ♕xd2 0-0 8 c3

Other moves promise little:

a) 8 f4 ♘bc6! (the most accurate move-order; on 8...a6 9 ♘d6 cxd4 10 ♘f3 ♘bc6 White has attacking prospects after 11 ♗d3) 9 ♘f3 (9 dxc5 is

perhaps best met by 9...b6!? with excellent compensation for Black) 9...a6 10 ♘d6 ♘xd4 (this is what makes the difference; exchanging knights minimizes White's hopes of an attack) 11 ♘xd4 cxd4 12 ♗d3 (12 ♕xd4 f6 ∓) 12...♕b6 13 0-0 ♗d7 14 ♕f2 f5 15 ♔h1 ♘c8 16 ♘xc8 ♖axc8 17 c3 ♗b5! ± Dean-Vaganian, Groningen 1999.

b) 8 dxc5 ♘d7 (8...♘bc6!? 9 ♘f3 and now either 9...b6 or 9...f6 is possible) 9 f4 ♘xc5 10 ♘d4 ♕b6 11 0-0-0 ♗d7 12 ♘gf3 ♖fc8 and Black had no problems in Karpov-Nogueiras, Rotterdam 1989.

8...♘bc6 9 f4 a6 10 ♘d6 cxd4 11 cxd4

Timman has had good results with White from this position, but theoretically Black need not worry:

a) 11...♘f5 12 ♘xf5 exf5 13 ♘f3 ♗e6 14 ♗e2 ♖c8 15 ♖c1 ♕b6 16 ♔f2 f6!? (Vaganian gives 16...♘a5 17 b3 ♖xc1 18 ♖xc1 ♖c8 19 ♖xc8+ ♗xc8 as equal; this is an important assessment for the whole line, because if Black has no problems in this type of ending, White has no chance of an advantage in this variation) 17 exf6 gxf6 18 ♖c3 ♗f7 19 ♖hc1 ♖ce8 with counterplay, Timman-Vaganian, Linares 1985.

b) 11...f6 12 ♘f3 ♘g6!? (threatening ...♘xf4) 13 ♘xc8 (13 g3? fxe5 14 dxe5 ♘gxe5 is much better for Black) 13...fxe5 14 dxe5 ♖xc8 (Agdestein also suggests the interesting 14...♖xf4 15 ♘d6 ♖xf3 16 gxf3 ♘cxe5, which he assesses as unclear after 17 ♘xb7; Black indeed seems to have splendid compensation) 15 g3 ♕b6 16 ♗h3 ♔h8! and Black cannot be dissatisfied with the opening, Timman-Agdestein, Taxco/Montetaxco IZ 1985.

H432)

6 dxc5 ♘bc6 7 ♕g4 *(D)*

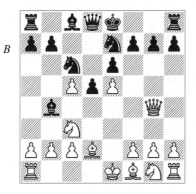

This sharp set-up might win games if Black is unprepared. On the other hand, if Black is prepared his chances shouldn't be worse.

7...0-0

7...♘f5 is a playable alternative. Leko-Hertneck, Moscow OL 1994 led to a mess after 8 ♘f3 ♗xc5 9 ♗d3 h5 10 ♕f4 ♘ce7! 11 ♘h4!? d4!? (also possible is 11...♘g6 12 ♘xg6 fxg6 13 0-0-0 0-0) 12 ♘a4 ♘d5 13 ♕e4 ♗b4 14 ♘xf5 ♗xd2+ 15 ♔xd2 exf5 16 ♕xd4 ♕g5+ 17 ♔e2 ♘f4+ 18 ♔e1 ♗d7 when Black has clear compensation.

8 0-0-0 *(D)*

This has been White's choice recently. After other moves Black can reach a satisfactory position:

a) 8 ♘f3 f5 9 exf6 ♖xf6 10 ♕h5 e5 11 0-0-0 ♗xc3!?, Van der Veen-Barsov, Haarlem 1999, 12 ♗xc3 ♖f5 13 ♕h4 (13 ♘g5? rebounds on White due to 13...h6 14 h4 ♕f8!, intending ...g6 and White's knight is lost) 13...♖f4 14 ♕g3 ♖g4 15 ♕h3 ♘g6 (McDonald). Black has a pleasant position.

b) 8 ♗d3!? ♘g6 (8...f5!?) 9 ♘f3 ♗xc5 10 ♕h5 ♘b4 11 ♘g5 h6 12 ♘f3 ♘xd3+ 13 cxd3 ♕e8! 14 d4 ♗e7 and Black was doing fine in Al Modiahki-Tukmakov, Erevan 1996.

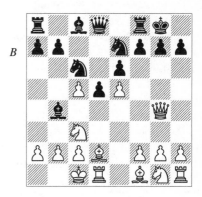

8...f5

An interesting idea is 8...b6!? 9 ♘f3 (9 cxb6 axb6 gives Black compensation) 9...bxc5 10 ♗d3 ♘g6 11 ♕h5 and now rather than 11...♕a5 12 ♘g5 h6 13 ♘xf7 ♖xf7 14 ♕xg6, which looked speculative but went well for Black in Chapman-B.Martin, Melbourne 2000, Black could also try 11...♕e8!? when both 12 ♘b5 c4! and 12 ♘g5 h6, with the point 13 ♘xf7(?) ♘gxe5!, look good for Black.

9 exf6 ♖xf6 10 ♗d3 ♕f8!?

10...e5 11 ♕h5 h6 12 g4 gives White a strong attack.

11 ♘f3

Now Black should try 11...♗xc5. Instead, 11...e5 12 ♕h4 h6 13 ♘xe5! ♘xe5 14 ♕xb4 ♘xd3+ 15 cxd3 ♘c6 16 ♕b3 ♗e6 and Black's compensation for the two pawns is probably not sufficient, Sutovsky-Cu.Hansen, Essen 2000.

H44)
5 a3 ♗xc3+

The only real alternative to this and the Armenian Variation (5...♗a5 – Chapter 15) is 5...cxd4. It is a common turn of moves that we also see in the Nimzo-Indian but here it has never been very popular. A key game is Nunn-Eingorn, Reykjavik tt 1990, which went 6 axb4 dxc3 7 ♘f3 (7 ♕g4!? is not bad either) 7...♘e7 8 ♗d3 ♘d7 (on 8...♕c7, Nunn gives 9 ♖a3! cxb2 10 ♗xb2 as good for White) 9 0-0 ♘c6 10 ♖e1 ♘xb4 (if 10...cxb2 11 ♗xb2 ♘xb4 12 ♗a3! ♘xd3 13 cxd3 Black is in trouble because his king is caught in the centre and the opposite-coloured bishops work greatly in White's favour) 11 bxc3 ♘xd3 12 cxd3 0-0 13 ♖a4! with good compensation for White as the rook is about to swing over to the kingside.

6 bxc3 *(D)*

Now we consider three moves for Black:

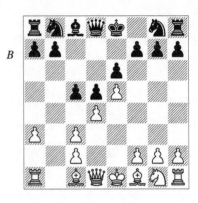

B

H441)
6...♕a5 7 ♗d2 ♕a4

This old idea has become topical recently – Black immediately blockades the queenside. Unfortunately, it is the queen who acts as the key blockader. Amongst others, Psakhis plays this line with great expertise.

8 ♕g4

This looks like the most dangerous for Black. Another idea is 8 ♕b1 c4, and now:

a) 9 h4 ♘c6 10 h5 h6 11 ♘e2 ♘ge7 with roughly equal chances, Nijboer-P.Nikolić, Rotterdam 1997.

b) 9 ♘h3 ♘c6 10 g3 ♗d7 11 ♘f4 0-0-0 12 ♗h3 (12 h4 is also interesting, but then Black can maybe break with 12...f6) 12...h5 (12...f5!? deserves attention) 13 ♕d1 h4 14 g4 f6 15 0-0 is slightly better for White, Kruppa-Krivoshei, Nikolaev 1995.

8...g6

8...♔f8 is probably best met by 9 ♕d1, although 9 c4!? ♘c6 10 dxc5 ♕xc2 11 ♘f3 ♘xe5 12 ♕g3, Vogt-Krivoshei, Leutersdorf 1998, also looks interesting. White has good compensation.

9 ♕d1 *(D)*

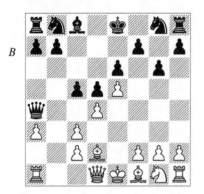

A typical manoeuvre. White has induced weaknesses on Black's kingside and does not mind the wasted tempi.

9...b6!

This is much safer than 9...cxd4 10 ♖b1! d3 11 ♗xd3 ♕xa3 12 ♘f3 ♕c5 13 h4 h6 14 0-0 ♘d7 15 ♖e1, when White was better in Anand-P.Nikolić, Groningen FIDE 1997.

10 h4 h5

The immediate 10...♗a6 is also interesting.

11 ♘f3 ♗a6 12 ♗xa6 ♕xa6 13 ♗g5 ♘d7 14 ♕d3 ♕xd3 15 cxd3 ♖c8 16 ♔d2 ♘e7

The position is about equal, Chandler-N.Pert, British League (4NCL) 2000/1.

H442)

6...♕c7!?

Depending on which line you intend to play as Black and which lines your opponent plays, this can be quite a clever move-order. Now Black threatens 7...cxd4, which rules out moves like 7 a4 and 7 h4, which are both seen frequently against 6...♘e7.

7 ♕g4 *(D)*

7 ♘f3 is the other try, when Black cannot really take advantage of the move-order, and consequently does best to play 7...♘e7 – *6...♘e7 7 ♘f3 ♕c7*.

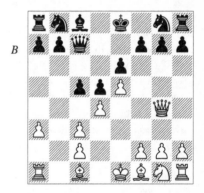

7...f5

Or:

a) 7...cxd4? 8 ♕xg7 ♕xc3+ 9 ♔d1 ♕xa1 10 ♕xh8 ♔f8 11 ♗d3 is very bad for Black.

b) 7...♘e7 – *6...♘e7 7 ♕g4 ♕c7*.

c) 7...f6 seems more in the French spirit but is very risky. White has two options:

c1) 8 ♘f3 c4 9 ♕g3 ♕f7 10 h4 h5 11 a4 ♘c6 12 ♗a3 ♗d7 13 ♕f4 0-0-0 14 g3 ± Djurhuus-Johannessen, Oslo 1997.

c2) 8 ♗b5+ is the most common, as Black should move his king:

c21) 8...♘c6 9 ♘f3 ♕f7 10 ♗xc6+ bxc6 11 0-0 ♘e7 12 dxc5 ♘g6 13 ♖e1 0-0 14 ♕g3 was very good for White in Oll-Ermolinsky, Sverdlovsk 1987.

c22) 8...♗f8 9 ♘f3 a6 (9...c4?! 10 a4 a6? 11 ♗a3+ ♘e7 12 ♗d6 ♕d8 13 exf6 gxf6 14 ♕f4 ±) 10 ♗d3 cxd4 11 0-0 dxc3 12 a4 f5 13 ♗a3+ ♘e7 14 ♕h5 ♘bc6 15 g4!? and White had a strong attack in Kindermann-Mohr, Altensteig 1989.

c23) 8...♗f7 9 ♘f3 (9 ♗d3? cxd4 10 ♘e2 fxe5 11 ♕h5+ ♔f8 looks very good for Black) 9...c4?! (a consistent attempt but unfortunately not very good) 10 ♕h5+! (10 ♘g5+ fxg5 11 ♕f3+ ♘f6 12 exf6 g6 13 ♗xg5 a6 14 h4 h5 15 ♗f4 ♕a5 16 ♕g3 e5 17 ♗xe5 ♗f5 won material for Black in Djurhuus-Johannessen, Gausdal 1999) 10...g6 11 ♕h4 f5 12 ♗g5 ±.

8 ♕h5+

Other moves:

a) 8 exf6 is rarely played. After 8...♘xf6 9 ♕g3 the inferior 9...♕e7 was chosen in Shirov-Short, Sarajevo 2000. Even though Short might have been OK later on in that game, it still remains to be answered what Shirov would have done against the more natural 9...♕a5! 10 ♗d2 0-0 ∓, which has given Black good results in several games.

b) 8 ♕g3 and now:

b1) 8...♘e7 9 ♕xg7 ♖g8 10 ♕xh7 cxd4 11 ♔d1!? (11 ♘e2 ♘bc6 12 f4 dxc3 13 ♕h3 ♗d7 14 ♕xc3 0-0-0 = R.Byrne-Botvinnik, Monte Carlo 1968) 11...♗d7 12 ♘f3 ♕xc3 13 ♖b1 ♗a4

14 ♘e1 ♕c7 15 h4 ♘bc6 16 ♗g5 0-0-0 17 ♗f6! ♖d7 18 f4 ♖g3 19 ♖h3 ♖xh3 20 gxh3 d3 21 ♗xd3 d4 22 ♗xe7 ♘xe7 23 ♖b4 ♘d5 24 ♕g8+ ♕d8 25 ♕xe6 ♘xb4 26 axb4 ± Winsnes. However, I have a feeling that Black should be alright in this line with an improvement somewhere around move 17-20.

b2) 8...cxd4 9 cxd4 ♘e7 10 ♗d2 0-0 11 ♗d3 b6 12 ♘e2 ♗a6 13 ♘f4 ♕d7 14 h4 ♗xd3 15 ♕xd3 ♖c8! (a tiny improvement over the more common 15...♘bc6) 16 ♖h3 ♖c4 17 ♖g3 ♘bc6 18 c3 ♔h8 19 ♕e2 ♘a5 20 ♕d1 ♖c6 21 ♔f1 ♘c4 22 ♗c1 b5 gave Black good counterplay in Svidler-Cu.Hansen, Esbjerg 2000.

8...g6 9 ♕d1

White has lost time with his queen over the last three moves but he has also succeeded in provoking weaknesses on the black kingside.

9...♗d7

9...cxd4 10 cxd4 ♕c3+ 11 ♗d2 ♕xd4 12 ♘f3 ♕e4+ 13 ♗e2 ♘c6 14 0-0 needs to be investigated but it is clear that White has compensation in the form of better development and the bishop-pair.

10 ♘f3 *(D)*

10...cxd4!

10...♗a4 is a typical French idea where Black aims to blockade the queenside, which will hopefully give him a reasonably safe shelter for his king and to some extent limit the power of White's bishops. Then Chandler-Kinsman, British League (4NCL) 1997/8 went 11 dxc5!? ♘d7 12 ♕d4

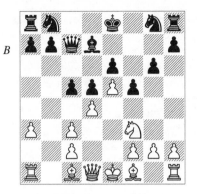

B

♘xc5 13 ♗d3 h6 14 0-0 ♘e7 15 ♗e3 b6 16 ♕h4 ±.

11 cxd4 ♗a4 12 ♗d2

12 ♗d3 ♕c3+ 13 ♗d2 ♕xd3 14 cxd3 ♗xd1 15 ♔xd1 h6 16 h4 ♘c6 17 ♔e2 ♘ge7 has arisen in several games, amongst others Stefansson-Short, Reykjavik 2000. Black has no problems and may even have reasonable prospects of playing for a win if White becomes overambitious.

12...♘c6

Now:

a) 13 ♗d3 h6 14 h4 0-0-0 15 ♔f1 ♔b8 16 ♖h3 ♖c8 gave Black at least equality in J.Polgar-Short, Dos Hermanas 1997. White needs an improvement in this line. Otherwise, it looks very simple for Black to equalize.

b) One idea is 13 h4 h6 14 ♕b1!?, perhaps aiming for a quick c4.

H443)

6...♘e7 7 ♕g4

White has several other 7th moves. 7 ♘f3, 7 a4 and 7 h4 are examined in Chapter 14.

7...♔f8 (D)

Here we examine only this slightly unusual but perfectly playable way of defending the pawn. 7...0-0 is Chapter 13 and 7...♕c7 is Chapter 12.

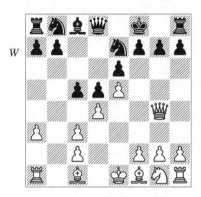

W

8 h4!?

This straightforward move intends to bring the rook into an attack on the black king with ♖h3, but other moves should also be considered. In particular, 8 ♗d2 has attracted some strong players lately. One idea is to discourage ...♕a5-a4. Black has then tried:

a) 8...♕a5 9 a4!? ♘bc6 10 ♘f3 ♕b6 11 dxc5 ♕xc5 12 ♗d3 h6 13 0-0 ♕b6 14 ♖fe1 ♗d7 15 c4 ♕c7 16 cxd5 exd5 17 ♕f4 ♗e6 18 h4 and White was better in Short-P.Nikolić, London Intel rpd 1994.

b) 8...♕b6 9 dxc5 ♕c7 10 ♘f3 ♘d7 11 ♗e2 ♘xe5 12 ♘xe5 ♕xe5 13 0-0 h5 14 ♕f3 ± Kamsky-Ljubojević, Monte Carlo Amber blindfold 1995.

c) 8...♕c7 9 ♗d3 b6 10 ♘h3!? (10 ♘f3 ♗a6 11 dxc5 bxc5 12 ♗xa6 ♘xa6 13 c4 ♕c6 14 cxd5 exd5 15 0-0 h6 16

♖fe1 ♕e6 17 ♕a4 with an edge for White, Timman-P.Nikolić, Pula Echt 1997) 10...♗a6 11 0-0 ♗xd3 12 cxd3 ♘d7 (12...♘bc6 13 dxc5 bxc5 14 ♖fe1 ♘g6 15 d4 ± Gdanski-Socko, Polish Ch (Warsaw) 2001) 13 ♘f4! ♕c6 14 ♘h5 g6?! 15 ♗h6+ ♔e8 16 ♘g7+ ♔d8 17 ♕h4 +− Vallejo Pons-Nogueiras, Havana 2001.

8...♕a5

8...♕c7 was employed in the famous game Kasparov-P.Nikolić, Horgen 1994, which continued 9 ♕d1! (White must defend against ...cxd4, and 9 ♗d2 cxd4 10 cxd4 ♕xc2 11 ♖c1 ♕e4+ 12 ♕xe4 dxe4 13 f3 exf3 14 ♘xf3 isn't necessarily enough compensation) 9...cxd4 10 cxd4 ♕c3+ 11 ♗d2 ♕xd4 12 ♘f3 ♕e4+ 13 ♗e2 b6 14 0-0 ♗a6 15 c4! with adequate compensation for White.

9 ♗d2 ♕a4 10 ♖h3! *(D)*

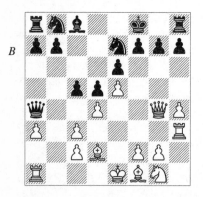

There is no need to take time to defend the c-pawn since 10...♕xc2 would

now be too risky in view of 11 ♗d3 ♕b2 12 ♖b1 ♕xa3 13 ♖g3 g6 14 ♕f4.

10...♘bc6 11 h5 h6

11...♘xe5? 12 ♕f4 followed by 13 h6 would again be too dangerous for Black.

12 ♕f4 b6

After this Black's knight becomes very passive on d8. An interesting and possibly better option is 12...♗d7!? which intends to cover f7 with ...♗e8. A major advantage of this is that the knight is kept on c6 to maintain the pressure on White's centre. Hraček-Bobrowska, Koszalin 1999 continued 13 ♖f3 ♗e8 14 ♖b1 b6 15 g4!? ♕xc2 (15...cxd4 16 ♗d3 gives White compensation) 16 ♗d3 ♕a4 17 g5 c4 18 ♗e2 (18 gxh6!? ♖xh6 19 ♕g4 ♖h8 20 ♖g3 g6 21 hxg6 fxg6 22 ♕xe6 cxd3 23 ♖f3+ ♘f5 24 ♕f6+ ♔g8 =) 18...♕c2 19 ♖c1 hxg5 20 ♕xg5 ♕h7 21 ♖h3 ♘g8, intending ...f6 with a dynamically balanced position.

13 ♖f3 ♘d8 14 dxc5 ♕xf4 15 ♖xf4 bxc5 16 ♗e3

16 c4!?.

16...c4 17 ♖b1 ♘dc6 18 ♘f3 g5 19 hxg6 ♘xg6 20 ♖g4

Now:

a) 20...♔g7 21 ♘h4! ♗d7 22 ♘xg6 fxg6 23 ♖b7 ♖hd8 24 ♗e2 and White is better, Atlas-Psakhis, Geneva 1992.

b) 20...♘cxe5 21 ♘xe5 ♘xe5 22 ♗c5+ ♔e8 23 ♖g7 gives White compensation according to Gelfand and Atlas.

17 Rare Third Moves for Black

1 e4 e6 2 d4 d5 3 ♘c3 *(D)*

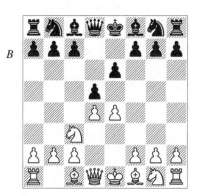

There are a variety of relatively rare third moves for Black that need a mention. None of these are established lines for Black but the following three aren't particularly bad:

A: 3...♗e7   249
B: 3...a6   251
C: 3...♘c6   251

Other moves are very rare, and easily lead to an advantage for White:

a) 3...f5 4 exf5 exf5 (compare this to the Dutch line *1 d4 f5 2 ♘c3 d5*, and I am sure you wouldn't mind having the pawns swapped as White) 5 ♗f4 c6 6 ♕h5+! g6 7 ♕e2+ ♔f7 8 ♘f3 ♘f6 9 ♘e5+ ♔g7 10 f3 h6 11 0-0-0 ♘a6 12 g4 ± Perdomo-A.Georghiou, Elista OL 1998.

b) 3...♘e7 4 ♘f3 dxe4 5 ♘xe4 ♘f5 6 ♗d3 ♗e7 7 0-0 0-0 8 c3 b6 9 ♕e2 ♗b7 10 ♗f4 ♘d7 11 ♗a6 ± T.Georgadze-Gurgenidze, USSR 1956.

c) 3...c5 4 exd5 exd5 5 dxc5 d4 6 ♗b5+ ♘c6 7 ♕e2+!? ♗e6 8 ♘e4 ♘f6 9 ♗g5 ♕a5+ 10 ♗d2 ♕d8 11 ♘g5 ♕d5 12 ♘xe6 fxe6 13 ♘f3 ♗xc5 14 0-0 ± Rausis-Tarira, Lisbon 1999.

A)

3...♗e7

A number of strong players like this as an offbeat try once in while. Like 3...a6, Black argues that White's next move is going to have certain drawbacks with respect to White's set-up later on.

4 ♘f3

This is White's most natural. Obviously, Black can now transpose to the Rubinstein Variation with 4...dxe4. White has two ways to avoid this:

a) 4 e5!? and now:

a1) 4...c5 5 ♕g4 ♔f8 6 dxc5 ♘c6 7 ♘f3 ♗xc5 8 ♗d3 ♘ge7 9 0-0 ♘b4 10 ♗e3 ♘xd3 11 cxd3 ♗b6 12 ♘e2 ♗d7

13 ♘g3 h6 14 h4 ± Gofshtein-Efimov, Genoa 1998.

a2) 4...b6 is also seen, but I have my doubts about it. In the Winawer line 3...♗b4 4 e5 b6 5 a3, Black usually retreats the bishop to f8, to make room for ...♘e7, or exchanges it on c3. Now the bishop occupies the knight's square. Babula-Dietz, Bad Mergentheim 1989 continued in White's favour: 5 h4!? h5 6 ♘f3 ♘h6 (possibly this is questionable and Black should play 6...♗a6 immediately) 7 ♗g5 ♗a6 8 ♘b5!? ♕d7 9 a4 ♘f5 10 ♗d3 ±.

b) 4 ♗d3 and then:

b1) 4...dxe4 5 ♗xe4 ±.

b2) 4...♘f6 5 e5 ♘fd7 6 ♘ce2 c5 7 c3 is very good for White. In the Shirov/Anand Variation (3...♘f6 4 e5 ♘fd7 5 ♘ce2) White would obviously be very happy to have his bishop already on d3.

b3) 4...b6 5 exd5 exd5 6 ♕f3 ♘f6 7 ♗g5 c6 8 ♘ge2 0-0 9 h3 ♗a6 10 g4 ♖e8 11 0-0-0 and White is better, Yakovenko-Riazantsev, Moscow 2000.

b4) 4...c5 5 exd5 exd5 6 dxc5 ♘f6 7 ♘ge2 ♗xc5 8 0-0 ♗e6 9 ♗g5 ♘c6 10 ♘f4 ± Galkin-Nikolenko, Moscow 1998.

b5) 4...♘c6 5 ♘f3 ♗b4 6 ♗e2 (6 ♗b5+ c6 7 ♗e2 can also be considered; even 6 0-0 is interesting) 6...dxe4 7 ♘xe4 ♘f6 8 ♘xf6+ ♗xf6 9 0-0 0-0 10 c3 ♘d5 11 ♖e1 b6 12 ♘e5 ♗b7 13 ♗f3 ± Ibragimov-Atalik, Athens 1995.

4...♘f6 (D)

4...dxe4 5 ♘xe4 – 3...dxe4 4 ♘xe4 ♗e7 5 ♘f3.

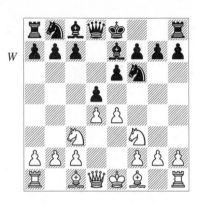

5 ♗d3

After 5 e5 Black has a choice between:

a) 5...♘fd7 – 3...♘f6 4 e5 ♘fd7 5 ♘f3 ♗e7 ±.

b) 5...♘e4 6 ♗d3 ♘xc3 7 bxc3 b6 intending ...♗a6 gives Black chances of equality.

5...c5

Other moves:

a) 5...dxe4 6 ♘xe4 ♘bd7 – 3...dxe4 4 ♘xe4 ♘d7 5 ♘f3 ♘gf6 6 ♗d3 ♗e7 ±.

b) 5...b6 6 e5 ♘fd7 – 3...♘f6 4 e5 ♘fd7 5 ♘f3 ♗e7 6 ♗d3 b6 ±.

6 exd5 cxd4

6...exd5 offers White a pleasant choice:

a) 7 dxc5 ♘bd7 8 0-0 0-0 9 ♗g5 ♘xc5 10 ♗e2 ± Kaminski.

b) 7 0-0 c4 8 ♗e2 0-0 9 ♘e5 a6 10 ♗f3 ♗e6 11 ♖e1 ♖e8 12 ♗f4 is also better for White, Timoshenko-Piskov, Belgrade 1995.

7 ♗b5+ ♗d7 8 ♗xd7+ ♘bxd7

Instead, 8...♕xd7 9 dxe6 ♕xe6+ 10 ♘e2 ♗b4+ 11 ♗d2 ♗c5 12 0-0 was very good for White in Lukin-Romanishin, USSR 1978.

9 ♘xd4 ♘xd5 10 ♘xd5 exd5 11 0-0

± Christiansen-Seirawan, USA Ch (Chandler) 1997.

B)

3...a6 *(D)*

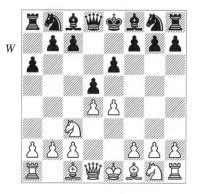

4 ♗d3

The other main line is 4 ♘f3 ♘f6. Now:

a) 5 e5 ♘fd7 6 ♗d3 c5 7 dxc5 is a type of position that Ian Rogers likes to play as White. Here White can even argue that he has an extra tempo compared to the line *3...♘f6 4 e5 ♘fd7 5 ♘f3 c5 6 dxc5*, because Black's ...a6 is not very useful.

b) 5 ♗d3 ♗b4 (perhaps the alternative 5...c5, which Prié has played, is better; then 6 exd5 exd5 7 dxc5 is a type of position that is probably slightly better for White) 6 e5 ♘e4 7 ♗d2 ♗xc3 8 bxc3 ♘xd2 9 ♕xd2 c5 10 0-0 ±.

4...c5

Alternatives are:

a) 4...♘f6 5 e5 ♘fd7 6 ♘ce2 ±.

b) 4...♘c6 5 ♘f3 ♗b4 6 0-0!? (6 ♗e2) 6...♘f6 (6...dxe4 7 ♘xe4 ♗e7 ± Glek) 7 e5 ♘d7 8 ♘g5! ♘xd3 9 cxd3 ♗e7 10 ♕h5 g6 11 ♕h6 ♗f8 12 ♕h3 ± Glek-Liogky, Dubai 1993.

5 dxc5 ♗xc5 6 exd5 exd5 7 ♘xd5! ♗xf2+ 8 ♔xf2 ♕xd5 9 ♕f3 ♘f6 10 ♕xd5 ♘xd5 11 ♘f3 0-0 12 ♗d2

White is slightly better due to his bishop-pair and three-vs-two majority on the queenside, Rantanen-Kovačević, Palma de Mallorca 1989.

C)

3...♘c6 *(D)*

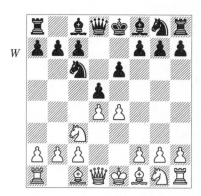

4 e5

This is very logical. White argues that Black's knight is misplaced on c6, and gains space while Black cannot attack White's centre with ...c5. White also has tried many other things here. Another line that seems to give White good chances of an advantage is 4 ♘f3 ♘f6, and now:

a) 5 e5 ♘e4!? 6 ♗d3 ♗b4 7 ♗d2 ♘xd2 8 ♕xd2 f6 9 a3 ♗xc3 (9...♗e7 10 exf6 ♗xf6 11 ♗b5 0-0 12 ♗xc6 bxc6 13 ♘a4 ± Stefansson-Hjartarson, Reykjavik 1992) 10 ♕xc3 fxe5 11 dxe5 ♗d7 12 b4!? a6 13 h4 ♕e7 14 ♔f1 ± Kuczynski-Bany, Warsaw 1990.

b) 5 ♗g5 ♗e7 6 ♗d3!? dxe4 7 ♘xe4 ♘xe4 (7...♘b4 should be considered) 8 ♗xe7 and now:

b1) 8...♕xe7 9 ♗xe4 ♕b4+?! (this is too ambitious; Black should resign himself to a slightly inferior position after 9...♗d7) 10 c3 ♕xb2 11 0-0 ♕b5 12 ♖b1 ♕h5 13 ♕a4 0-0 (13...♗d7 14 ♖fe1 ♕a5 15 ♕c2 gives White a strong initiative – Vuković) 14 ♗xc6 bxc6 15 ♘e5 ± Vuković-Vlat.Kovačević, Senec ECC 1998.

b2) 8...♘xf2 9 ♗xd8 ♘xd1 10 ♗xc7 ♘xb2 11 ♗e2 ♘a4 12 ♔d2 ♔d7 13 ♗g3 ♔e7 14 c4 ♖d8 15 ♔e3 ♘b6 16 ♖hc1 f6 17 ♖ab1 and White has excellent compensation for the pawn, Nataf-Short, New Delhi FIDE 2000.

4...♘ge7

Black has also tried 4...f6 but then White has achieved very good results with 5 ♗b5 ♗d7 6 ♘f3. After 6...a6 White has two options:

a) 7 ♗xc6 ♗xc6 8 exf6 gxf6 9 0-0 ♕d7 10 ♗f4 ♘e7 11 ♖e1 0-0-0 12 ♕d3 ♘g6 13 ♗g3 ♗d6 14 ♖ab1 ♖he8 15 b4 e5 was unclear in Movsesian-Lipka, Slovakian Cht 1997.

b) 7 ♗d3 ♕e7 8 0-0 fxe5 9 dxe5 g6 10 ♖e1 ♗g7 11 a3 ♘h6 12 ♗g5 ♕f7 13 h3 0-0 14 ♕d2 is slightly better for White, Lanc-Lipka, Slovakian Cht 1997.

5 ♘f3 b6 (D)

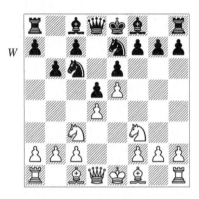

6 a3

This avoids the bishop getting harassed by ...♘b4 after White plays ♗d3. Now Dolmatov-Riazantsev, St Petersburg 2000 continued 6...♗b7 7 ♗d3 ♕d7 8 0-0 h6 9 b4 0-0-0 10 ♘e2 and White was better.

Index of Variations

Chapter Guide

1: Rubinstein Variation: 4...♗d7 and others

1 e4 e6 2 d4 d5 3 ♘c3 dxe4 4 ♘xe4 *8*
A: **4...♕d5** *8*

B: **4...♗e7** *10*
C: **4...♘f6** *11*
D: **4...♗d7** *11* **5 ♘f3 ♗c6 6 ♗d3** *12*
D1: 6...♗xe4 *13*
D2: 6...♘d7 *14*

2: Rubinstein Variation: 4...♘d7
1 e4 e6 2 d4 d5 3 ♘c3 dxe4 4 ♘xe4 ♘d7 *17*
A: **5 g3** *17*
B: **5 ♘f3** *19* **5...♘gf6** *19*
B1: **6 ♗d3** *19*
B2: **6 ♘xf6+** *21* **6...♘xf6** *21*
B21: 7 ♗g5 *21*
B22: 7 ♗d3 *25*
C: **5 ♗d3** *30*

3: Burn Variation: 5...♘bd7
1 e4 e6 2 d4 d5 3 ♘c3 ♘f6 4 ♗g5 dxe4 5 ♘xe4 ♘bd7 *34* **6 ♘f3** *34*
A: **6...h6** *34*
B: **6...♗e7** *35* **7 ♘xf6+ ♗xf6** *35*
B1: **8 ♕d2** *35*
B2: **8 ♗xf6** *36*
B3: **8 h4** *38*
B31: 8...h6 *38*
B32: 8...0-0 *39*

4: Burn Variation: 6...gxf6
1 e4 e6 2 d4 d5 3 ♘c3 ♘f6 4 ♗g5 dxe4 5 ♘xe4 ♗e7 6 ♗xf6 gxf6 *41*
A: **7 ♗c4** *41*
B: **7 g3** *42*
C: **7 ♕d3** *45*
D: **7 ♘f3** *46*
D1: 7...f5 *46*
D2: 7...♘d7 *50*
D3: 7...b6 *51*
D4: 7...a6 *53*

5: Burn Variation: 6...♗xf6
1 e4 e6 2 d4 d5 3 ♘c3 ♘f6 4 ♗g5 dxe4 5 ♘xe4 ♗e7 6 ♗xf6 ♗xf6 *57* **7 ♘f3** *57*
A: **7...0-0** *58*
A1: 8 c3 *58*
A2: 8 ♕d2 *59*
A3: 8 ♕d3!? *60*
A4: 8 ♗c4 *60*
B: **7...♘d7** *61*
B1: **8 ♗c4** *62*
B2: **8 ♕d2** *63* **8...0-0 9 0-0-0** *63*
B21: 9...♗e7 *63*
B22: 9...b6 *64*

6: Steinitz Variation: Introduction
1 e4 e6 2 d4 d5 3 ♘c3 ♘f6 4 e5 *67*
A: **4...♘e4** *67*
B: **4...♘fd7** *68*
B1: 5 ♘f3 *69*
B2: 5 f4 *70* 5...c5 6 ♘f3 *70* 6...a6 *71* 7 ♗e3 *71*

7: Steinitz Variation: Main Line (7 ♗e3)
1 e4 e6 2 d4 d5 3 ♘c3 ♘f6 4 e5 ♘fd7 5 f4 c5 6 ♘f3 ♘c6 7 ♗e3 *74*
A: **7...♗e7** *74*
B: **7...♕b6** *75* **8 ♘a4 ♕a5+ 9 c3** *75*
B1: 9...cxd4?! *75*
B2: 9...c4 *76*
B3: 9...b6!? *78*
C: **7...a6** *80*
D: **7...cxd4** *83* **8 ♘xd4** *83*
D1: **8...♘xd4** *83*
D2: **8...♕b6** *84*
D3: **8...♗c5** *87* **9 ♕d2** *87*
D31: 9...♘xd4 *87*
D32: 9...0-0 *90*